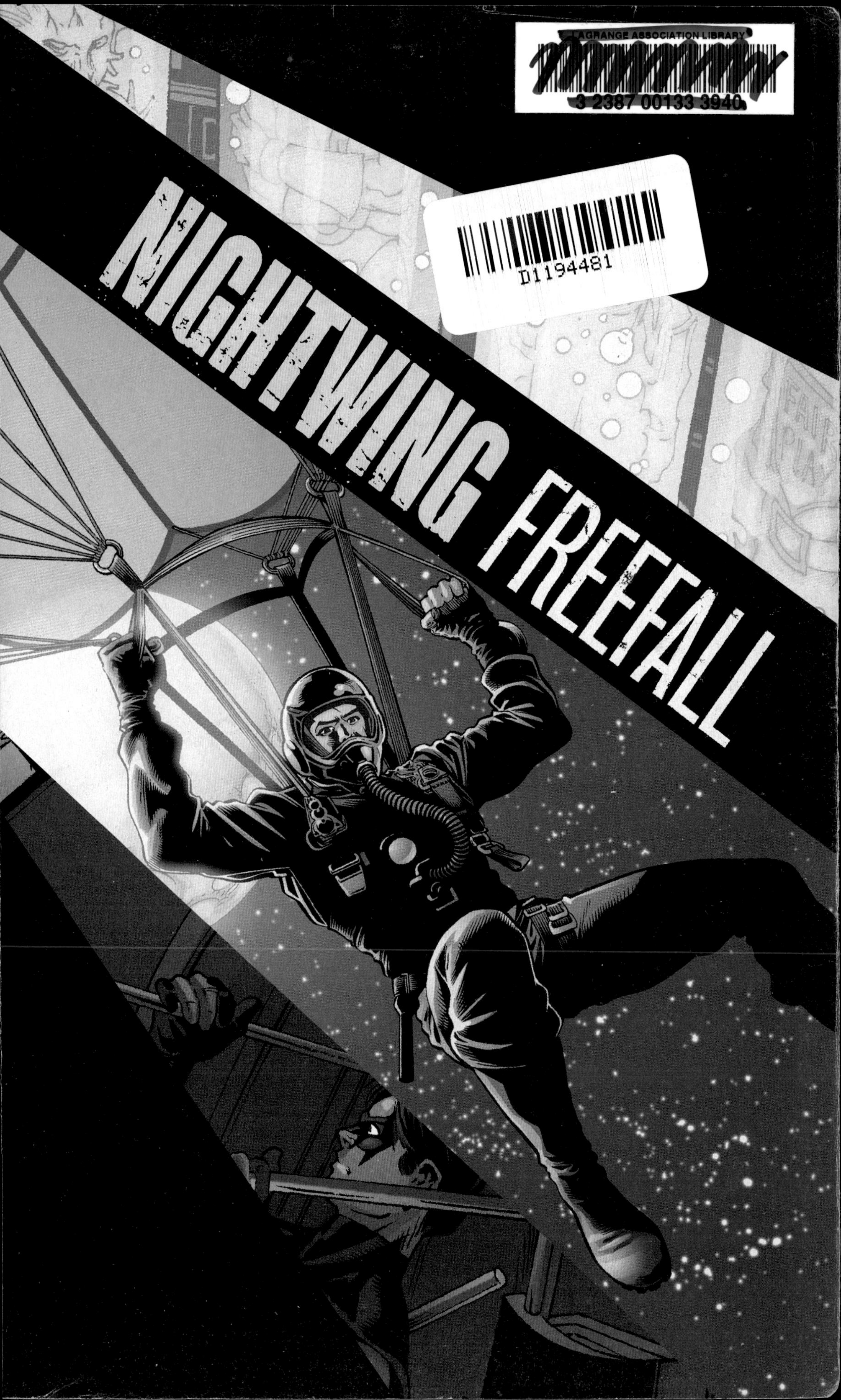
NIGHTWING
FREEFALL
FAIR PLAY

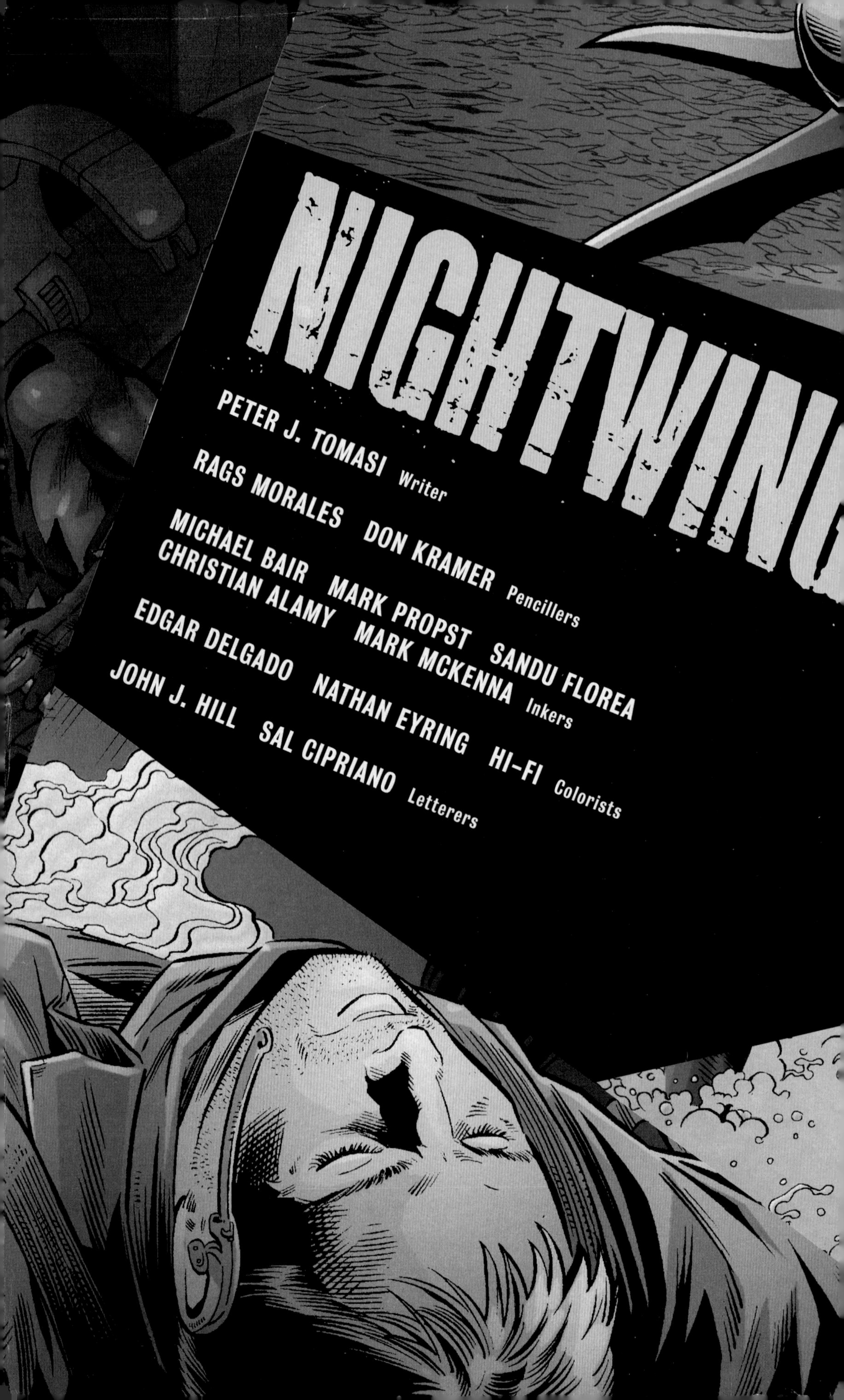
NIGHTWING
PETER J. TOMASI Writer
RAGS MORALES DON KRAMER Pencillers
MICHAEL BAIR MARK PROPST SANDU FLOREA
CHRISTIAN ALAMY MARK MCKENNA Inkers
EDGAR DELGADO NATHAN EYRING HI-FI Colorists
JOHN J. HILL SAL CIPRIANO Letterers

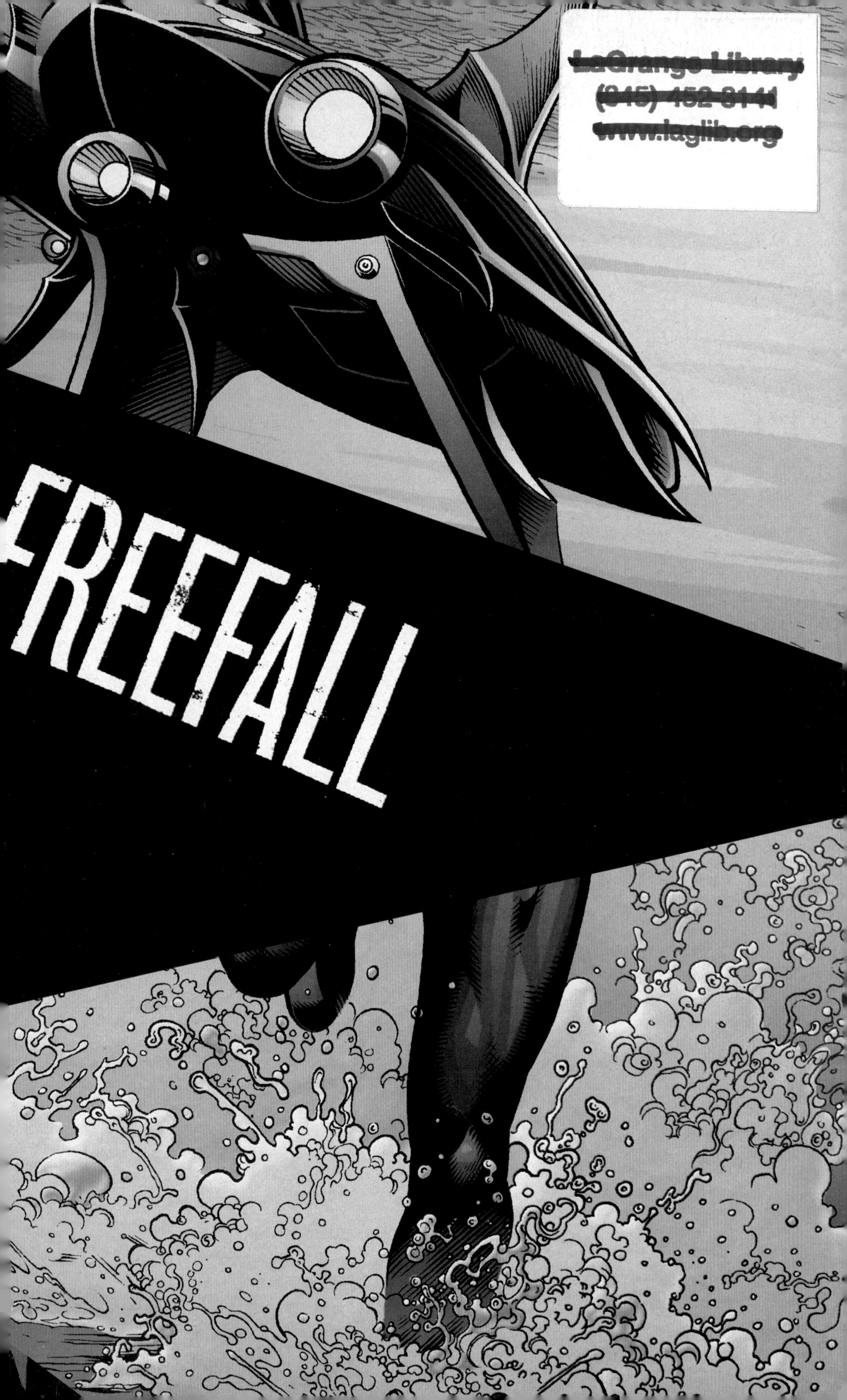
FREEFALL

Cover by Andy Kubert and Laura Martin.

NIGHTWING: FREEFALL

Published by DC Comics. Cover, text and compilation
Copyright © 2008 DC Comics. All Rights Reserved.

Originally published in single magazine form in NIGHTWING
140-146. Copyright © 2008 DC Comics. All Rights Reserved. All
characters, their distinctive likenesses and related elements
featured in this publication are trademarks of DC Comics. The
stories, characters and incidents featured in this publication
are entirely fictional. DC Comics does not read or accept
unsolicited submissions of ideas, stories or artwork.

DC Comics, 1700 Broadway, New York, NY 10019
A Warner Bros. Entertainment Company
Printed in Canada. First Printing.
ISBN: 978-1-4012-1965-9

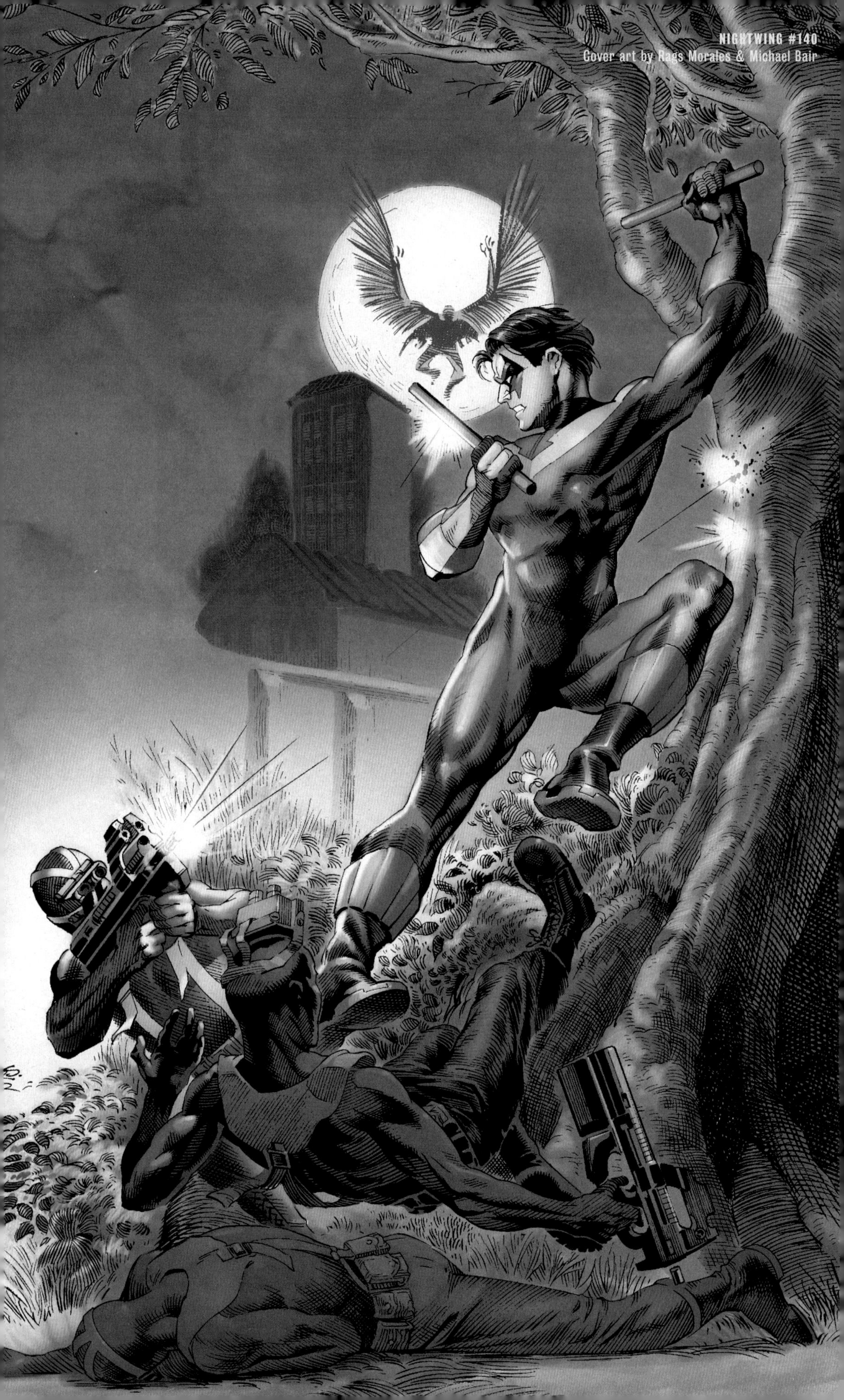

NIGHTWING #140
Cover art by Rags Morales & Michael Bair

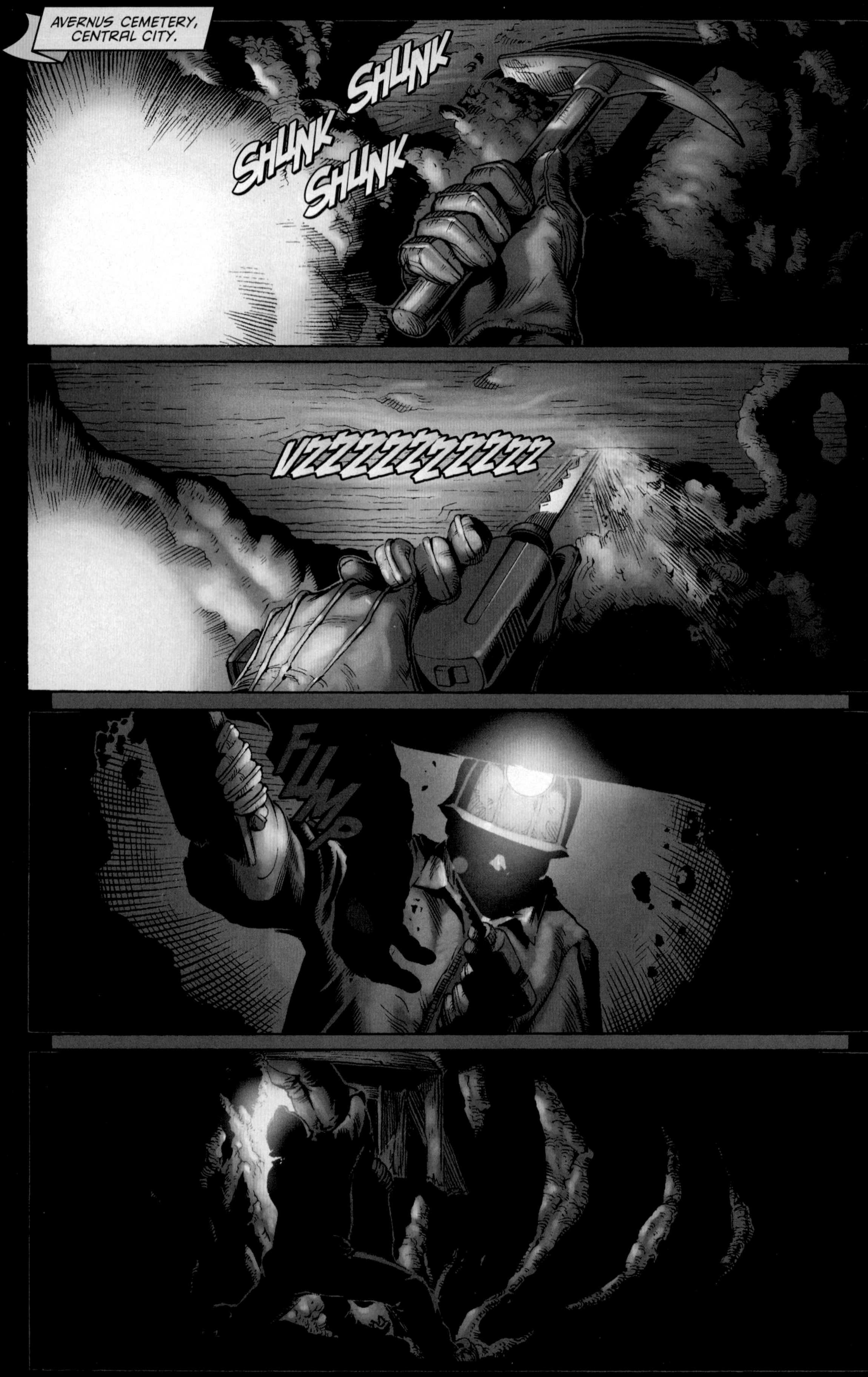
AVERNUS CEMETERY, CENTRAL CITY.
SHUNK SHUNK
SHUNK
V Z Z Z Z Z Z Z Z Z Z Z
FUMP

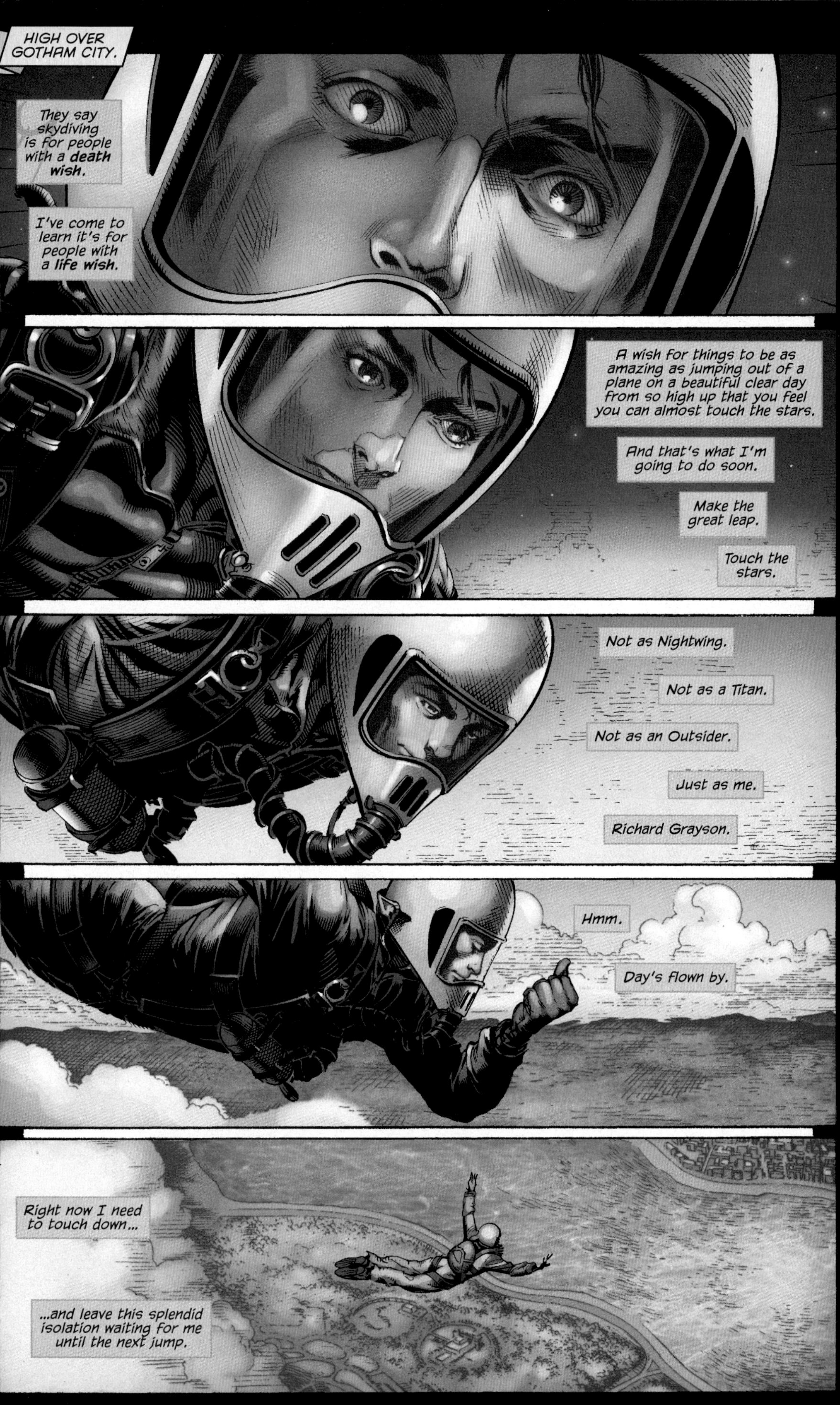
HIGH OVER GOTHAM CITY.
They say skydiving is for people with a death wish.
I've come to learn it's for people with a life wish.
A wish for things to be as amazing as jumping out of a plane on a beautiful clear day from so high up that you feel you can almost touch the stars.
And that's what I'm going to do soon.
Make the great leap.
Touch the stars.
Not as Nightwing.
Not as a Titan.
Not as an Outsider.
Just as me.
Richard Grayson.
Hmm.
Day's flown by.
Right now I need to touch down...
...and leave this splendid isolation waiting for me until the next jump.

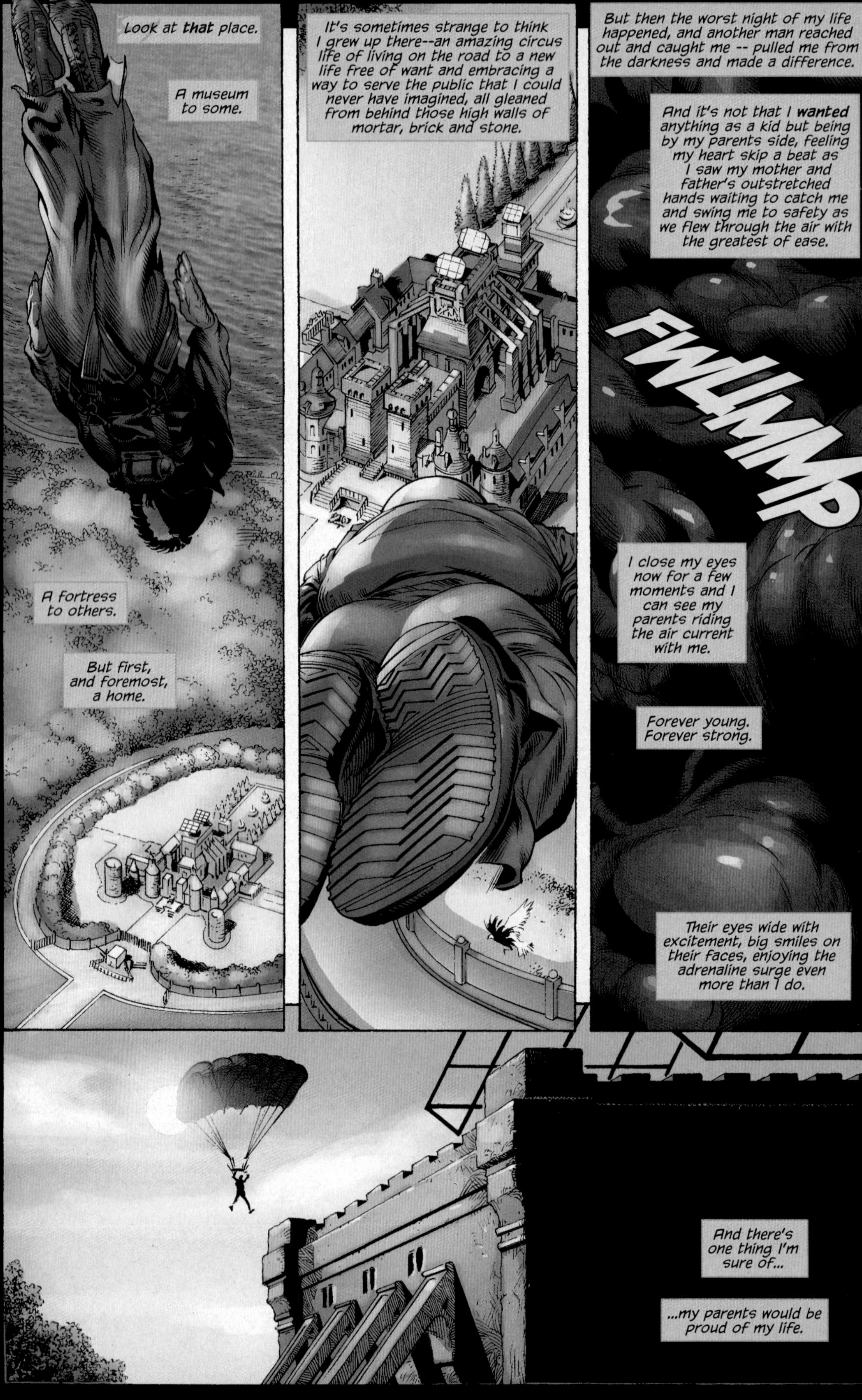

Look at **that** place.
A museum to some.
A fortress to others.
But first, and foremost, a home.
It's sometimes strange to think I grew up there--an amazing circus life of living on the road to a new life free of want and embracing a way to serve the public that I could never have imagined, all gleaned from behind those high walls of mortar, brick and stone.
But then the worst night of my life happened, and another man reached out and caught me -- pulled me from the darkness and made a difference.
And it's not that I **wanted** anything as a kid but being by my parents side, feeling my heart skip a beat as I saw my mother and father's outstretched hands waiting to catch me and swing me to safety as we flew through the air with the greatest of ease.
FWUMMP
I close my eyes now for a few moments and I can see my parents riding the air current with me.
Forever young. Forever strong.
Their eyes wide with excitement, big smiles on their faces, enjoying the adrenaline surge even more than I do.
And there's one thing I'm sure of...
...my parents would be proud of my life.

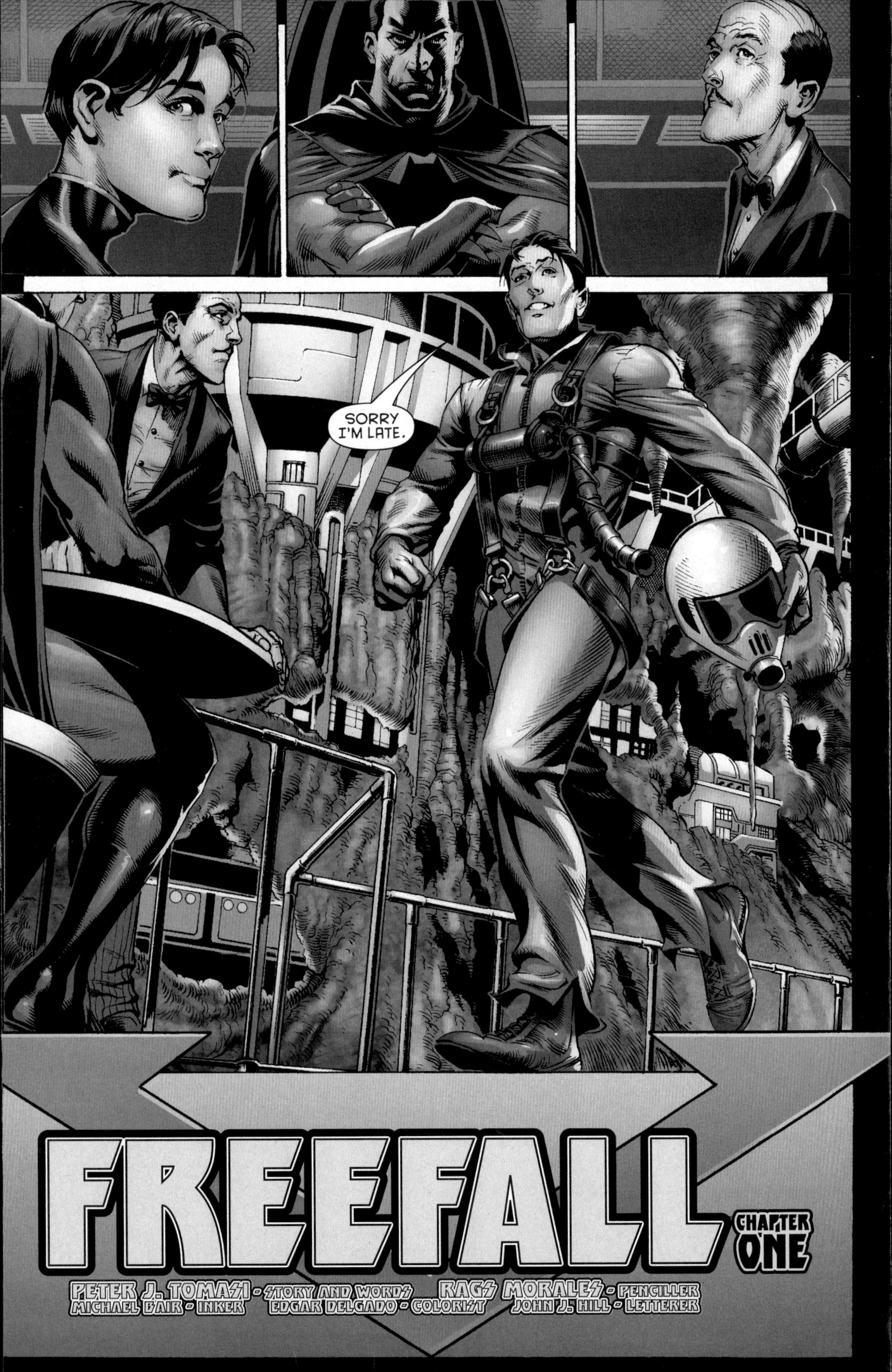
SORRY I'M LATE.
FREEFALL
CHAPTER ONE
PETER J. TOMASI - STORY AND WORDS RAGS MORALES - PENCILLER
MICHAEL BAIR - INKER EDGAR DELGADO - COLORIST JOHN J. HILL - LETTERER

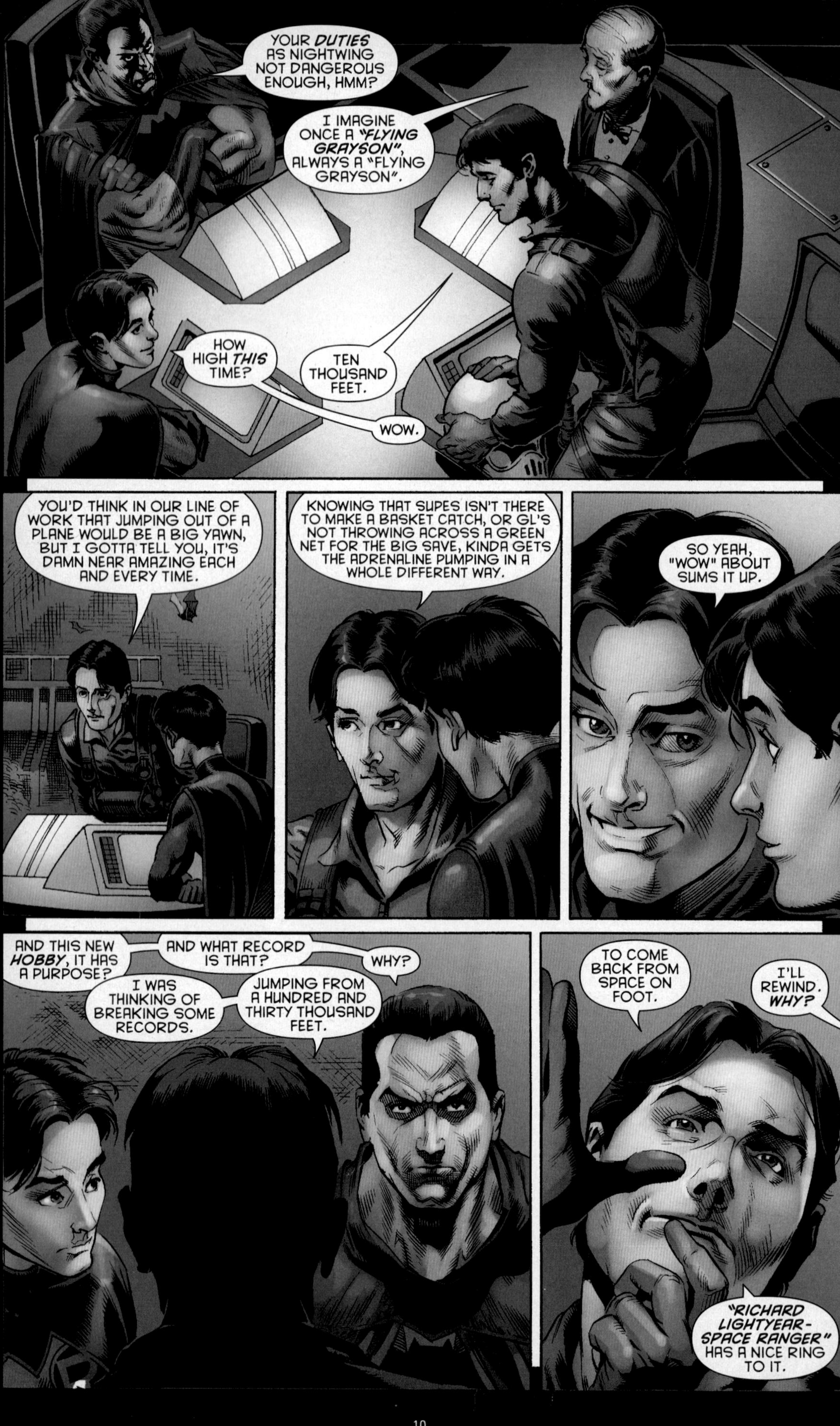
YOUR DUTIES AS NIGHTWING NOT DANGEROUS ENOUGH, HMM?
I IMAGINE ONCE A "FLYING GRAYSON", ALWAYS A "FLYING GRAYSON".
HOW HIGH THIS TIME?
TEN THOUSAND FEET.
WOW.
YOU'D THINK IN OUR LINE OF WORK THAT JUMPING OUT OF A PLANE WOULD BE A BIG YAWN, BUT I GOTTA TELL YOU, IT'S DAMN NEAR AMAZING EACH AND EVERY TIME.
KNOWING THAT SUPES ISN'T THERE TO MAKE A BASKET CATCH, OR GL'S NOT THROWING ACROSS A GREEN NET FOR THE BIG SAVE, KINDA GETS THE ADRENALINE PUMPING IN A WHOLE DIFFERENT WAY.
SO YEAH, "WOW" ABOUT SUMS IT UP.
AND THIS NEW HOBBY, IT HAS A PURPOSE?
I WAS THINKING OF BREAKING SOME RECORDS.
AND WHAT RECORD IS THAT?
JUMPING FROM A HUNDRED AND THIRTY THOUSAND FEET.
WHY?
TO COME BACK FROM SPACE ON FOOT.
I'LL REWIND. WHY?
"RICHARD LIGHTYEAR-SPACE RANGER" HAS A NICE RING TO IT.

HNN

I CALLED THIS MEETING BECAUSE WITH *RA'S* AND *TALIA* STILL A VERY OBVIOUS THREAT, I THINK IT'S BEST WE KEEP THEM ON A PERPETUAL FRONT-BURNER.

TIM'S BEEN PULLING DOUBLE DUTY, PUSHING OUR CRAYS TO THE LIMIT, PICKING UP A LOT OF CHATTER ALONG THE PERIPHERALS CENTERING ON THE *LEAGUE OF ASSASSINS*.

NOTHING SPECIFIC, HEAVILY CODED STUFF, BUT THE SHEER AMOUNT OF IT THAT'S SUDDENLY MOVING ACROSS THE NET IS POPPING RED FLAGS.

SOMETHING'S UP. I JUST DON'T KNOW WHAT.

YET.

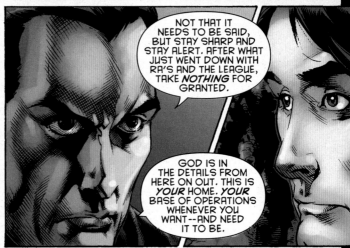

NOT THAT IT NEEDS TO BE SAID, BUT STAY SHARP AND STAY ALERT. AFTER WHAT JUST WENT DOWN WITH RA'S AND THE LEAGUE, TAKE *NOTHING* FOR GRANTED.

GOD IS IN THE DETAILS FROM HERE ON OUT. THIS IS *YOUR* HOME. *YOUR* BASE OF OPERATIONS WHENEVER YOU WANT--AND NEED IT TO BE.

PLAIN AND SIMPLE. WE'RE FAMILY.

THERE IS NO ONE ELSE IN THE WORLD I TRUST AND RESPECT MORE.

NO ONE.

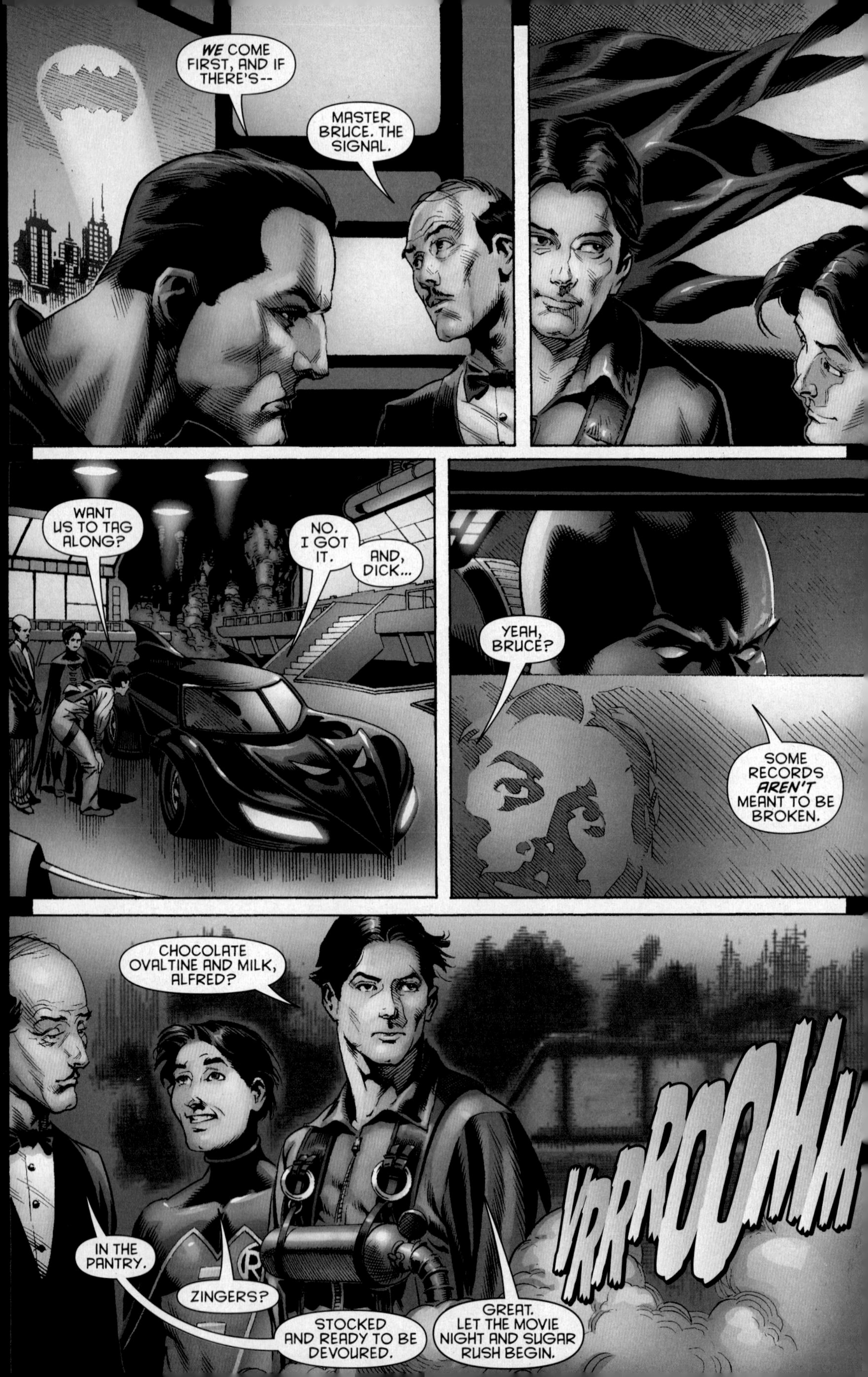
WE COME FIRST, AND IF THERE'S--
MASTER BRUCE. THE SIGNAL.
WANT US TO TAG ALONG?
NO. I GOT IT.
AND, DICK...
YEAH, BRUCE?
SOME RECORDS AREN'T MEANT TO BE BROKEN.
CHOCOLATE OVALTINE AND MILK, ALFRED?
IN THE PANTRY.
ZINGERS?
STOCKED AND READY TO BE DEVOURED.
GREAT. LET THE MOVIE NIGHT AND SUGAR RUSH BEGIN.
VRRROOMM

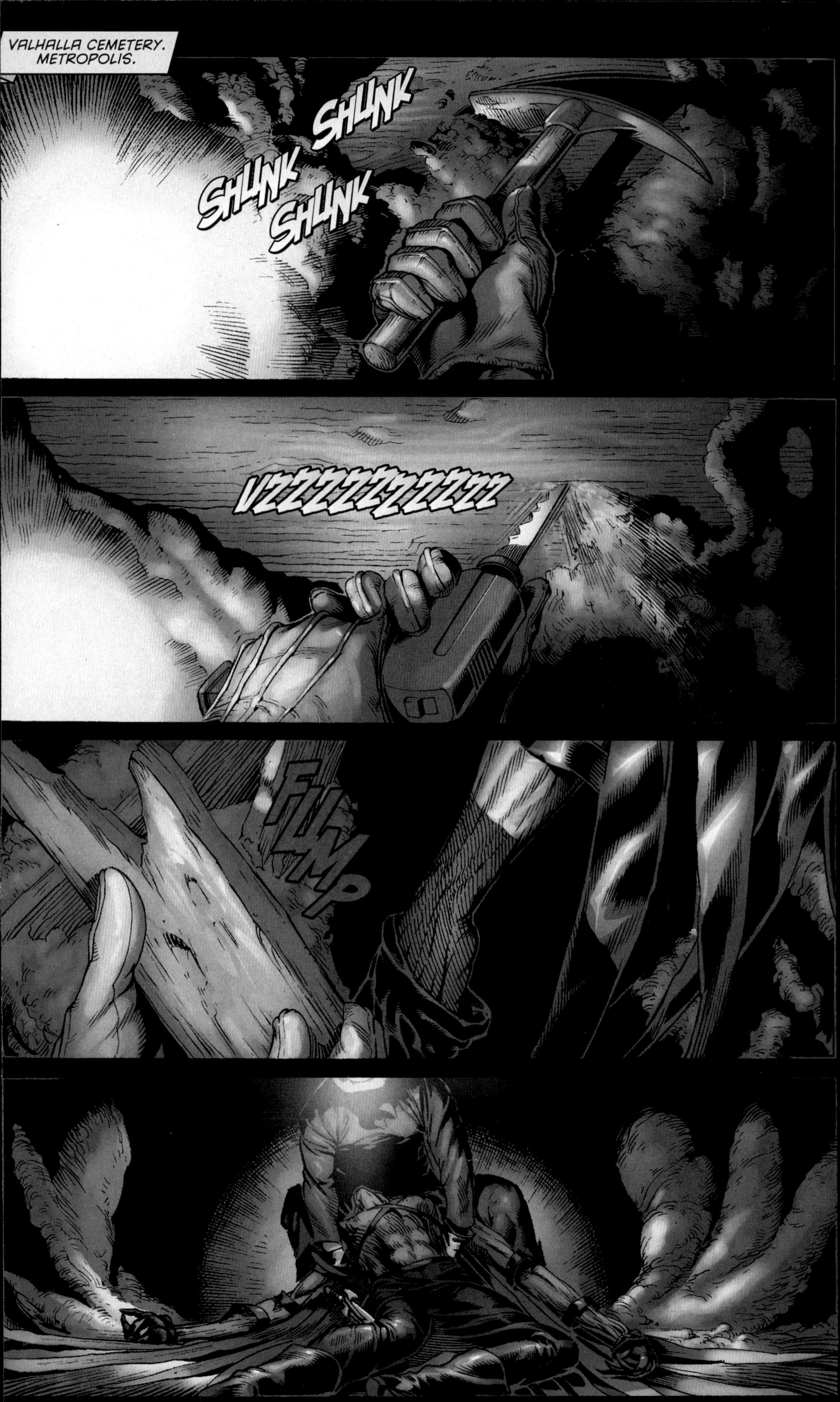
VALHALLA CEMETERY.
METROPOLIS.
SHUNK SHUNK
SHUNK
V Z Z Z Z Z Z Z Z Z Z Z
FLUMP

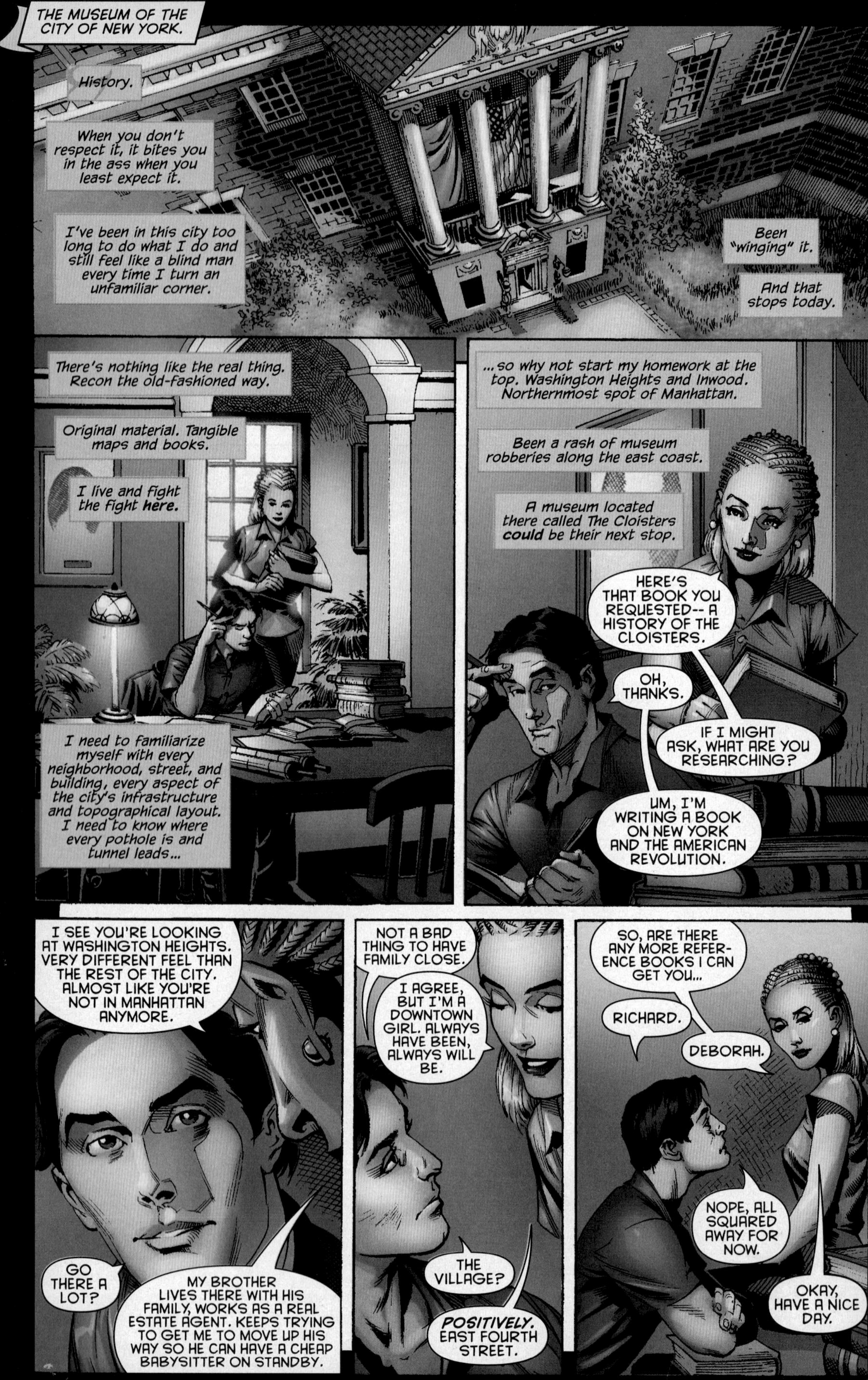

THE MUSEUM OF THE CITY OF NEW YORK.
History.
When you don't respect it, it bites you in the ass when you least expect it.
I've been in this city too long to do what I do and still feel like a blind man every time I turn an unfamiliar corner.
Been "winging" it.
And that stops today.
There's nothing like the real thing. Recon the old-fashioned way.
Original material. Tangible maps and books.
I live and fight the fight here.
I need to familiarize myself with every neighborhood, street, and building, every aspect of the city's infrastructure and topographical layout. I need to know where every pothole is and tunnel leads...
...so why not start my homework at the top. Washington Heights and Inwood. Northernmost spot of Manhattan.
Been a rash of museum robberies along the east coast.
A museum located there called The Cloisters could be their next stop.
HERE'S THAT BOOK YOU REQUESTED-- A HISTORY OF THE CLOISTERS.
OH, THANKS.
IF I MIGHT ASK, WHAT ARE YOU RESEARCHING?
UM, I'M WRITING A BOOK ON NEW YORK AND THE AMERICAN REVOLUTION.
I SEE YOU'RE LOOKING AT WASHINGTON HEIGHTS. VERY DIFFERENT FEEL THAN THE REST OF THE CITY. ALMOST LIKE YOU'RE NOT IN MANHATTAN ANYMORE.
GO THERE A LOT?
MY BROTHER LIVES THERE WITH HIS FAMILY, WORKS AS A REAL ESTATE AGENT. KEEPS TRYING TO GET ME TO MOVE UP HIS WAY SO HE CAN HAVE A CHEAP BABYSITTER ON STANDBY.
NOT A BAD THING TO HAVE FAMILY CLOSE.
I AGREE, BUT I'M A DOWNTOWN GIRL. ALWAYS HAVE BEEN, ALWAYS WILL BE.
THE VILLAGE?
POSITIVELY. EAST FOURTH STREET.
SO, ARE THERE ANY MORE REFERENCE BOOKS I CAN GET YOU...
RICHARD.
DEBORAH.
NOPE, ALL SQUARED AWAY FOR NOW.
OKAY, HAVE A NICE DAY.

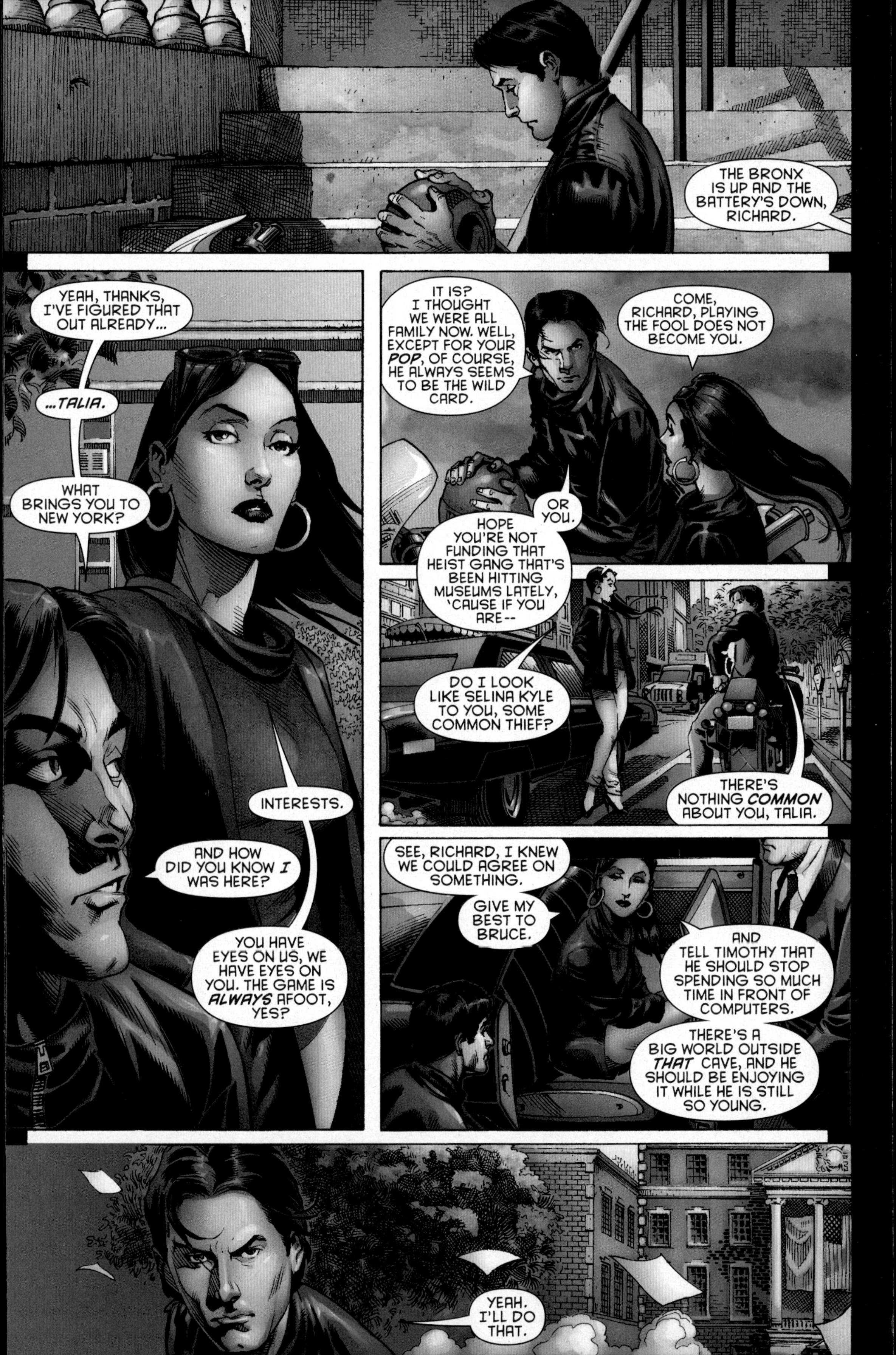
THE BRONX IS UP AND THE BATTERY'S DOWN, RICHARD.
YEAH, THANKS, I'VE FIGURED THAT OUT ALREADY...
...TALIA.
WHAT BRINGS YOU TO NEW YORK?
INTERESTS.
AND HOW DID YOU KNOW *I* WAS HERE?
YOU HAVE EYES ON US, WE HAVE EYES ON YOU. THE GAME IS *ALWAYS* AFOOT, YES?
IT IS? I THOUGHT WE WERE ALL FAMILY NOW. WELL, EXCEPT FOR YOUR *POP*, OF COURSE, HE ALWAYS SEEMS TO BE THE WILD CARD.
COME, RICHARD, PLAYING THE FOOL DOES NOT BECOME YOU.
OR YOU.
HOPE YOU'RE NOT FUNDING THAT HEIST GANG THAT'S BEEN HITTING MUSEUMS LATELY, 'CAUSE IF YOU ARE--
DO I LOOK LIKE SELINA KYLE TO YOU, SOME COMMON THIEF?
THERE'S NOTHING *COMMON* ABOUT YOU, TALIA.
SEE, RICHARD, I KNEW WE COULD AGREE ON SOMETHING.
GIVE MY BEST TO BRUCE.
AND TELL TIMOTHY THAT HE SHOULD STOP SPENDING SO MUCH TIME IN FRONT OF COMPUTERS.
THERE'S A BIG WORLD OUTSIDE *THAT* CAVE, AND HE SHOULD BE ENJOYING IT WHILE HE IS STILL SO YOUNG.
YEAH. I'LL DO THAT.

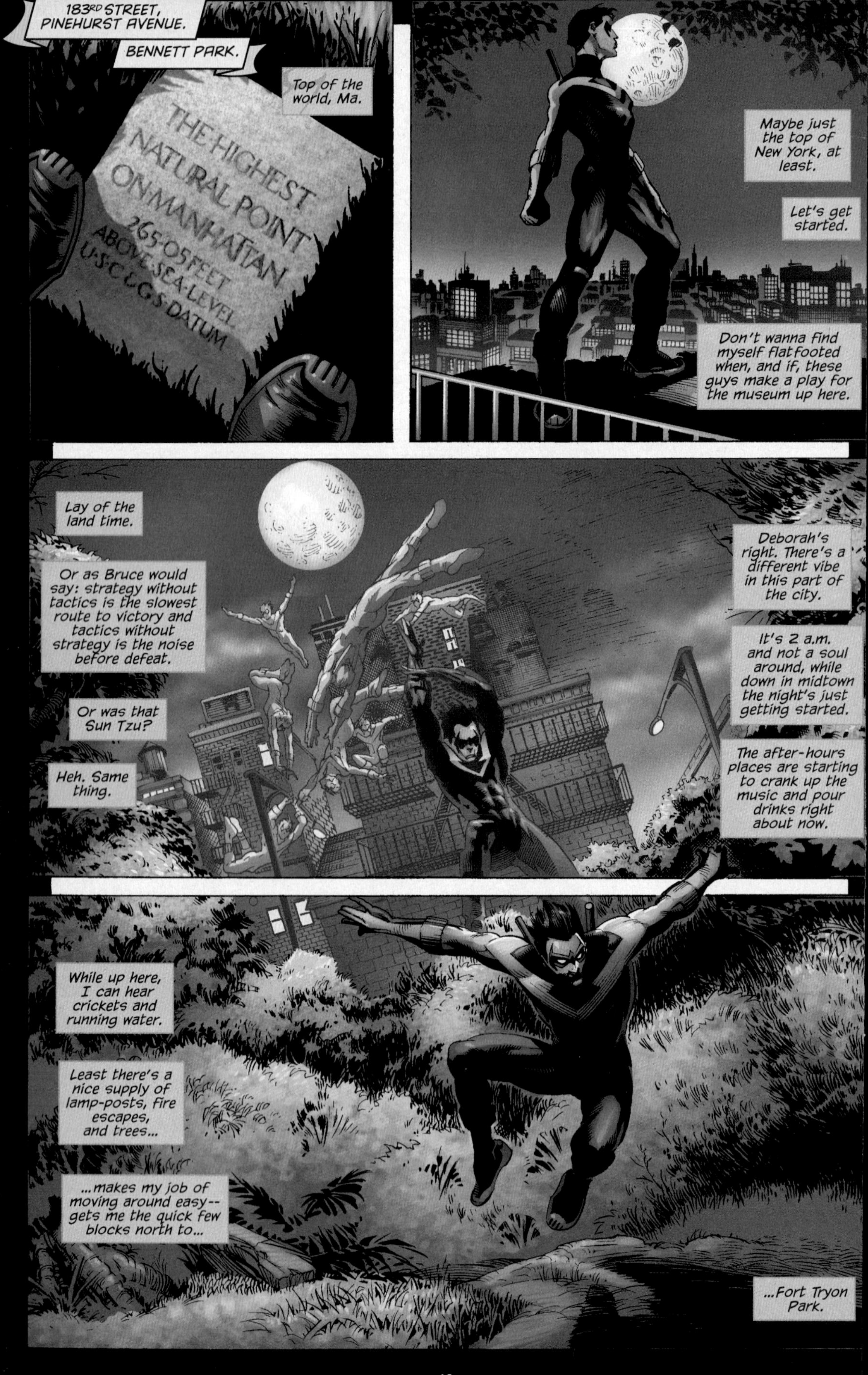
183RD STREET, PINEHURST AVENUE.
BENNETT PARK.
Top of the world, Ma.
THE HIGHEST NATURAL POINT ON MANHATTAN 265.05 FEET ABOVE SEA LEVEL U.S.C.&G.S. DATUM
Maybe just the top of New York, at least.
Let's get started.
Don't wanna find myself flatfooted when, and if, these guys make a play for the museum up here.
Lay of the land time.
Or as Bruce would say: strategy without tactics is the slowest route to victory and tactics without strategy is the noise before defeat.
Or was that Sun Tzu?
Heh. Same thing.
Deborah's right. There's a different vibe in this part of the city.
It's 2 a.m. and not a soul around, while down in midtown the night's just getting started.
The after-hours places are starting to crank up the music and pour drinks right about now.
While up here, I can hear crickets and running water.
Least there's a nice supply of lamp-posts, fire escapes, and trees...
...makes my job of moving around easy--gets me the quick few blocks north to...
...Fort Tryon Park.

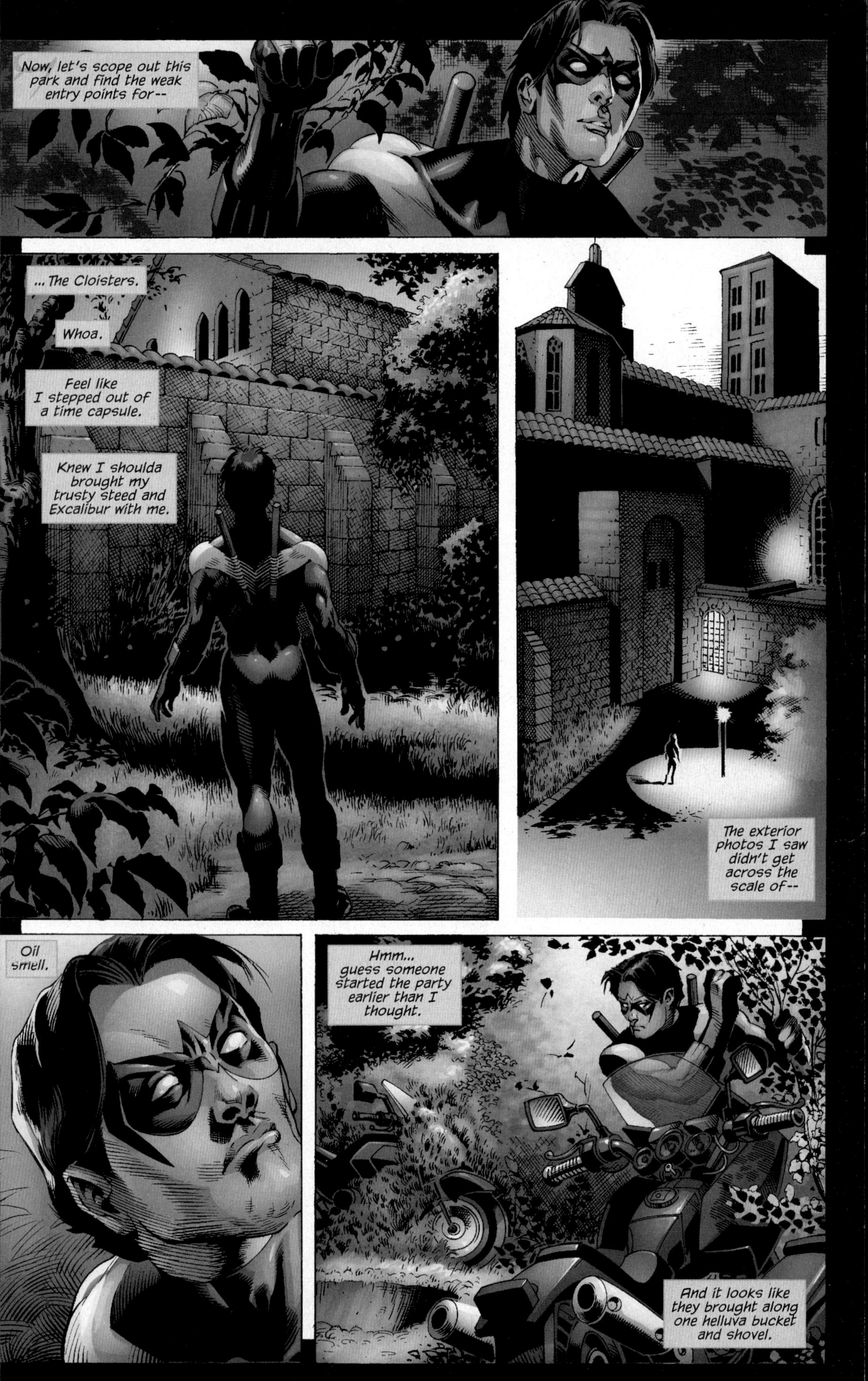
Now, let's scope out this park and find the weak entry points for--
...The Cloisters.
Whoa.
Feel like I stepped out of a time capsule.
Knew I shoulda brought my trusty steed and Excalibur with me.
The exterior photos I saw didn't get across the scale of--
Oil smell.
Hmm... guess someone started the party earlier than I thought.
And it looks like they brought along one helluva bucket and shovel.

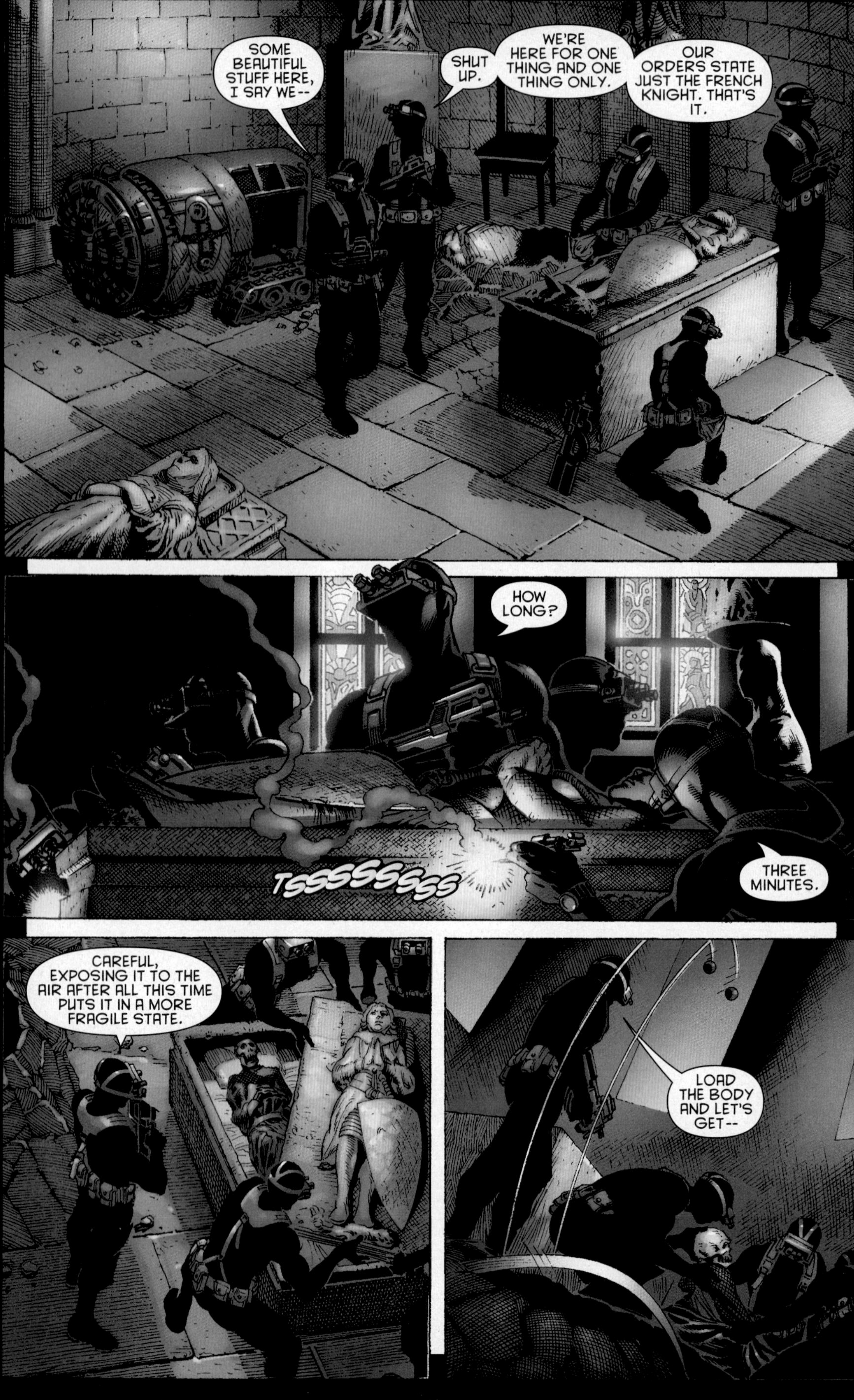
SOME BEAUTIFUL STUFF HERE, I SAY WE--
SHUT UP.
WE'RE HERE FOR ONE THING AND ONE THING ONLY.
OUR ORDERS STATE JUST THE FRENCH KNIGHT. THAT'S IT.
HOW LONG?
TSSSSSSSS
THREE MINUTES.
CAREFUL, EXPOSING IT TO THE AIR AFTER ALL THIS TIME PUTS IT IN A MORE FRAGILE STATE.
LOAD THE BODY AND LET'S GET--

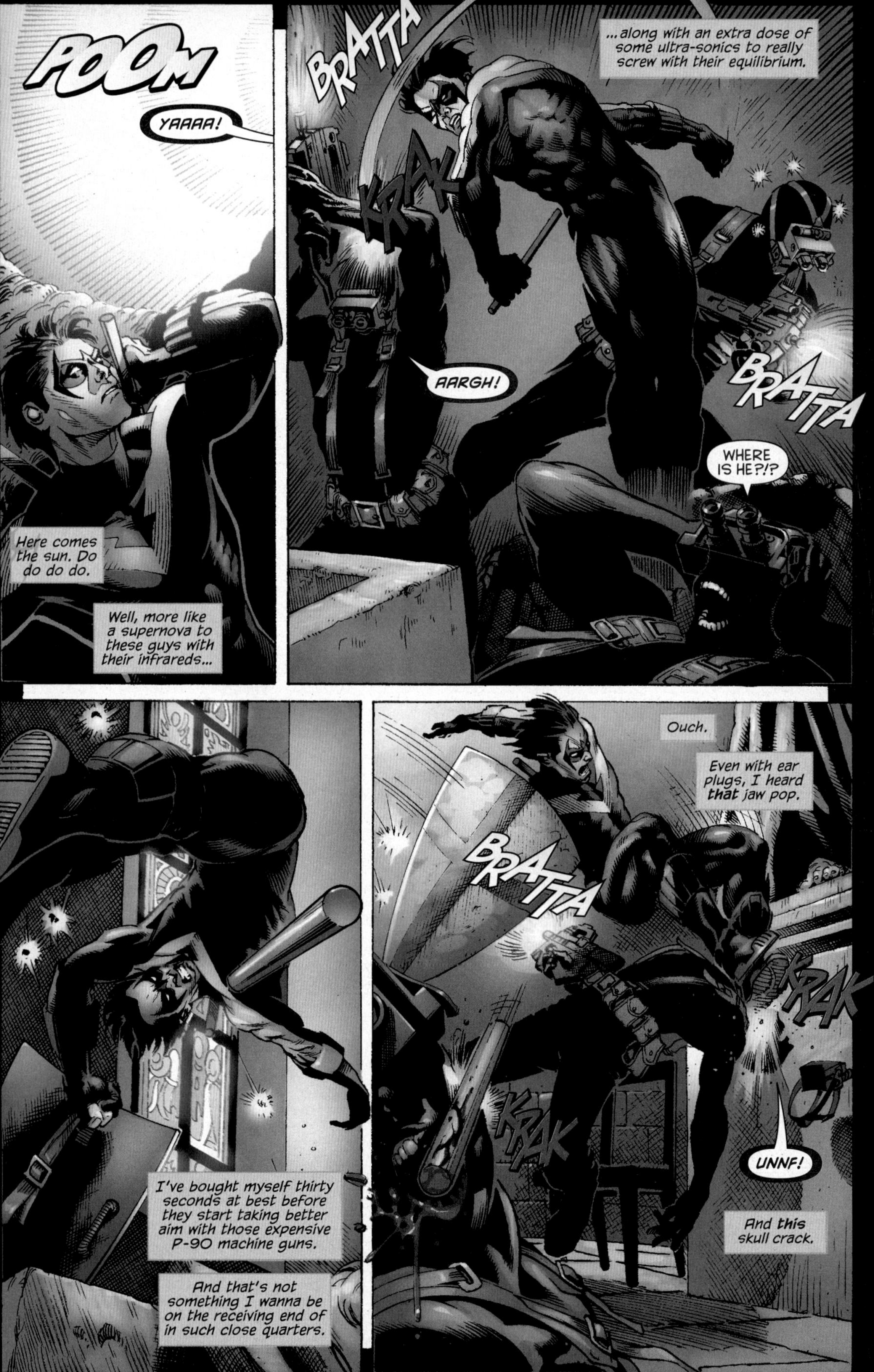
POOM
YAAAA!
Here comes the sun. Do do do do.
Well, more like a supernova to these guys with their infrareds...
BRATTA
...along with an extra dose of some ultra-sonics to really screw with their equilibrium.
KRAK
AARGH!
BRATTA
WHERE IS HE?!?
I've bought myself thirty seconds at best before they start taking better aim with those expensive P-90 machine guns.
And that's not something I wanna be on the receiving end of in such close quarters.
Ouch.
Even with ear plugs, I heard that jaw pop.
BRATTA
KRAK
KRAK
UNNF!
And this skull crack.

This one's got the shakes.

Still reeling from the effects of the sonics and lightshow.

KLANG

Put him down before he draws a bead on--

Crap.

Memo to self intensify the sturm and amplify the drang next time.

POK POK POK POK POK POK POK POK POK

ARGH!

PANG PANG

BRATTA BRATTA BRATTA

Taking cover inside a tomb--not my favorite way to spend an evening.

But damn if it isn't more comfortable than my mattress at home.

PANG PANG PANG

Not sure I wanna wait and see how much longer this shield is gonna hold up.

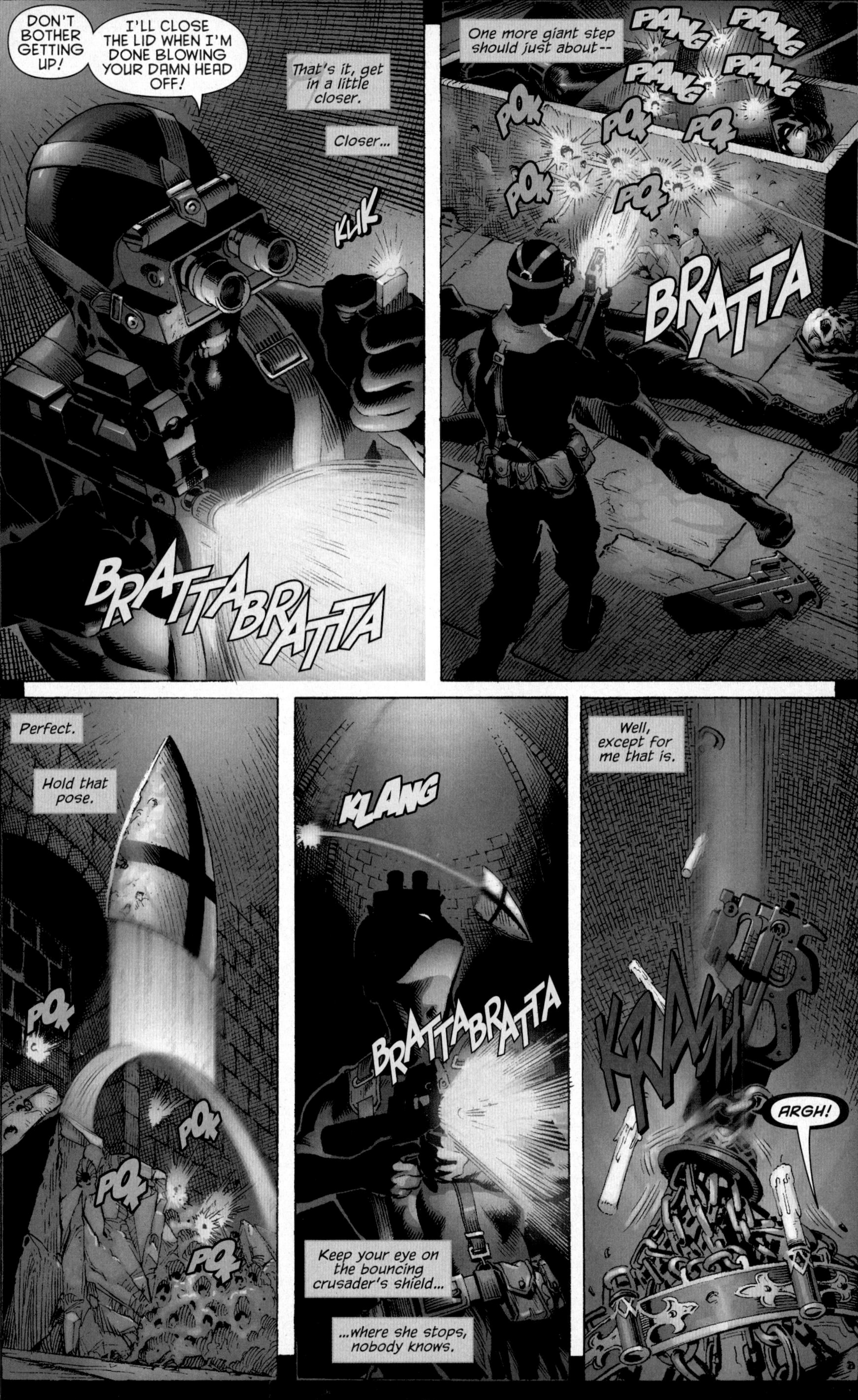
DON'T BOTHER GETTING UP!
I'LL CLOSE THE LID WHEN I'M DONE BLOWING YOUR DAMN HEAD OFF!
That's it, get in a little closer.
Closer...
KLIK
BRATTABRATTA
One more giant step should just about--
PANG PANG PANG PANG
POK POK POK POK POK
BRATTA
Perfect.
Hold that pose.
POK POK POK POK
KLANG
BRATTABRATTA
Keep your eye on the bouncing crusader's shield...
...where she stops, nobody knows.
Well, except for me that is.
KLANG
ARGH!

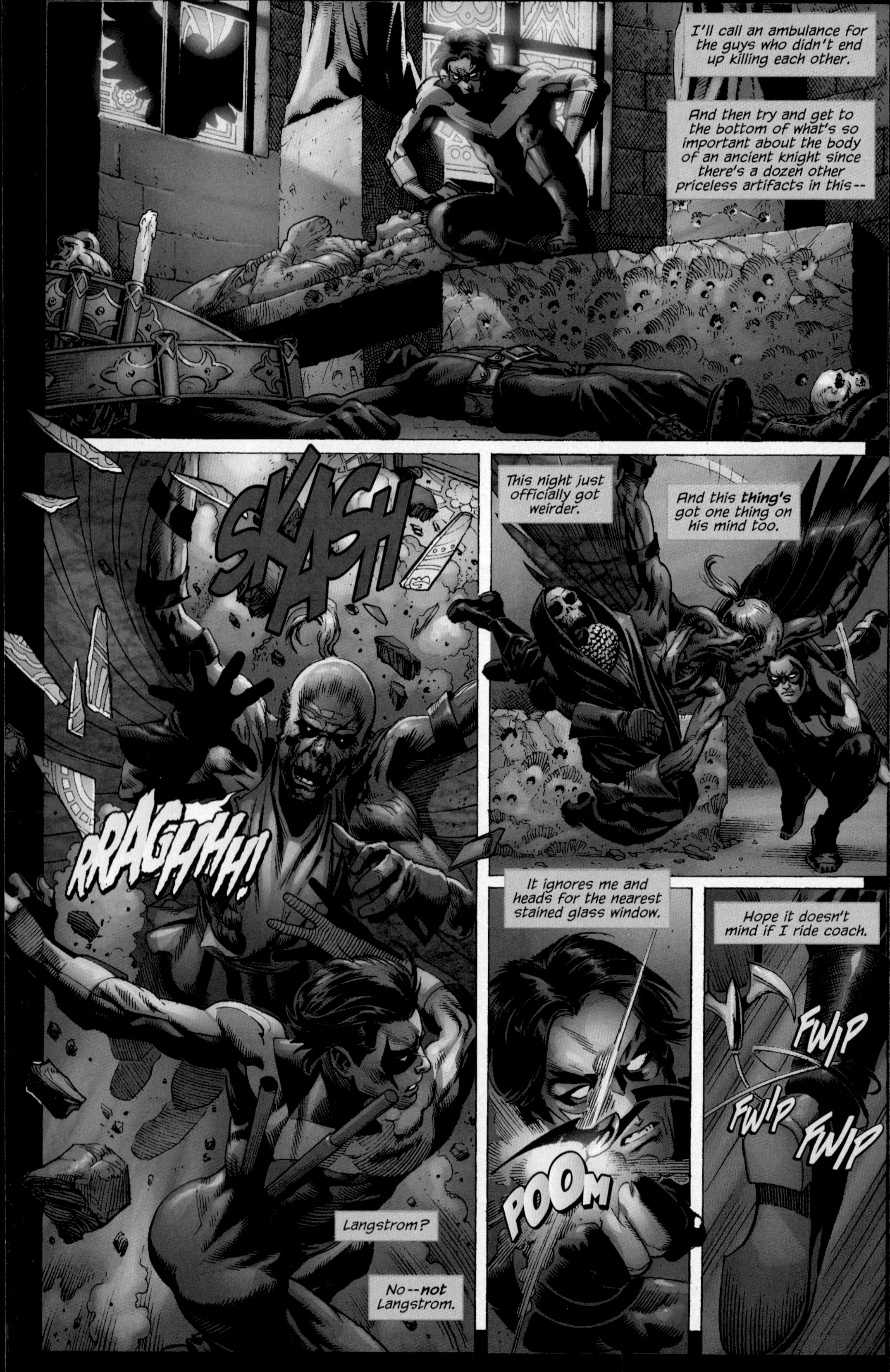

I'll call an ambulance for the guys who didn't end up killing each other.
And then try and get to the bottom of what's so important about the body of an ancient knight since there's a dozen other priceless artifacts in this--
SKASH
RRAGHHH!
Langstrom?
No--**not** Langstrom.
This night just officially got weirder.
And this **thing's** got one thing on his mind too.
It ignores me and heads for the nearest stained glass window.
POOM
Hope it doesn't mind if I ride coach.
FWIP
FWIP
FWIP

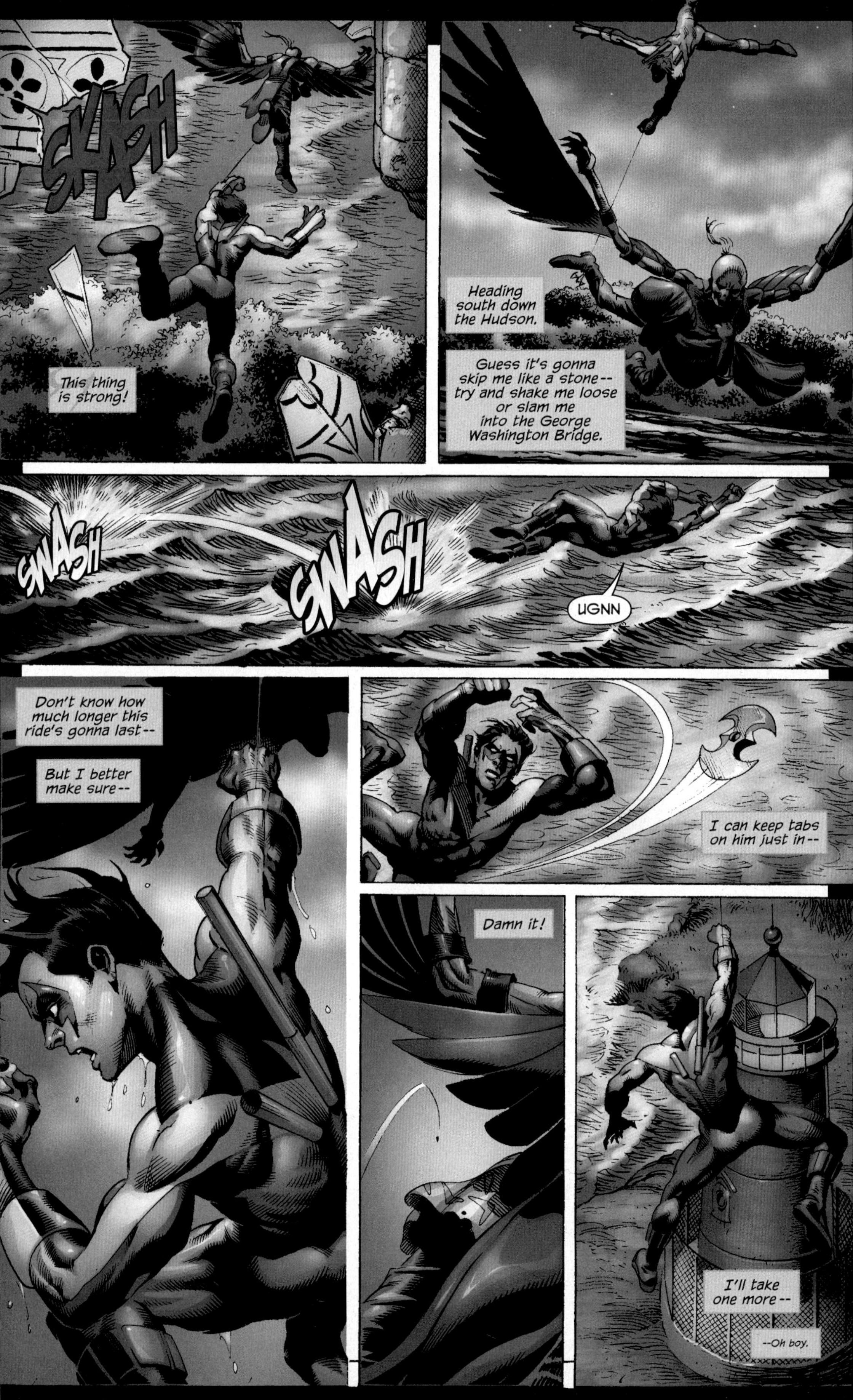
SKASH
This thing is strong!
Heading south down the Hudson.
Guess it's gonna skip me like a stone-- try and shake me loose or slam me into the George Washington Bridge.
SWASH
SWASH
UGNN
Don't know how much longer this ride's gonna last--
But I better make sure--
I can keep tabs on him just in--
Damn it!
I'll take one more--
--Oh boy.

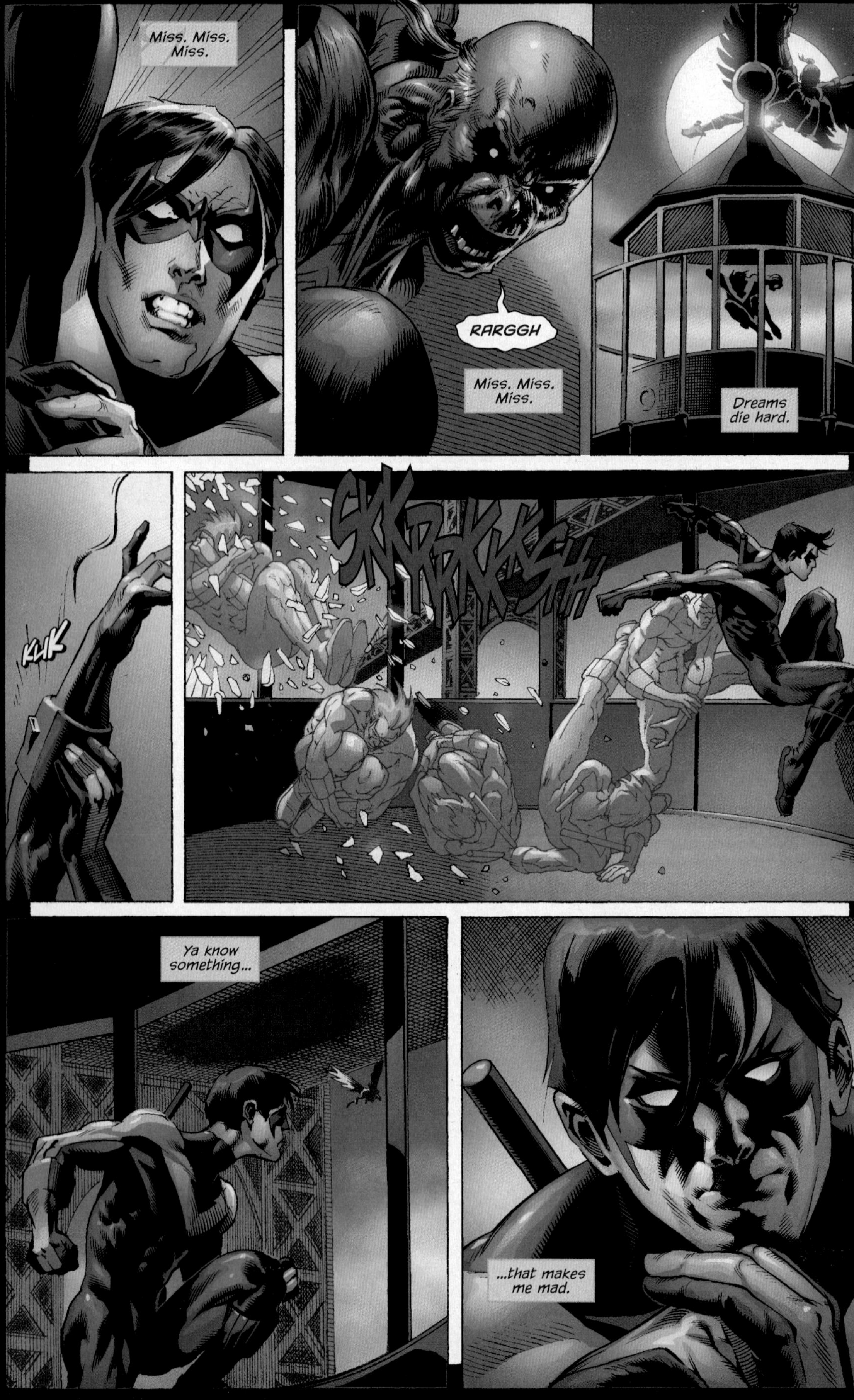

Miss. Miss.
Miss.
RARGGH
Miss. Miss.
Miss.
Dreams
die hard.
KLIK
SKKRKKKSH
Ya know
something...
...that makes
me mad.

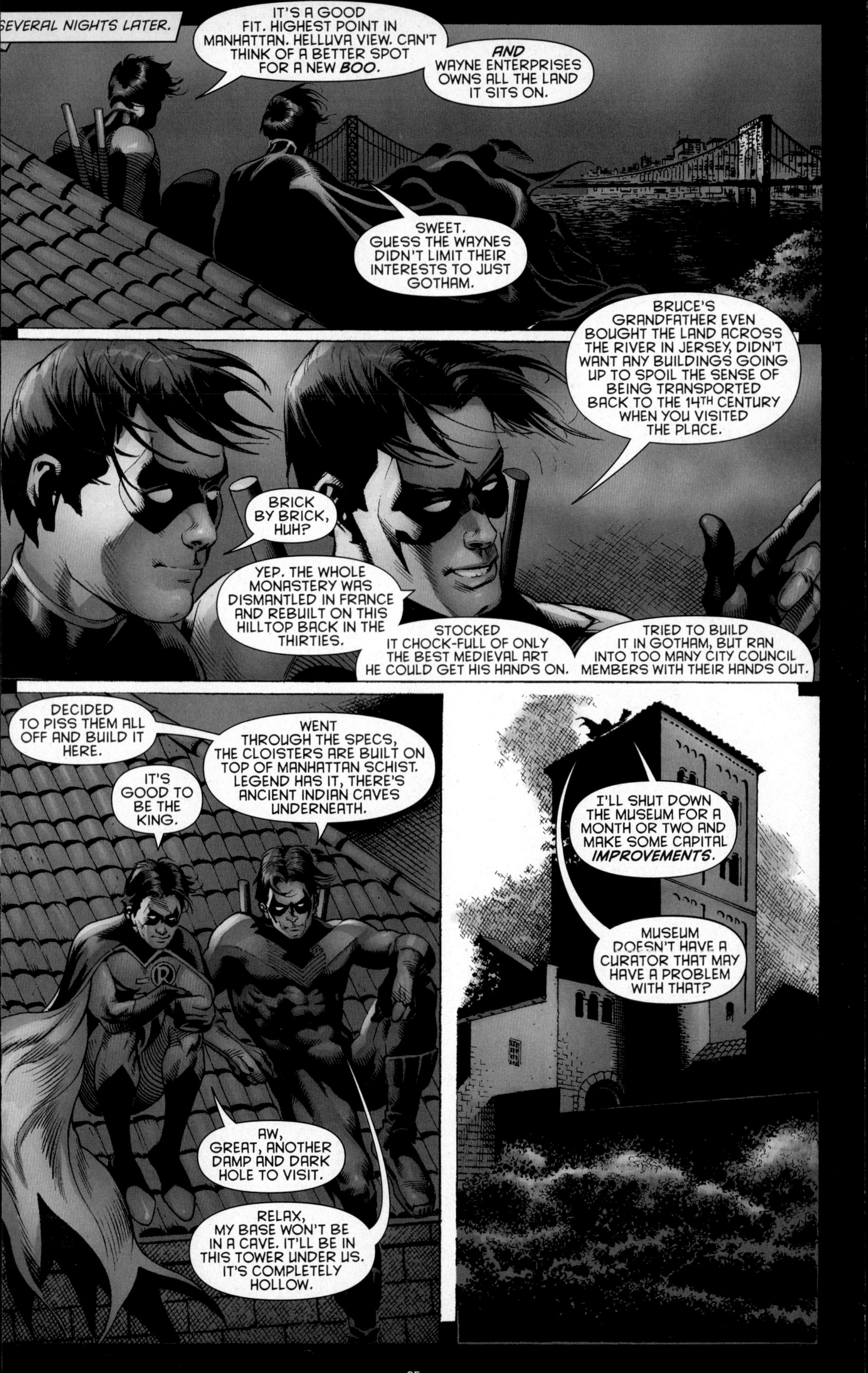
SEVERAL NIGHTS LATER.
IT'S A GOOD FIT. HIGHEST POINT IN MANHATTAN. HELLUVA VIEW. CAN'T THINK OF A BETTER SPOT FOR A NEW BOO.
AND WAYNE ENTERPRISES OWNS ALL THE LAND IT SITS ON.
SWEET. GUESS THE WAYNES DIDN'T LIMIT THEIR INTERESTS TO JUST GOTHAM.
BRUCE'S GRANDFATHER EVEN BOUGHT THE LAND ACROSS THE RIVER IN JERSEY, DIDN'T WANT ANY BUILDINGS GOING UP TO SPOIL THE SENSE OF BEING TRANSPORTED BACK TO THE 14TH CENTURY WHEN YOU VISITED THE PLACE.
BRICK BY BRICK, HUH?
YEP. THE WHOLE MONASTERY WAS DISMANTLED IN FRANCE AND REBUILT ON THIS HILLTOP BACK IN THE THIRTIES.
STOCKED IT CHOCK-FULL OF ONLY THE BEST MEDIEVAL ART HE COULD GET HIS HANDS ON.
TRIED TO BUILD IT IN GOTHAM, BUT RAN INTO TOO MANY CITY COUNCIL MEMBERS WITH THEIR HANDS OUT.
DECIDED TO PISS THEM ALL OFF AND BUILD IT HERE.
IT'S GOOD TO BE THE KING.
WENT THROUGH THE SPECS, THE CLOISTERS ARE BUILT ON TOP OF MANHATTAN SCHIST. LEGEND HAS IT, THERE'S ANCIENT INDIAN CAVES UNDERNEATH.
AW, GREAT, ANOTHER DAMP AND DARK HOLE TO VISIT.
RELAX, MY BASE WON'T BE IN A CAVE. IT'LL BE IN THIS TOWER UNDER US. IT'S COMPLETELY HOLLOW.
I'LL SHUT DOWN THE MUSEUM FOR A MONTH OR TWO AND MAKE SOME CAPITAL IMPROVEMENTS.
MUSEUM DOESN'T HAVE A CURATOR THAT MAY HAVE A PROBLEM WITH THAT?

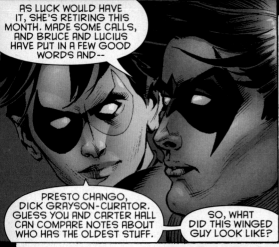

AS LUCK WOULD HAVE IT, SHE'S RETIRING THIS MONTH. MADE SOME CALLS, AND BRUCE AND LUCIUS HAVE PUT IN A FEW GOOD WORDS AND--

PRESTO CHANGO, DICK GRAYSON-CURATOR. GUESS YOU AND CARTER HALL CAN COMPARE NOTES ABOUT WHO HAS THE OLDEST STUFF.

SO, WHAT DID THIS WINGED GUY LOOK LIKE?

DIDN'T GET A GOOD LOOK. DOWNWIND OF HIS SMELLY FEET MOST OF THE TIME.

Hate to lie to Tim, but there's no way I'm telling him that thing was wearing Boomerang's tunic until I get a handle on whoever--or whatever that thing was.

WELL, AT LEAST THE LIGHTHOUSE'S STILL STANDING.

IF YOU IDIOTS SMASHED IT UP, YOU WOULD'VE HAD A LOTTA PEOPLE WHO GREW UP READING THAT BOOK PAYING DEATHSTROKE A HEFTY FEE TO TAKE YOU DOWN.

RIGHT, I ALMOST FORGOT ABOUT THAT, "THE LITTLE RED LIGHTHOUSE AND THE GREAT GREY BRIDGE."

MY DAD USED TO READ ME THAT BOOK AT NIGHT. I THINK HE LOVED IT EVEN MORE THAN I DID.

YEAH. MY DAD TOO. THIS CITY AND THE RED LIGHTHOUSE SEEMED A MILLION MILES AWAY FROM THE CIRCUS AND THE ELEPHANT DUNG.

EVEN READ IT TO MY DAD BACK WHEN HE WAS IN THAT COMA.

C'MON, LET'S GO CHECK IT OUT. I'D LIKE TO GO INSIDE.

SURE, I SENT AN ANONYMOUS DONATION TO COVER THE DAMAGES TO THE GLASS. MAYBE THEY FIXED IT.

BREEP--BREEP

TITANS EMERGENCY. GOTTA GO, DICK. RAIN-CHECK.

YOU BET. RAIN CHECK.

DICK.

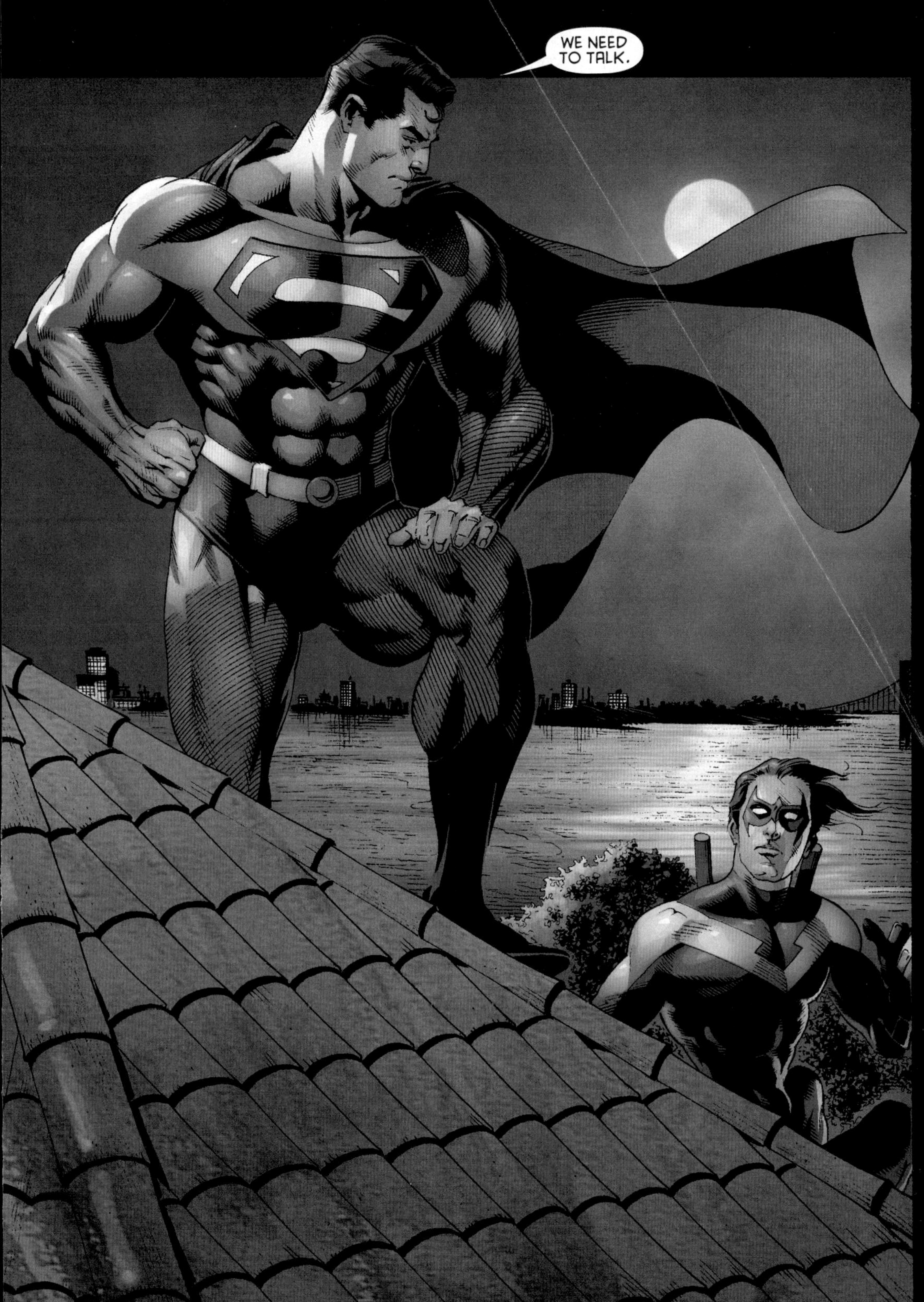
WE NEED TO TALK.

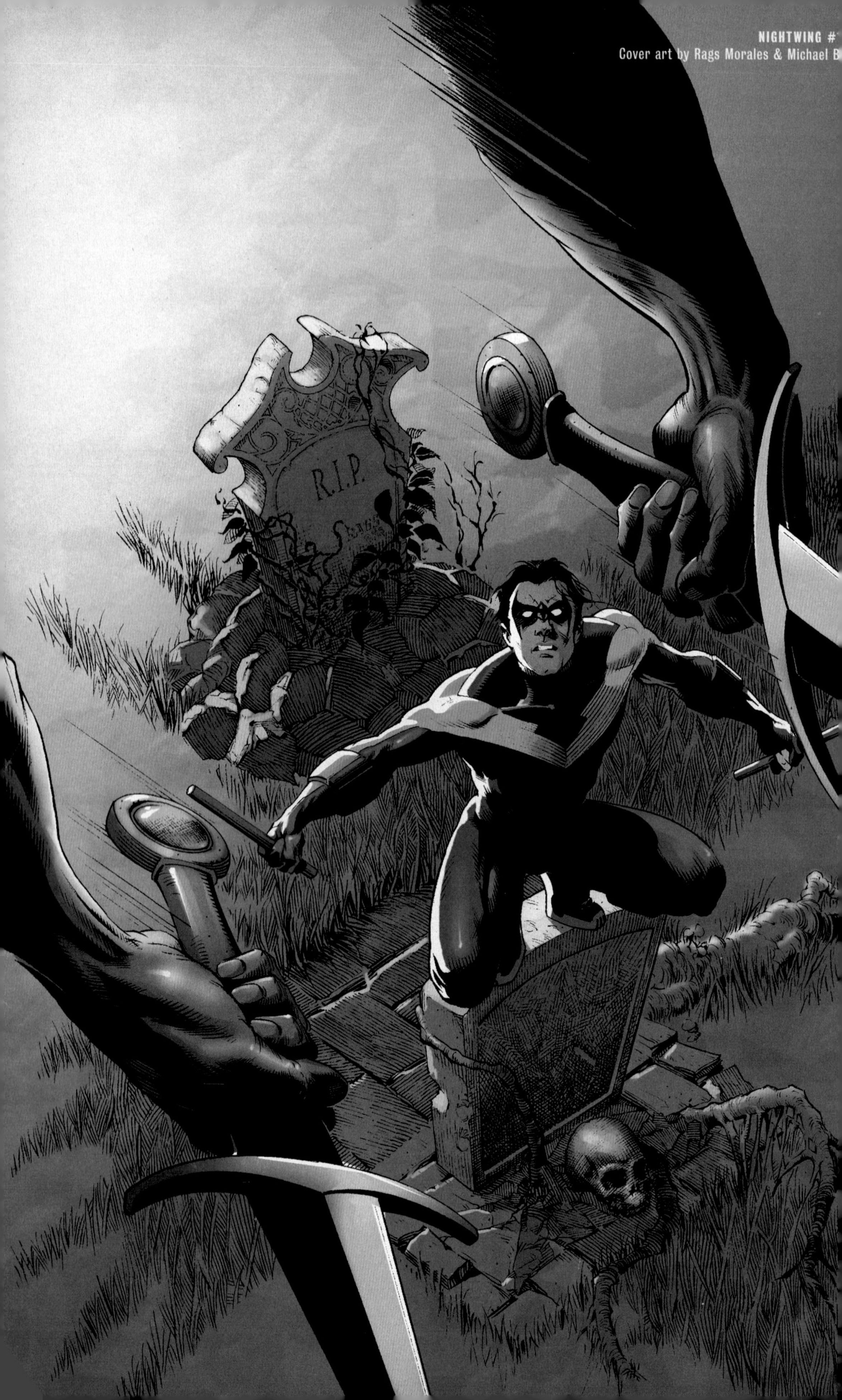
R.I.P.

NIGHTWING #
Cover art by Rags Morales & Michael B

WELL, FIRST THINGS FIRST.

FORT TRYON TAL

WHAT DO WE KNOW?

I KNOW I'VE GOT A WINGED CREATURE AND SECRET OPS GUYS STEALING THE BODY OF A 13TH CENTURY FRENCH KNIGHT.

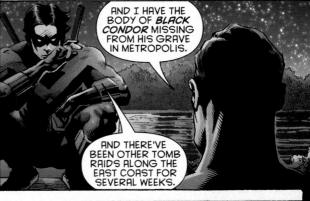

AND I HAVE THE BODY OF *BLACK CONDOR* MISSING FROM HIS GRAVE IN METROPOLIS.

AND THERE'VE BEEN OTHER TOMB RAIDS ALONG THE EAST COAST FOR SEVERAL WEEKS.

ANY ANSWERS FROM THE OPERATIVES YOU HELPED PUT IN CUSTODY?

NOPE. NOT A PEEP. THEY LAWYERED UP AND ARE AWAITING TRIAL.

WHEN I HEARD ABOUT YOUR FRENCH KNIGHT I THOUGHT WE SHOULD COMPARE NOTES.

HOW DID YOU FIND OUT ABOUT CONDOR?

BY ACCIDENT.

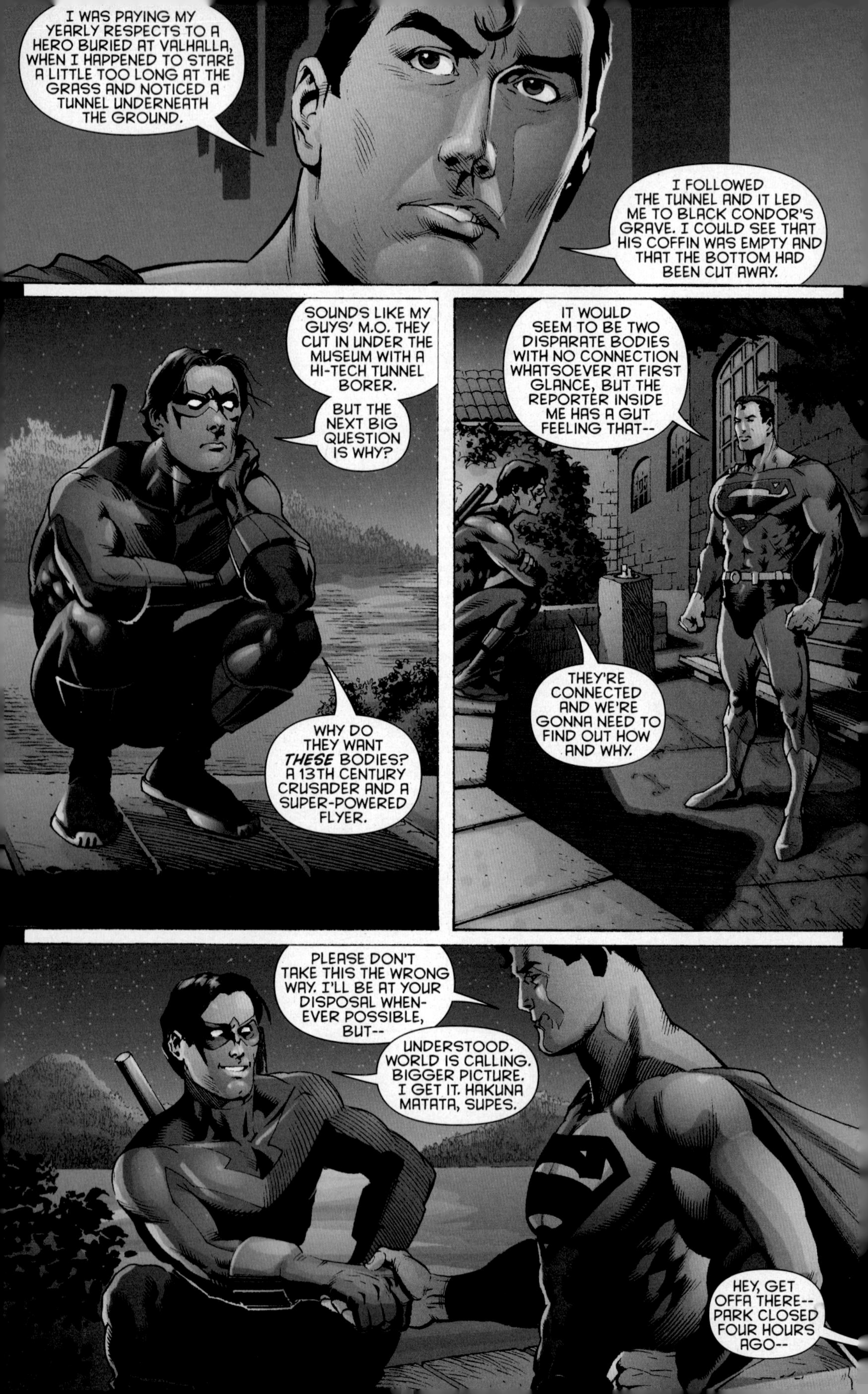
I WAS PAYING MY YEARLY RESPECTS TO A HERO BURIED AT VALHALLA, WHEN I HAPPENED TO STARE A LITTLE TOO LONG AT THE GRASS AND NOTICED A TUNNEL UNDERNEATH THE GROUND.
I FOLLOWED THE TUNNEL AND IT LED ME TO BLACK CONDOR'S GRAVE. I COULD SEE THAT HIS COFFIN WAS EMPTY AND THAT THE BOTTOM HAD BEEN CUT AWAY.
SOUNDS LIKE MY GUYS' M.O. THEY CUT IN UNDER THE MUSEUM WITH A HI-TECH TUNNEL BORER.
BUT THE NEXT BIG QUESTION IS WHY?
WHY DO THEY WANT *THESE* BODIES? A 13TH CENTURY CRUSADER AND A SUPER-POWERED FLYER.
IT WOULD SEEM TO BE TWO DISPARATE BODIES WITH NO CONNECTION WHATSOEVER AT FIRST GLANCE, BUT THE REPORTER INSIDE ME HAS A GUT FEELING THAT--
THEY'RE CONNECTED AND WE'RE GONNA NEED TO FIND OUT HOW AND WHY.
PLEASE DON'T TAKE THIS THE WRONG WAY. I'LL BE AT YOUR DISPOSAL WHEN-EVER POSSIBLE, BUT--
UNDERSTOOD. WORLD IS CALLING. BIGGER PICTURE. I GET IT. HAKUNA MATATA, SUPES.
HEY, GET OFFA THERE-- PARK CLOSED FOUR HOURS AGO--

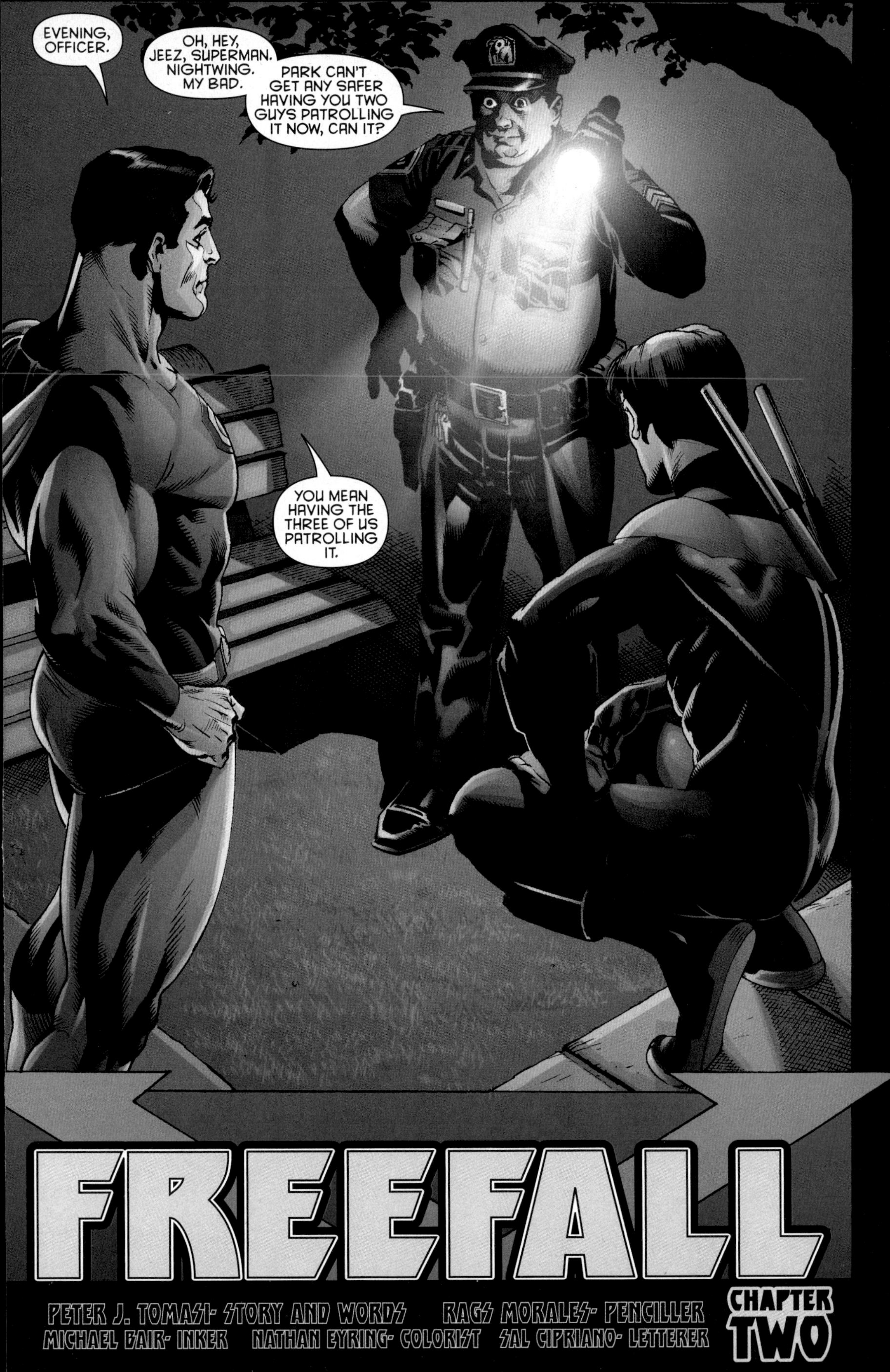
EVENING, OFFICER.
OH, HEY, JEEZ, SUPERMAN. NIGHTWING. MY BAD.
PARK CAN'T GET ANY SAFER HAVING YOU TWO GUYS PATROLLING IT NOW, CAN IT?
YOU MEAN HAVING THE THREE OF US PATROLLING IT.
FREEFALL
PETER J. TOMASI- STORY AND WORDS
RAGS MORALES- PENCILLER
MICHAEL BAIR- INKER
NATHAN EYRING- COLORIST
SAL CIPRIANO- LETTERER
CHAPTER TWO

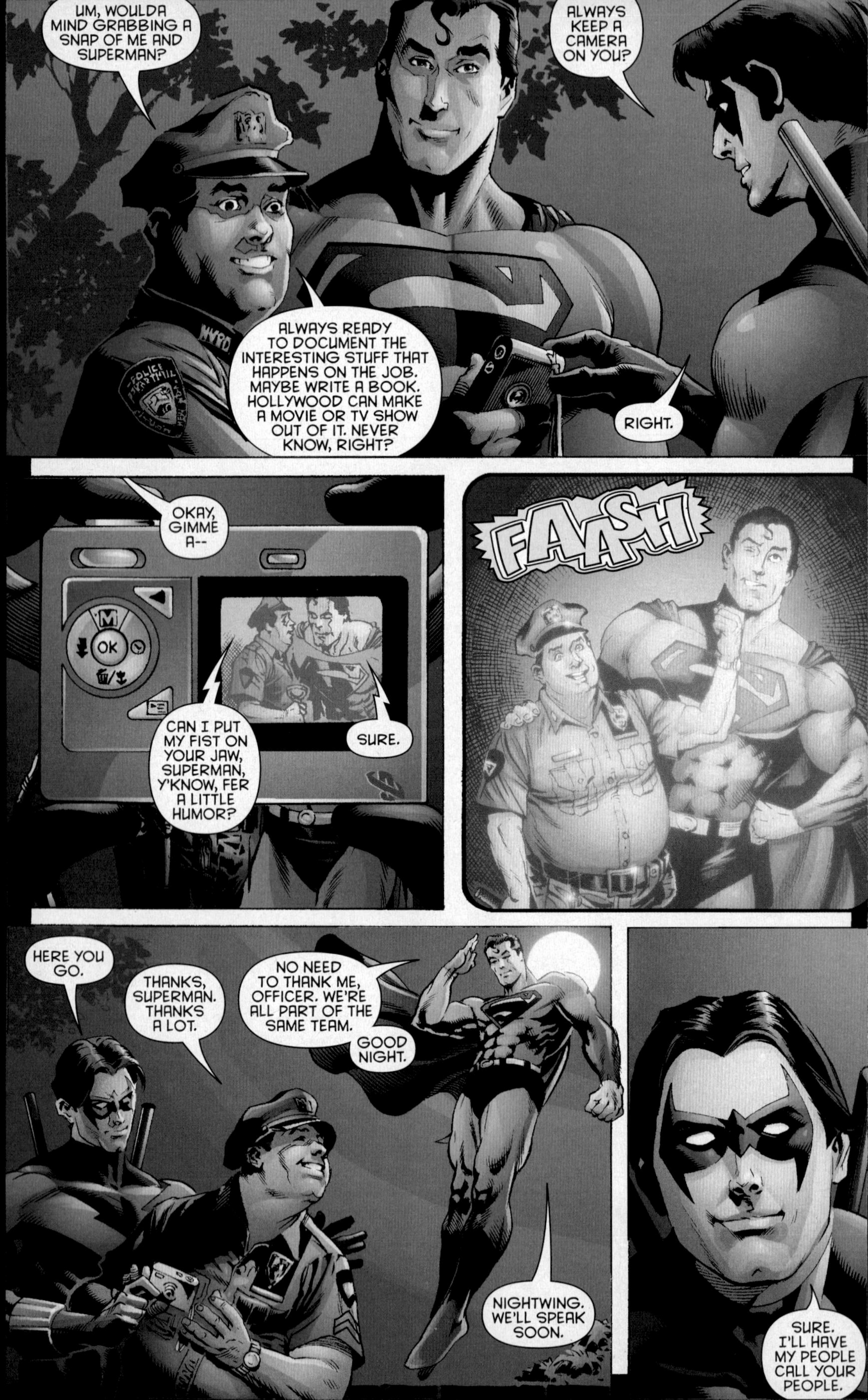
UM, WOULDA MIND GRABBING A SNAP OF ME AND SUPERMAN?
ALWAYS KEEP A CAMERA ON YOU?
ALWAYS READY TO DOCUMENT THE INTERESTING STUFF THAT HAPPENS ON THE JOB. MAYBE WRITE A BOOK. HOLLYWOOD CAN MAKE A MOVIE OR TV SHOW OUT OF IT. NEVER KNOW, RIGHT?
RIGHT.
OKAY, GIMME A--
CAN I PUT MY FIST ON YOUR JAW, SUPERMAN, Y'KNOW, FER A LITTLE HUMOR?
SURE.
FAASH
HERE YOU GO.
THANKS, SUPERMAN. THANKS A LOT.
NO NEED TO THANK ME, OFFICER. WE'RE ALL PART OF THE SAME TEAM.
GOOD NIGHT.
NIGHTWING. WE'LL SPEAK SOON.
SURE. I'LL HAVE MY PEOPLE CALL YOUR PEOPLE.

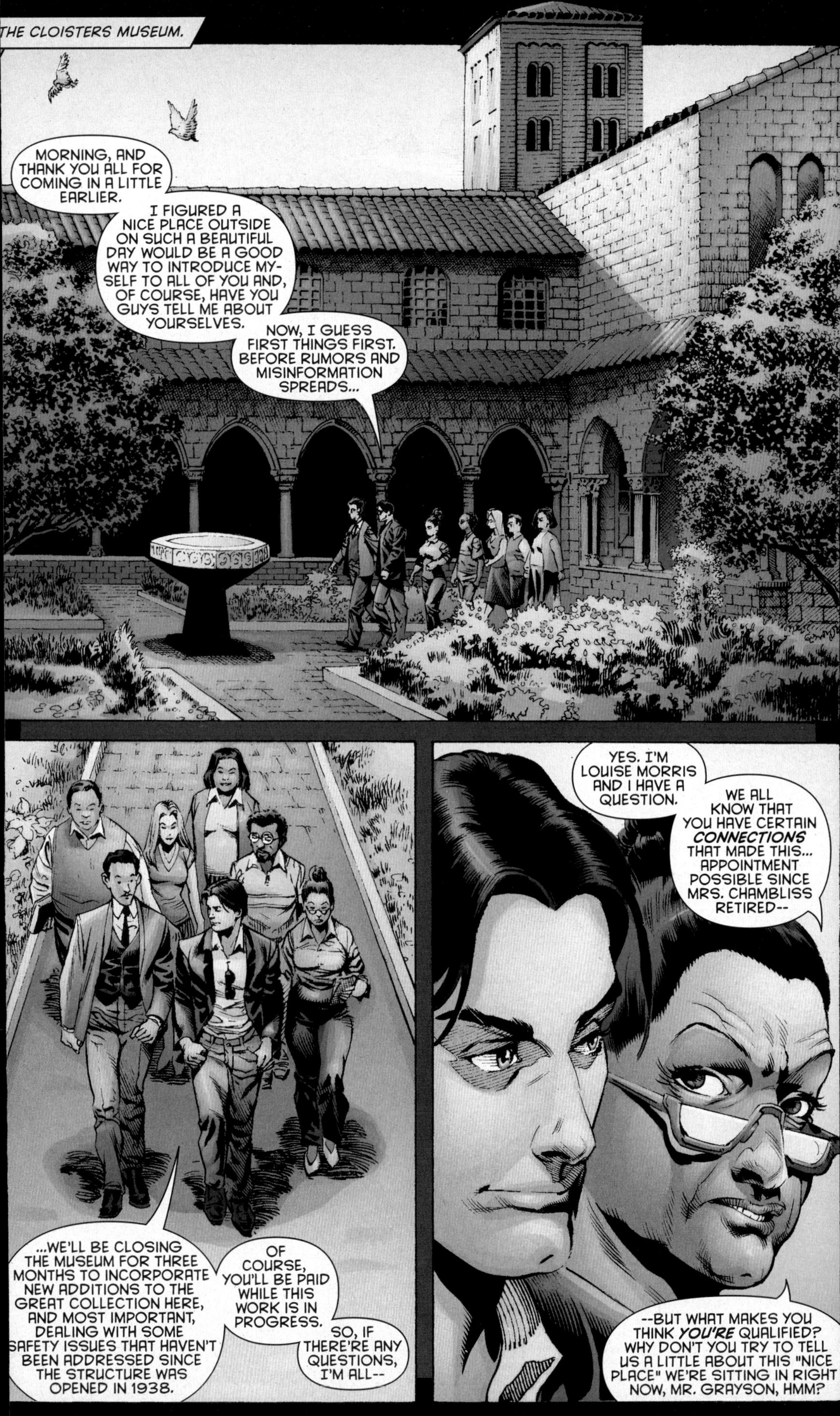
THE CLOISTERS MUSEUM.
MORNING, AND THANK YOU ALL FOR COMING IN A LITTLE EARLIER.
I FIGURED A NICE PLACE OUTSIDE ON SUCH A BEAUTIFUL DAY WOULD BE A GOOD WAY TO INTRODUCE MY-SELF TO ALL OF YOU AND, OF COURSE, HAVE YOU GUYS TELL ME ABOUT YOURSELVES.
NOW, I GUESS FIRST THINGS FIRST. BEFORE RUMORS AND MISINFORMATION SPREADS...
...WE'LL BE CLOSING THE MUSEUM FOR THREE MONTHS TO INCORPORATE NEW ADDITIONS TO THE GREAT COLLECTION HERE, AND MOST IMPORTANT, DEALING WITH SOME SAFETY ISSUES THAT HAVEN'T BEEN ADDRESSED SINCE THE STRUCTURE WAS OPENED IN 1938.
OF COURSE, YOU'LL BE PAID WHILE THIS WORK IS IN PROGRESS.
SO, IF THERE'RE ANY QUESTIONS, I'M ALL--
YES. I'M LOUISE MORRIS AND I HAVE A QUESTION.
WE ALL KNOW THAT YOU HAVE CERTAIN *CONNECTIONS* THAT MADE THIS... APPOINTMENT POSSIBLE SINCE MRS. CHAMBLISS RETIRED--
--BUT WHAT MAKES YOU THINK *YOU'RE* QUALIFIED? WHY DON'T YOU TRY TO TELL US A LITTLE ABOUT THIS "NICE PLACE" WE'RE SITTING IN RIGHT NOW, MR. GRAYSON, HMM?

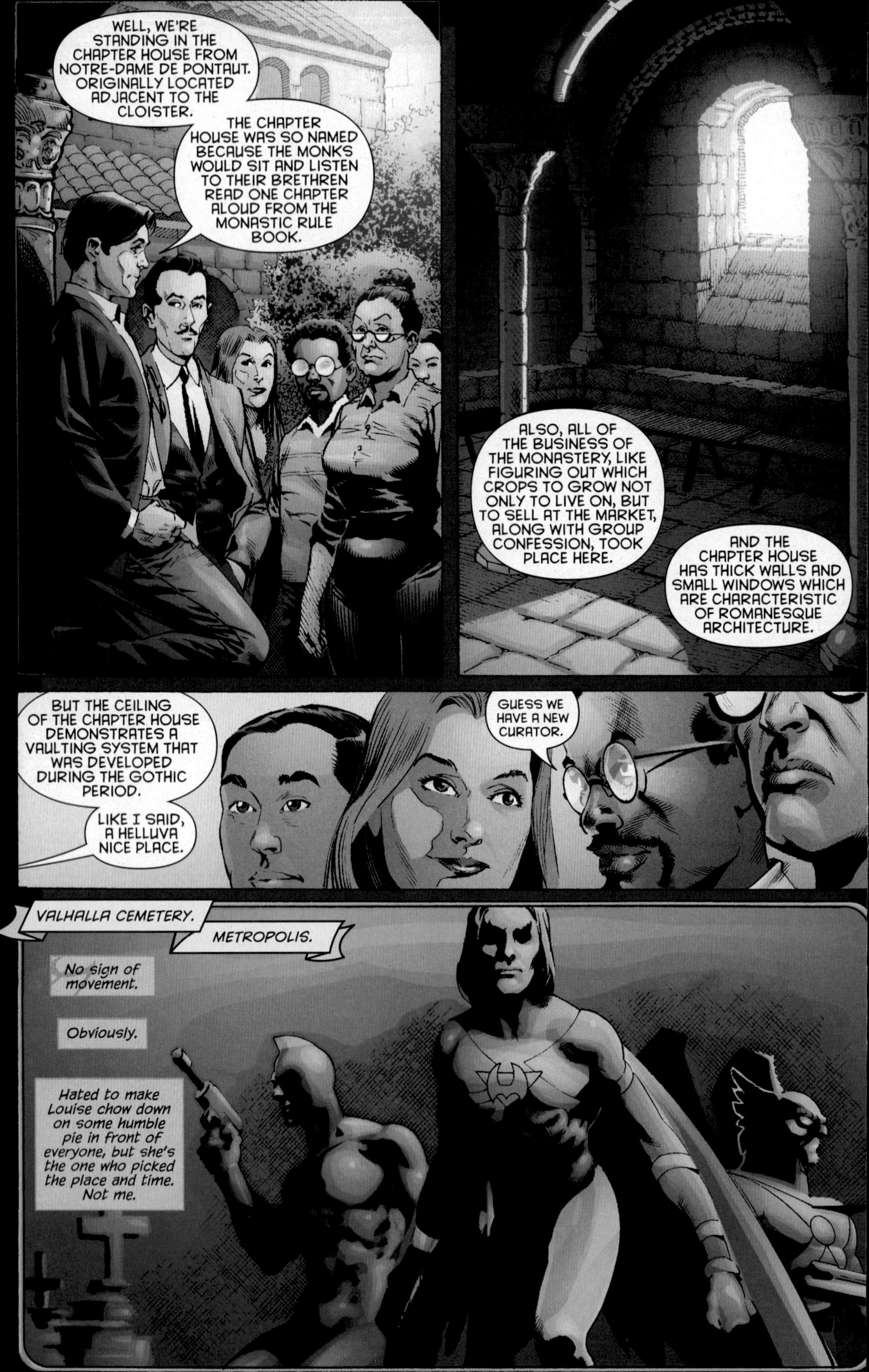
WELL, WE'RE STANDING IN THE CHAPTER HOUSE FROM NOTRE-DAME DE PONTAUT. ORIGINALLY LOCATED ADJACENT TO THE CLOISTER.
THE CHAPTER HOUSE WAS SO NAMED BECAUSE THE MONKS WOULD SIT AND LISTEN TO THEIR BRETHREN READ ONE CHAPTER ALOUD FROM THE MONASTIC RULE BOOK.
ALSO, ALL OF THE BUSINESS OF THE MONASTERY, LIKE FIGURING OUT WHICH CROPS TO GROW NOT ONLY TO LIVE ON, BUT TO SELL AT THE MARKET, ALONG WITH GROUP CONFESSION, TOOK PLACE HERE.
AND THE CHAPTER HOUSE HAS THICK WALLS AND SMALL WINDOWS WHICH ARE CHARACTERISTIC OF ROMANESQUE ARCHITECTURE.
BUT THE CEILING OF THE CHAPTER HOUSE DEMONSTRATES A VAULTING SYSTEM THAT WAS DEVELOPED DURING THE GOTHIC PERIOD.
LIKE I SAID, A HELLUVA NICE PLACE.
GUESS WE HAVE A NEW CURATOR.
VALHALLA CEMETERY.
METROPOLIS.
No sign of movement.
Obviously.
Hated to make Louise chow down on some humble pie in front of everyone, but she's the one who picked the place and time. Not me.

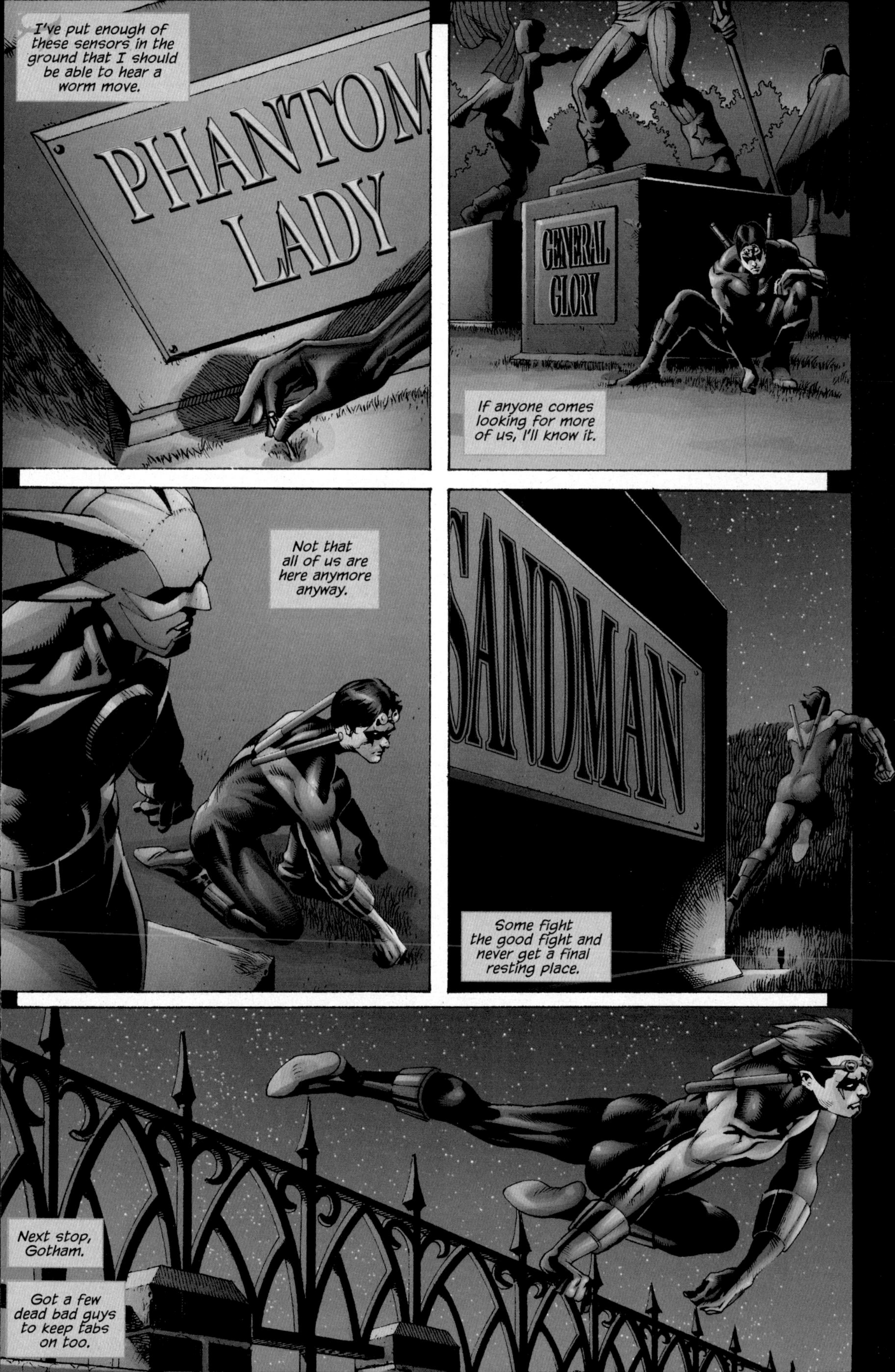
I've put enough of these sensors in the ground that I should be able to hear a worm move.
PHANTOM LADY
GENERAL GLORY
If anyone comes looking for more of us, I'll know it.
Not that all of us are here anymore anyway.
SANDMAN
Some fight the good fight and never get a final resting place.
Next stop, Gotham.
Got a few dead bad guys to keep tabs on too.

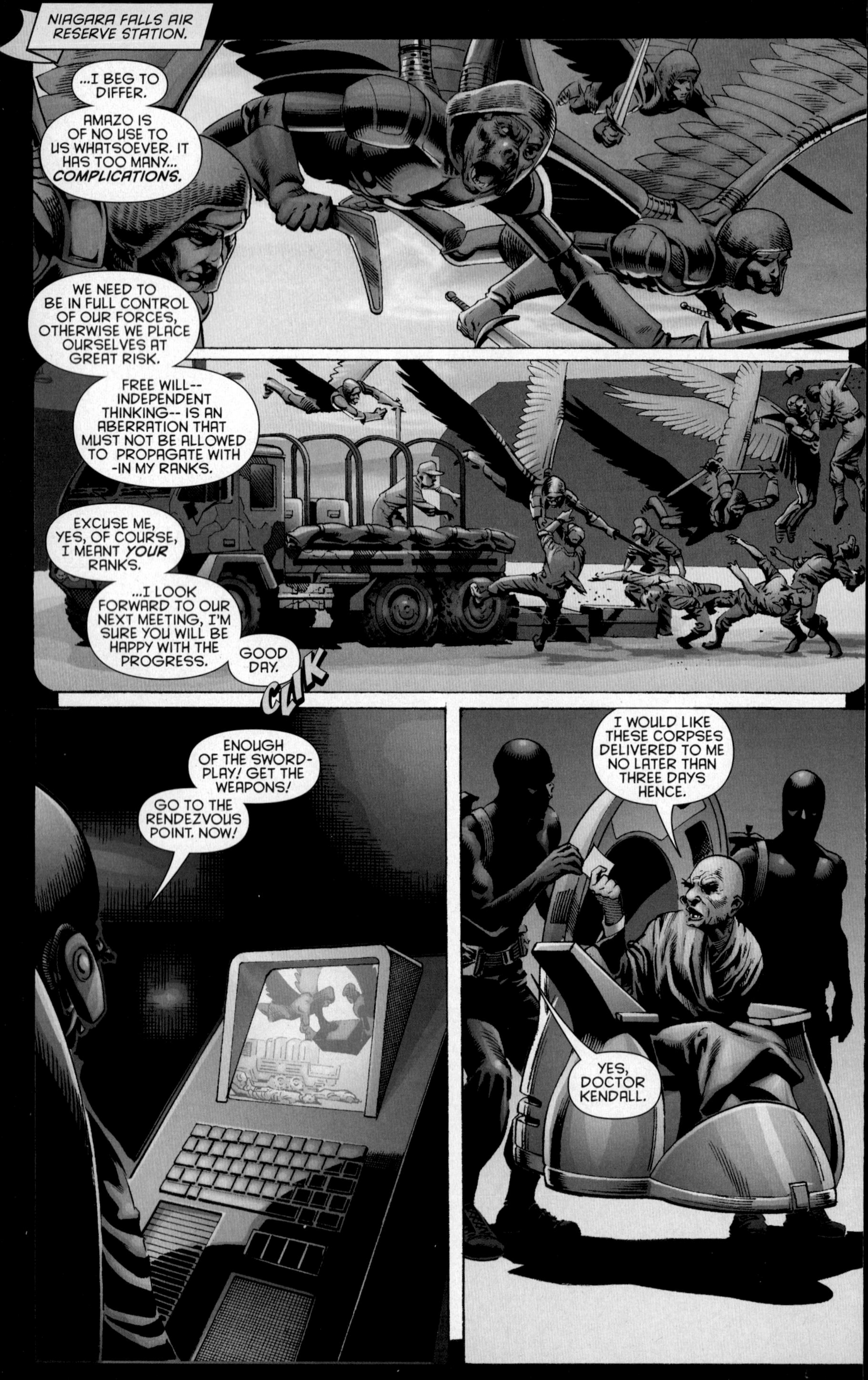
NIAGARA FALLS AIR RESERVE STATION.
...I BEG TO DIFFER.
AMAZO IS OF NO USE TO US WHATSOEVER. IT HAS TOO MANY... COMPLICATIONS.
WE NEED TO BE IN FULL CONTROL OF OUR FORCES, OTHERWISE WE PLACE OURSELVES AT GREAT RISK.
FREE WILL-- INDEPENDENT THINKING-- IS AN ABERRATION THAT MUST NOT BE ALLOWED TO PROPAGATE WITH -IN MY RANKS.
EXCUSE ME, YES, OF COURSE, I MEANT YOUR RANKS.
...I LOOK FORWARD TO OUR NEXT MEETING, I'M SURE YOU WILL BE HAPPY WITH THE PROGRESS.
GOOD DAY.
CLIK
ENOUGH OF THE SWORD-PLAY! GET THE WEAPONS!
GO TO THE RENDEZVOUS POINT. NOW!
I WOULD LIKE THESE CORPSES DELIVERED TO ME NO LATER THAN THREE DAYS HENCE.
YES, DOCTOR KENDALL.

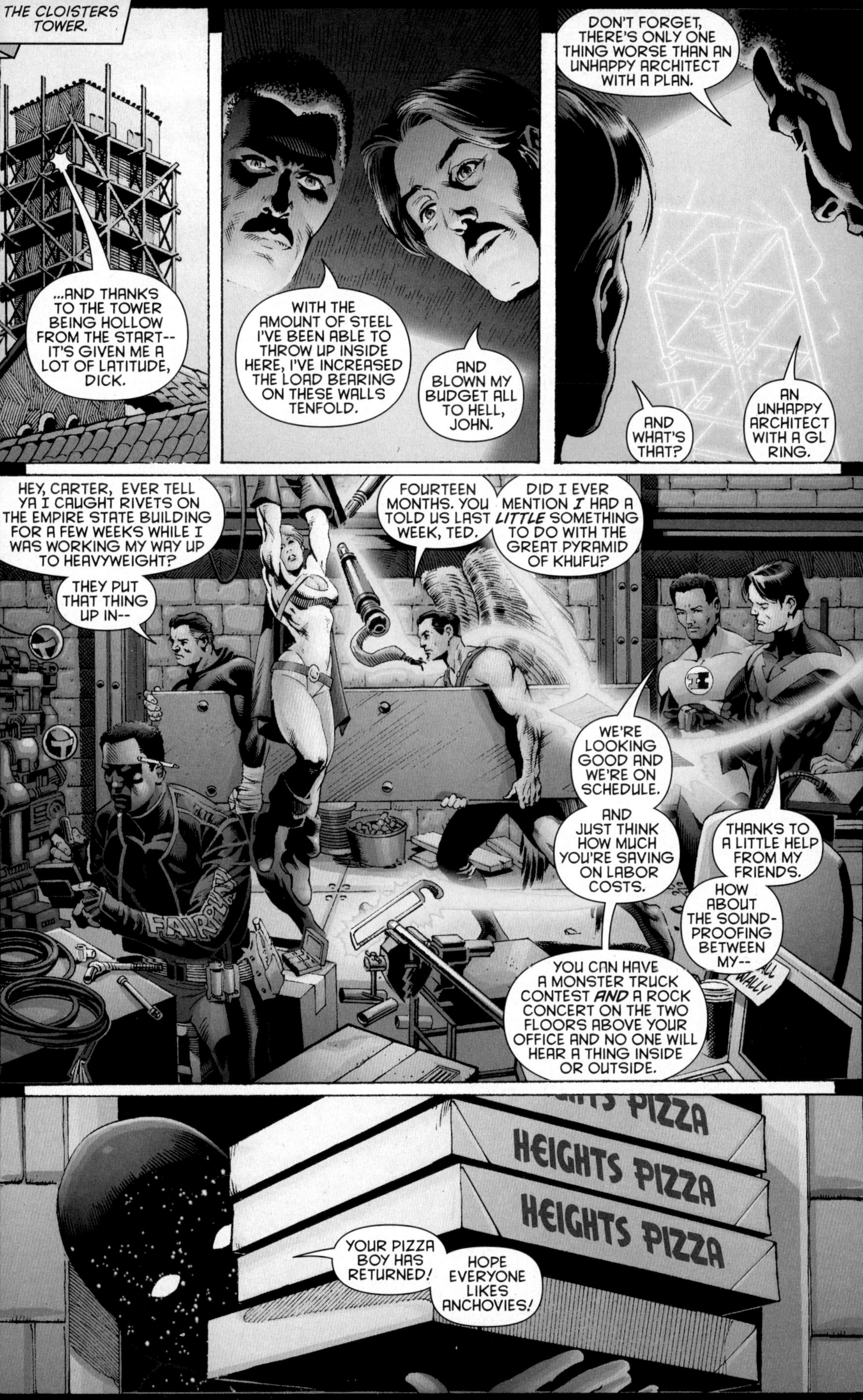
THE CLOISTERS TOWER.
...AND THANKS TO THE TOWER BEING HOLLOW FROM THE START-- IT'S GIVEN ME A LOT OF LATITUDE, DICK.
WITH THE AMOUNT OF STEEL I'VE BEEN ABLE TO THROW UP INSIDE HERE, I'VE INCREASED THE LOAD BEARING ON THESE WALLS TENFOLD.
AND BLOWN MY BUDGET ALL TO HELL, JOHN.
DON'T FORGET, THERE'S ONLY ONE THING WORSE THAN AN UNHAPPY ARCHITECT WITH A PLAN.
AND WHAT'S THAT?
AN UNHAPPY ARCHITECT WITH A GL RING.
HEY, CARTER, EVER TELL YA I CAUGHT RIVETS ON THE EMPIRE STATE BUILDING FOR A FEW WEEKS WHILE I WAS WORKING MY WAY UP TO HEAVYWEIGHT?
THEY PUT THAT THING UP IN--
FOURTEEN MONTHS. YOU TOLD US LAST WEEK, TED.
DID I EVER MENTION *I* HAD A *LITTLE* SOMETHING TO DO WITH THE GREAT PYRAMID OF KHUFU?
WE'RE LOOKING GOOD AND WE'RE ON SCHEDULE.
AND JUST THINK HOW MUCH YOU'RE SAVING ON LABOR COSTS.
THANKS TO A LITTLE HELP FROM MY FRIENDS.
HOW ABOUT THE SOUND-PROOFING BETWEEN MY--
YOU CAN HAVE A MONSTER TRUCK CONTEST *AND* A ROCK CONCERT ON THE TWO FLOORS ABOVE YOUR OFFICE AND NO ONE WILL HEAR A THING INSIDE OR OUTSIDE.
HEIGHTS PIZZA
HEIGHTS PIZZA
HEIGHTS PIZZA
YOUR PIZZA BOY HAS RETURNED!
HOPE EVERYONE LIKES ANCHOVIES!

MUSEUM OF THE CITY OF NEW YORK.

WELL, YOU *ARE* PERSISTENT, AREN'T YOU, RICHARD?

I DO TRY, DEBORAH. I DO TRY.

SO, IF YOU DON'T HAVE ANY BOYFRIENDS OR HUSBANDS THAT WOULD OBJECT, HOW ABOUT DINNER?

THE POWER BROKER

GOTHAM

DOWNTOWN

STREETSCAPES

HERE IS NEW YORK

EMPIRE CITY

LAST I CHECKED, NO ON BOTH COUNTS.

THAT'S GOOD.

DINNER SOUNDS GOOD, TOO.

I KNOW A NICE *LITTLE PLACE.* NO FRILLS, BUT FOOD IS GOOD AND FILLING.

I GET OFF IN THIRTY MINUTES.

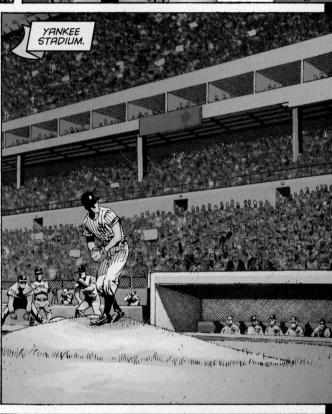

YANKEE STADIUM.

"LITTLE PLACE," HMM?

I MEANT THE KNEE ROOM IN THE BOX SEATS.

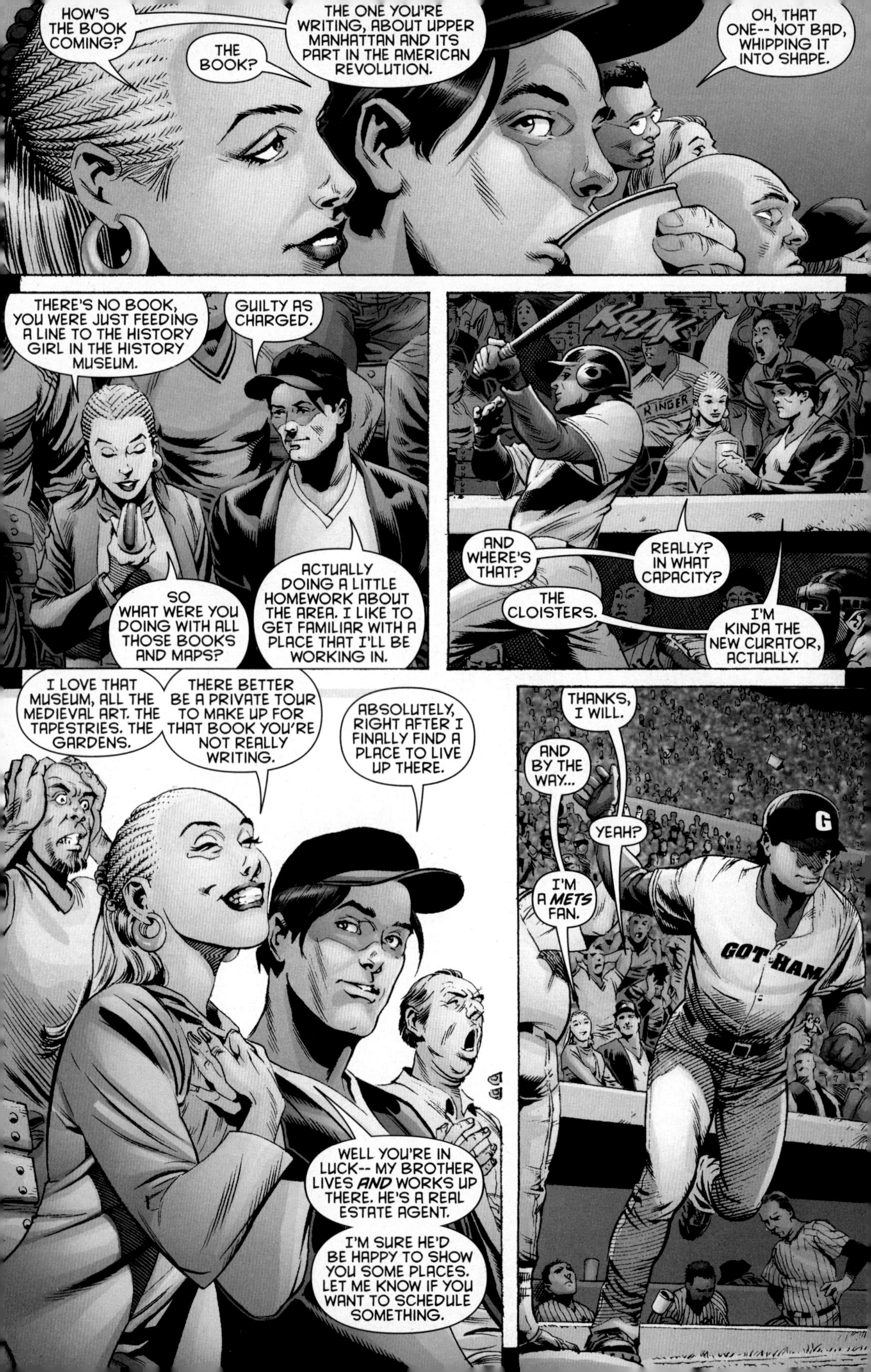
HOW'S THE BOOK COMING?
THE BOOK?
THE ONE YOU'RE WRITING, ABOUT UPPER MANHATTAN AND ITS PART IN THE AMERICAN REVOLUTION.
OH, THAT ONE-- NOT BAD, WHIPPING IT INTO SHAPE.
THERE'S NO BOOK, YOU WERE JUST FEEDING A LINE TO THE HISTORY GIRL IN THE HISTORY MUSEUM.
GUILTY AS CHARGED.
SO WHAT WERE YOU DOING WITH ALL THOSE BOOKS AND MAPS?
ACTUALLY DOING A LITTLE HOMEWORK ABOUT THE AREA. I LIKE TO GET FAMILIAR WITH A PLACE THAT I'LL BE WORKING IN.
KRAK
RINGER
AND WHERE'S THAT?
THE CLOISTERS.
REALLY? IN WHAT CAPACITY?
I'M KINDA THE NEW CURATOR, ACTUALLY.
I LOVE THAT MUSEUM, ALL THE MEDIEVAL ART. THE TAPESTRIES. THE GARDENS.
THERE BETTER BE A PRIVATE TOUR TO MAKE UP FOR THAT BOOK YOU'RE NOT REALLY WRITING.
ABSOLUTELY, RIGHT AFTER I FINALLY FIND A PLACE TO LIVE UP THERE.
WELL YOU'RE IN LUCK-- MY BROTHER LIVES **AND** WORKS UP THERE. HE'S A REAL ESTATE AGENT.
I'M SURE HE'D BE HAPPY TO SHOW YOU SOME PLACES. LET ME KNOW IF YOU WANT TO SCHEDULE SOMETHING.
THANKS, I WILL.
AND BY THE WAY...
YEAH?
I'M A **METS** FAN.
G
GOTHAM

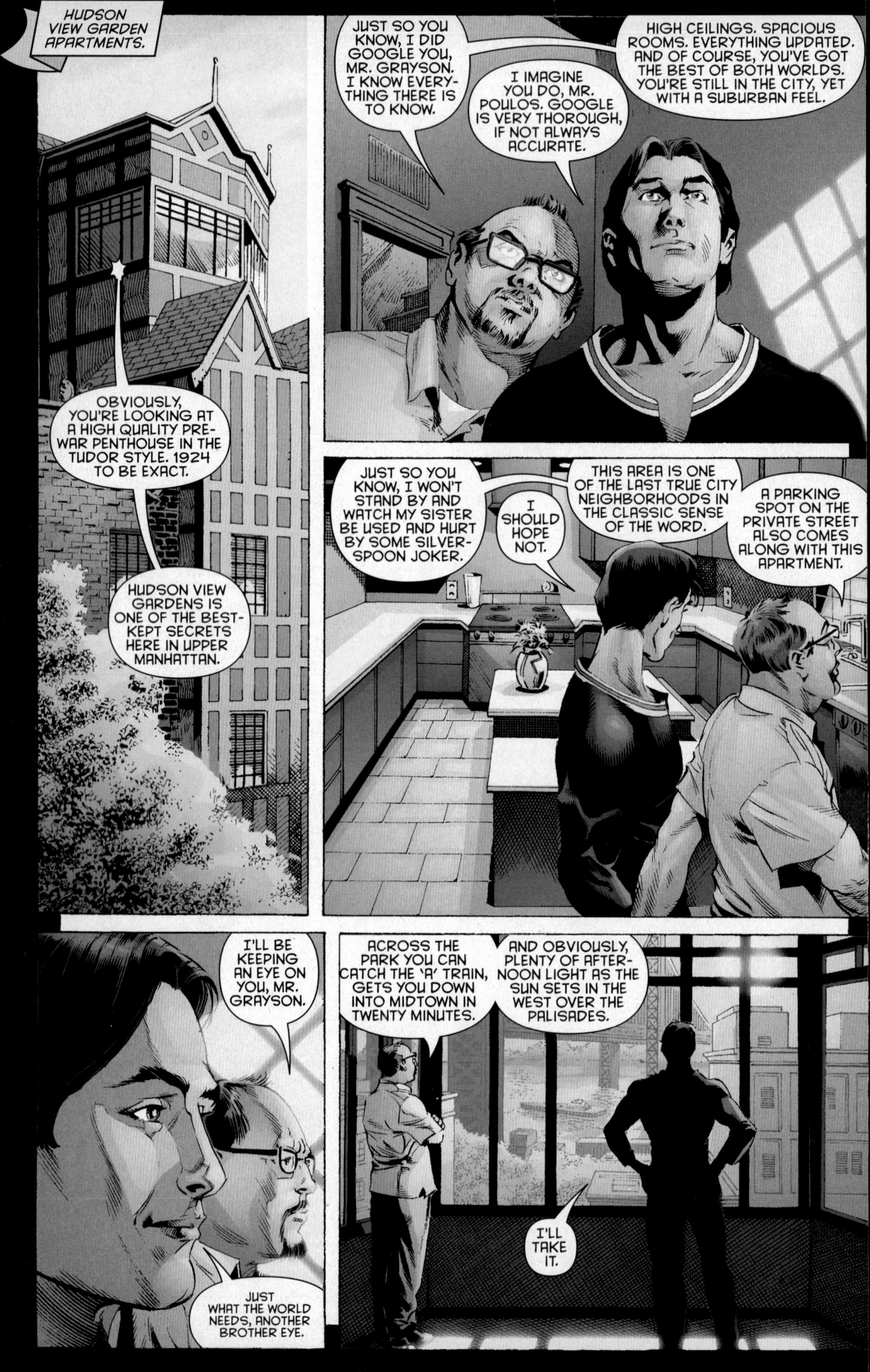

HUDSON VIEW GARDEN APARTMENTS.
OBVIOUSLY, YOU'RE LOOKING AT A HIGH QUALITY PRE-WAR PENTHOUSE IN THE TUDOR STYLE. 1924 TO BE EXACT.
HUDSON VIEW GARDENS IS ONE OF THE BEST-KEPT SECRETS HERE IN UPPER MANHATTAN.
HIGH CEILINGS. SPACIOUS ROOMS. EVERYTHING UPDATED. AND OF COURSE, YOU'VE GOT THE BEST OF BOTH WORLDS. YOU'RE STILL IN THE CITY, YET WITH A SUBURBAN FEEL.
JUST SO YOU KNOW, I DID GOOGLE YOU, MR. GRAYSON. I KNOW EVERYTHING THERE IS TO KNOW.
I IMAGINE YOU DO, MR. POULOS. GOOGLE IS VERY THOROUGH, IF NOT ALWAYS ACCURATE.
THIS AREA IS ONE OF THE LAST TRUE CITY NEIGHBORHOODS IN THE CLASSIC SENSE OF THE WORD.
JUST SO YOU KNOW, I WON'T STAND BY AND WATCH MY SISTER BE USED AND HURT BY SOME SILVER-SPOON JOKER.
I SHOULD HOPE NOT.
A PARKING SPOT ON THE PRIVATE STREET ALSO COMES ALONG WITH THIS APARTMENT.
I'LL BE KEEPING AN EYE ON YOU, MR. GRAYSON.
JUST WHAT THE WORLD NEEDS, ANOTHER BROTHER EYE.
ACROSS THE PARK YOU CAN CATCH THE 'A' TRAIN, GETS YOU DOWN INTO MIDTOWN IN TWENTY MINUTES.
AND OBVIOUSLY, PLENTY OF AFTERNOON LIGHT AS THE SUN SETS IN THE WEST OVER THE PALISADES.
I'LL TAKE IT.

Think it's time to take the ol' moniker to heart from here on in.

Time is of the essence...

...when it comes to helping people in a city this size.

I can't be faster than a speeding bullet, but I sure as hell need to be quicker than a motorcycle on these congested streets...

...if I'm going to get to where I need to be to make a difference.

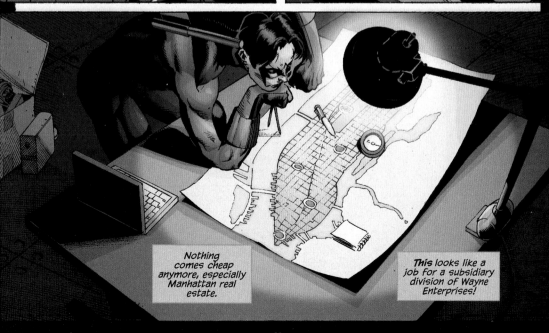

Nothing comes cheap anymore, especially Manhattan real estate.

This looks like a job for a subsidiary division of Wayne Enterprises!

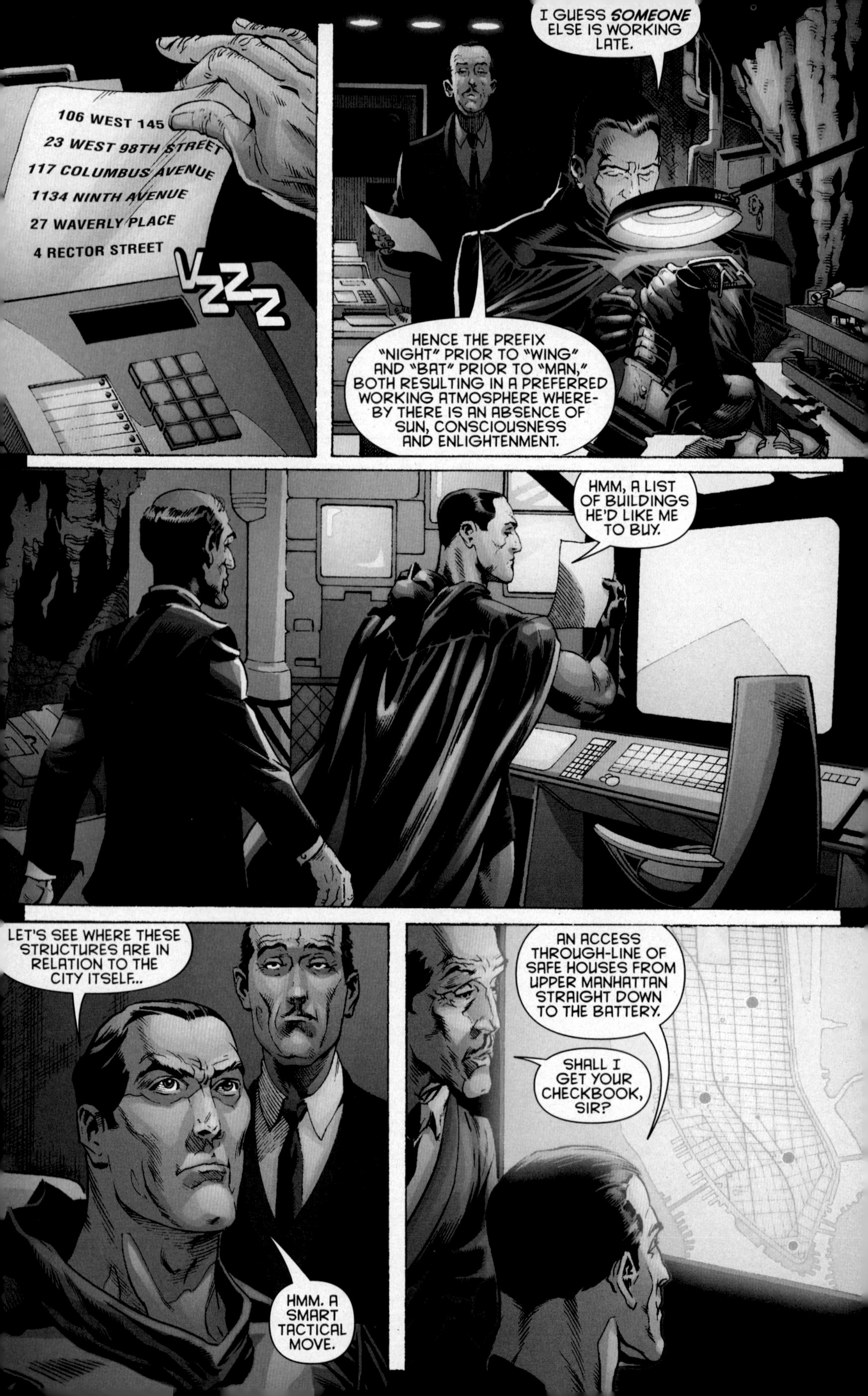

106 WEST 145
23 WEST 98TH STREET
117 COLUMBUS AVENUE
1134 NINTH AVENUE
27 WAVERLY PLACE
4 RECTOR STREET
VZZZ
I GUESS *SOMEONE* ELSE IS WORKING LATE.
HENCE THE PREFIX "NIGHT" PRIOR TO "WING" AND "BAT" PRIOR TO "MAN," BOTH RESULTING IN A PREFERRED WORKING ATMOSPHERE WHERE-BY THERE IS AN ABSENCE OF SUN, CONSCIOUSNESS AND ENLIGHTENMENT.
HMM, A LIST OF BUILDINGS HE'D LIKE ME TO BUY.
LET'S SEE WHERE THESE STRUCTURES ARE IN RELATION TO THE CITY ITSELF...
HMM. A SMART TACTICAL MOVE.
AN ACCESS THROUGH-LINE OF SAFE HOUSES FROM UPPER MANHATTAN STRAIGHT DOWN TO THE BATTERY.
SHALL I GET YOUR CHECKBOOK, SIR?

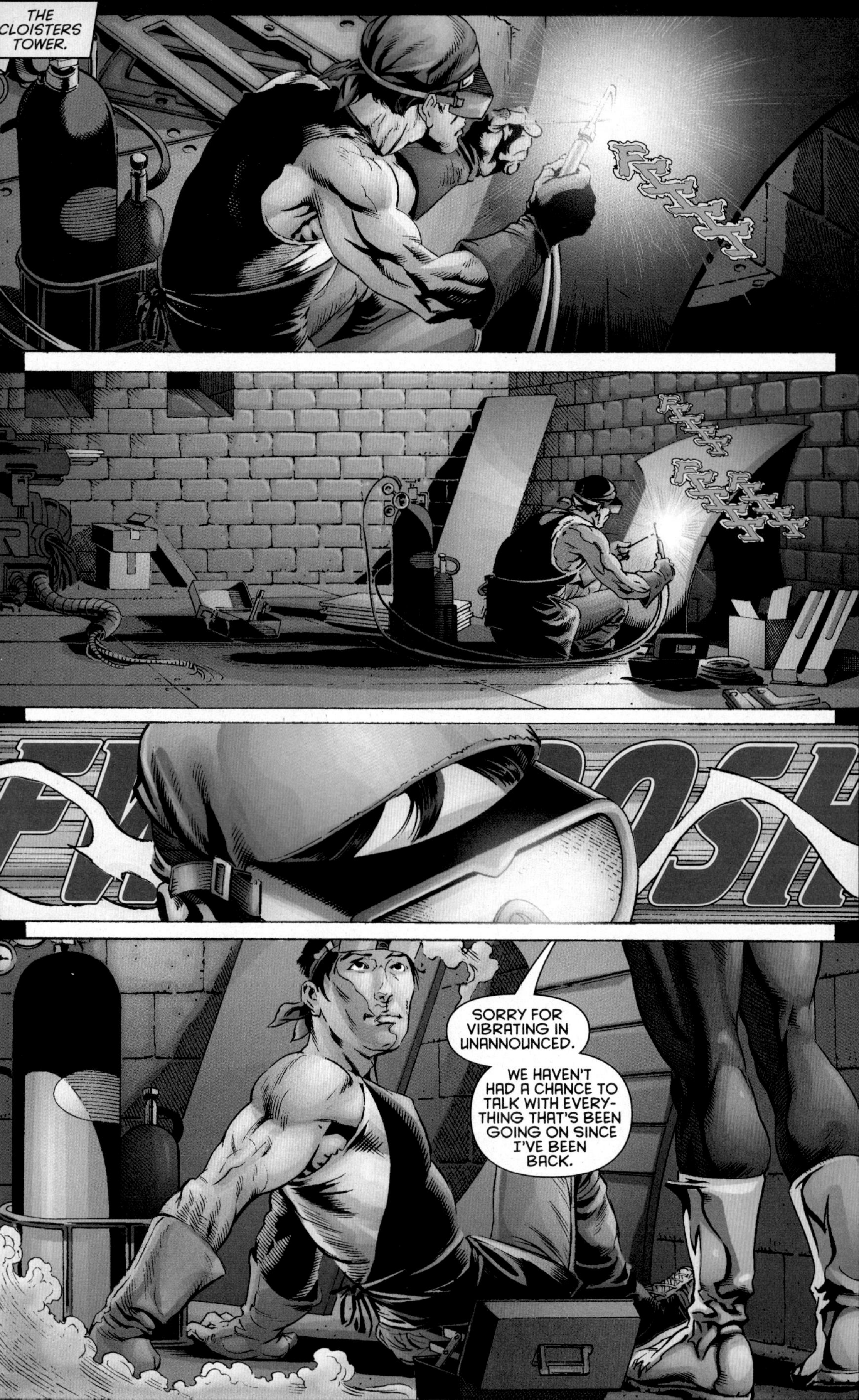
THE CLOISTERS TOWER.
SORRY FOR VIBRATING IN UNANNOUNCED.
WE HAVEN'T HAD A CHANCE TO TALK WITH EVERY-THING THAT'S BEEN GOING ON SINCE I'VE BEEN BACK.

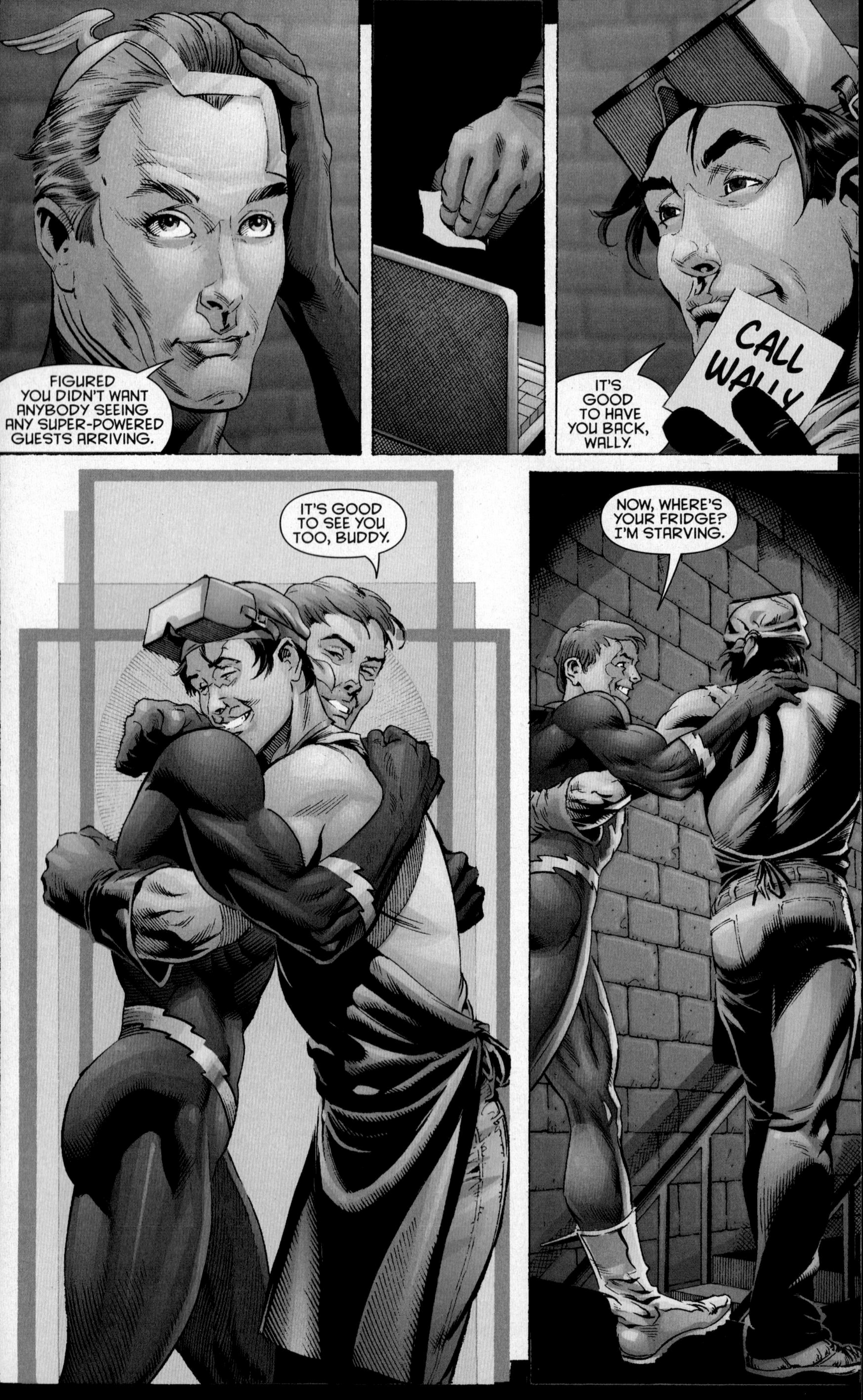
FIGURED YOU DIDN'T WANT ANYBODY SEEING ANY SUPER-POWERED GUESTS ARRIVING.
CALL WALLY
IT'S GOOD TO HAVE YOU BACK, WALLY.
IT'S GOOD TO SEE YOU TOO, BUDDY.
NOW, WHERE'S YOUR FRIDGE? I'M STARVING.

HERE'S TO OLD FRIENDS.

BROTHERS IN ARMS.

BEST FRIENDS.

CLINK

AND HERE'S TO BART.

TO BART.

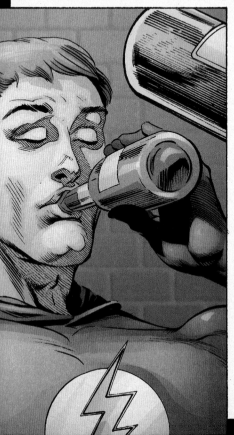

SO, SHAKING THINGS UP, HMM?

JUST A LITTLE.

A MUSEUM CURATOR, HUH?

YEAH.

COULDN'T GET ROY TO STOP LAUGHING FOR AN HOUR.

KITCHE

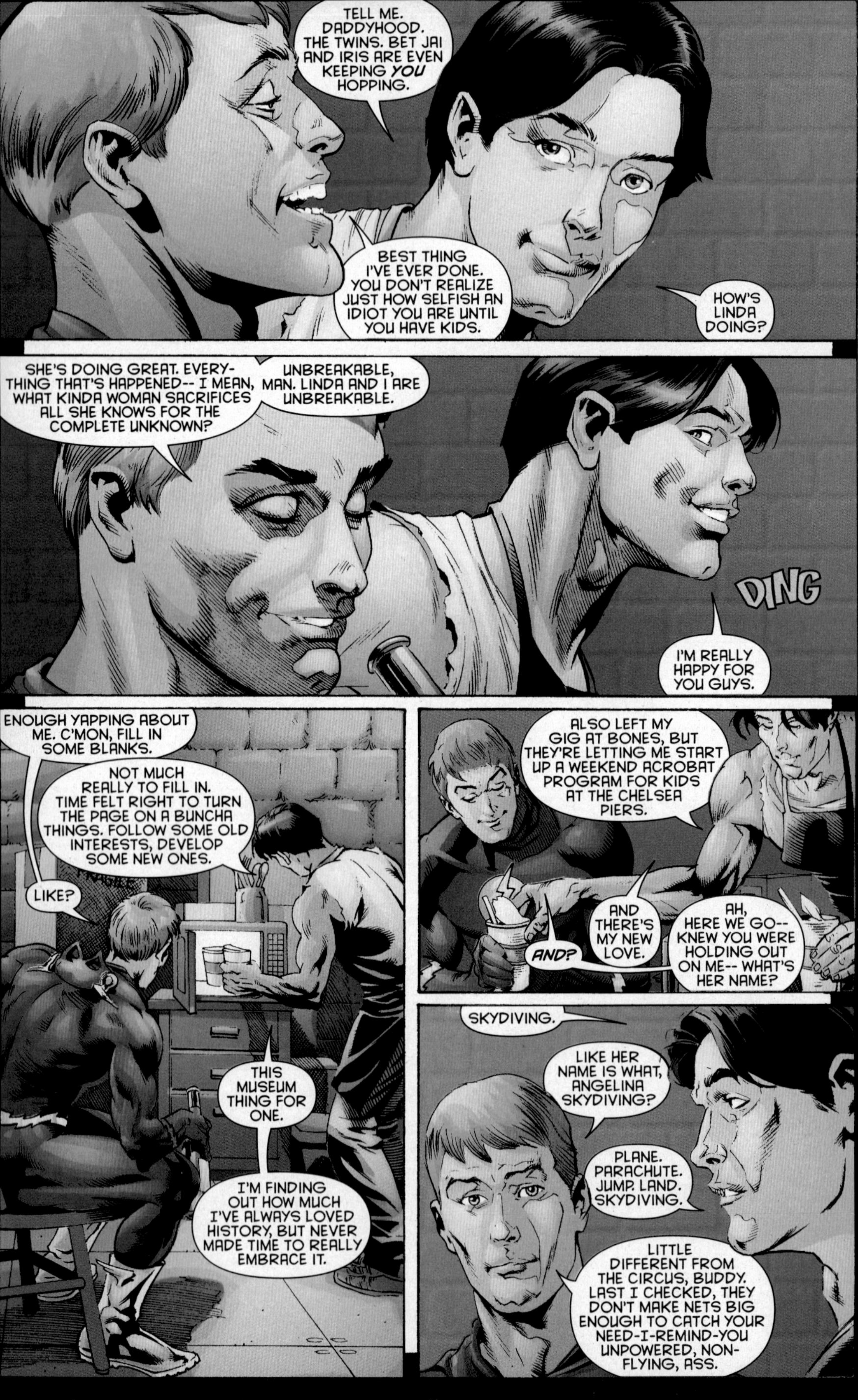
TELL ME. DADDYHOOD. THE TWINS. BET JAI AND IRIS ARE EVEN KEEPING *YOU* HOPPING.
BEST THING I'VE EVER DONE. YOU DON'T REALIZE JUST HOW SELFISH AN IDIOT YOU ARE UNTIL YOU HAVE KIDS.
HOW'S LINDA DOING?
SHE'S DOING GREAT. EVERY-THING THAT'S HAPPENED-- I MEAN, WHAT KINDA WOMAN SACRIFICES ALL SHE KNOWS FOR THE COMPLETE UNKNOWN?
UNBREAKABLE, MAN. LINDA AND I ARE UNBREAKABLE.
DING
I'M REALLY HAPPY FOR YOU GUYS.
ENOUGH YAPPING ABOUT ME. C'MON, FILL IN SOME BLANKS.
NOT MUCH REALLY TO FILL IN. TIME FELT RIGHT TO TURN THE PAGE ON A BUNCHA THINGS. FOLLOW SOME OLD INTERESTS, DEVELOP SOME NEW ONES.
LIKE?
THIS MUSEUM THING FOR ONE.
I'M FINDING OUT HOW MUCH I'VE ALWAYS LOVED HISTORY, BUT NEVER MADE TIME TO REALLY EMBRACE IT.
ALSO LEFT MY GIG AT BONES, BUT THEY'RE LETTING ME START UP A WEEKEND ACROBAT PROGRAM FOR KIDS AT THE CHELSEA PIERS.
AND?
AND THERE'S MY NEW LOVE.
AH, HERE WE GO-- KNEW YOU WERE HOLDING OUT ON ME-- WHAT'S HER NAME?
SKYDIVING.
LIKE HER NAME IS WHAT, ANGELINA SKYDIVING?
PLANE. PARACHUTE. JUMP. LAND. SKYDIVING.
LITTLE DIFFERENT FROM THE CIRCUS, BUDDY. LAST I CHECKED, THEY DON'T MAKE NETS BIG ENOUGH TO CATCH YOUR NEED-I-REMIND-YOU UNPOWERED, NON-FLYING, ASS.

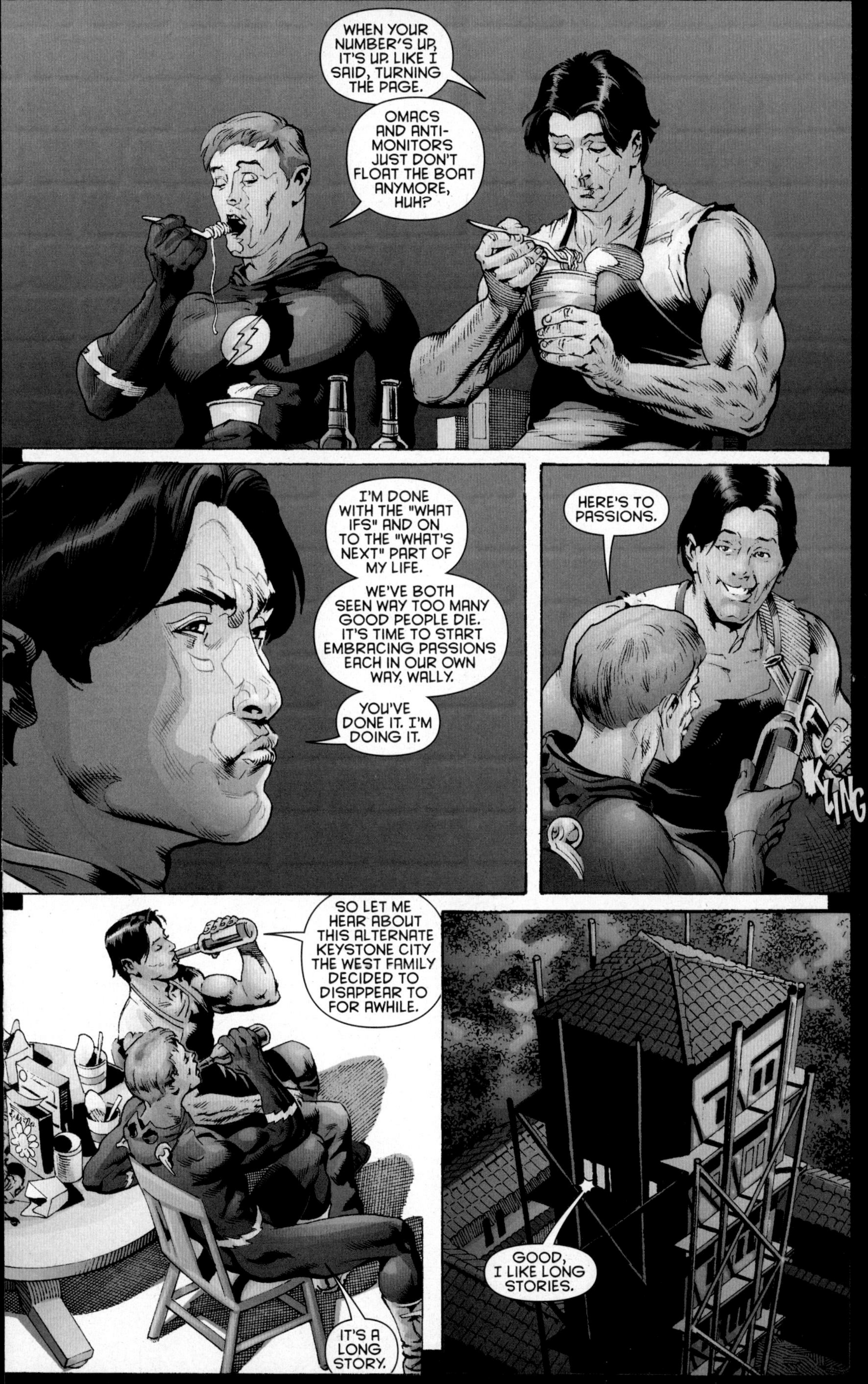
WHEN YOUR NUMBER'S UP, IT'S UP. LIKE I SAID, TURNING THE PAGE.
OMACS AND ANTI-MONITORS JUST DON'T FLOAT THE BOAT ANYMORE, HUH?
I'M DONE WITH THE "WHAT IFS" AND ON TO THE "WHAT'S NEXT" PART OF MY LIFE.
WE'VE BOTH SEEN WAY TOO MANY GOOD PEOPLE DIE. IT'S TIME TO START EMBRACING PASSIONS EACH IN OUR OWN WAY, WALLY.
YOU'VE DONE IT. I'M DOING IT.
HERE'S TO PASSIONS.
KLING
SO LET ME HEAR ABOUT THIS ALTERNATE KEYSTONE CITY THE WEST FAMILY DECIDED TO DISAPPEAR TO FOR AWHILE.
IT'S A LONG STORY.
GOOD, I LIKE LONG STORIES.

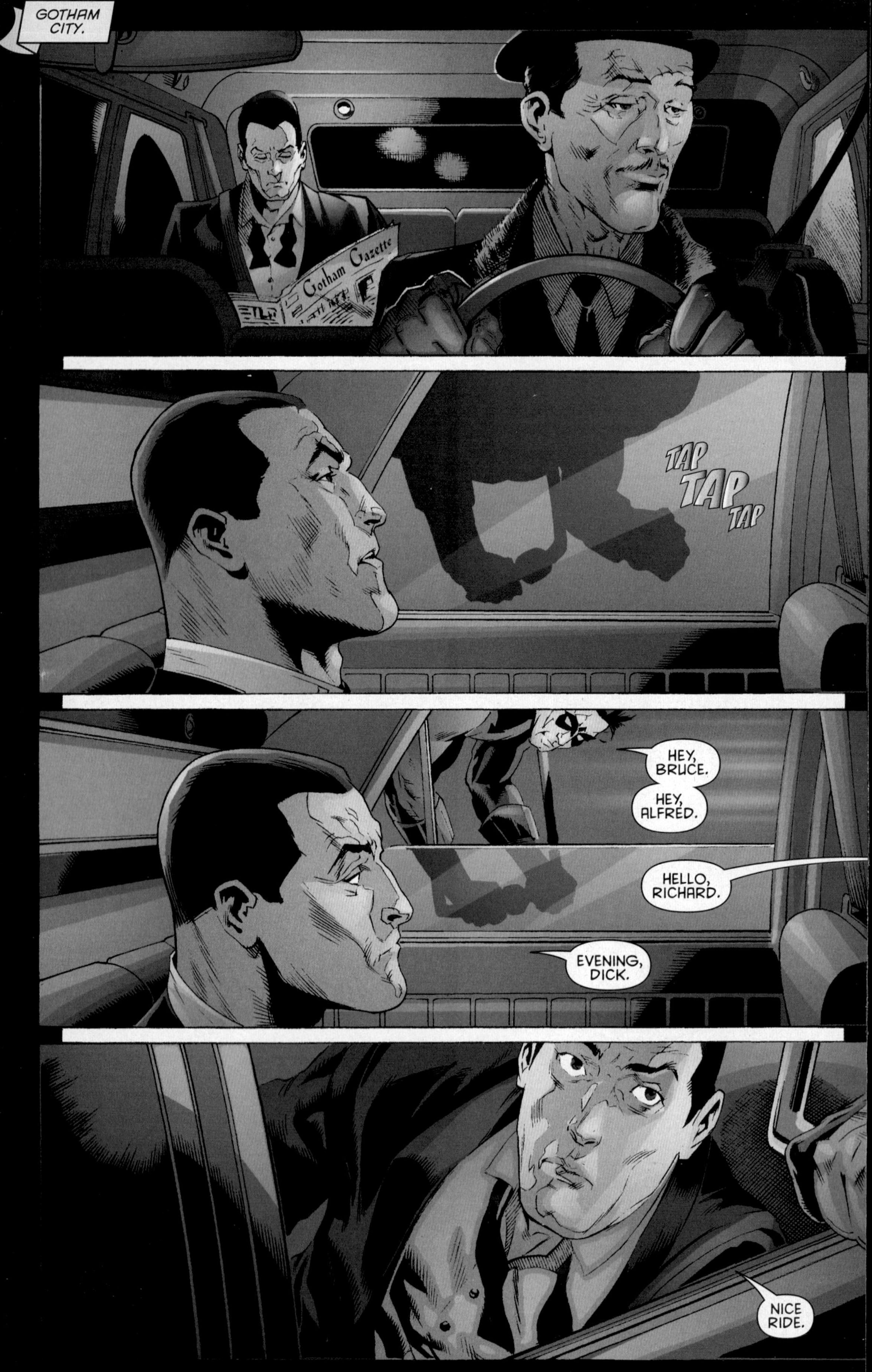
GOTHAM CITY.
Gotham Gazette
TAP TAP TAP
HEY, BRUCE.
HEY, ALFRED.
HELLO, RICHARD.
EVENING, DICK.
NICE RIDE.

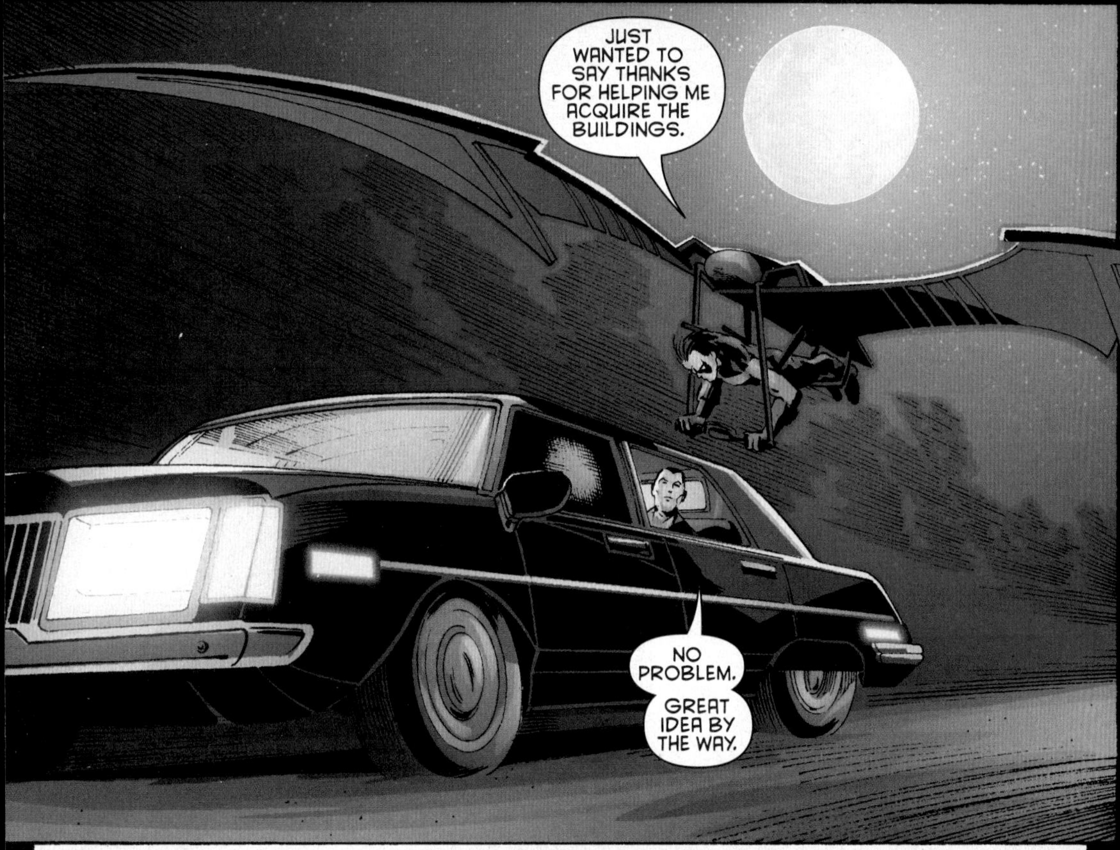
JUST WANTED TO SAY THANKS FOR HELPING ME ACQUIRE THE BUILDINGS.
NO PROBLEM.
GREAT IDEA BY THE WAY.

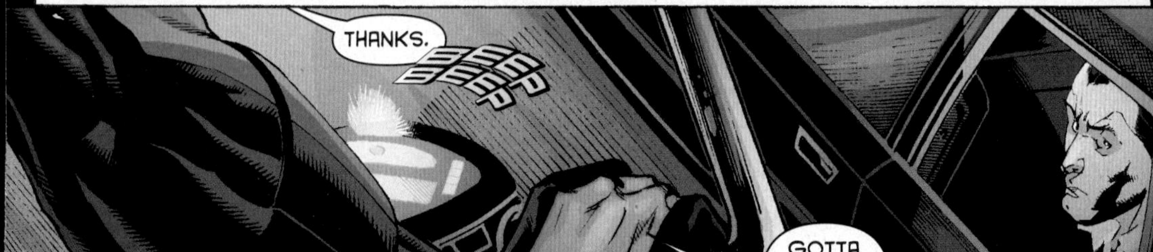
THANKS.
BEEP BEEP
GOTTA TAKE THIS. SEE YA, BRUCE.

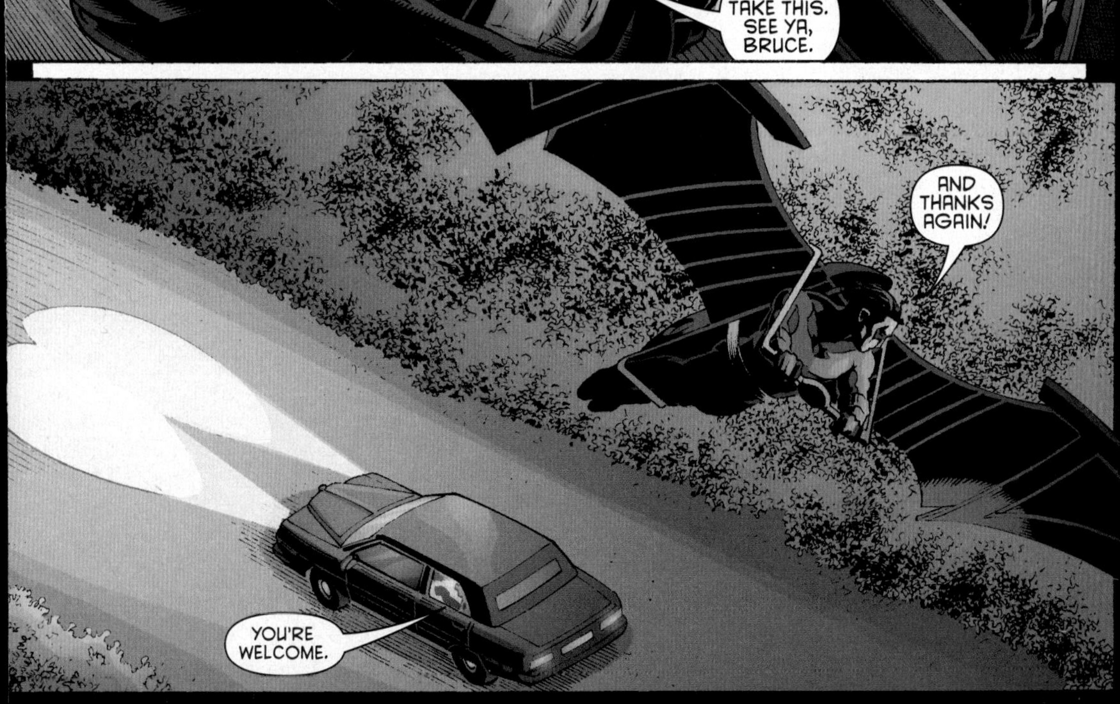
AND THANKS AGAIN!
YOU'RE WELCOME.

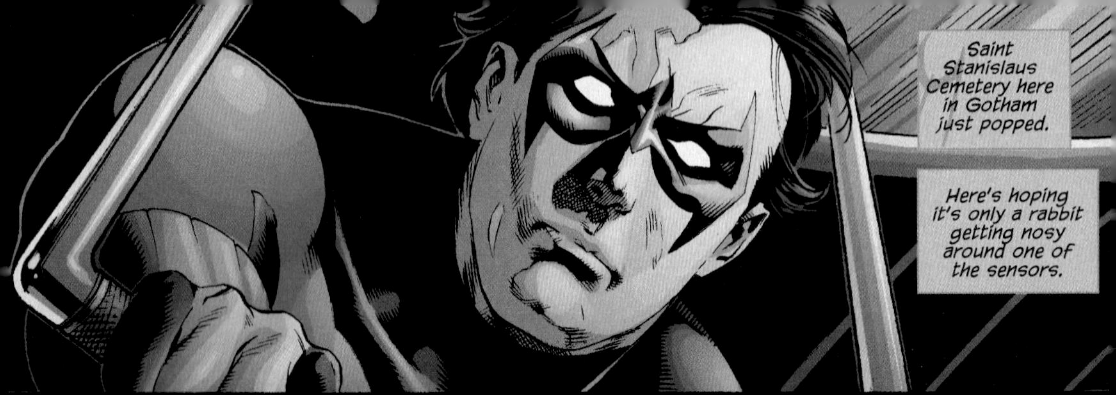
Saint Stanislaus Cemetery here in Gotham just popped.
Here's hoping it's only a rabbit getting nosy around one of the sensors.

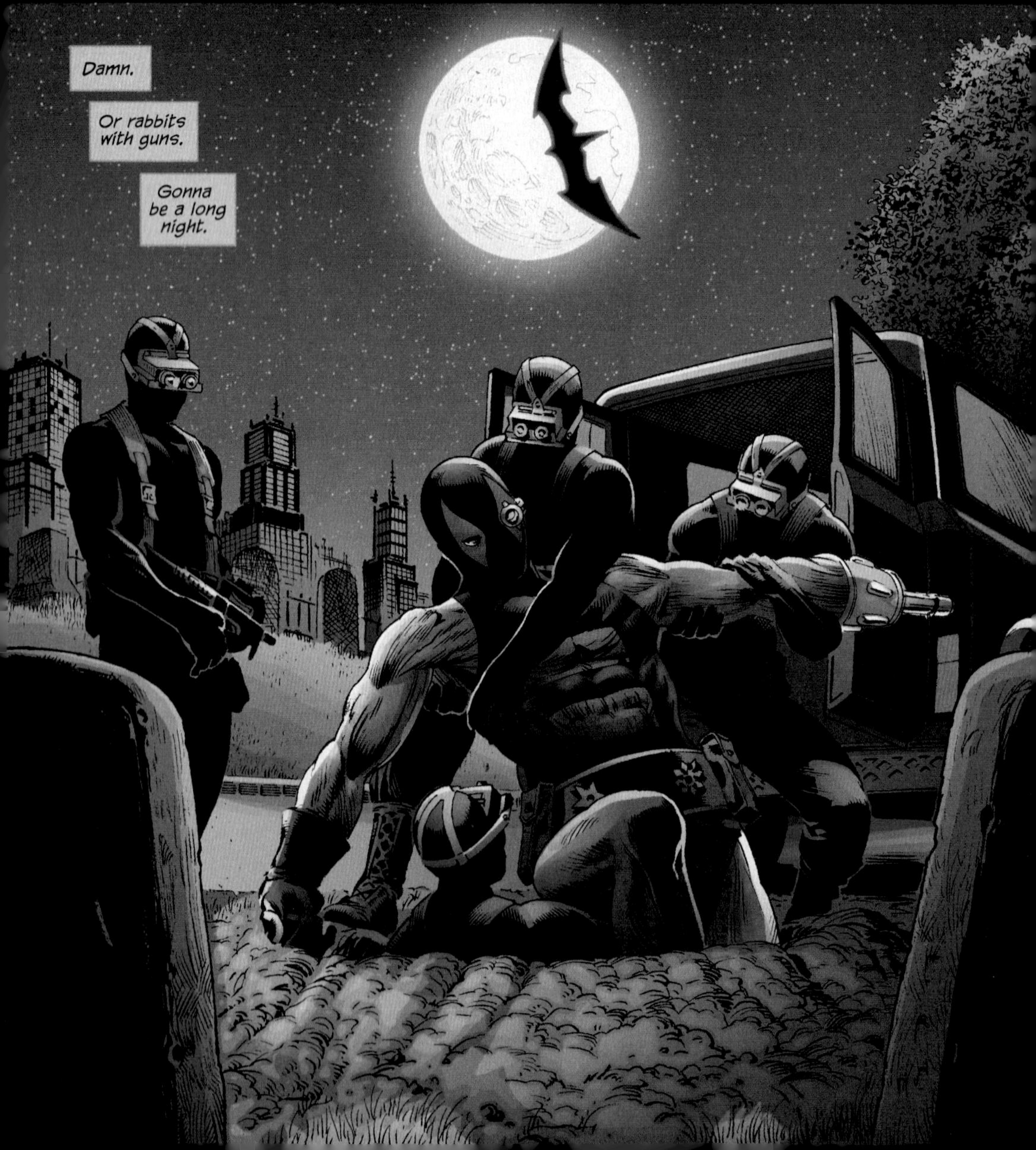
Damn.
Or rabbits with guns.
Gonna be a long night.

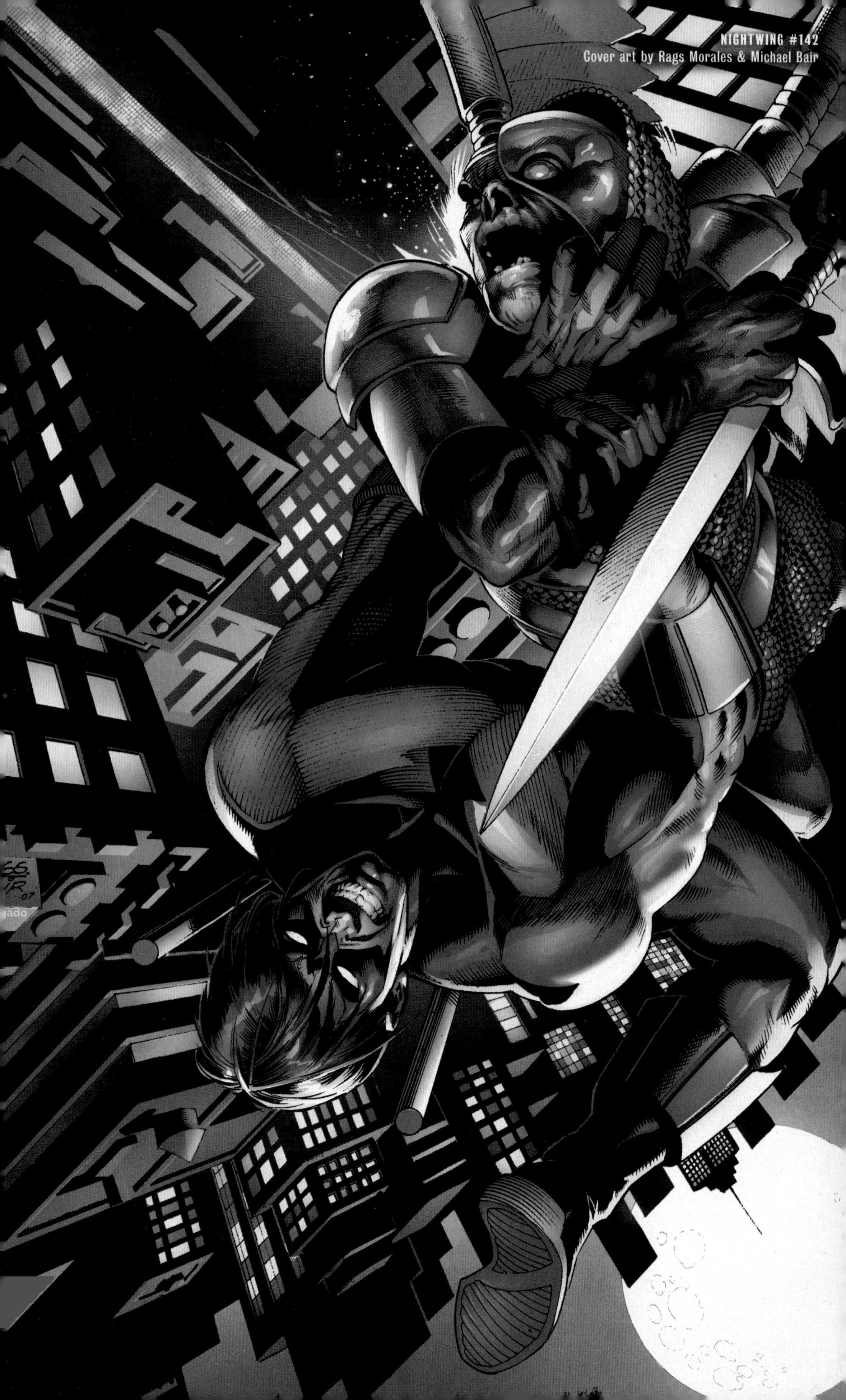

NIGHTWING #142
Cover art by Rags Morales & Michael Bair

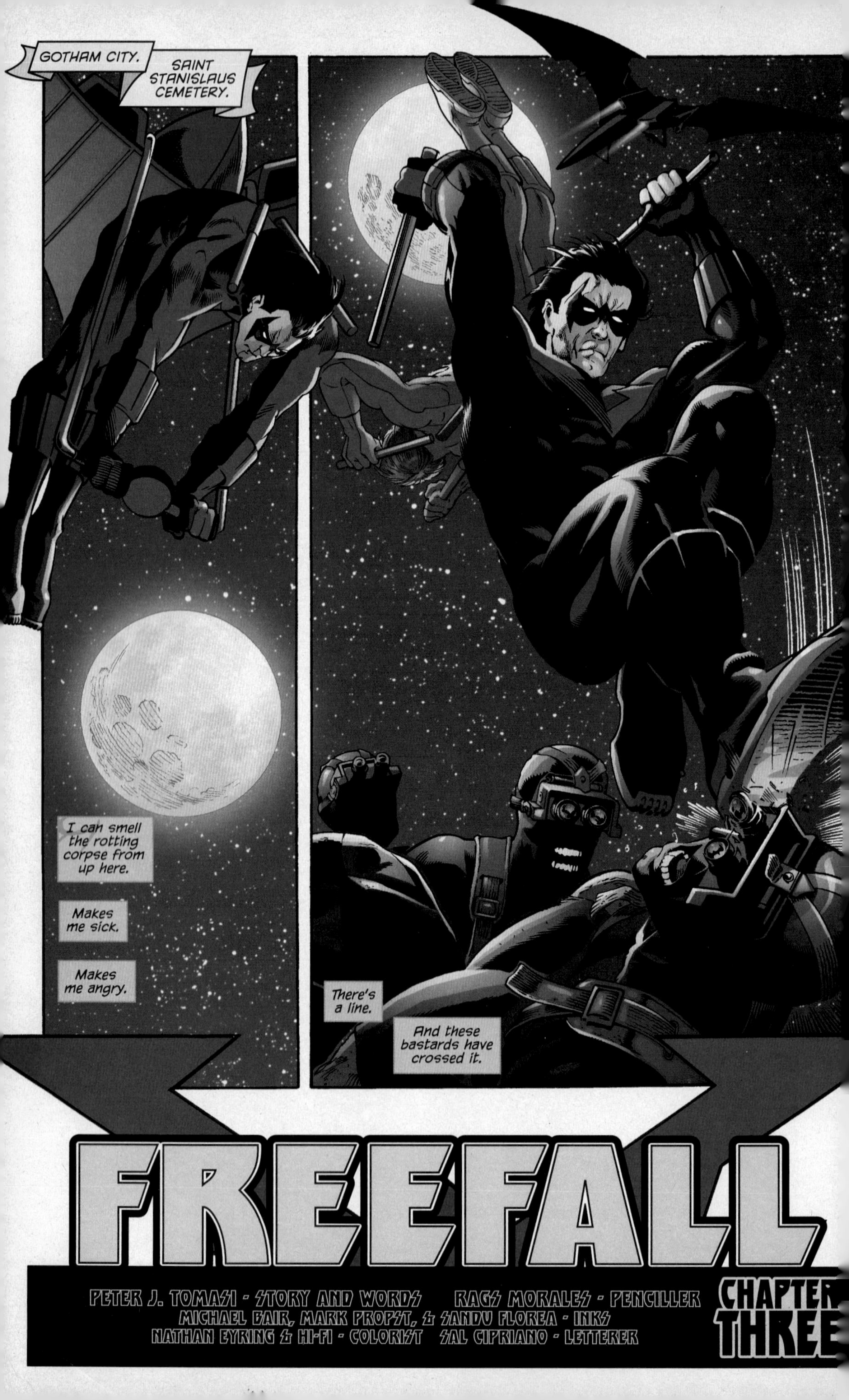
GOTHAM CITY.
SAINT STANISLAUS CEMETERY.
I can smell the rotting corpse from up here.
Makes me sick.
Makes me angry.
There's a line.
And these bastards have crossed it.
FREEFALL
CHAPTER THREE
PETER J. TOMASI - STORY AND WORDS
RAGS MORALES - PENCILLER
MICHAEL BAIR, MARK PROPST, & SANDU FLOREA - INKS
NATHAN EYRING & HI-FI - COLORIST
SAL CIPRIANO - LETTERER

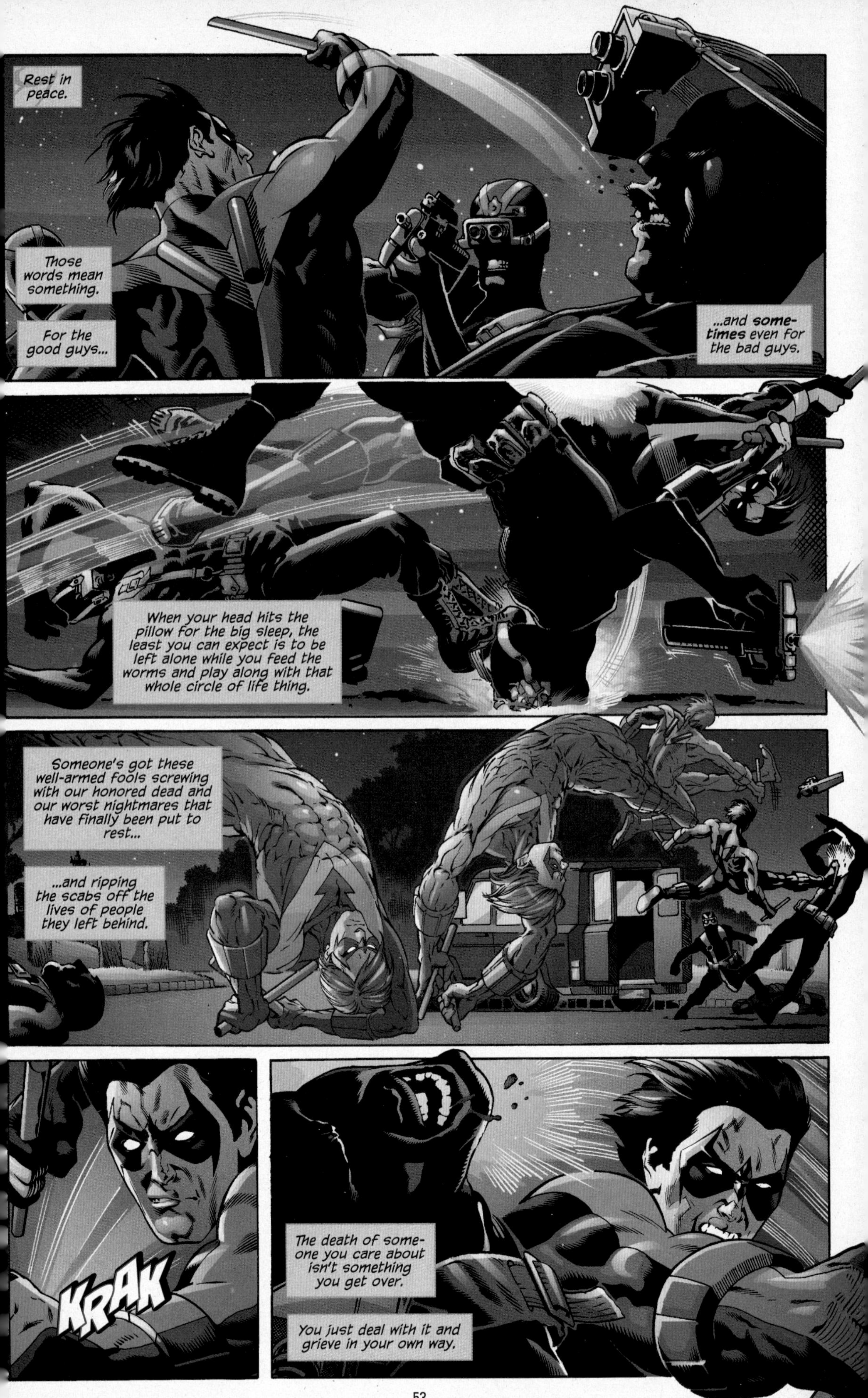

Rest in peace.
Those words mean something.
For the good guys...
...and sometimes even for the bad guys.
When your head hits the pillow for the big sleep, the least you can expect is to be left alone while you feed the worms and play along with that whole circle of life thing.
Someone's got these well-armed fools screwing with our honored dead and our worst nightmares that have finally been put to rest...
...and ripping the scabs off the lives of people they left behind.
KRAK
The death of someone you care about isn't something you get over.
You just deal with it and grieve in your own way.

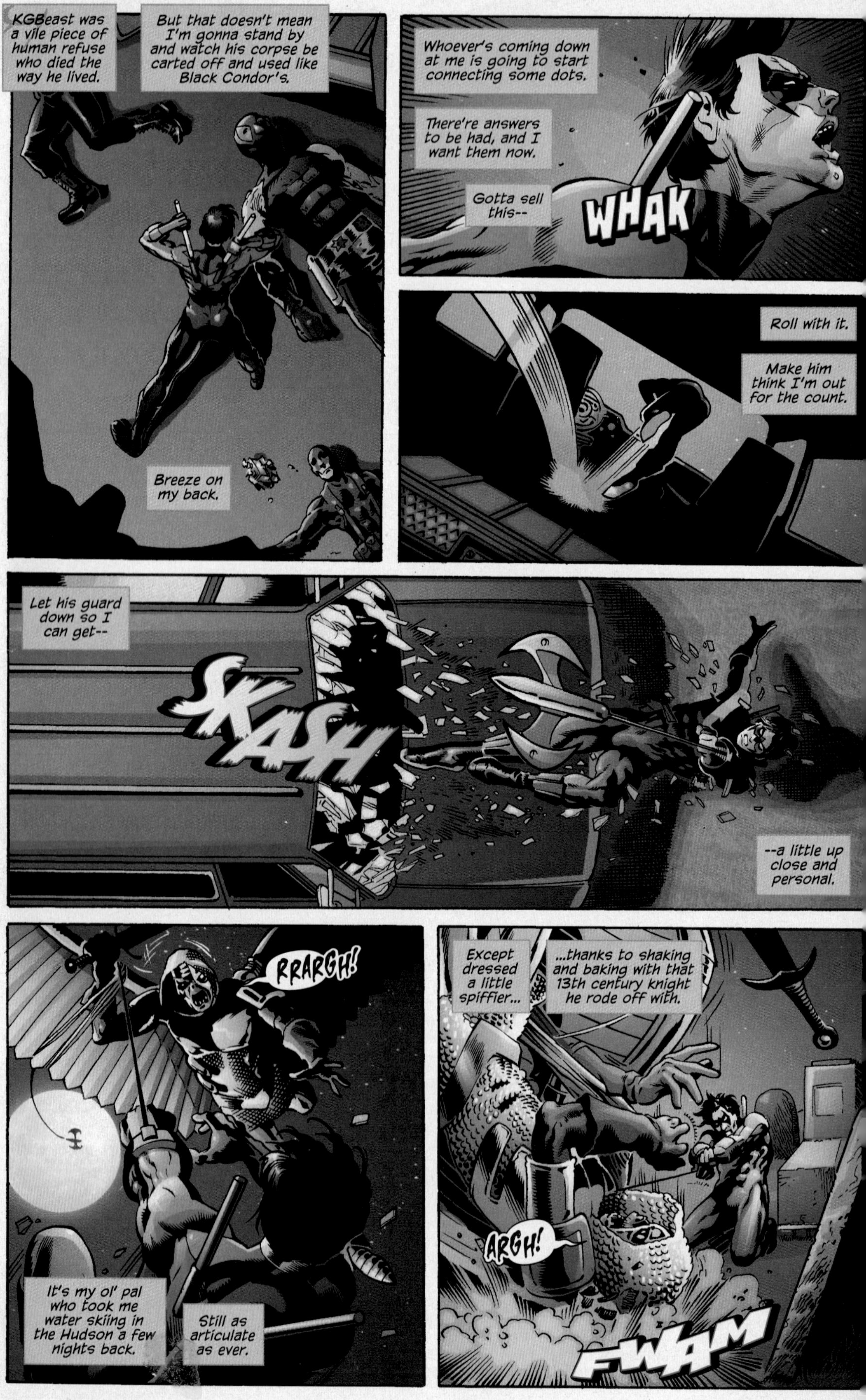
KGBeast was a vile piece of human refuse who died the way he lived.
But that doesn't mean I'm gonna stand by and watch his corpse be carted off and used like Black Condor's.
Breeze on my back.
Whoever's coming down at me is going to start connecting some dots.
There're answers to be had, and I want them now.
Gotta sell this--
WHAK
Roll with it.
Make him think I'm out for the count.
Let his guard down so I can get--
SKASH
--a little up close and personal.
RRARGH!
It's my ol' pal who took me water skiing in the Hudson a few nights back.
Still as articulate as ever.
Except dressed a little spiffier...
...thanks to shaking and baking with that 13th century knight he rode off with.
ARGH!
FWAM

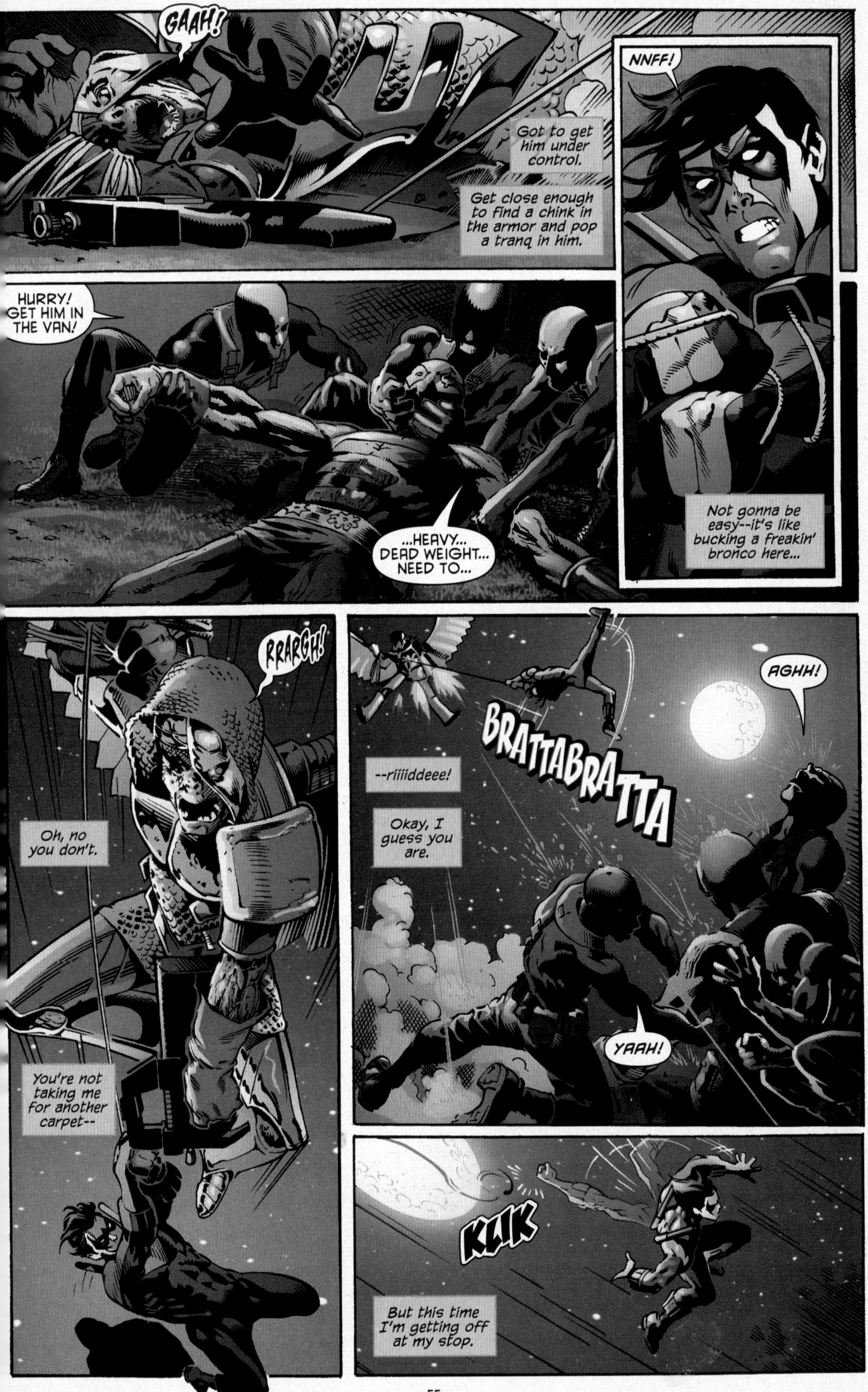
GAAH!
Got to get him under control.
Get close enough to find a chink in the armor and pop a tranq in him.
NNFF!
HURRY! GET HIM IN THE VAN!
...HEAVY... DEAD WEIGHT... NEED TO...
Not gonna be easy--it's like bucking a freakin' bronco here...
RRARGH!
Oh, no you don't.
You're not taking me for another carpet--
--riiiiddeee!
Okay, I guess you are.
BRATTABRATTA
AGHH!
YAAH!
KLIK
But this time I'm getting off at my stop.

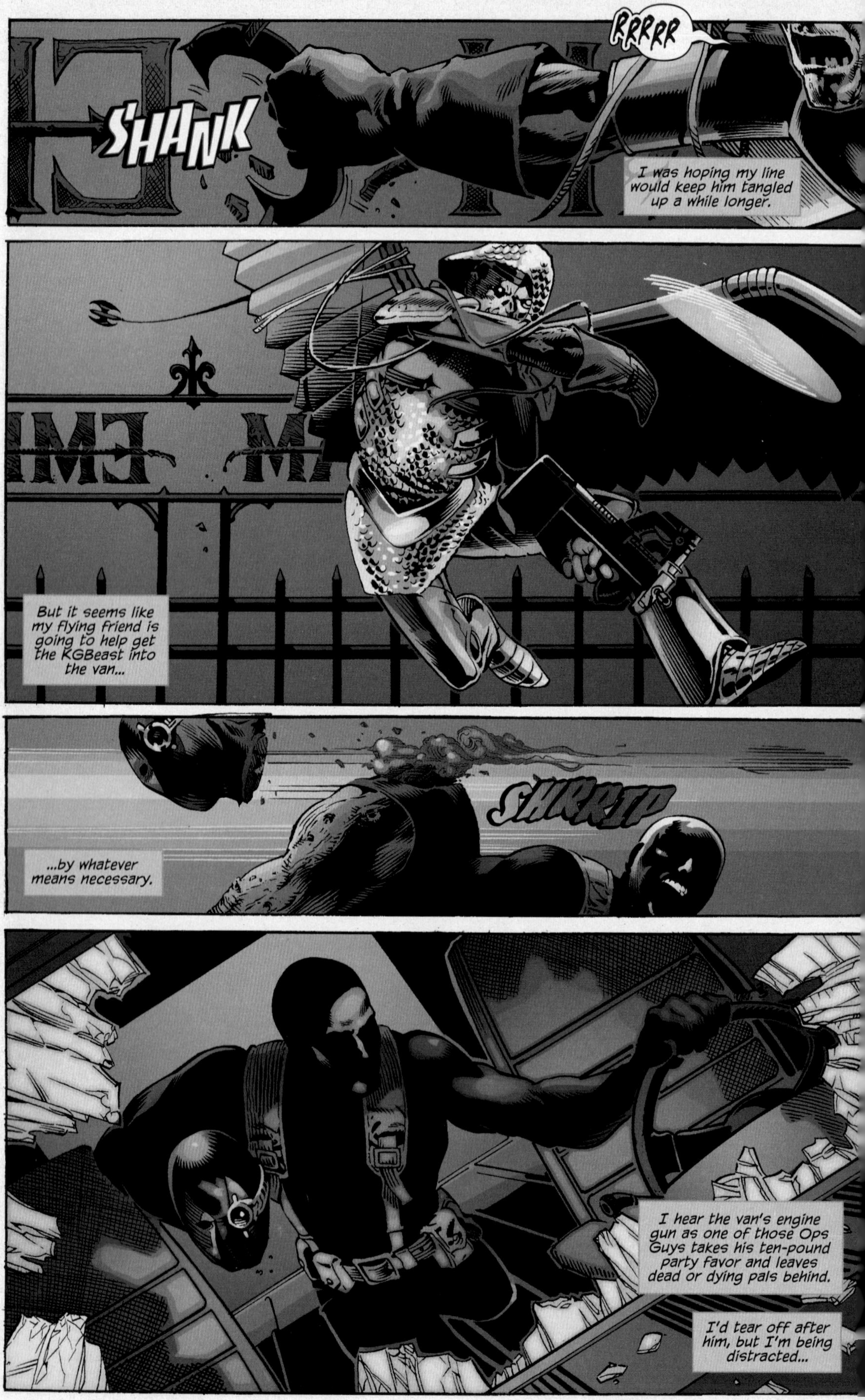
RRRRR
SHANK
I was hoping my line would keep him tangled up a while longer.
But it seems like my flying friend is going to help get the KGBeast into the van...
...by whatever means necessary.
SHRRIP
I hear the van's engine gun as one of those Ops Guys takes his ten-pound party favor and leaves dead or dying pals behind.
I'd tear off after him, but I'm being distracted...

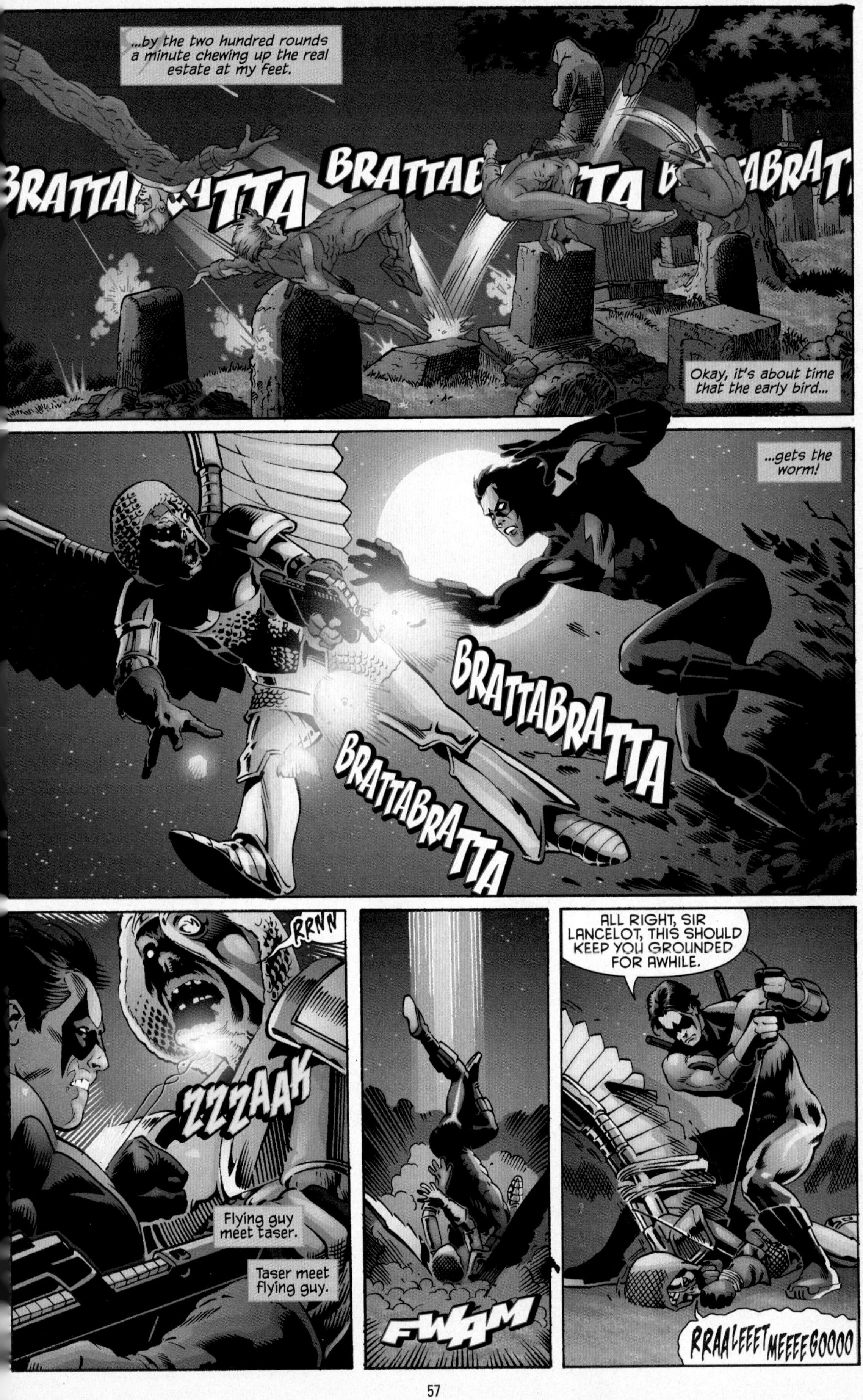
...by the two hundred rounds a minute chewing up the real estate at my feet.
BRATTATATTA
BRATTAB TA
BRATTABRAT
Okay, it's about time that the early bird...
...gets the worm!
BRATTABRATTA
BRATTABRATTA
RRNN
ZZZAAK
Flying guy meet taser.
Taser meet flying guy.
FWAM
ALL RIGHT, SIR LANCELOT, THIS SHOULD KEEP YOU GROUNDED FOR AWHILE.
RRAALEEETMEEEEGOOOO

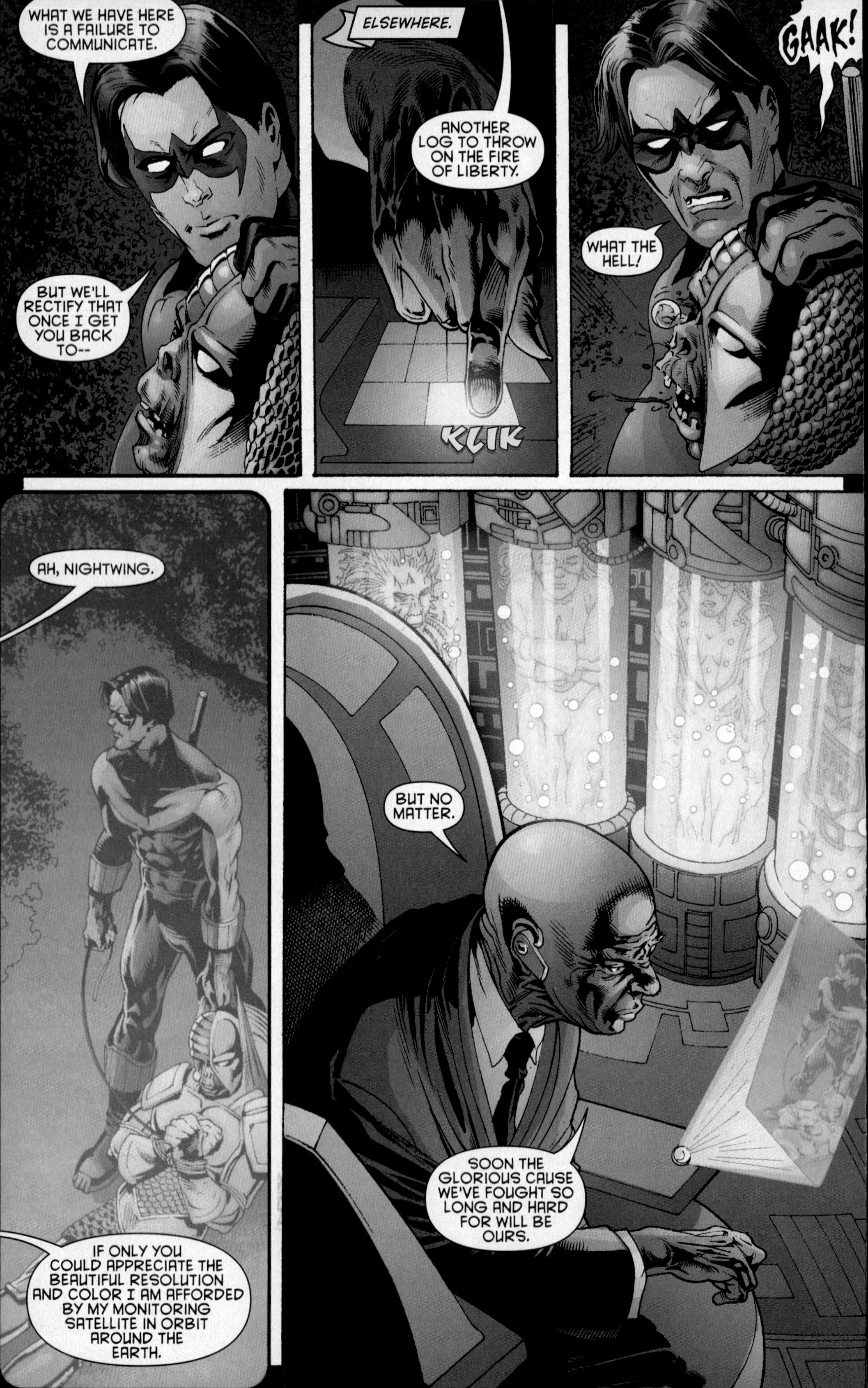
WHAT WE HAVE HERE IS A FAILURE TO COMMUNICATE.
BUT WE'LL RECTIFY THAT ONCE I GET YOU BACK TO--
ELSEWHERE.
ANOTHER LOG TO THROW ON THE FIRE OF LIBERTY.
KLIK
GAAK!
WHAT THE HELL!
AH, NIGHTWING.
IF ONLY YOU COULD APPRECIATE THE BEAUTIFUL RESOLUTION AND COLOR I AM AFFORDED BY MY MONITORING SATELLITE IN ORBIT AROUND THE EARTH.
BUT NO MATTER.
SOON THE GLORIOUS CAUSE WE'VE FOUGHT SO LONG AND HARD FOR WILL BE OURS.

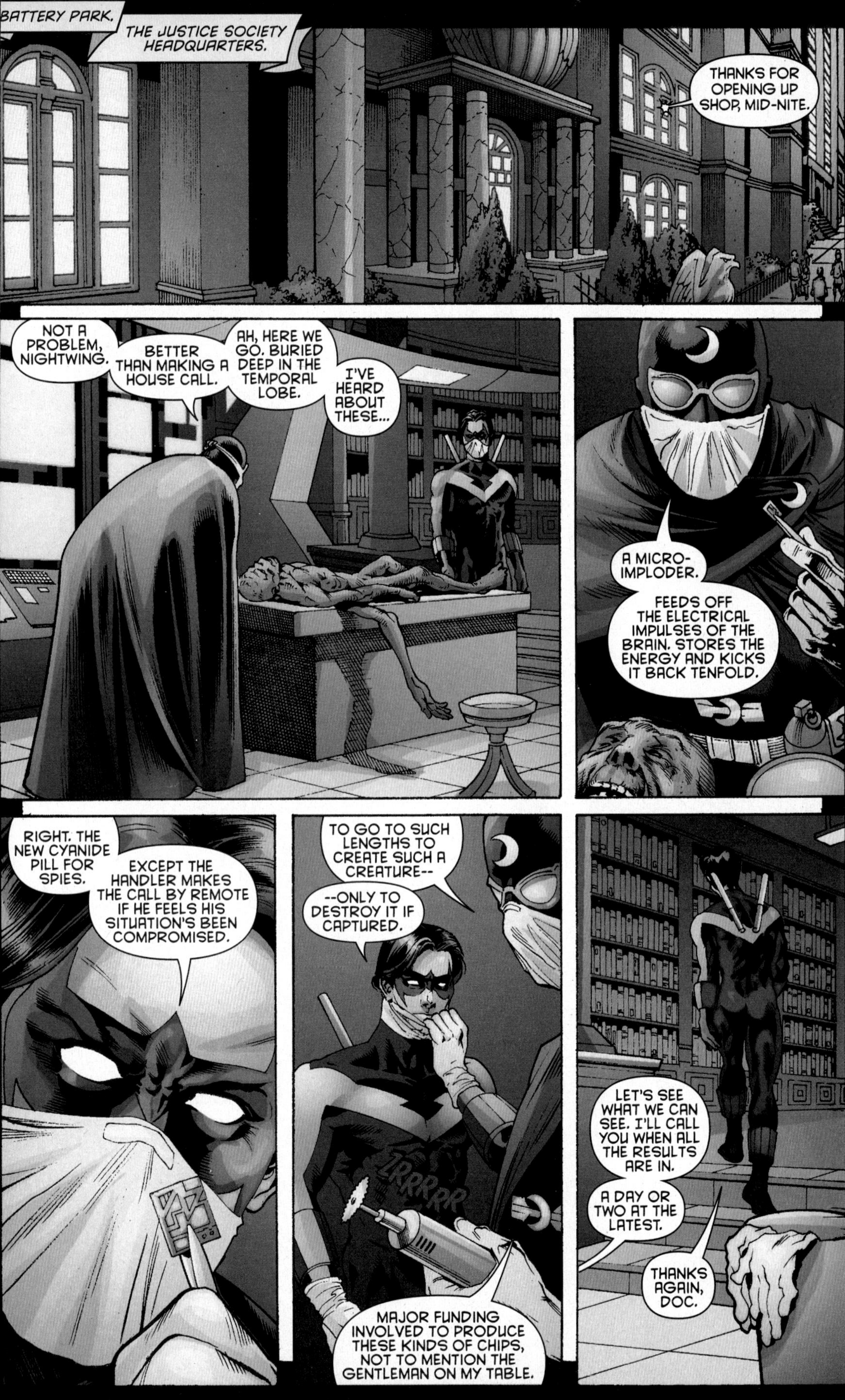

BATTERY PARK.
THE JUSTICE SOCIETY HEADQUARTERS.
THANKS FOR OPENING UP SHOP, MID-NITE.
NOT A PROBLEM, NIGHTWING.
BETTER THAN MAKING A HOUSE CALL.
AH, HERE WE GO. BURIED DEEP IN THE TEMPORAL LOBE.
I'VE HEARD ABOUT THESE...
A MICRO-IMPLODER.
FEEDS OFF THE ELECTRICAL IMPULSES OF THE BRAIN. STORES THE ENERGY AND KICKS IT BACK TENFOLD.
RIGHT. THE NEW CYANIDE PILL FOR SPIES.
EXCEPT THE HANDLER MAKES THE CALL BY REMOTE IF HE FEELS HIS SITUATION'S BEEN COMPROMISED.
TO GO TO SUCH LENGTHS TO CREATE SUCH A CREATURE--
--ONLY TO DESTROY IT IF CAPTURED.
ZRRRRR
MAJOR FUNDING INVOLVED TO PRODUCE THESE KINDS OF CHIPS, NOT TO MENTION THE GENTLEMAN ON MY TABLE.
LET'S SEE WHAT WE CAN SEE. I'LL CALL YOU WHEN ALL THE RESULTS ARE IN.
A DAY OR TWO AT THE LATEST.
THANKS AGAIN, DOC.

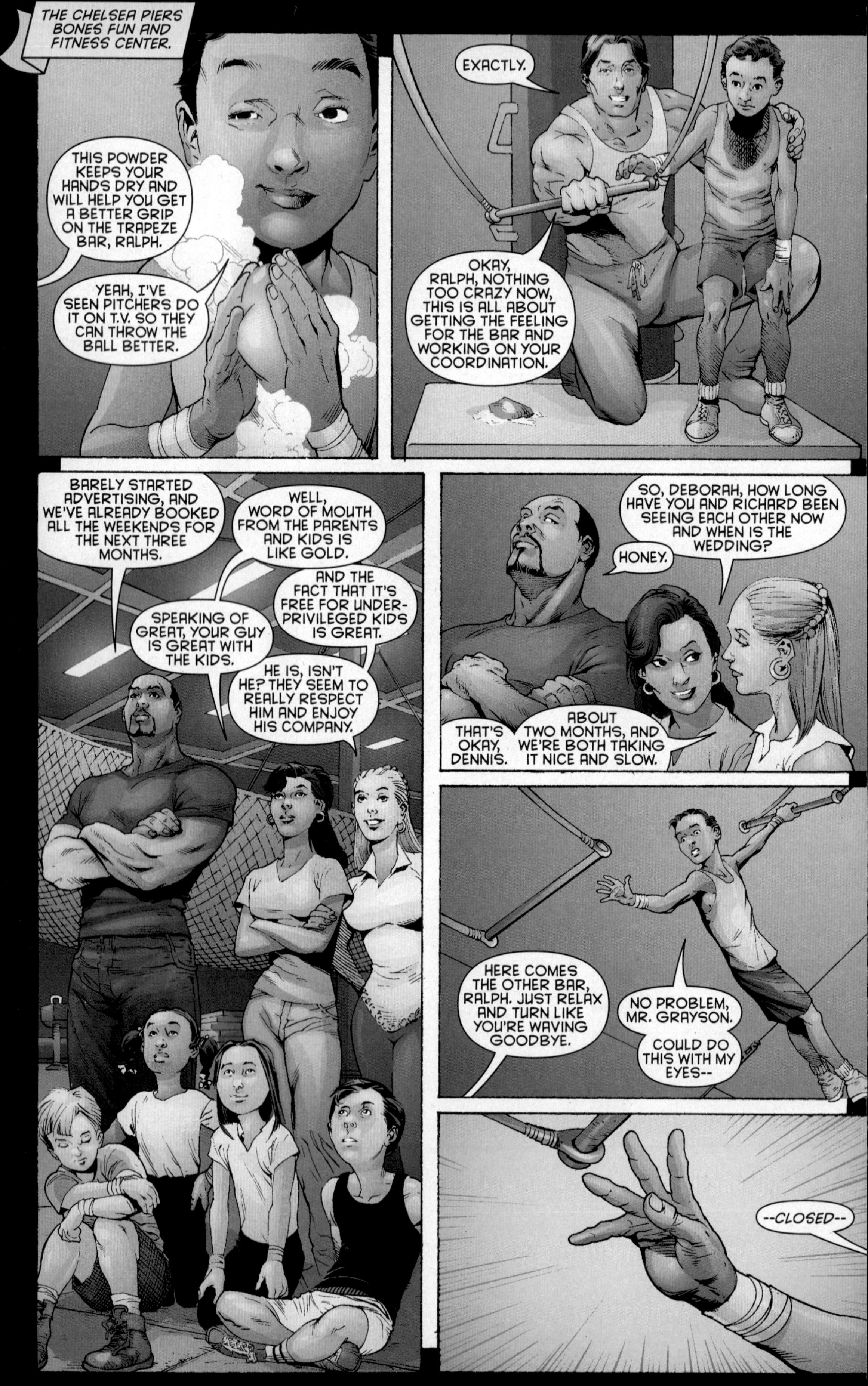
THE CHELSEA PIERS BONES FUN AND FITNESS CENTER.
THIS POWDER KEEPS YOUR HANDS DRY AND WILL HELP YOU GET A BETTER GRIP ON THE TRAPEZE BAR, RALPH.
YEAH, I'VE SEEN PITCHERS DO IT ON T.V. SO THEY CAN THROW THE BALL BETTER.
EXACTLY.
OKAY, RALPH, NOTHING TOO CRAZY NOW, THIS IS ALL ABOUT GETTING THE FEELING FOR THE BAR AND WORKING ON YOUR COORDINATION.
BARELY STARTED ADVERTISING, AND WE'VE ALREADY BOOKED ALL THE WEEKENDS FOR THE NEXT THREE MONTHS.
WELL, WORD OF MOUTH FROM THE PARENTS AND KIDS IS LIKE GOLD.
AND THE FACT THAT IT'S FREE FOR UNDER-PRIVILEGED KIDS IS GREAT.
SPEAKING OF GREAT, YOUR GUY IS GREAT WITH THE KIDS.
HE IS, ISN'T HE? THEY SEEM TO REALLY RESPECT HIM AND ENJOY HIS COMPANY.
SO, DEBORAH, HOW LONG HAVE YOU AND RICHARD BEEN SEEING EACH OTHER NOW AND WHEN IS THE WEDDING?
HONEY.
THAT'S OKAY, DENNIS.
ABOUT TWO MONTHS, AND WE'RE BOTH TAKING IT NICE AND SLOW.
HERE COMES THE OTHER BAR, RALPH. JUST RELAX AND TURN LIKE YOU'RE WAVING GOODBYE.
NO PROBLEM, MR. GRAYSON.
COULD DO THIS WITH MY EYES--
--CLOSED--

YAAAH!

ROLL OFF THE NET LIKE I SHOWED YOU LAST WEEK, RALPH.

GOOD. LEARNING HOW TO FALL IS JUST AS IMPORTANT AS LEARNING HOW TO SWING.

HMM, WHO'S NEXT?

STOP HIDING BEHIND THE KIDS AND GET GOING.

LOOKS LIKE WE HAVE A VOLUNTEER FROM THE AUDIENCE TODAY.

I DON'T THINK SO. I FORGOT TO BRING MY SWEATS...

...AND I'M AFRAID OF HEIGHTS.

AND WHAT DO WE SAY, TEAM?

WHO DARES WINS!

YOU HEARD 'EM, DEB. NOW GET UP HERE.

AFRAID OF HEIGHTS, HUH?

YES.

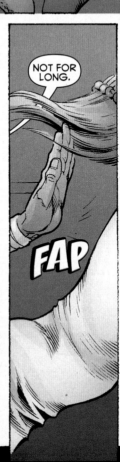

NOT FOR LONG.

FAP

I'M GOING TO GET YOU FOR THIS, GRAYSON!

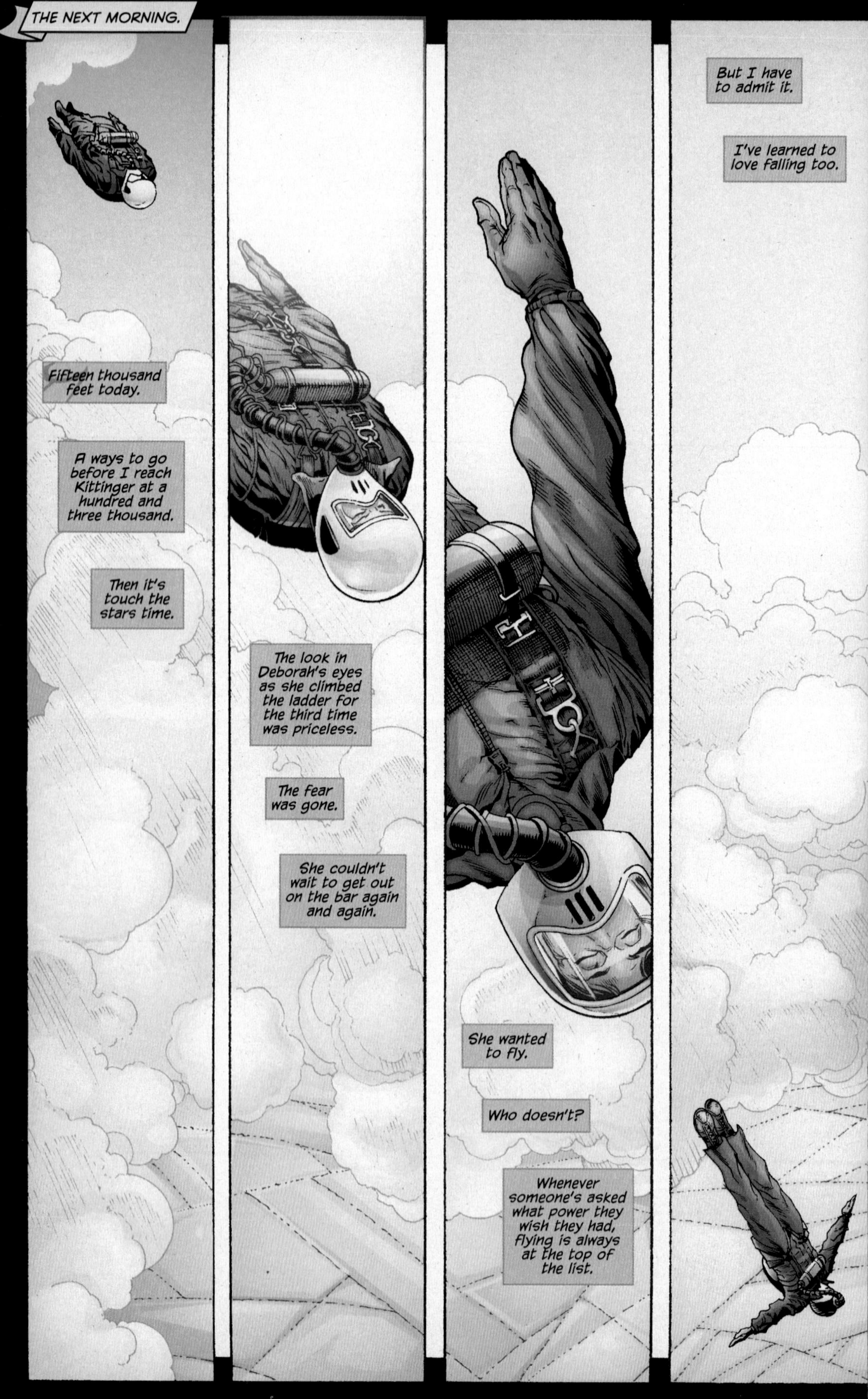
THE NEXT MORNING.
Fifteen thousand feet today.
A ways to go before I reach Kittinger at a hundred and three thousand.
Then it's touch the stars time.
The look in Deborah's eyes as she climbed the ladder for the third time was priceless.
The fear was gone.
She couldn't wait to get out on the bar again and again.
She wanted to fly.
Who doesn't?
Whenever someone's asked what power they wish they had, flying is always at the top of the list.
But I have to admit it.
I've learned to love falling too.

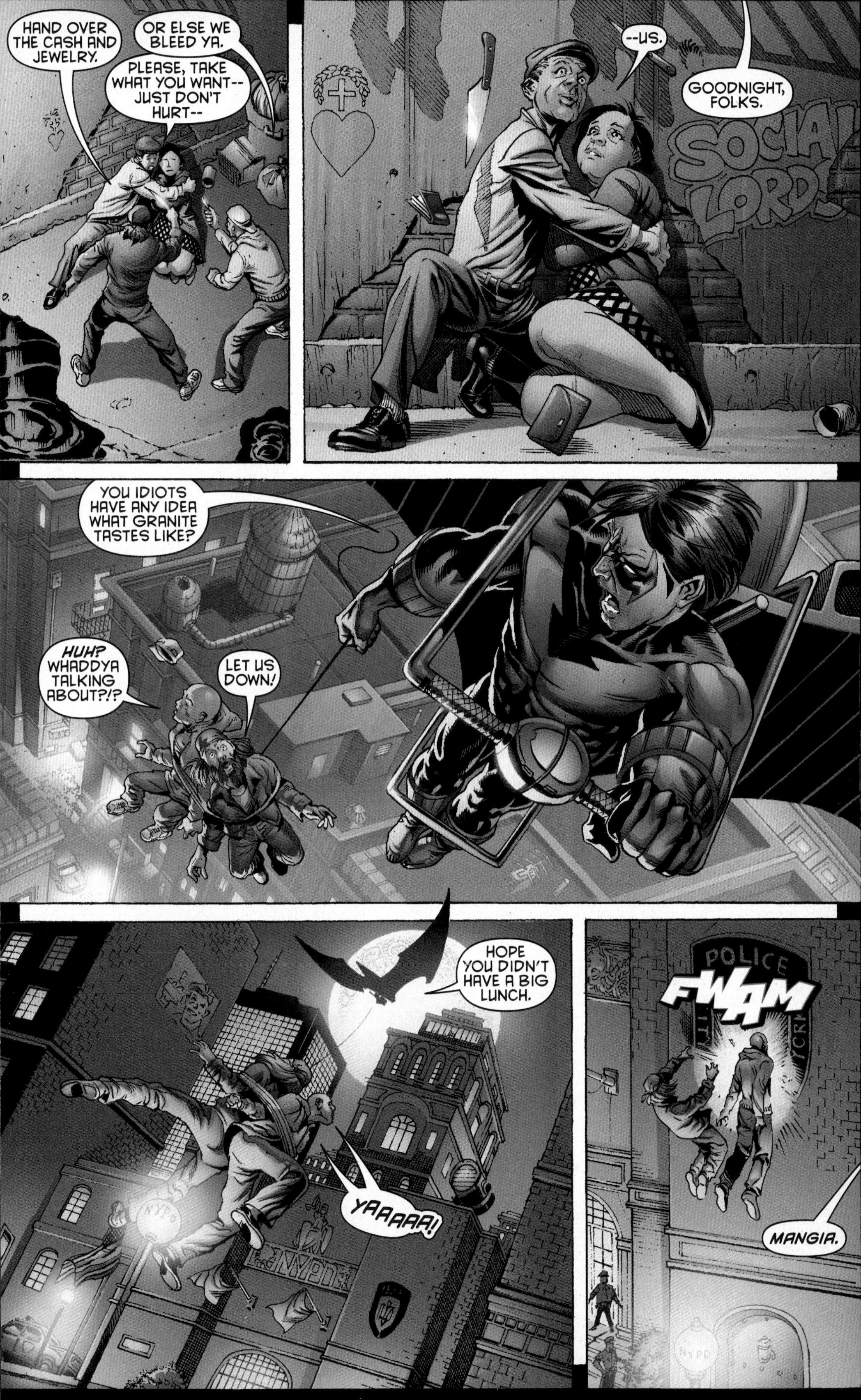
HAND OVER THE CASH AND JEWELRY.
OR ELSE WE BLEED YA.
PLEASE, TAKE WHAT YOU WANT-- JUST DON'T HURT--
--US.
GOODNIGHT, FOLKS.
SOCIAL LORDS
YOU IDIOTS HAVE ANY IDEA WHAT GRANITE TASTES LIKE?
HUH? WHADDYA TALKING ABOUT?!?
LET US DOWN!
HOPE YOU DIDN'T HAVE A BIG LUNCH.
YAAAAA!
POLICE
FWAM
MANGIA.

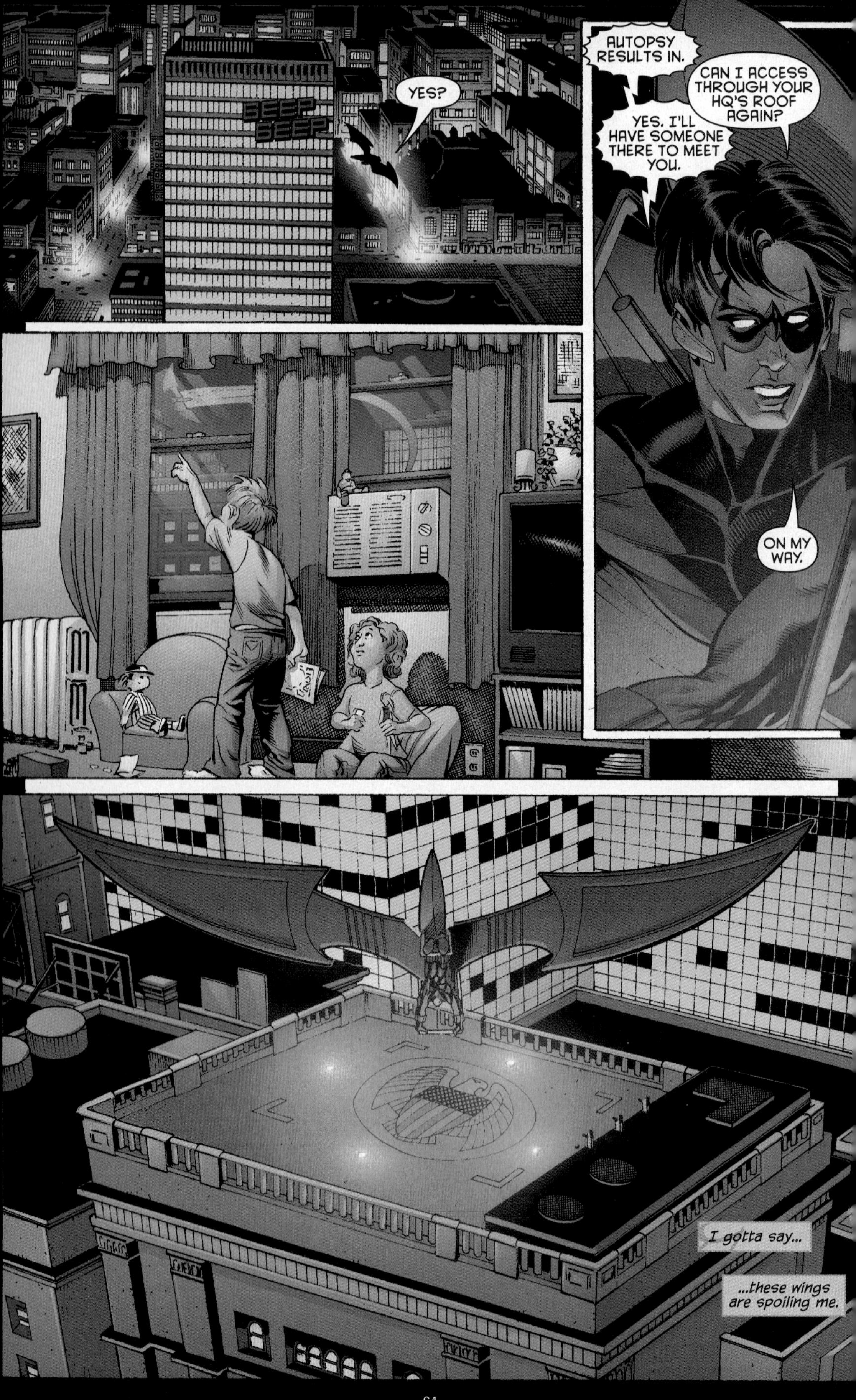

BEEP
BEEP
YES?
AUTOPSY RESULTS IN.
CAN I ACCESS THROUGH YOUR HQ'S ROOF AGAIN?
YES. I'LL HAVE SOMEONE THERE TO MEET YOU.
ON MY WAY.
I gotta say...
...these wings are spoiling me.

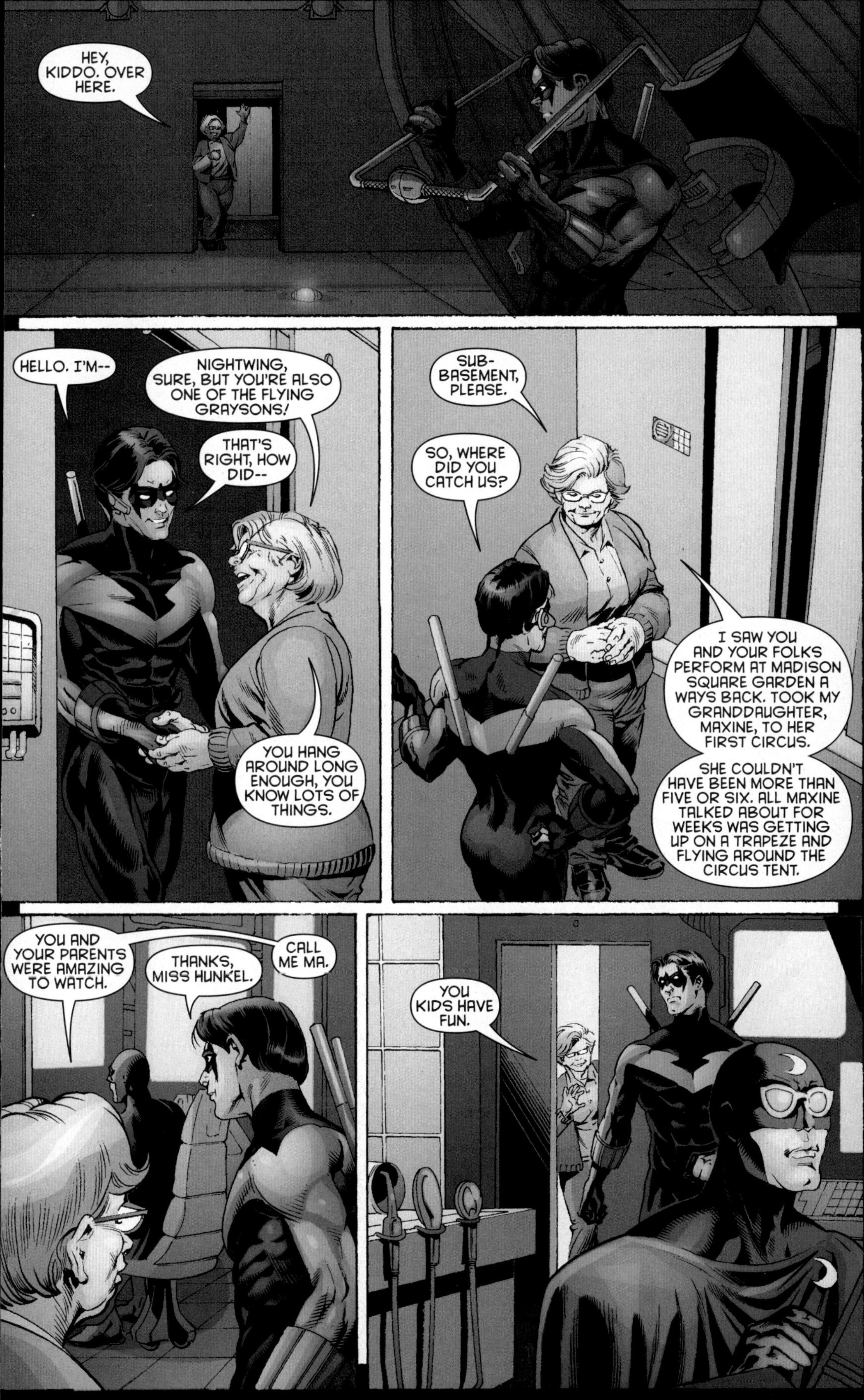
HEY, KIDDO. OVER HERE.
HELLO. I'M--
NIGHTWING, SURE, BUT YOU'RE ALSO ONE OF THE FLYING GRAYSONS!
THAT'S RIGHT, HOW DID--
YOU HANG AROUND LONG ENOUGH, YOU KNOW LOTS OF THINGS.
SUB-BASEMENT, PLEASE.
SO, WHERE DID YOU CATCH US?
I SAW YOU AND YOUR FOLKS PERFORM AT MADISON SQUARE GARDEN A WAYS BACK. TOOK MY GRANDDAUGHTER, MAXINE, TO HER FIRST CIRCUS.
SHE COULDN'T HAVE BEEN MORE THAN FIVE OR SIX. ALL MAXINE TALKED ABOUT FOR WEEKS WAS GETTING UP ON A TRAPEZE AND FLYING AROUND THE CIRCUS TENT.
YOU AND YOUR PARENTS WERE AMAZING TO WATCH.
THANKS, MISS HUNKEL.
CALL ME MA.
YOU KIDS HAVE FUN.

THANKS FOR THE QUICK WORK.

NO PROBLEM. SOME INTERESTING REVELATIONS HAVE POPPED UP.

FOLLOW ME.

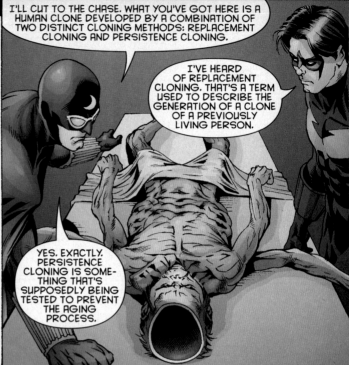

I'LL CUT TO THE CHASE. WHAT YOU'VE GOT HERE IS A HUMAN CLONE DEVELOPED BY A COMBINATION OF TWO DISTINCT CLONING METHODS: REPLACEMENT CLONING AND PERSISTENCE CLONING.

I'VE HEARD OF REPLACEMENT CLONING. THAT'S A TERM USED TO DESCRIBE THE GENERATION OF A CLONE OF A PREVIOUSLY LIVING PERSON.

YES. EXACTLY. PERSISTENCE CLONING IS SOMETHING THAT'S SUPPOSEDLY BEING TESTED TO PREVENT THE AGING PROCESS.

THERE HAVEN'T BEEN ANY REPORTED BREAKTHROUGHS.

NOW HERE'S THE *REALLY* STRANGE ASPECT OF THIS CASE.

THE CREATURE'S HANDS, HIS WINGS, AND HIS BODY, ALL HAVE SEPARATE AND DISTINCT NUCLEAR D.N.A. STRANDS.

WHAT YOU'RE SAYING IS THAT SOMEBODY BASICALLY THREW THE D.N.A. OF THREE SPECIFIC PEOPLE INTO A MIXER AND CREATED *THIS* POOR CREATURE?

EXACTLY.

ALONG WITH TRYING TO MAKE THEM SOMEWHAT IMMORTAL UNLESS SOMEONE BLOWS THEIR BRAINS OUT FROM THE INSIDE?

YES.

HAVE YOU IDENTIFIED A SPECIFIC TRIGGER THAT'S TRYING TO STOP THE AGING PROCESS?

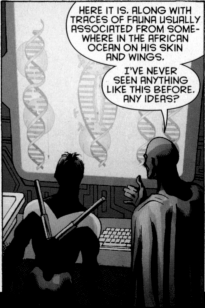

HERE IT IS. ALONG WITH TRACES OF FAUNA USUALLY ASSOCIATED FROM SOMEWHERE IN THE AFRICAN OCEAN ON HIS SKIN AND WINGS.

I'VE NEVER SEEN ANYTHING LIKE THIS BEFORE. ANY IDEAS?

TALIA.

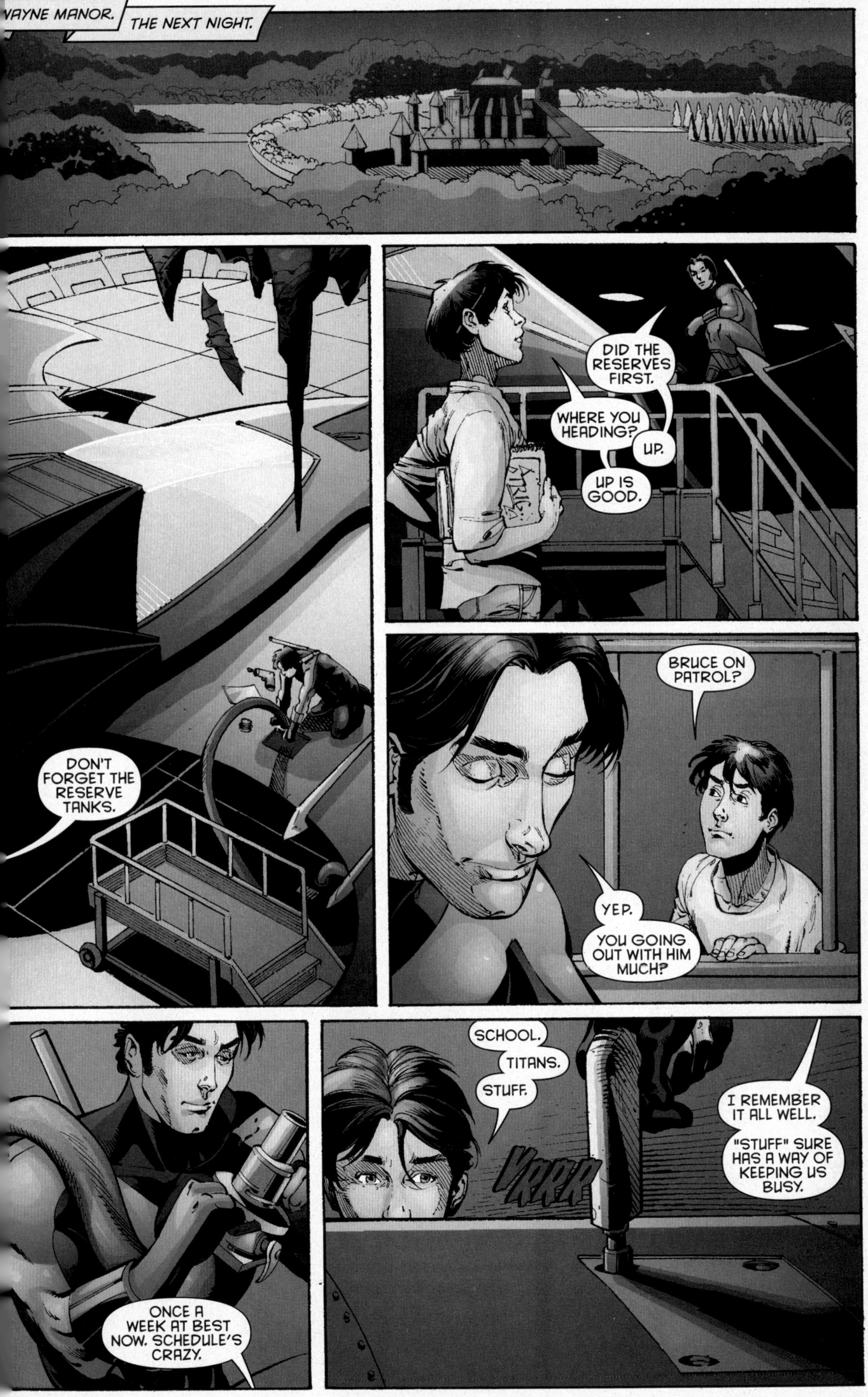

WAYNE MANOR.
THE NEXT NIGHT.
DON'T FORGET THE RESERVE TANKS.
DID THE RESERVES FIRST.
WHERE YOU HEADING?
UP.
UP IS GOOD.
BRUCE ON PATROL?
YEP.
YOU GOING OUT WITH HIM MUCH?
ONCE A WEEK AT BEST NOW. SCHEDULE'S CRAZY.
SCHOOL.
TITANS.
STUFF.
VRRR
I REMEMBER IT ALL WELL.
"STUFF" SURE HAS A WAY OF KEEPING US BUSY.

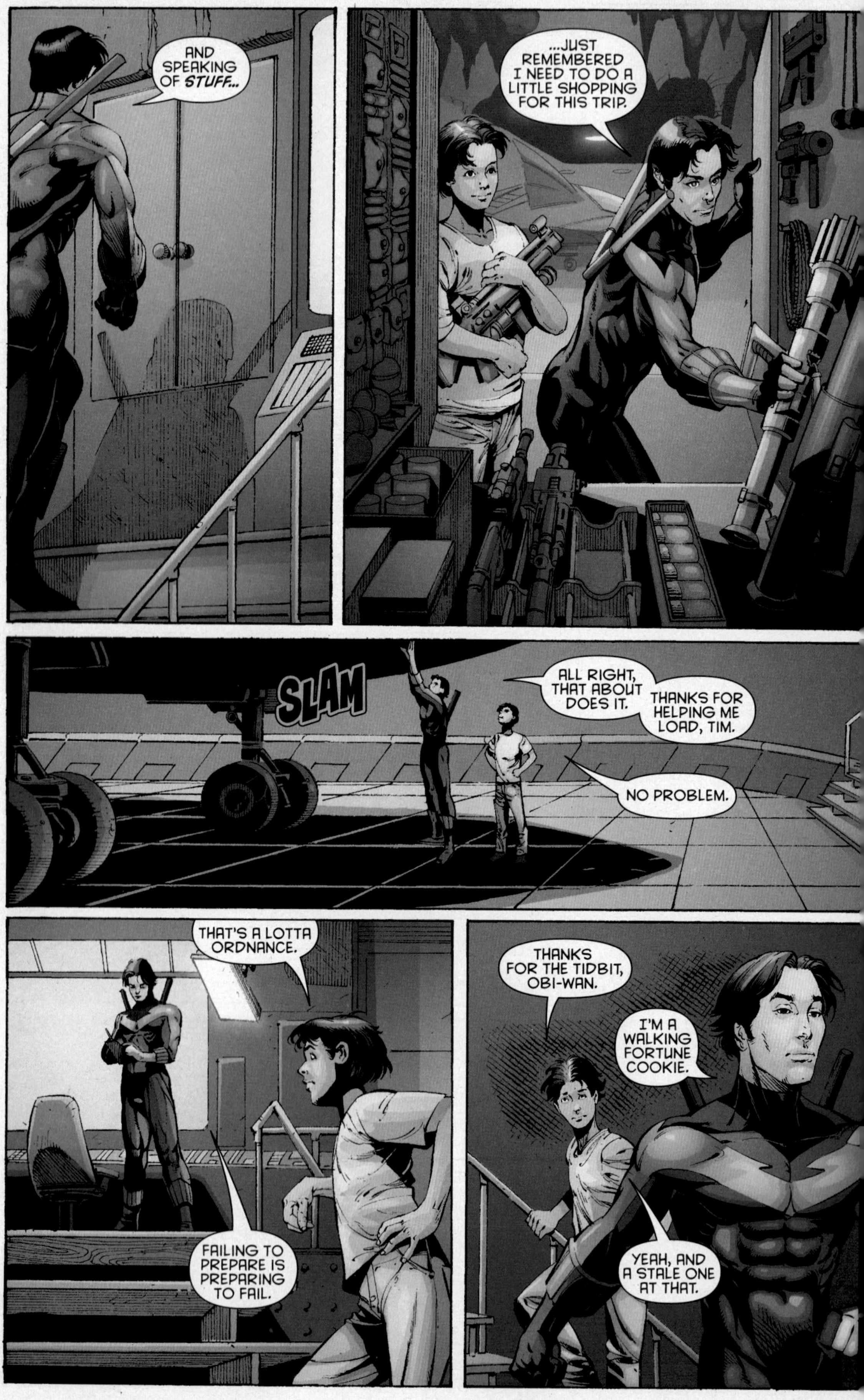
AND SPEAKING OF STUFF...
...JUST REMEMBERED I NEED TO DO A LITTLE SHOPPING FOR THIS TRIP.
SLAM
ALL RIGHT, THAT ABOUT DOES IT.
THANKS FOR HELPING ME LOAD, TIM.
NO PROBLEM.
THAT'S A LOTTA ORDNANCE.
FAILING TO PREPARE IS PREPARING TO FAIL.
THANKS FOR THE TIDBIT, OBI-WAN.
I'M A WALKING FORTUNE COOKIE.
YEAH, AND A STALE ONE AT THAT.

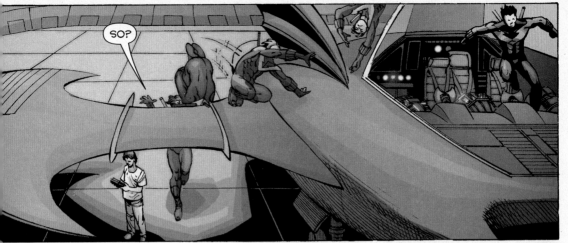

SO?

SO WHAT?

YOU COMING?

THOUGHT YOU'D NEVER ASK!

TIM.

YEAH?

FORGETTING SOMETHING? HAS A TOUCH OF RED IN IT, BIG LETTER *"R"* ON THE FRONT?

BE RIGHT BACK!

SO, NEW PLANE, HMM?

YEP.

I LIKE IT. WHAT HAPPENED TO THE LAST ONE?

BRUCE AND I WERE PAYING A VISIT TO AN ISLAND IN THE CARIBBEAN OWNED BY THIS BILLIONAIRE PHILANTHROPIST GUY BY THE NAME OF JOHN MAYHEW.

I REMEMBER HIM-- FINANCED THE CLUB OF HEROES. I TAGGED ALONG WITH BRUCE ON A FEW OF THOSE OCCASIONS.

HOW'S MY OL' PAL THE LEGIONARY AND WINGMAN DOING?

NOT GOOD.

LEGIONARY'S DEAD, STABBED 23 TIMES BY WINGMAN WHO WAS THEN KILLED BY THE RAVING LUNATIC, MAYHEW.

OH, AND MAYHEW BLEW UP THE PLANE JUST AS WE GOT READY TO GET THE HELL OUT OF THERE.

IT WAS A *LONG* WEEKEND.

YEAH, I'D SAY SO.

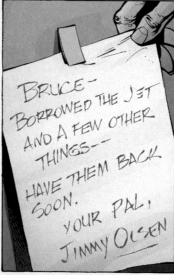

BRUCE--
BORROWED THE JET AND A FEW OTHER THINGS--
HAVE THEM BACK SOON.
YOUR PAL,
JIMMY OLSEN

"A FEW *OTHER* THINGS."

HNNN.

70

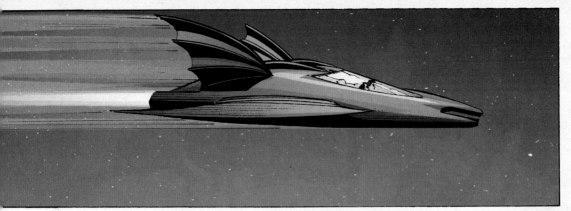

HOW'S THE NEW HQ SHAPING UP?

NOT BAD. ANOTHER MONTH OR SO AND IT SHOULD BE DONE.

KINDA NICE HAVING THE J.S.A. ONLY A FEW MILES SOUTH. THEY'VE BEEN A BIG HELP.

DID POWER GIRL DO SOME HEAVY LIFTING?

AS A MATTER OF FACT SHE DID.

UNIFORM OR CIVVIES?

UNIFORM.

THINK CLEAN THOUGHTS, CHUM.

BRUCE MENTIONED YOU'RE HITTING THE FRIENDLY SKIES NOW.

WHEN CAN I TAKE A SPIN IN THE ALL NEW, ALL DIFFERENT "WINGER"?

IF YOU CALL IT "WINGER" AGAIN, PROBABLY NEVER.

WHO BUILT THE PROPULSION UNITS?

JOHN IRONS.

SWEET.

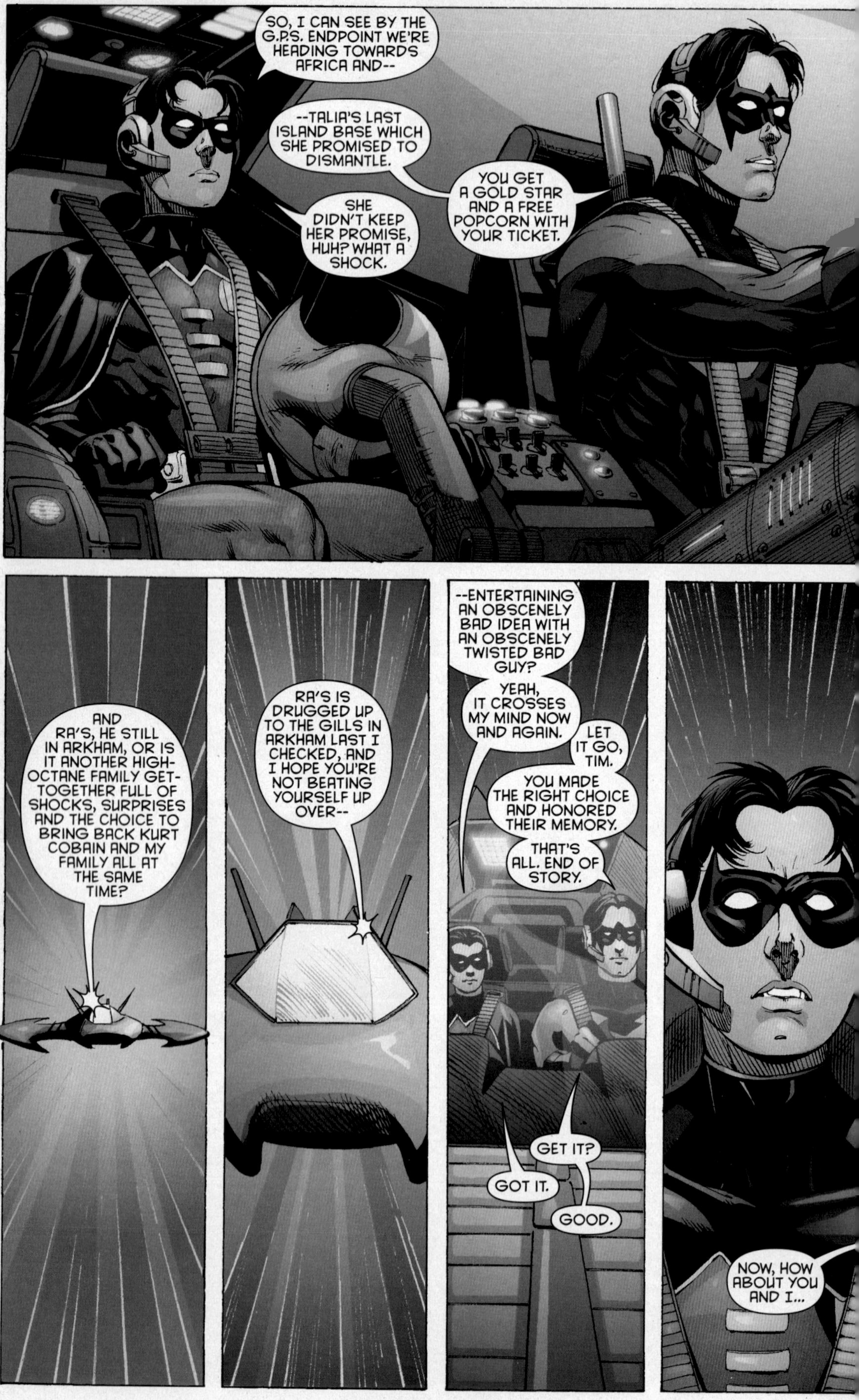
SO, I CAN SEE BY THE G.P.S. ENDPOINT WE'RE HEADING TOWARDS AFRICA AND--
--TALIA'S LAST ISLAND BASE WHICH SHE PROMISED TO DISMANTLE.
SHE DIDN'T KEEP HER PROMISE, HUH? WHAT A SHOCK.
YOU GET A GOLD STAR AND A FREE POPCORN WITH YOUR TICKET.
AND RA'S, HE STILL IN ARKHAM, OR IS IT ANOTHER HIGH-OCTANE FAMILY GET-TOGETHER FULL OF SHOCKS, SURPRISES AND THE CHOICE TO BRING BACK KURT COBAIN AND MY FAMILY ALL AT THE SAME TIME?
RA'S IS DRUGGED UP TO THE GILLS IN ARKHAM LAST I CHECKED, AND I HOPE YOU'RE NOT BEATING YOURSELF UP OVER--
--ENTERTAINING AN OBSCENELY BAD IDEA WITH AN OBSCENELY TWISTED BAD GUY?
YEAH, IT CROSSES MY MIND NOW AND AGAIN.
LET IT GO, TIM.
YOU MADE THE RIGHT CHOICE AND HONORED THEIR MEMORY.
THAT'S ALL. END OF STORY.
GET IT?
GOT IT.
GOOD.
NOW, HOW ABOUT YOU AND I...

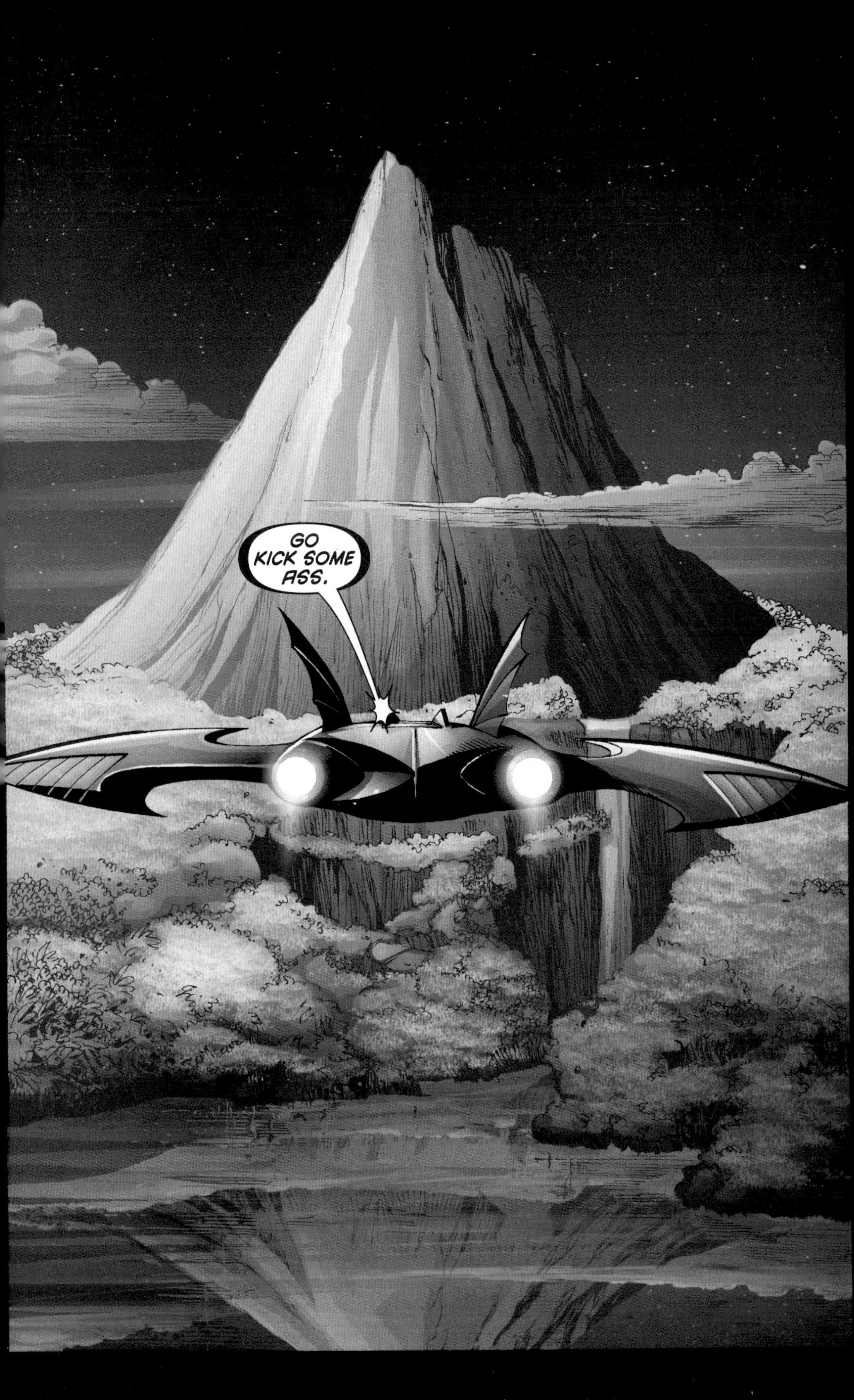
GO KICK SOME ASS.

NIGHTWING #1
Cover art by Rags Morales & Michael B

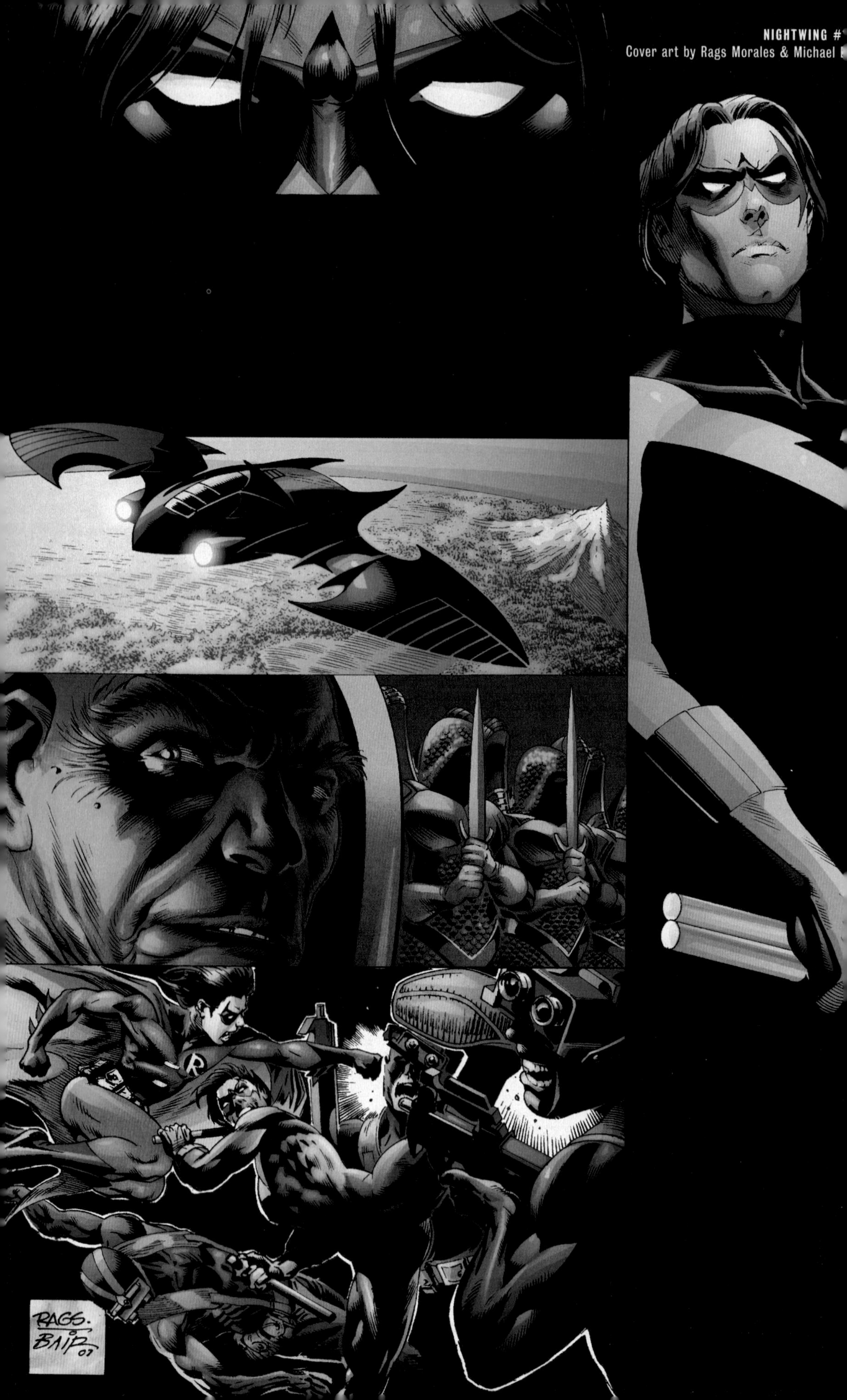
RAGS.
BAIR 07

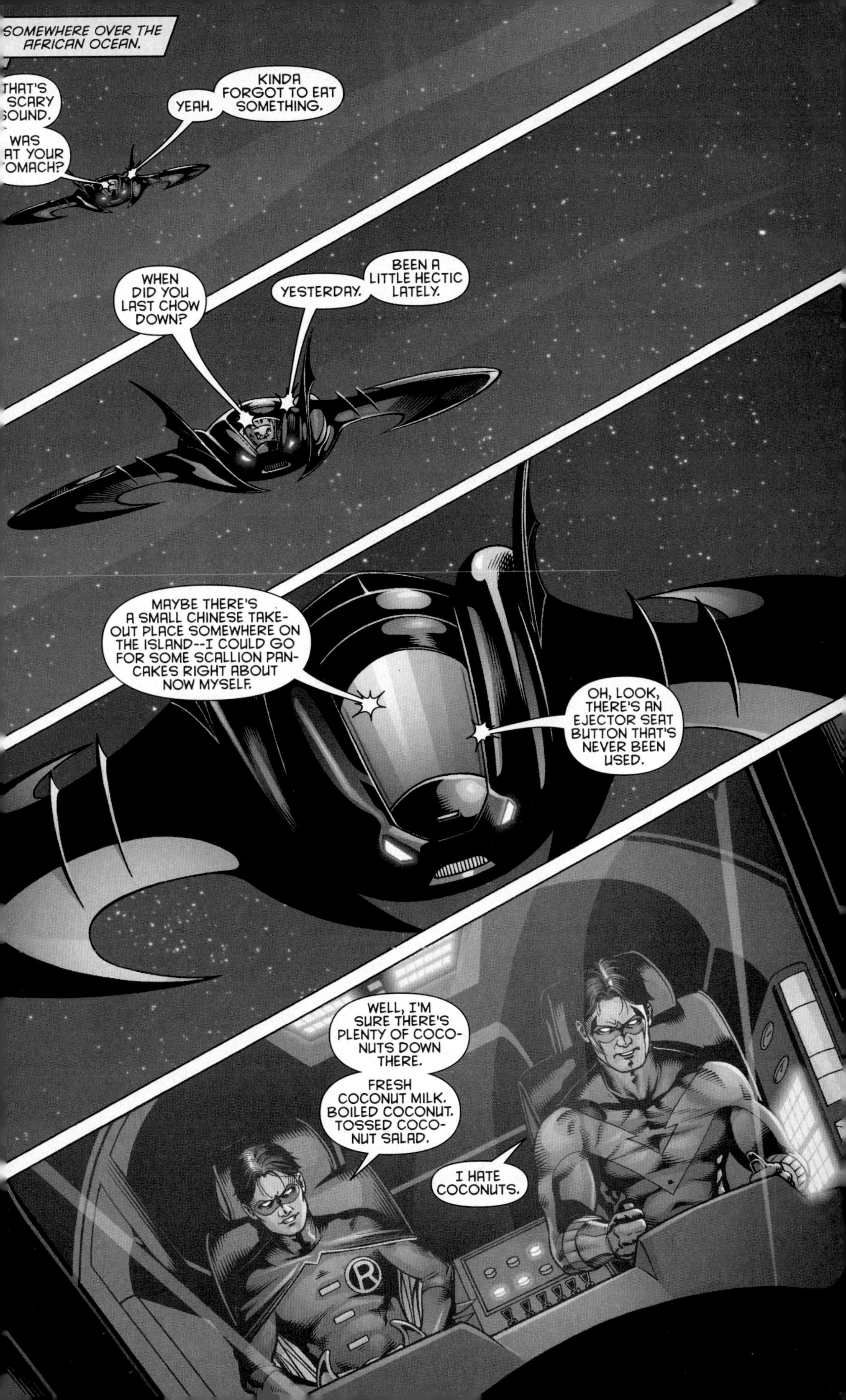

SOMEWHERE OVER THE AFRICAN OCEAN.
THAT'S SCARY SOUND.
WAS AT YOUR OMACH?
YEAH.
KINDA FORGOT TO EAT SOMETHING.
WHEN DID YOU LAST CHOW DOWN?
YESTERDAY.
BEEN A LITTLE HECTIC LATELY.
MAYBE THERE'S A SMALL CHINESE TAKE-OUT PLACE SOMEWHERE ON THE ISLAND--I COULD GO FOR SOME SCALLION PAN-CAKES RIGHT ABOUT NOW MYSELF.
OH, LOOK, THERE'S AN EJECTOR SEAT BUTTON THAT'S NEVER BEEN USED.
WELL, I'M SURE THERE'S PLENTY OF COCO-NUTS DOWN THERE.
FRESH COCONUT MILK. BOILED COCONUT. TOSSED COCO-NUT SALAD.
I HATE COCONUTS.

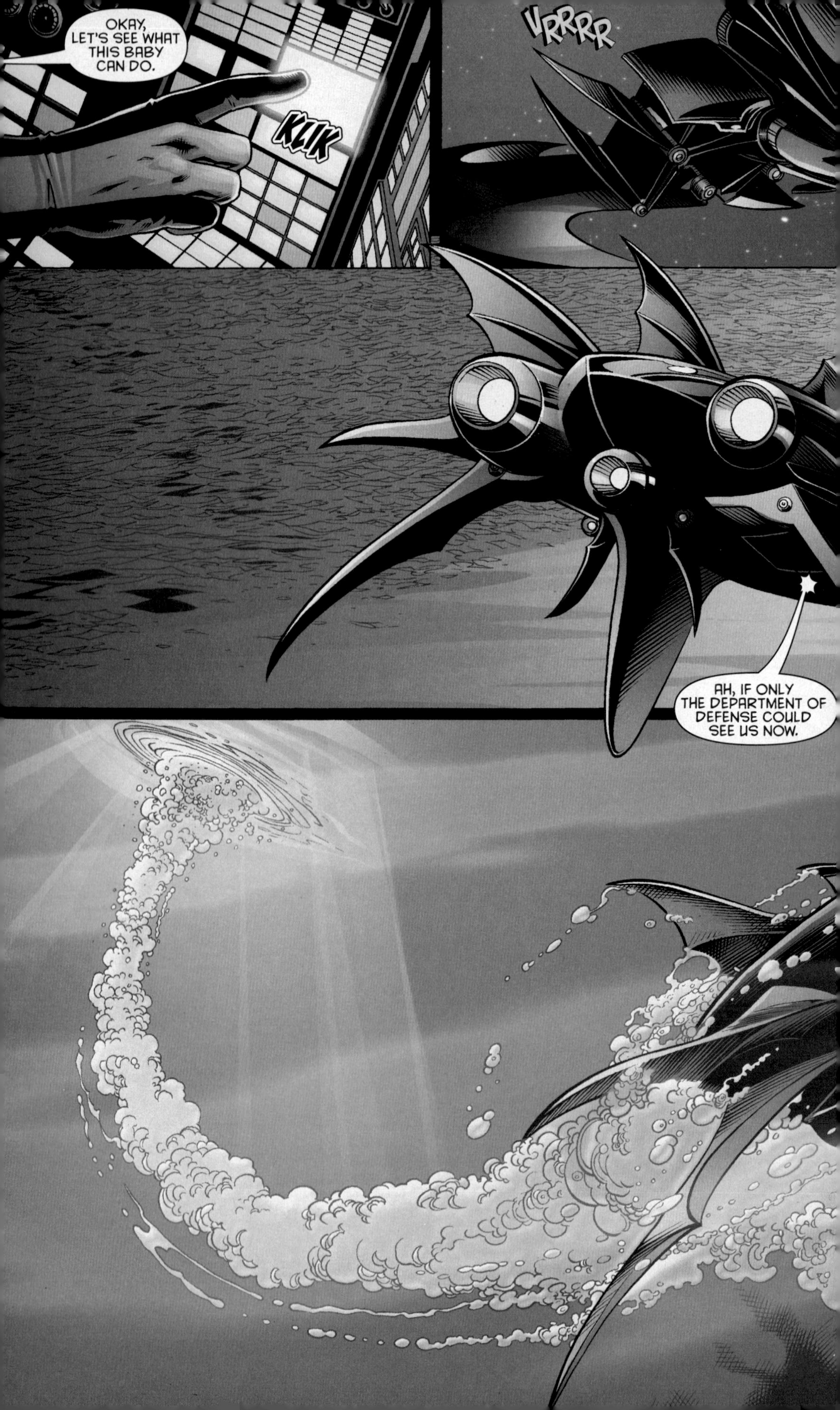
OKAY, LET'S SEE WHAT THIS BABY CAN DO.
KLIK
VRRRR
AH, IF ONLY THE DEPARTMENT OF DEFENSE COULD SEE US NOW.

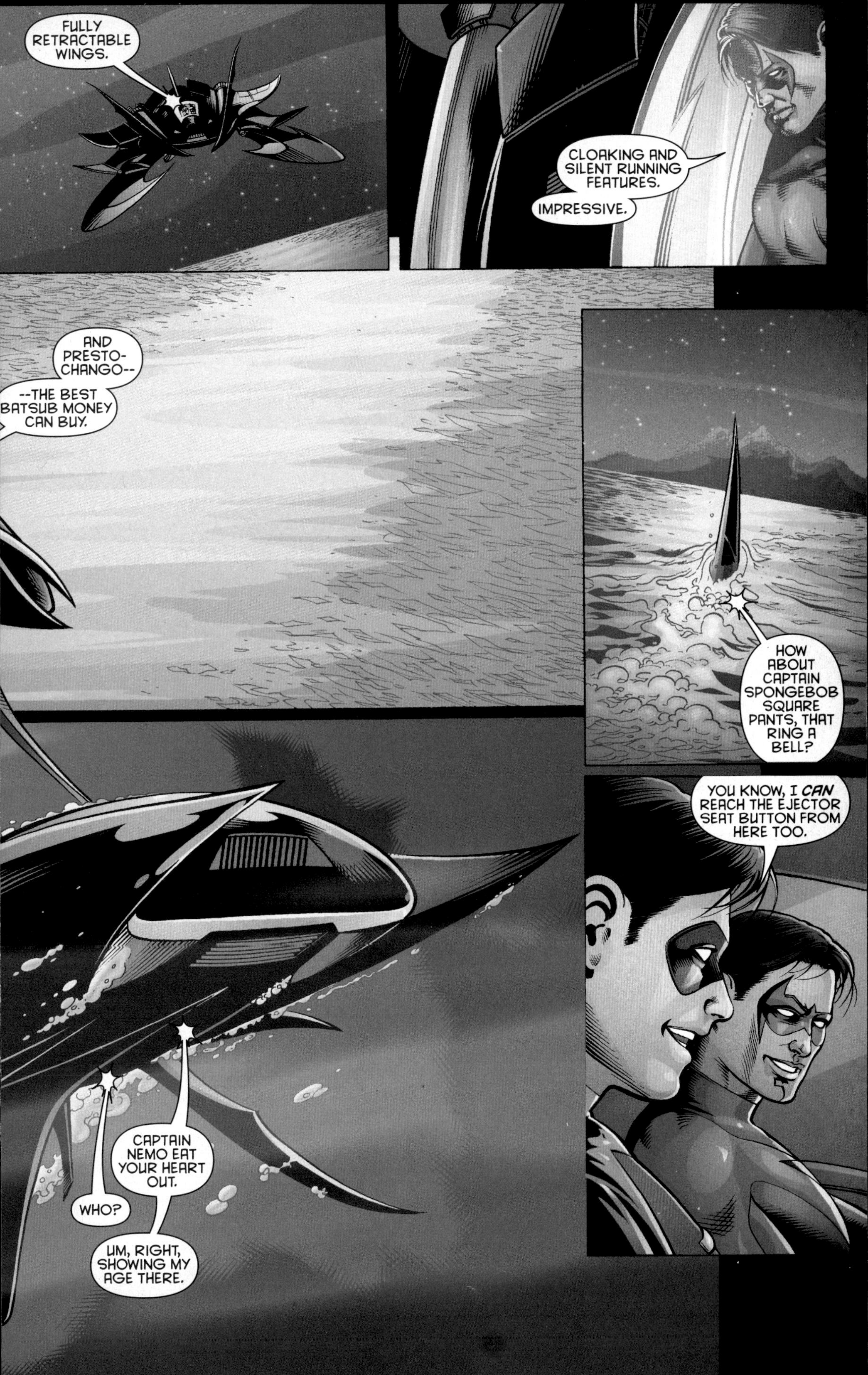
FULLY RETRACTABLE WINGS.
CLOAKING AND SILENT RUNNING FEATURES.
IMPRESSIVE.
AND PRESTO-CHANGO--
--THE BEST BATSUB MONEY CAN BUY.
HOW ABOUT CAPTAIN SPONGEBOB SQUARE PANTS, THAT RING A BELL?
CAPTAIN NEMO EAT YOUR HEART OUT.
WHO?
UM, RIGHT, SHOWING MY AGE THERE.
YOU KNOW, I CAN REACH THE EJECTOR SEAT BUTTON FROM HERE TOO.

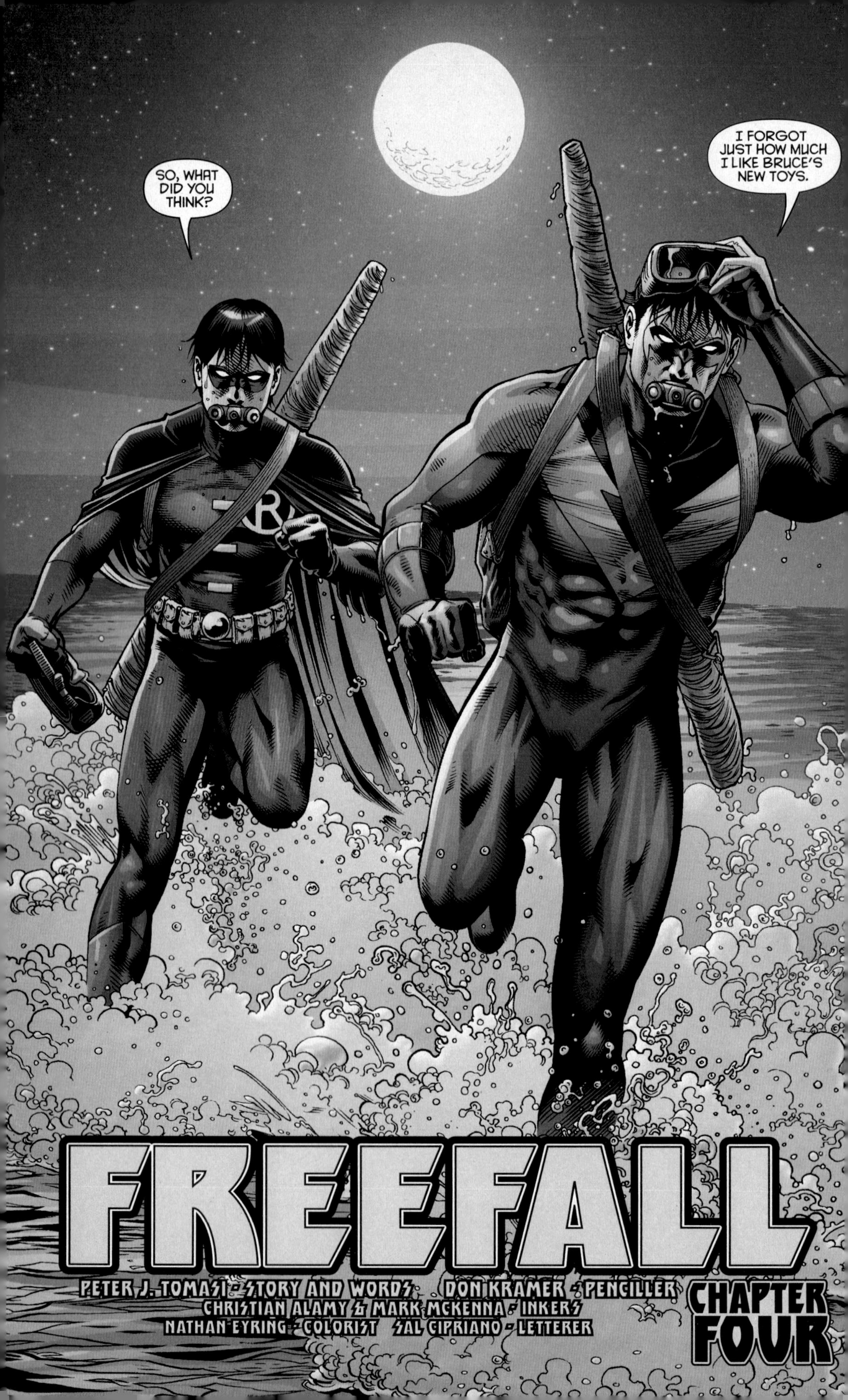
SO, WHAT DID YOU THINK?
I FORGOT JUST HOW MUCH I LIKE BRUCE'S NEW TOYS.
FREEFALL
PETER J. TOMASI - STORY AND WORDS
DON KRAMER - PENCILLER
CHRISTIAN ALAMY & MARK MCKENNA - INKERS
NATHAN EYRING - COLORIST
SAL CIPRIANO - LETTERER
CHAPTER FOUR

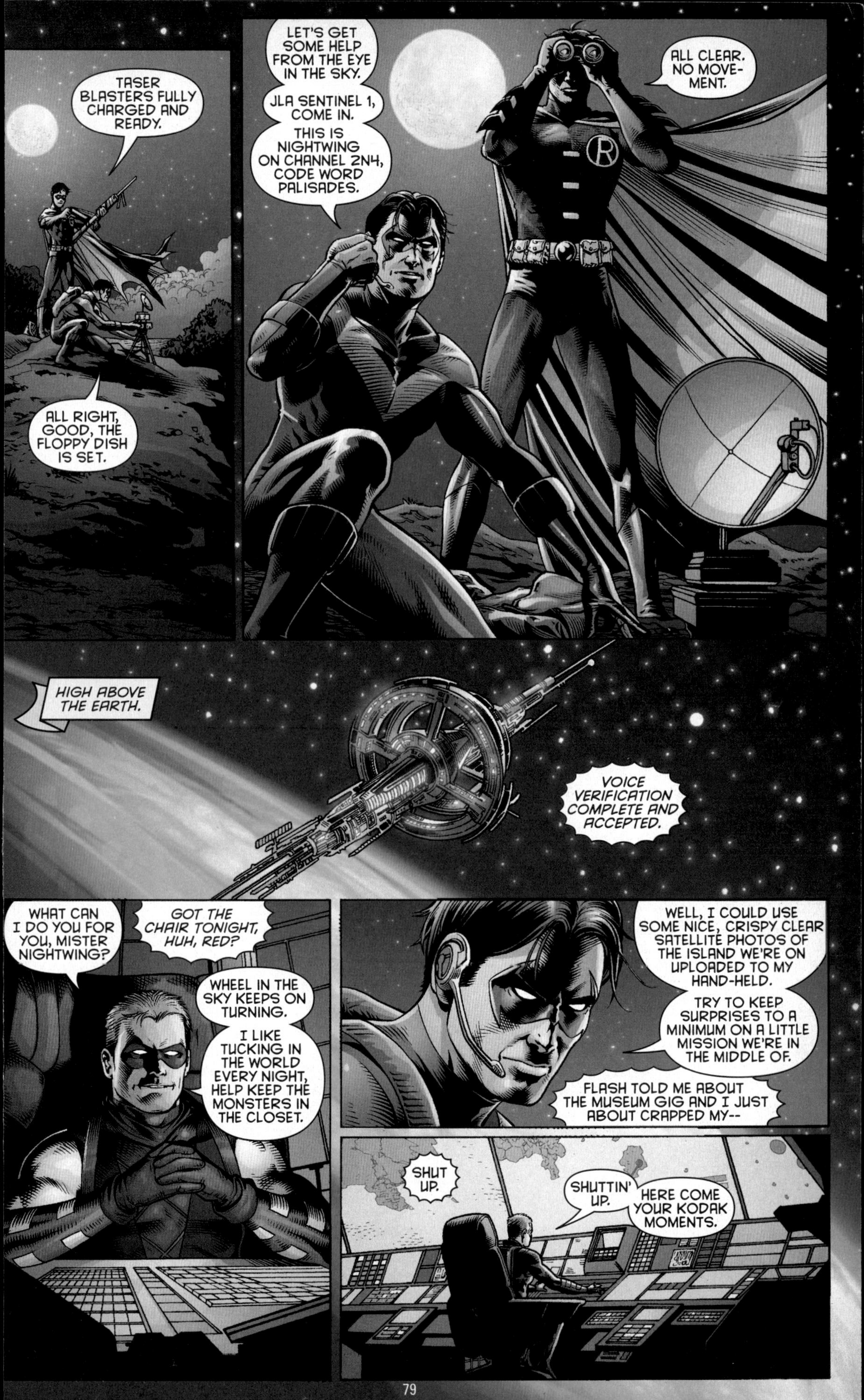
TASER BLASTERS FULLY CHARGED AND READY.
ALL RIGHT, GOOD, THE FLOPPY DISH IS SET.
LET'S GET SOME HELP FROM THE EYE IN THE SKY.
JLA SENTINEL 1, COME IN.
THIS IS NIGHTWING ON CHANNEL 2N4, CODE WORD PALISADES.
ALL CLEAR. NO MOVEMENT.
HIGH ABOVE THE EARTH.
VOICE VERIFICATION COMPLETE AND ACCEPTED.
WHAT CAN I DO YOU FOR YOU, MISTER NIGHTWING?
GOT THE CHAIR TONIGHT, HUH, RED?
WHEEL IN THE SKY KEEPS ON TURNING.
I LIKE TUCKING IN THE WORLD EVERY NIGHT, HELP KEEP THE MONSTERS IN THE CLOSET.
WELL, I COULD USE SOME NICE, CRISPY CLEAR SATELLITE PHOTOS OF THE ISLAND WE'RE ON UPLOADED TO MY HAND-HELD.
TRY TO KEEP SURPRISES TO A MINIMUM ON A LITTLE MISSION WE'RE IN THE MIDDLE OF.
FLASH TOLD ME ABOUT THE MUSEUM GIG AND I JUST ABOUT CRAPPED MY--
SHUT UP.
SHUTTIN' UP.
HERE COME YOUR KODAK MOMENTS.

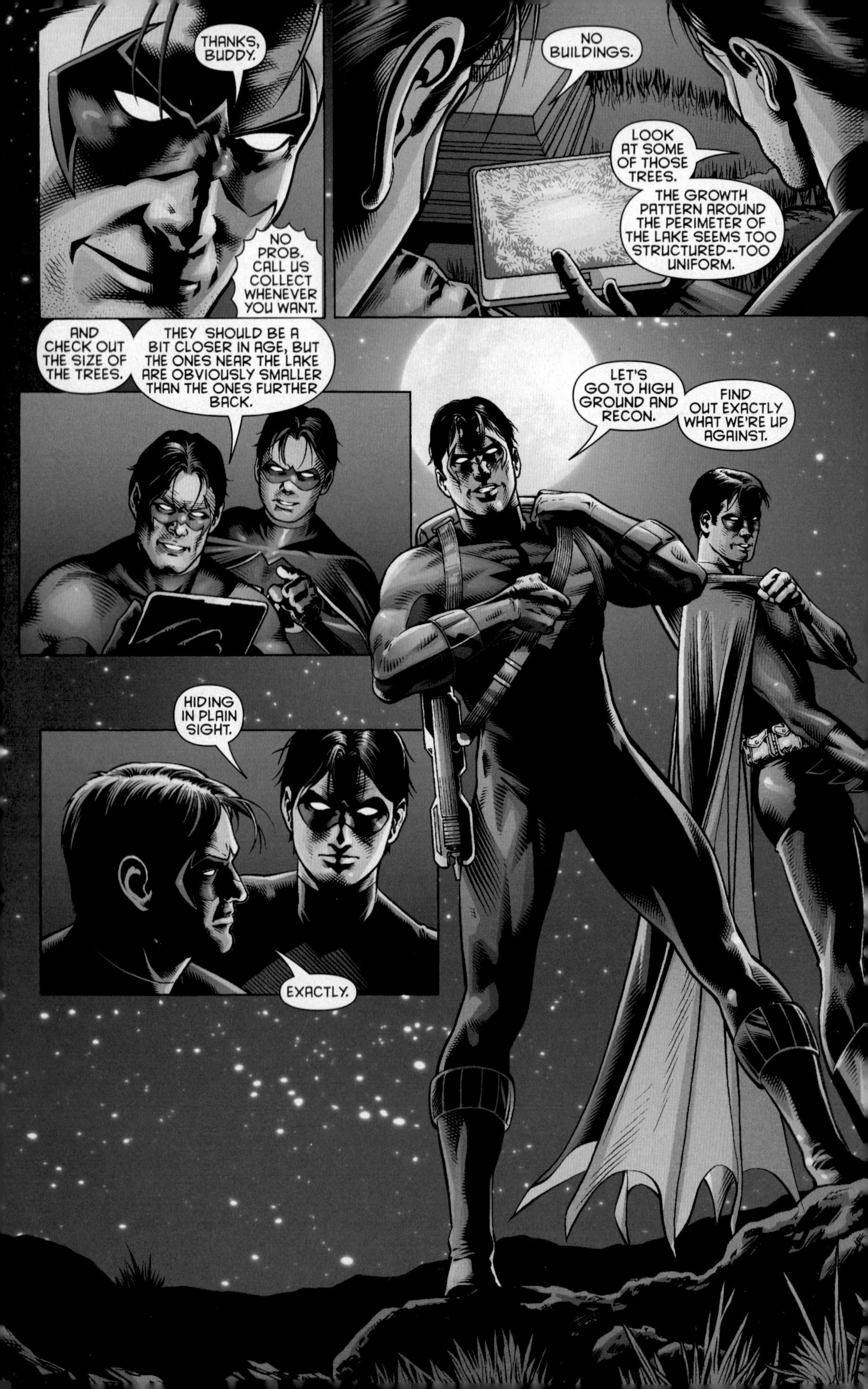
THANKS, BUDDY.
NO PROB. CALL US COLLECT WHENEVER YOU WANT.
NO BUILDINGS.
LOOK AT SOME OF THOSE TREES.
THE GROWTH PATTERN AROUND THE PERIMETER OF THE LAKE SEEMS TOO STRUCTURED--TOO UNIFORM.
AND CHECK OUT THE SIZE OF THE TREES.
THEY SHOULD BE A BIT CLOSER IN AGE, BUT THE ONES NEAR THE LAKE ARE OBVIOUSLY SMALLER THAN THE ONES FURTHER BACK.
HIDING IN PLAIN SIGHT.
EXACTLY.
LET'S GO TO HIGH GROUND AND RECON.
FIND OUT EXACTLY WHAT WE'RE UP AGAINST.

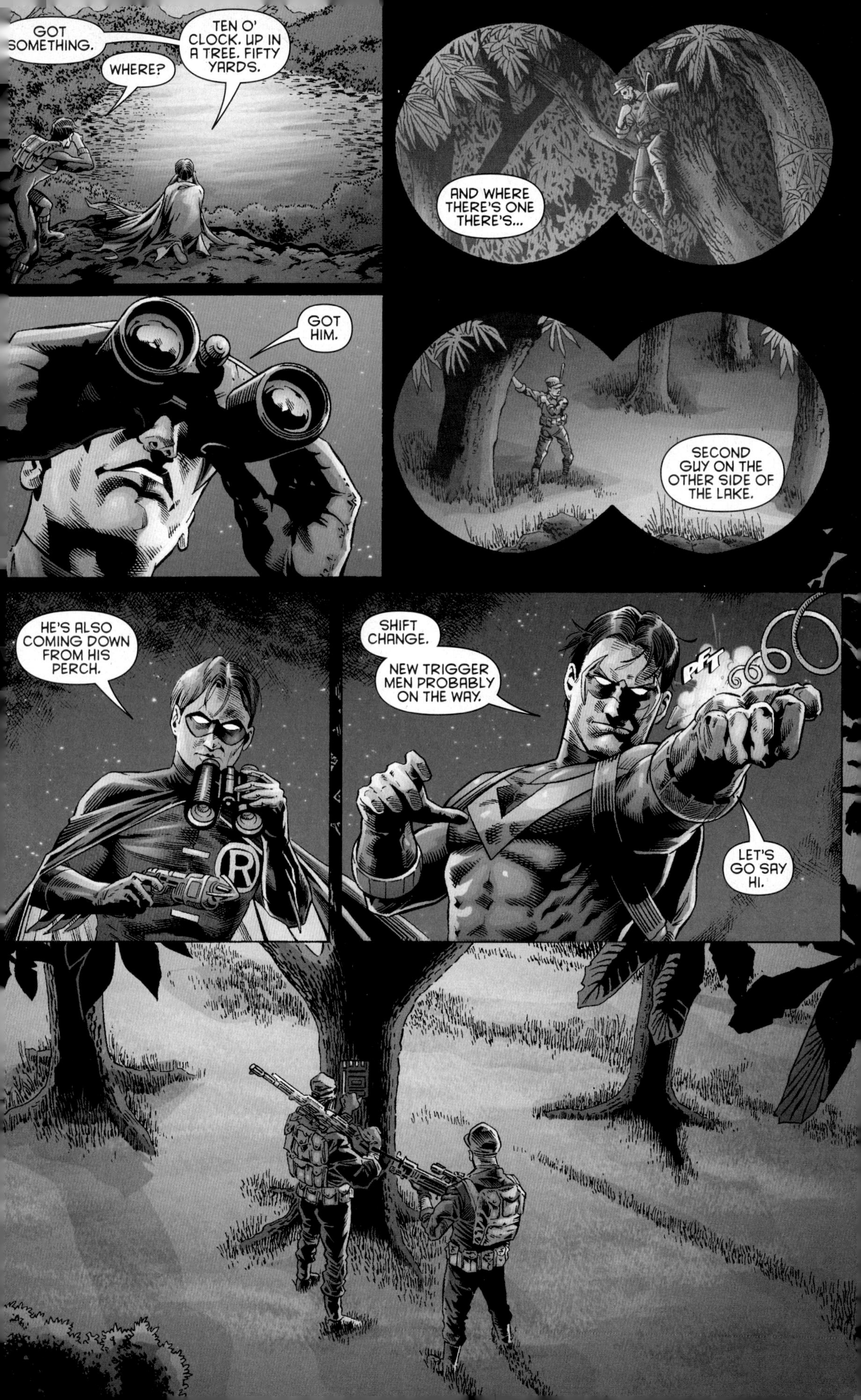
GOT SOMETHING.
WHERE?
TEN O' CLOCK. UP IN A TREE. FIFTY YARDS.
AND WHERE THERE'S ONE THERE'S...
GOT HIM.
SECOND GUY ON THE OTHER SIDE OF THE LAKE.
HE'S ALSO COMING DOWN FROM HIS PERCH.
SHIFT CHANGE.
NEW TRIGGER MEN PROBABLY ON THE WAY.
PFFT
LET'S GO SAY HI.

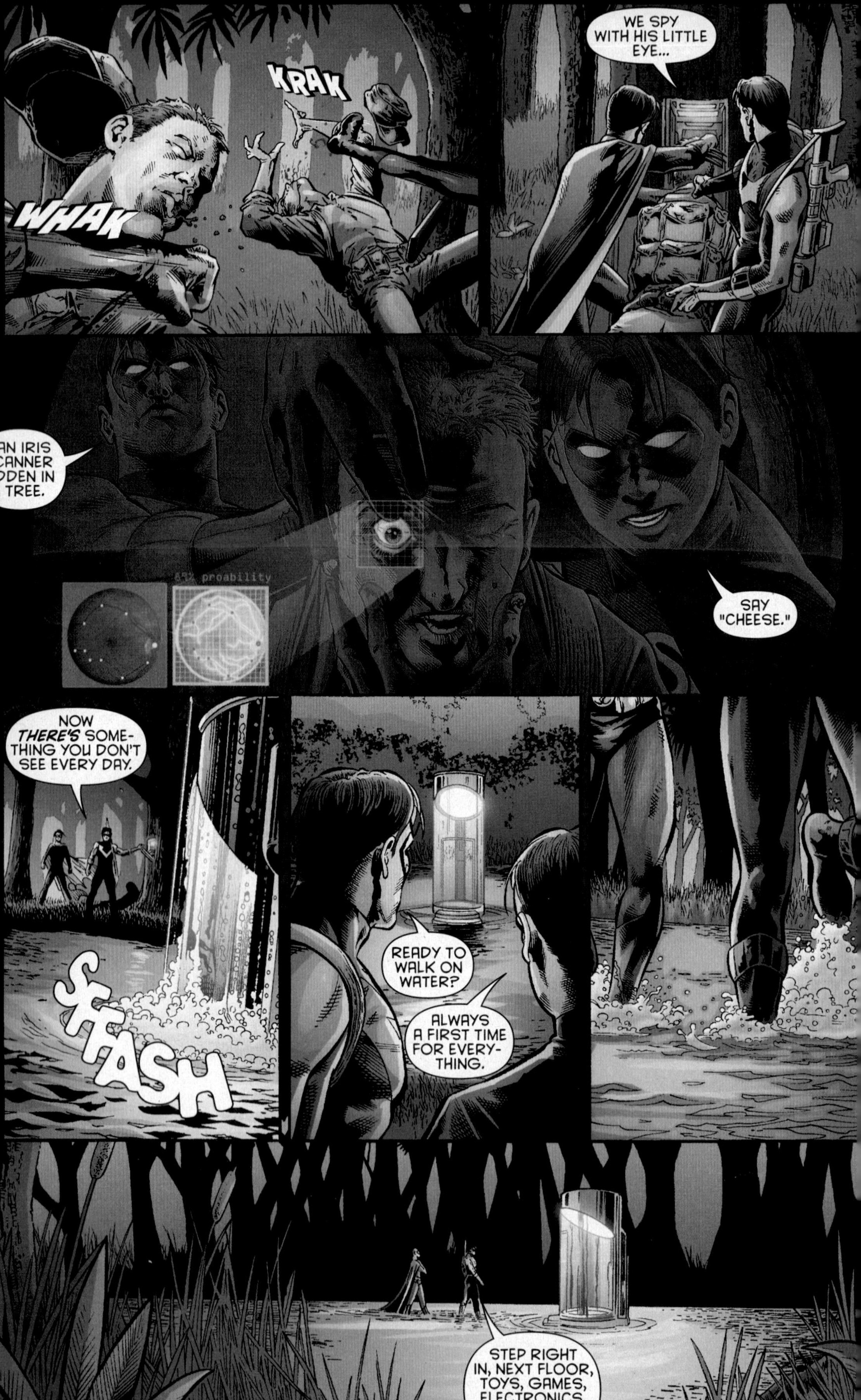
KRAK
WHAK
WE SPY WITH HIS LITTLE EYE...
...AN IRIS SCANNER HIDDEN IN A TREE.
SAY "CHEESE."
NOW THERE'S SOME-THING YOU DON'T SEE EVERY DAY.
SFFASH
READY TO WALK ON WATER?
ALWAYS A FIRST TIME FOR EVERY-THING.
STEP RIGHT IN, NEXT FLOOR, TOYS, GAMES, ELECTRONICS, CENTER OF THE EARTH.

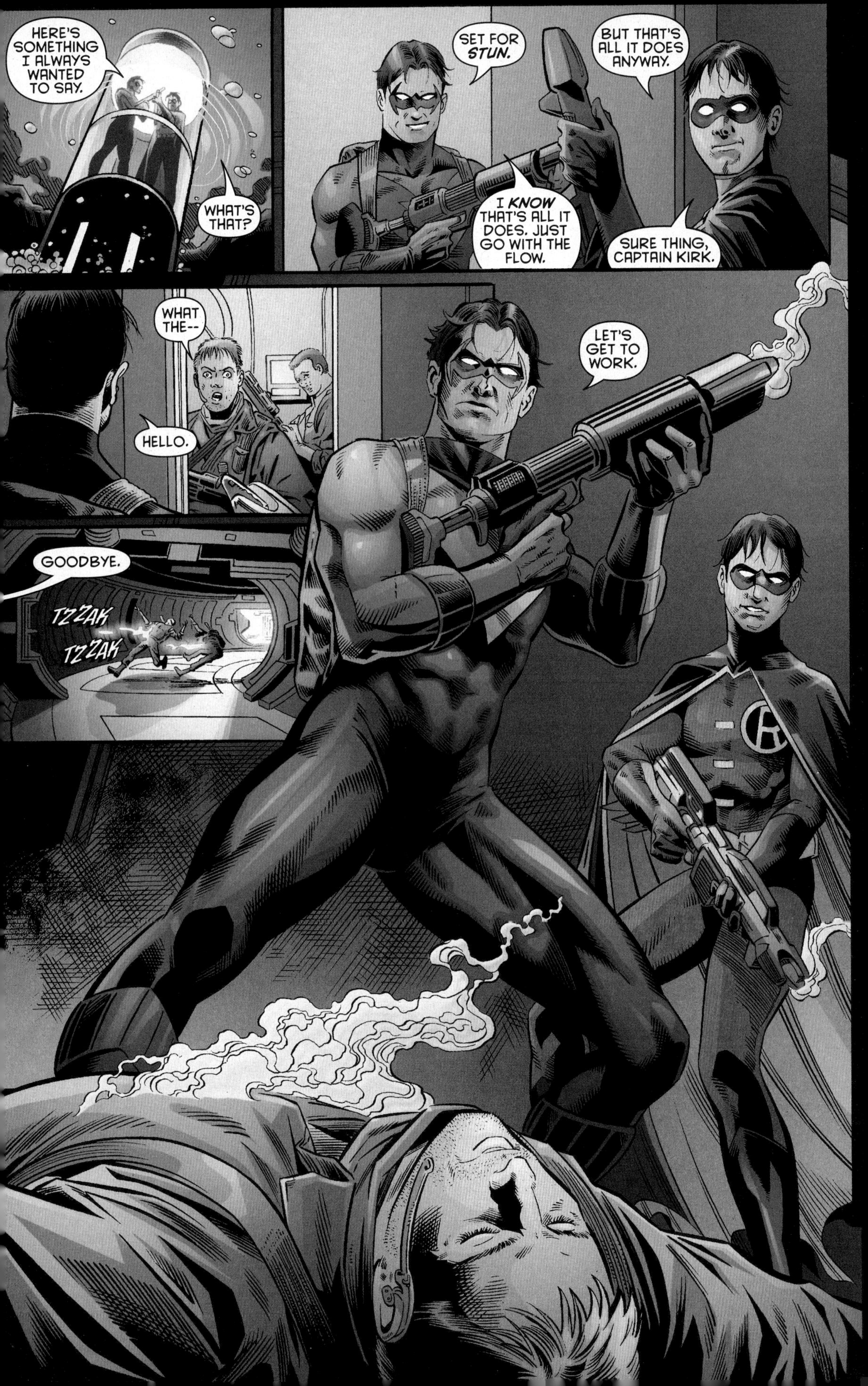
HERE'S SOMETHING I ALWAYS WANTED TO SAY.
WHAT'S THAT?
SET FOR *STUN.*
BUT THAT'S ALL IT DOES ANYWAY.
I *KNOW* THAT'S ALL IT DOES. JUST GO WITH THE FLOW.
SURE THING, CAPTAIN KIRK.
WHAT THE--
HELLO.
GOODBYE.
TZZAK
TZZAK
LET'S GET TO WORK.

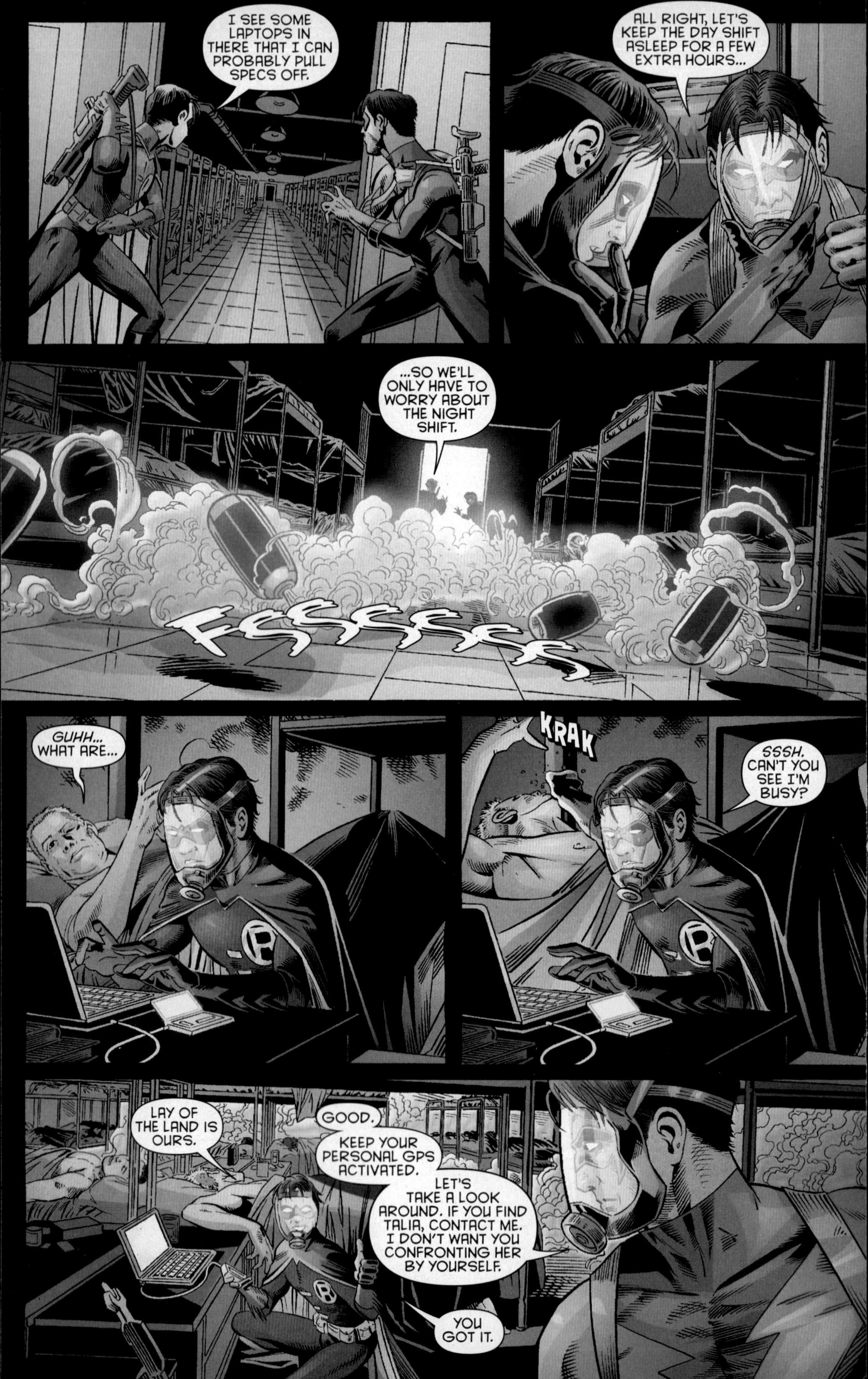

I SEE SOME LAPTOPS IN THERE THAT I CAN PROBABLY PULL SPECS OFF.
ALL RIGHT, LET'S KEEP THE DAY SHIFT ASLEEP FOR A FEW EXTRA HOURS...
...SO WE'LL ONLY HAVE TO WORRY ABOUT THE NIGHT SHIFT.
FSSSSSS
GUHH... WHAT ARE...
KRAK
SSSH. CAN'T YOU SEE I'M BUSY?
LAY OF THE LAND IS OURS.
GOOD.
KEEP YOUR PERSONAL GPS ACTIVATED.
LET'S TAKE A LOOK AROUND. IF YOU FIND TALIA, CONTACT ME. I DON'T WANT YOU CONFRONTING HER BY YOURSELF.
YOU GOT IT.

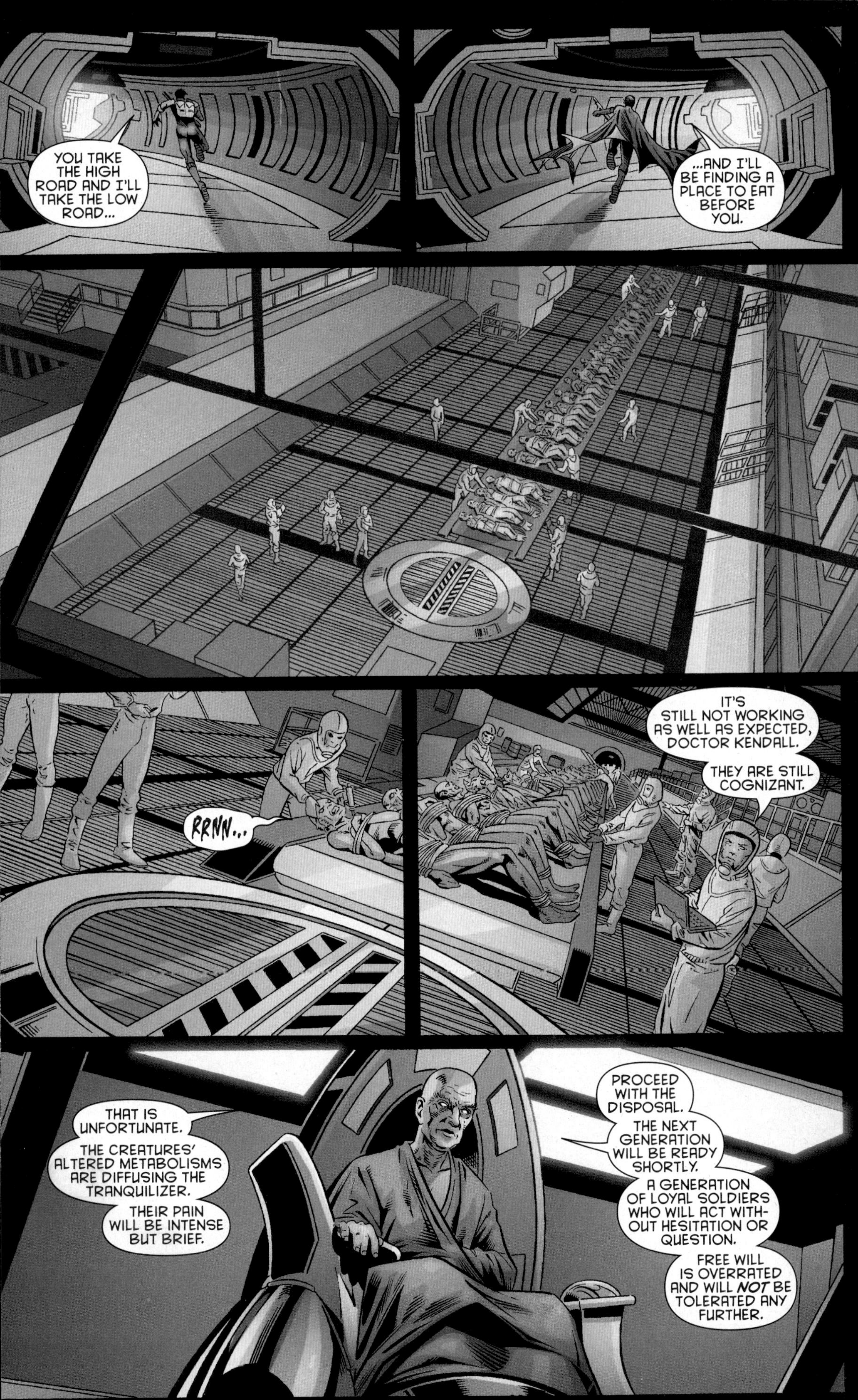
YOU TAKE THE HIGH ROAD AND I'LL TAKE THE LOW ROAD...
...AND I'LL BE FINDING A PLACE TO EAT BEFORE YOU.
RRNN...
IT'S STILL NOT WORKING AS WELL AS EXPECTED, DOCTOR KENDALL.
THEY ARE STILL COGNIZANT.
THAT IS UNFORTUNATE.
THE CREATURES' ALTERED METABOLISMS ARE DIFFUSING THE TRANQUILIZER.
THEIR PAIN WILL BE INTENSE BUT BRIEF.
PROCEED WITH THE DISPOSAL.
THE NEXT GENERATION WILL BE READY SHORTLY.
A GENERATION OF LOYAL SOLDIERS WHO WILL ACT WITHOUT HESITATION OR QUESTION.
FREE WILL IS OVERRATED AND WILL *NOT* BE TOLERATED ANY FURTHER.

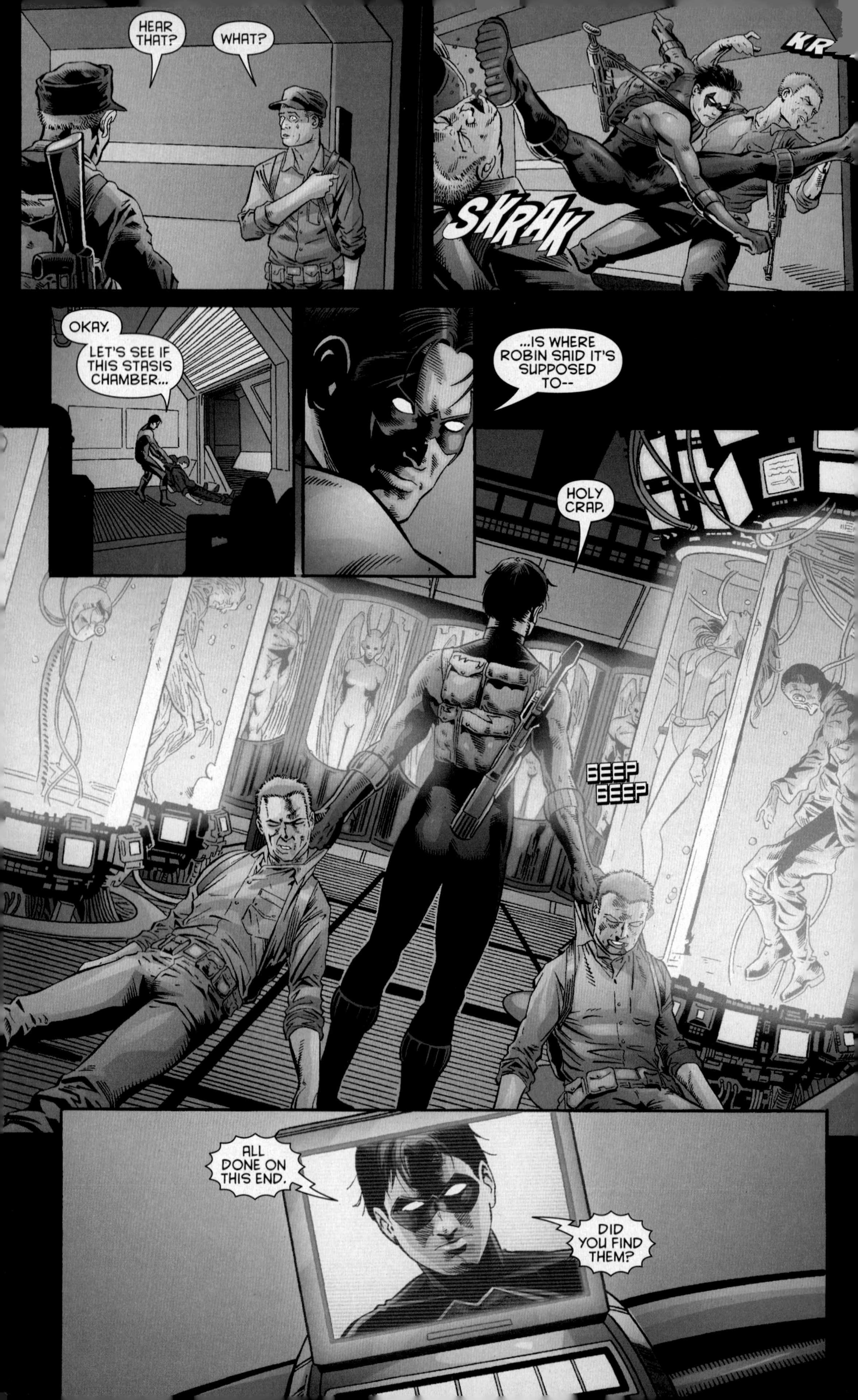
HEAR THAT?
WHAT?
KR--
SKRAK
OKAY. LET'S SEE IF THIS STASIS CHAMBER...
...IS WHERE ROBIN SAID IT'S SUPPOSED TO--
HOLY CRAP.
BEEP BEEP
ALL DONE ON THIS END.
DID YOU FIND THEM?

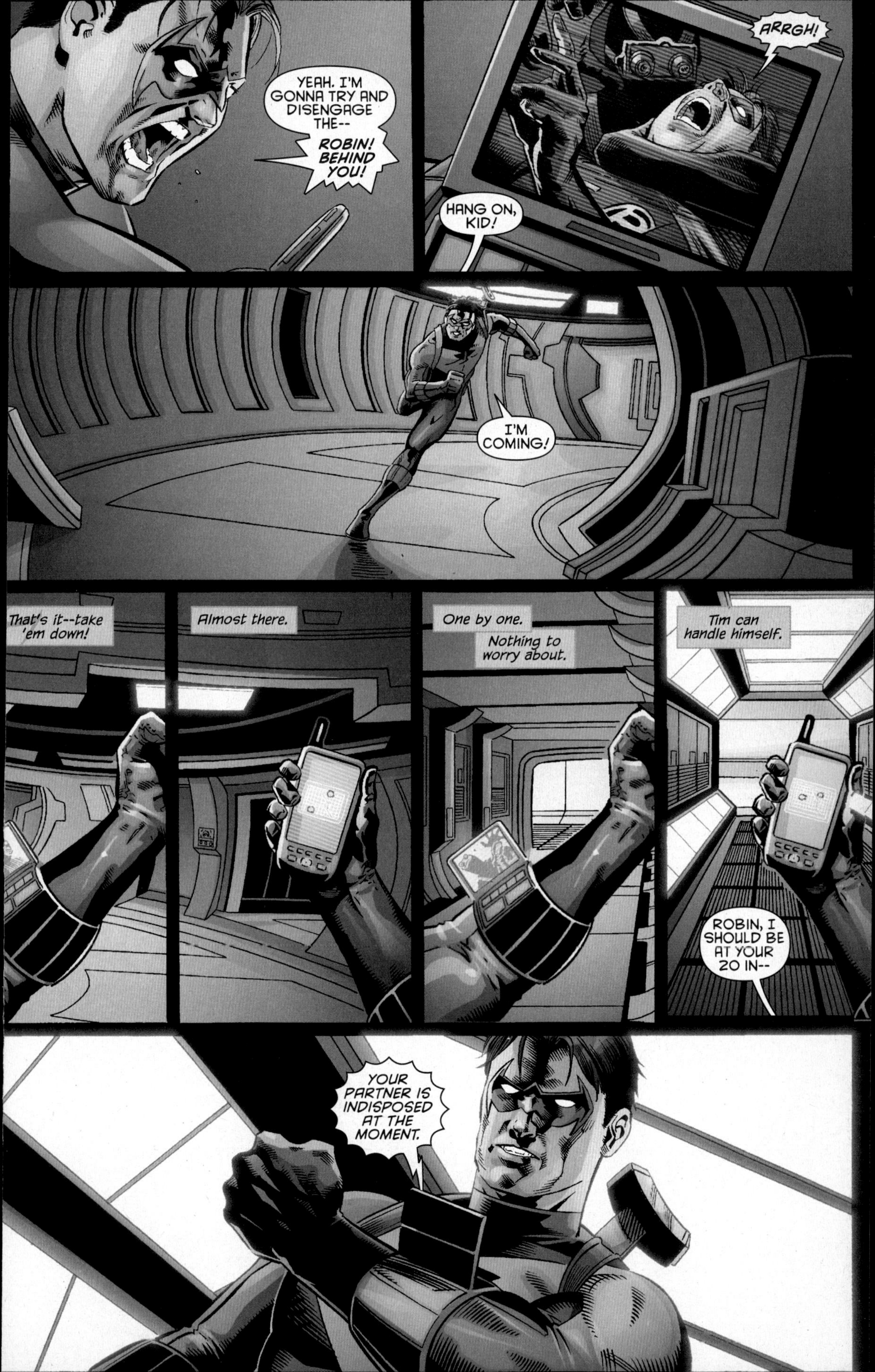
YEAH. I'M GONNA TRY AND DISENGAGE THE--
ROBIN! BEHIND YOU!
ARRGH!
HANG ON, KID!
I'M COMING!
That's it--take 'em down!
Almost there.
One by one.
Nothing to worry about.
Tim can handle himself.
ROBIN, I SHOULD BE AT YOUR 20 IN--
YOUR PARTNER IS INDISPOSED AT THE MOMENT.

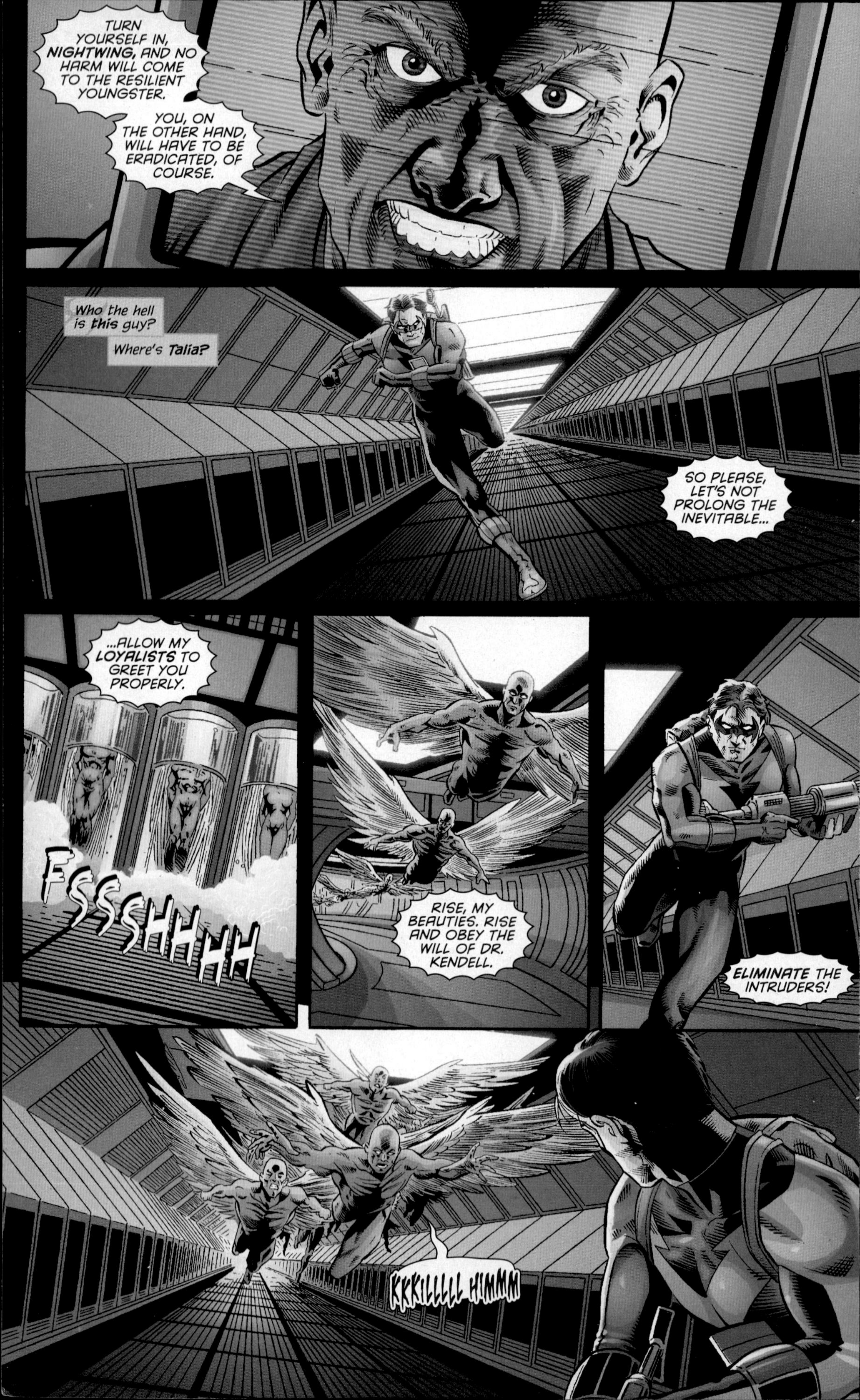
TURN YOURSELF IN, NIGHTWING, AND NO HARM WILL COME TO THE RESILIENT YOUNGSTER.
YOU, ON THE OTHER HAND, WILL HAVE TO BE ERADICATED, OF COURSE.
Who the hell is this guy?
Where's Talia?
SO PLEASE, LET'S NOT PROLONG THE INEVITABLE...
...ALLOW MY LOYALISTS TO GREET YOU PROPERLY.
FSSSHHHH
RISE, MY BEAUTIES. RISE AND OBEY THE WILL OF DR. KENDELL.
ELIMINATE THE INTRUDERS!
KKKILLLLL HIMMM

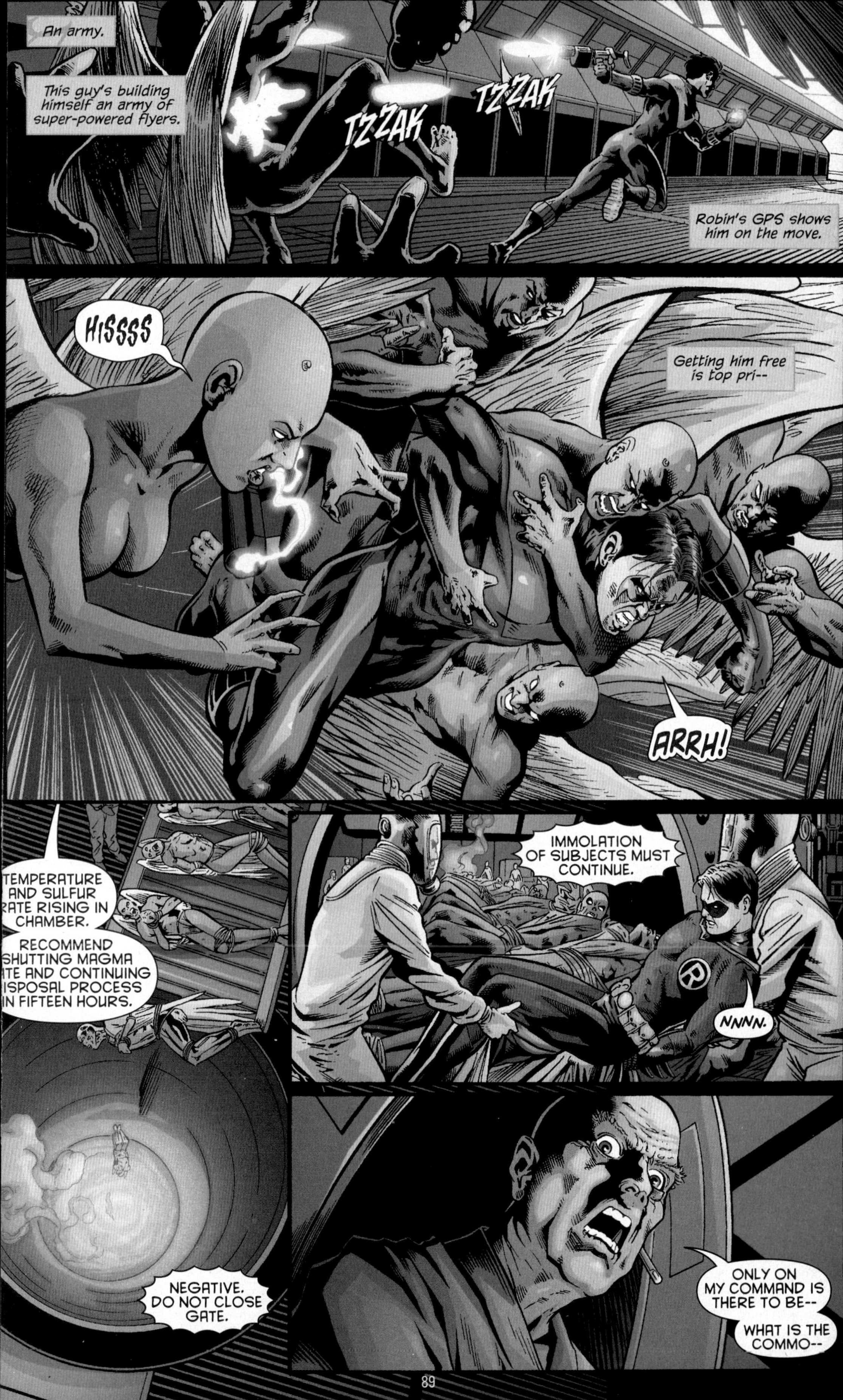

An army.
This guy's building himself an army of super-powered flyers.
TZZAK
TZZAK
Robin's GPS shows him on the move.
HISSSS
Getting him free is top pri--
ARRH!
TEMPERATURE AND SULFUR RATE RISING IN CHAMBER.
RECOMMEND SHUTTING MAGMA GATE AND CONTINUING DISPOSAL PROCESS IN FIFTEEN HOURS.
IMMOLATION OF SUBJECTS MUST CONTINUE.
NNNN.
NEGATIVE. DO NOT CLOSE GATE.
ONLY ON MY COMMAND IS THERE TO BE--
WHAT IS THE COMMO--

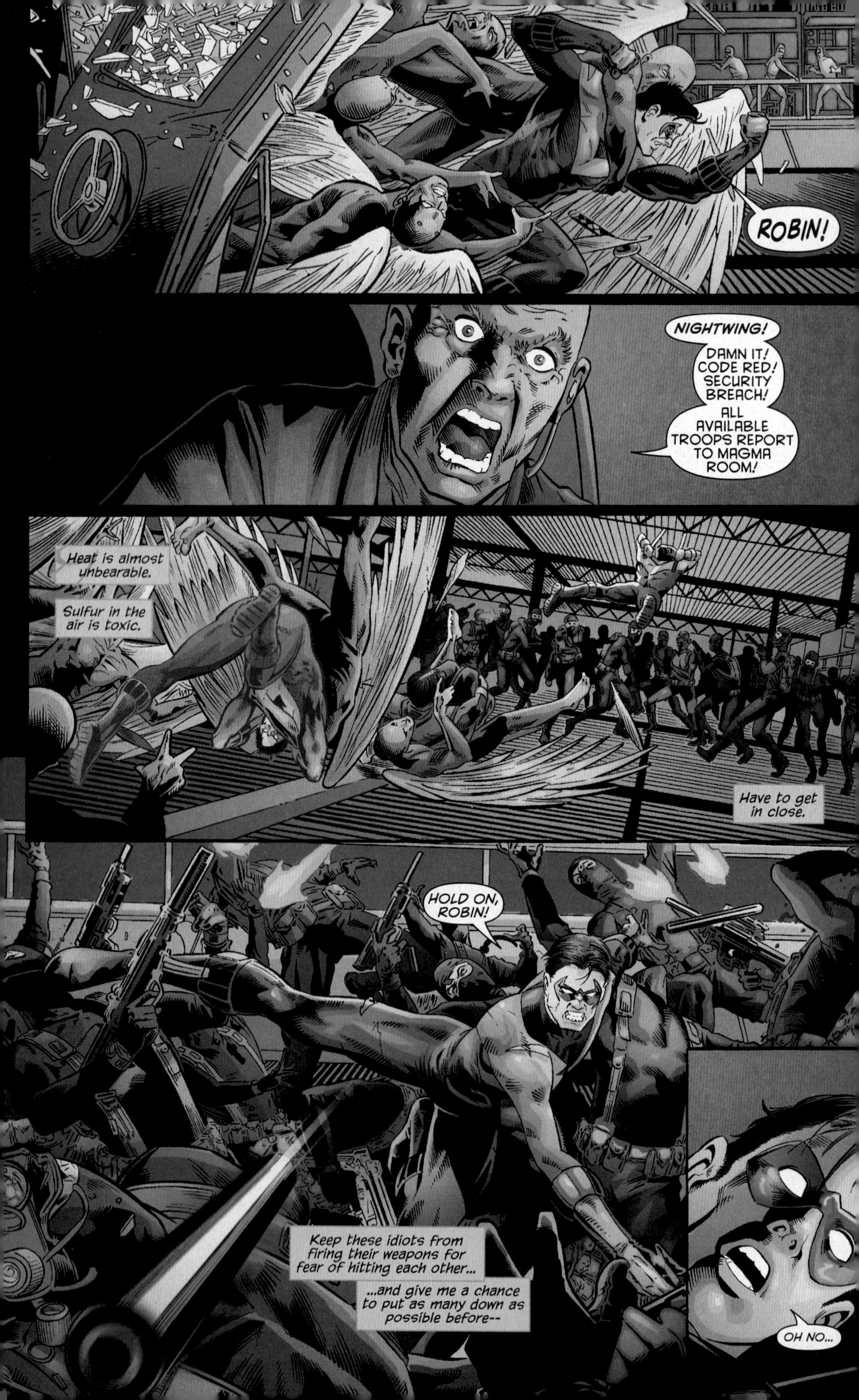
ROBIN!
NIGHTWING!
DAMN IT! CODE RED! SECURITY BREACH!
ALL AVAILABLE TROOPS REPORT TO MAGMA ROOM!
Heat is almost unbearable.
Sulfur in the air is toxic.
Have to get in close.
HOLD ON, ROBIN!
Keep these idiots from firing their weapons for fear of hitting each other...
...and give me a chance to put as many down as possible before--
OH NO...

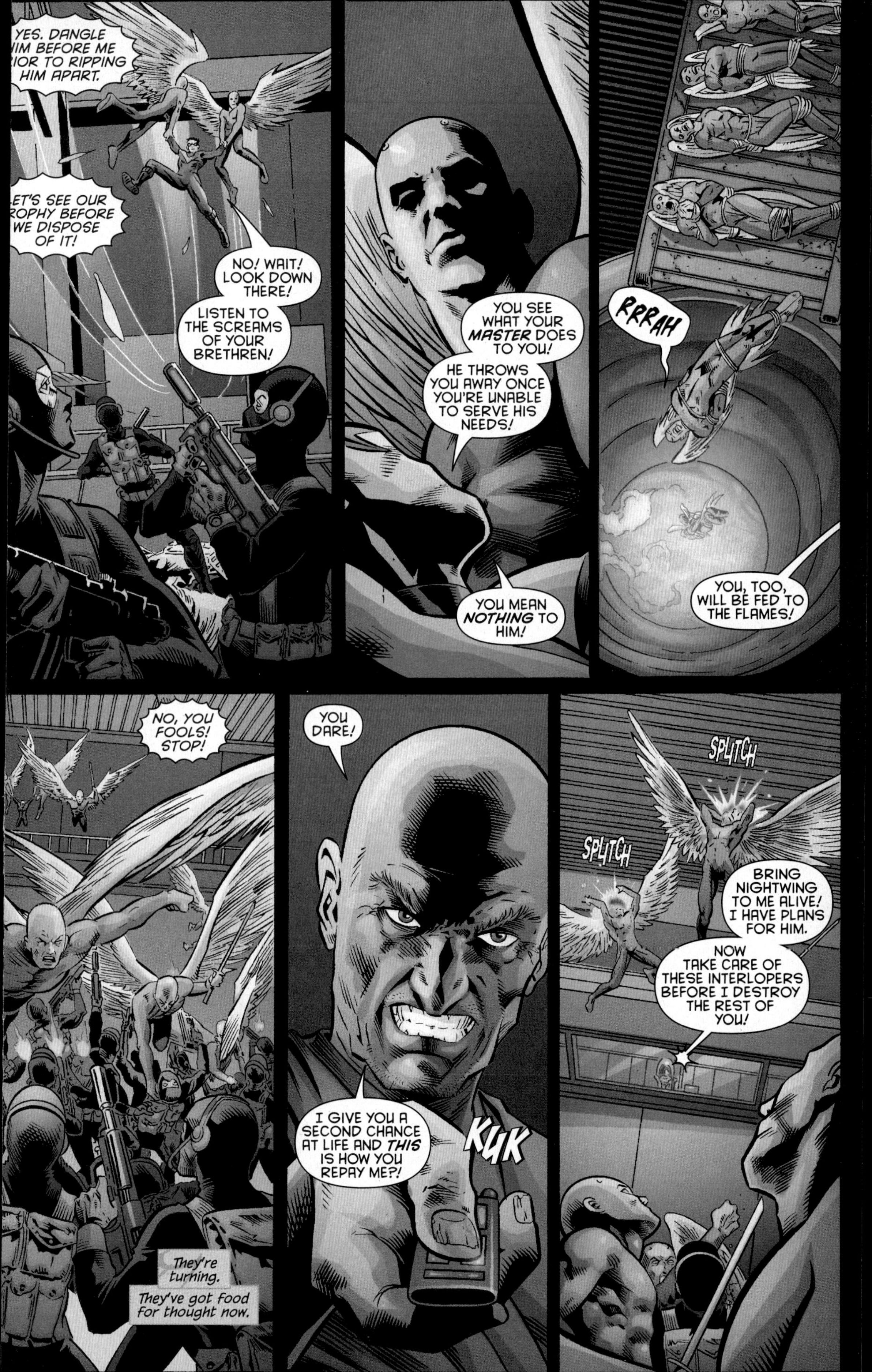
YES. DANGLE HIM BEFORE ME PRIOR TO RIPPING HIM APART.
LET'S SEE OUR TROPHY BEFORE WE DISPOSE OF IT!
NO! WAIT! LOOK DOWN THERE!
LISTEN TO THE SCREAMS OF YOUR BRETHREN!
YOU SEE WHAT YOUR MASTER DOES TO YOU!
HE THROWS YOU AWAY ONCE YOU'RE UNABLE TO SERVE HIS NEEDS!
YOU MEAN NOTHING TO HIM!
RRRAH
YOU, TOO, WILL BE FED TO THE FLAMES!
NO, YOU FOOLS! STOP!
They're turning.
They've got food for thought now.
YOU DARE!
I GIVE YOU A SECOND CHANCE AT LIFE AND THIS IS HOW YOU REPAY ME?!
KUK
SPLTCH
SPLTCH
BRING NIGHTWING TO ME ALIVE! I HAVE PLANS FOR HIM.
NOW TAKE CARE OF THESE INTERLOPERS BEFORE I DESTROY THE REST OF YOU!

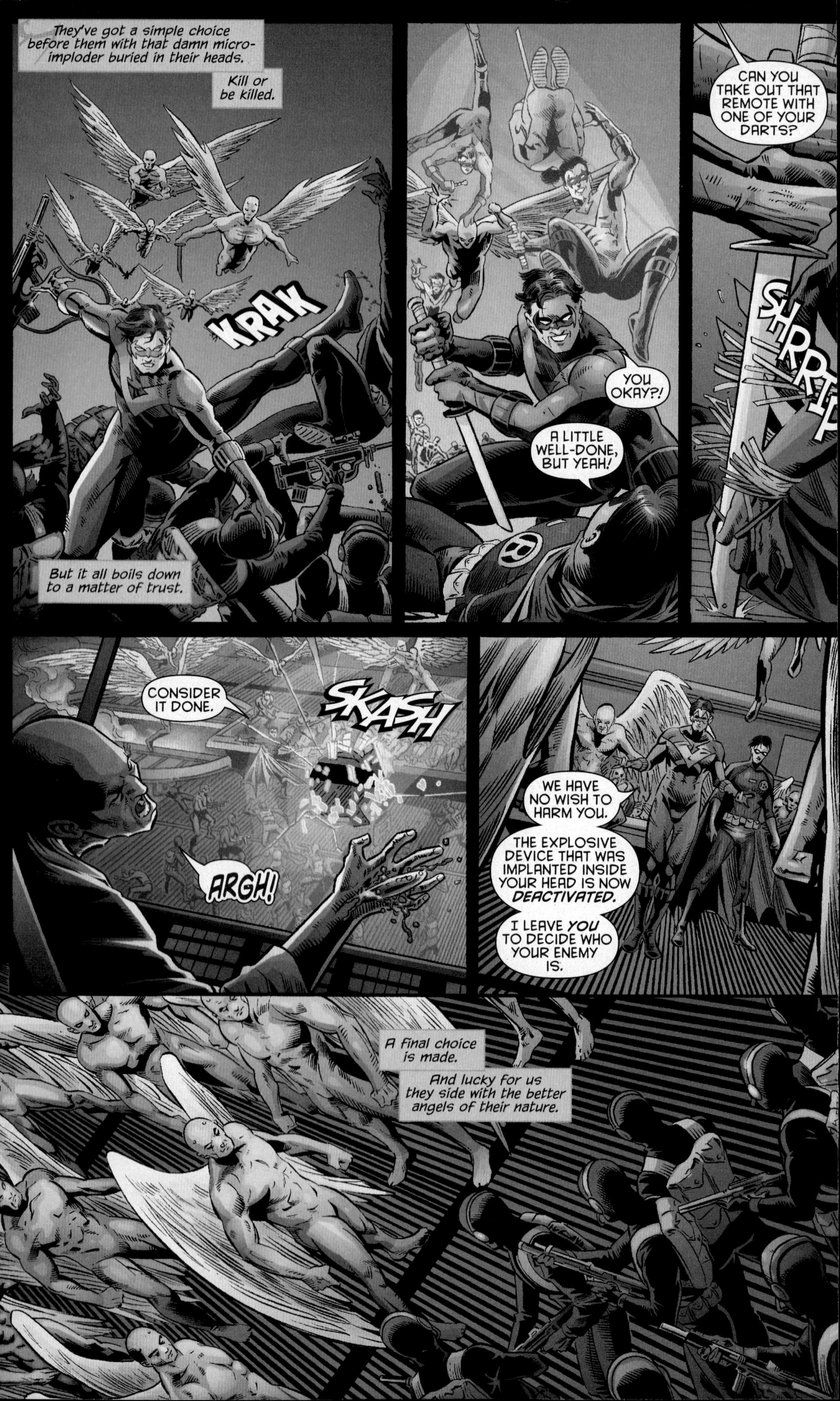

They've got a simple choice before them with that damn micro-imploder buried in their heads.
Kill or be killed.
KRAK
But it all boils down to a matter of trust.
YOU OKAY?!
A LITTLE WELL-DONE, BUT YEAH!
CAN YOU TAKE OUT THAT REMOTE WITH ONE OF YOUR DARTS?
SHRRIP
CONSIDER IT DONE.
SKASH
ARGH!
WE HAVE NO WISH TO HARM YOU.
THE EXPLOSIVE DEVICE THAT WAS IMPLANTED INSIDE YOUR HEAD IS NOW DEACTIVATED.
I LEAVE YOU TO DECIDE WHO YOUR ENEMY IS.
A final choice is made.
And lucky for us they side with the better angels of their nature.

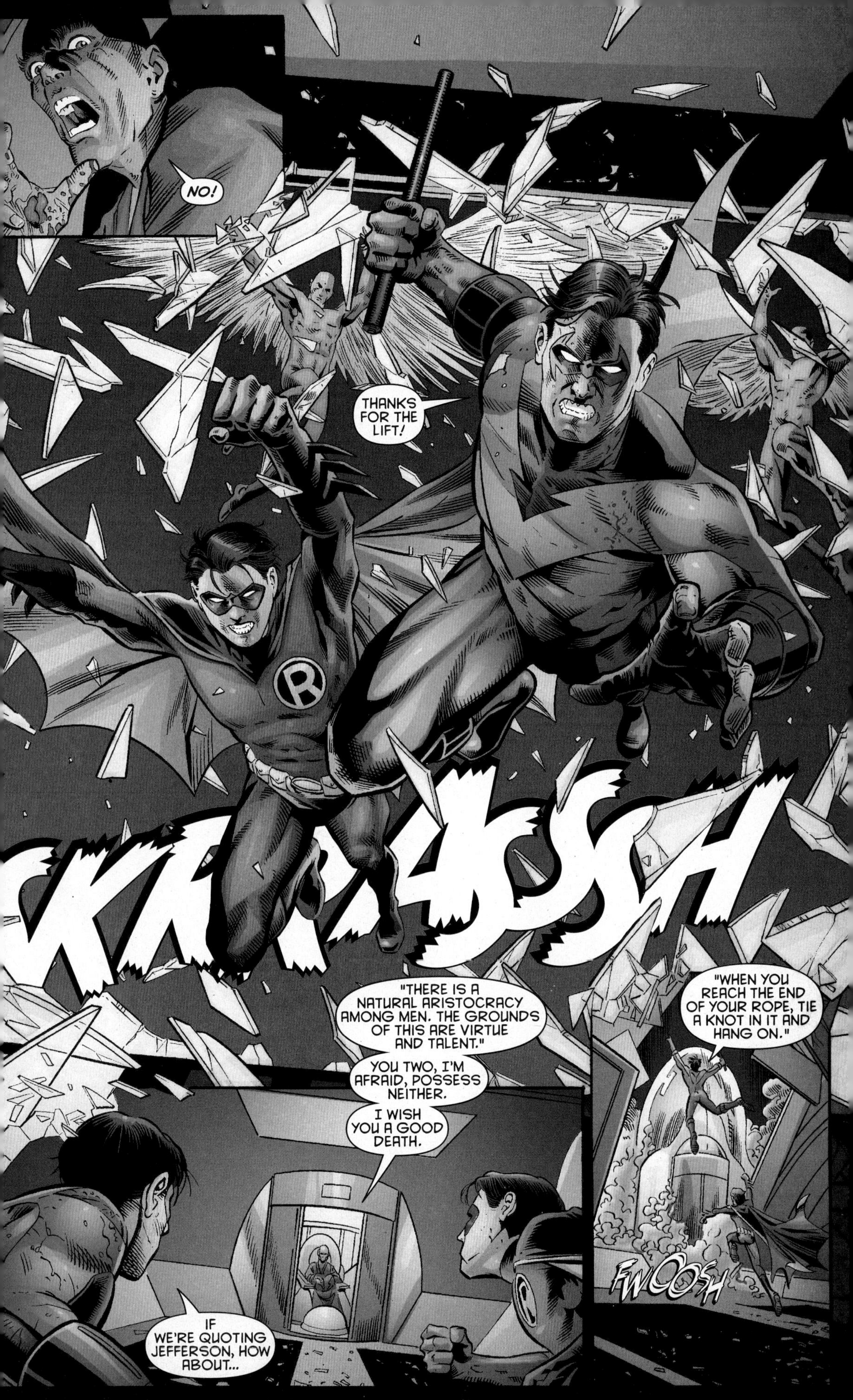
NO!
THANKS FOR THE LIFT!
"THERE IS A NATURAL ARISTOCRACY AMONG MEN. THE GROUNDS OF THIS ARE VIRTUE AND TALENT."
YOU TWO, I'M AFRAID, POSSESS NEITHER.
I WISH YOU A GOOD DEATH.
IF WE'RE QUOTING JEFFERSON, HOW ABOUT...
"WHEN YOU REACH THE END OF YOUR ROPE, TIE A KNOT IN IT AND HANG ON."
FWOOSH

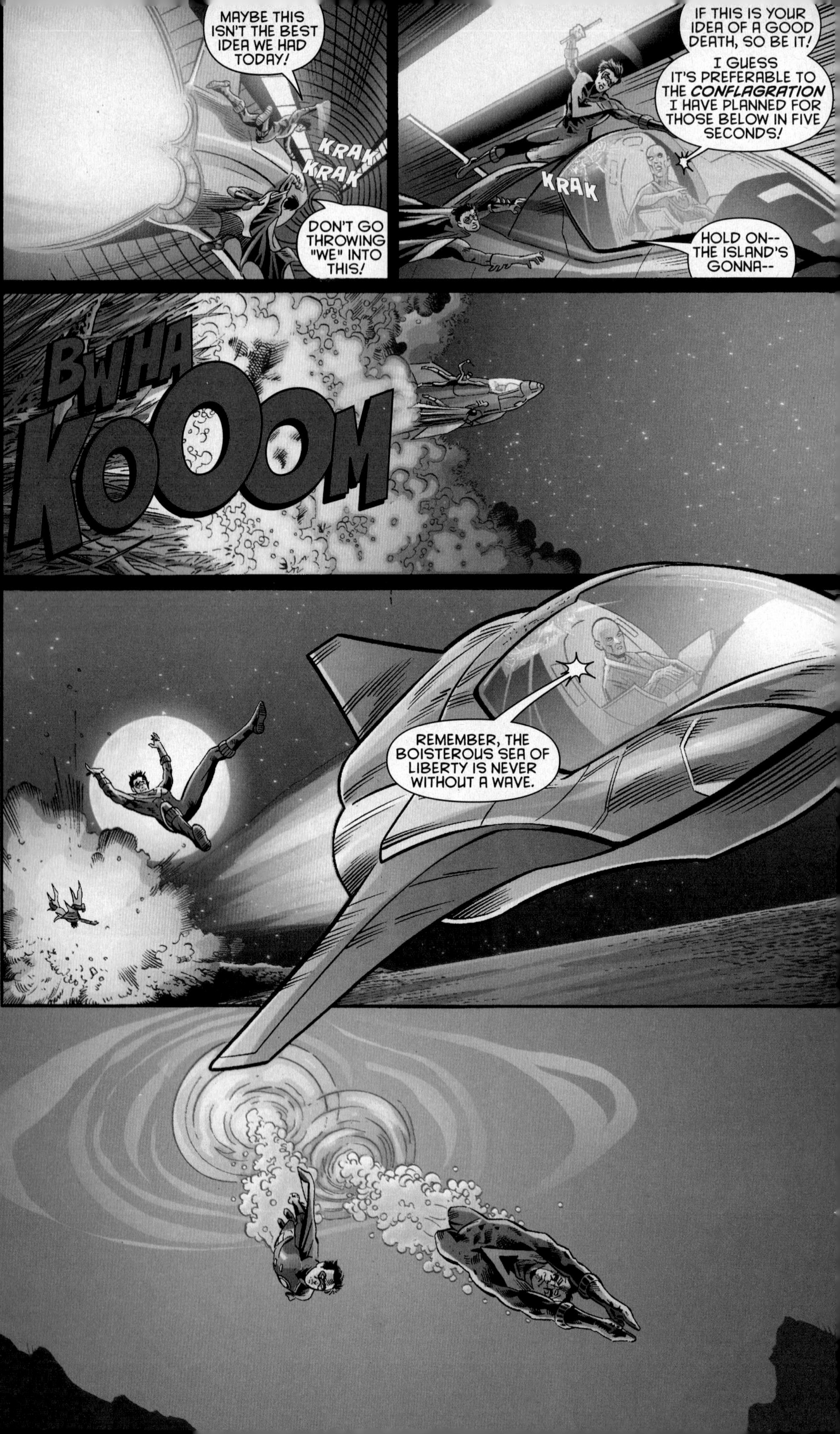
MAYBE THIS ISN'T THE BEST IDEA WE HAD TODAY!
KRAK
KRAK
DON'T GO THROWING "WE" INTO THIS!
IF THIS IS YOUR IDEA OF A GOOD DEATH, SO BE IT!
I GUESS IT'S PREFERABLE TO THE *CONFLAGRATION* I HAVE PLANNED FOR THOSE BELOW IN FIVE SECONDS!
KRAK
HOLD ON-- THE ISLAND'S GONNA--
BWHA KOOOM
REMEMBER, THE BOISTEROUS SEA OF LIBERTY IS NEVER WITHOUT A WAVE.

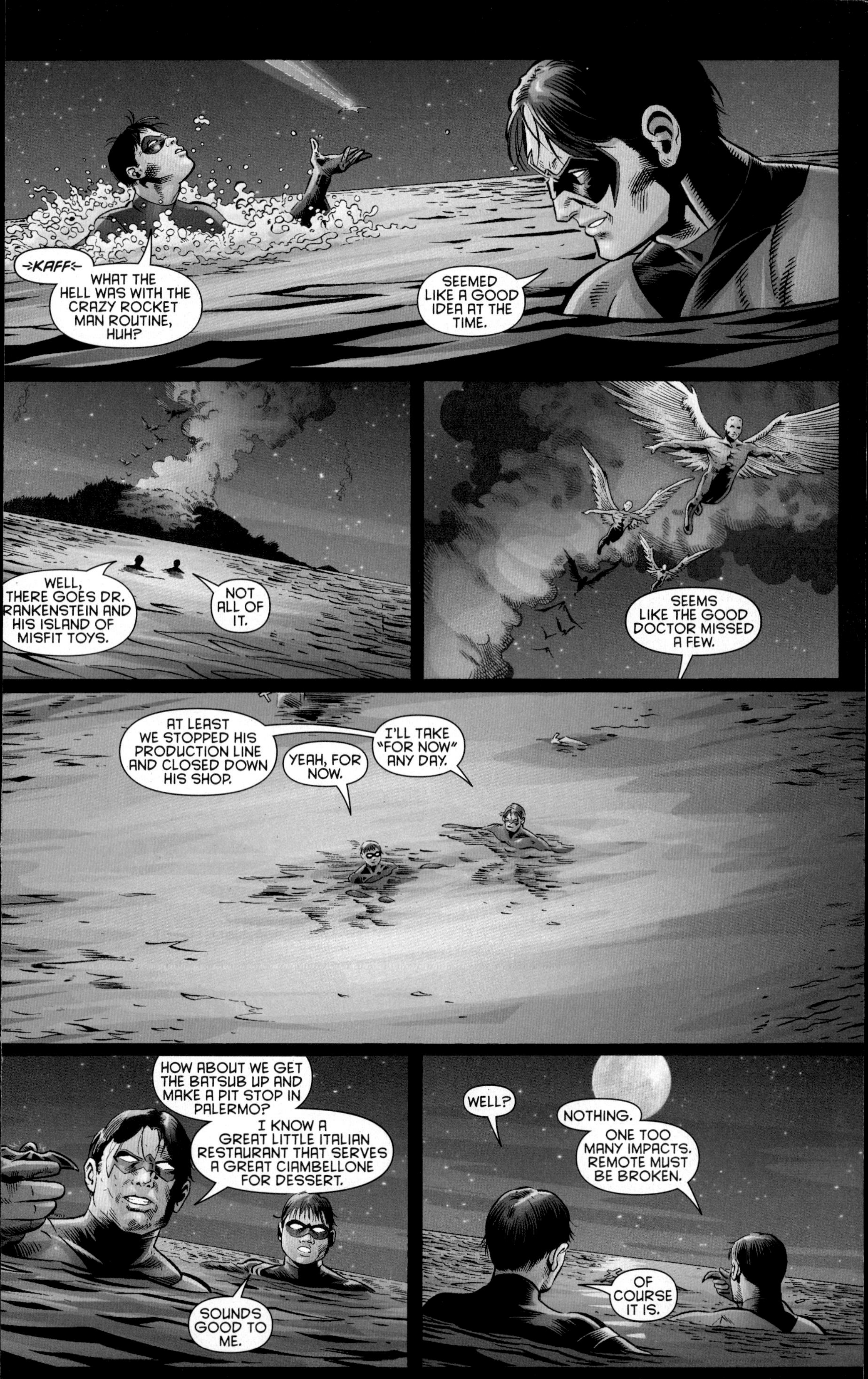

-KAFF- WHAT THE HELL WAS WITH THE CRAZY ROCKET MAN ROUTINE, HUH?
SEEMED LIKE A GOOD IDEA AT THE TIME.
WELL, THERE GOES DR. FRANKENSTEIN AND HIS ISLAND OF MISFIT TOYS.
NOT ALL OF IT.
SEEMS LIKE THE GOOD DOCTOR MISSED A FEW.
AT LEAST WE STOPPED HIS PRODUCTION LINE AND CLOSED DOWN HIS SHOP.
YEAH, FOR NOW.
I'LL TAKE "FOR NOW" ANY DAY.
HOW ABOUT WE GET THE BATSUB UP AND MAKE A PIT STOP IN PALERMO?
I KNOW A GREAT LITTLE ITALIAN RESTAURANT THAT SERVES A GREAT CIAMBELLONE FOR DESSERT.
SOUNDS GOOD TO ME.
WELL?
NOTHING.
ONE TOO MANY IMPACTS. REMOTE MUST BE BROKEN.
OF COURSE IT IS.

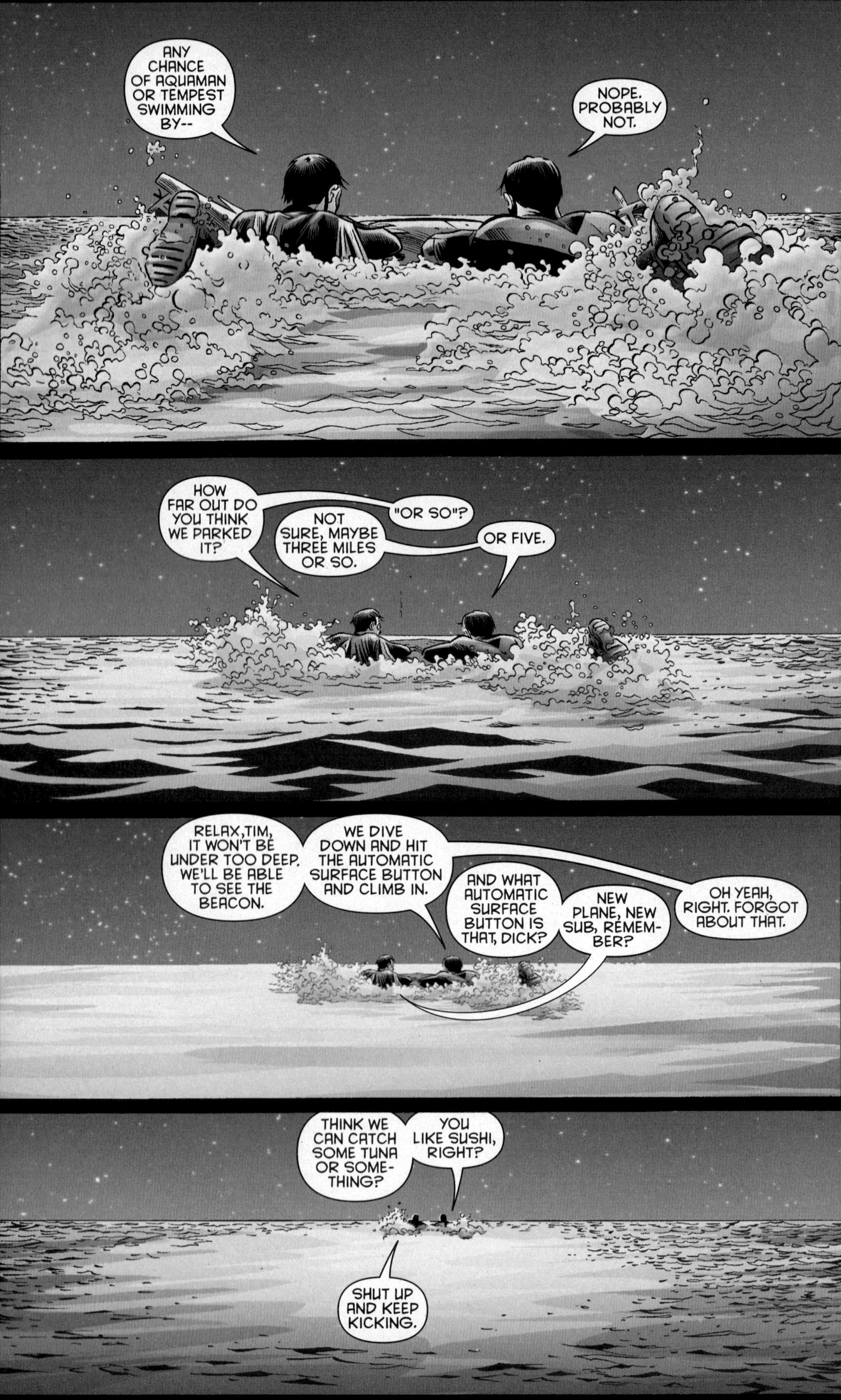
ANY CHANCE OF AQUAMAN OR TEMPEST SWIMMING BY--
NOPE. PROBABLY NOT.
HOW FAR OUT DO YOU THINK WE PARKED IT?
NOT SURE, MAYBE THREE MILES OR SO.
"OR SO"?
OR FIVE.
RELAX, TIM, IT WON'T BE UNDER TOO DEEP. WE'LL BE ABLE TO SEE THE BEACON.
WE DIVE DOWN AND HIT THE AUTOMATIC SURFACE BUTTON AND CLIMB IN.
AND WHAT AUTOMATIC SURFACE BUTTON IS THAT, DICK?
NEW PLANE, NEW SUB, REMEMBER?
OH YEAH, RIGHT. FORGOT ABOUT THAT.
THINK WE CAN CATCH SOME TUNA OR SOMETHING?
YOU LIKE SUSHI, RIGHT?
SHUT UP AND KEEP KICKING.

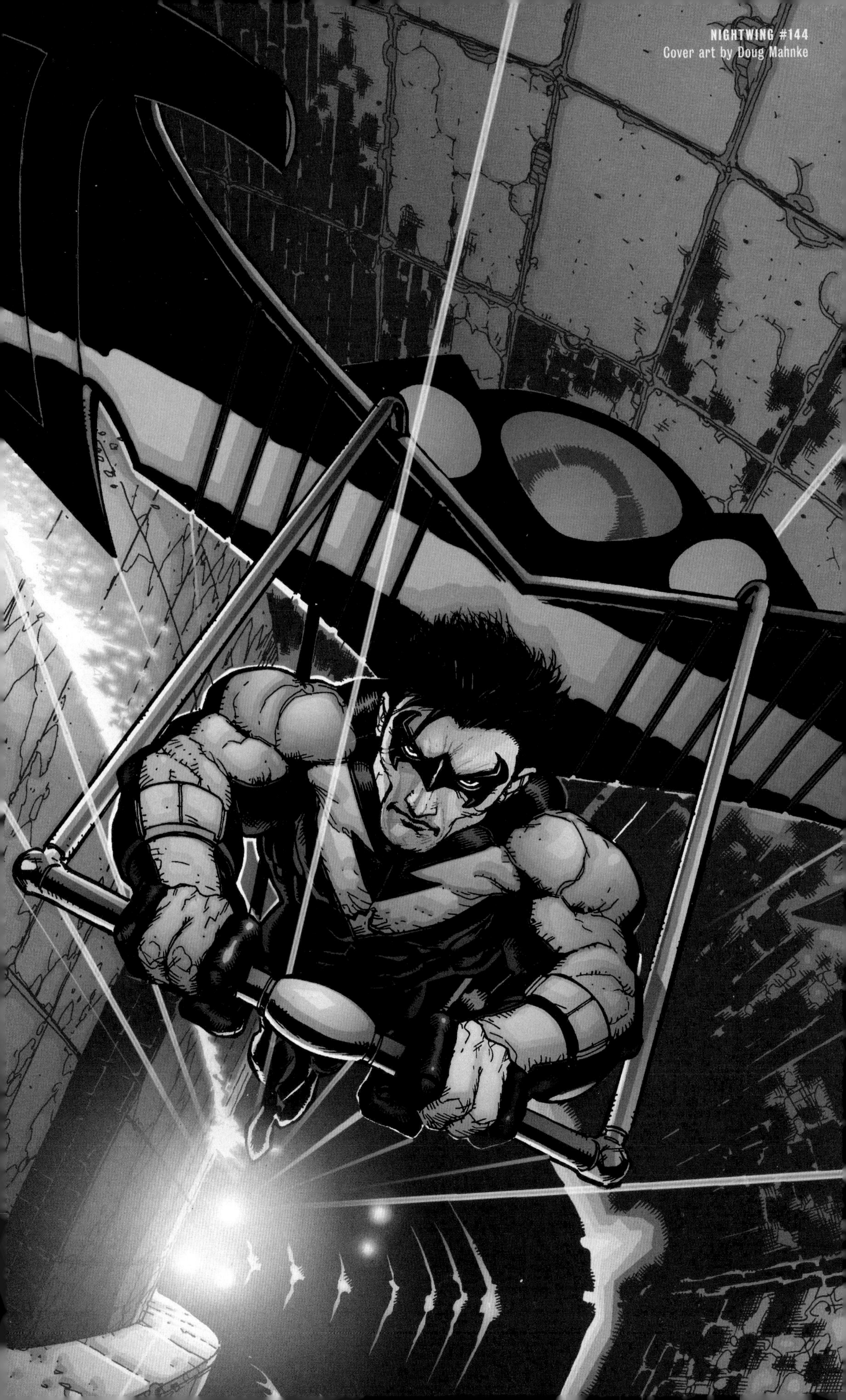

NIGHTWING #144
Cover art by Doug Mahnke

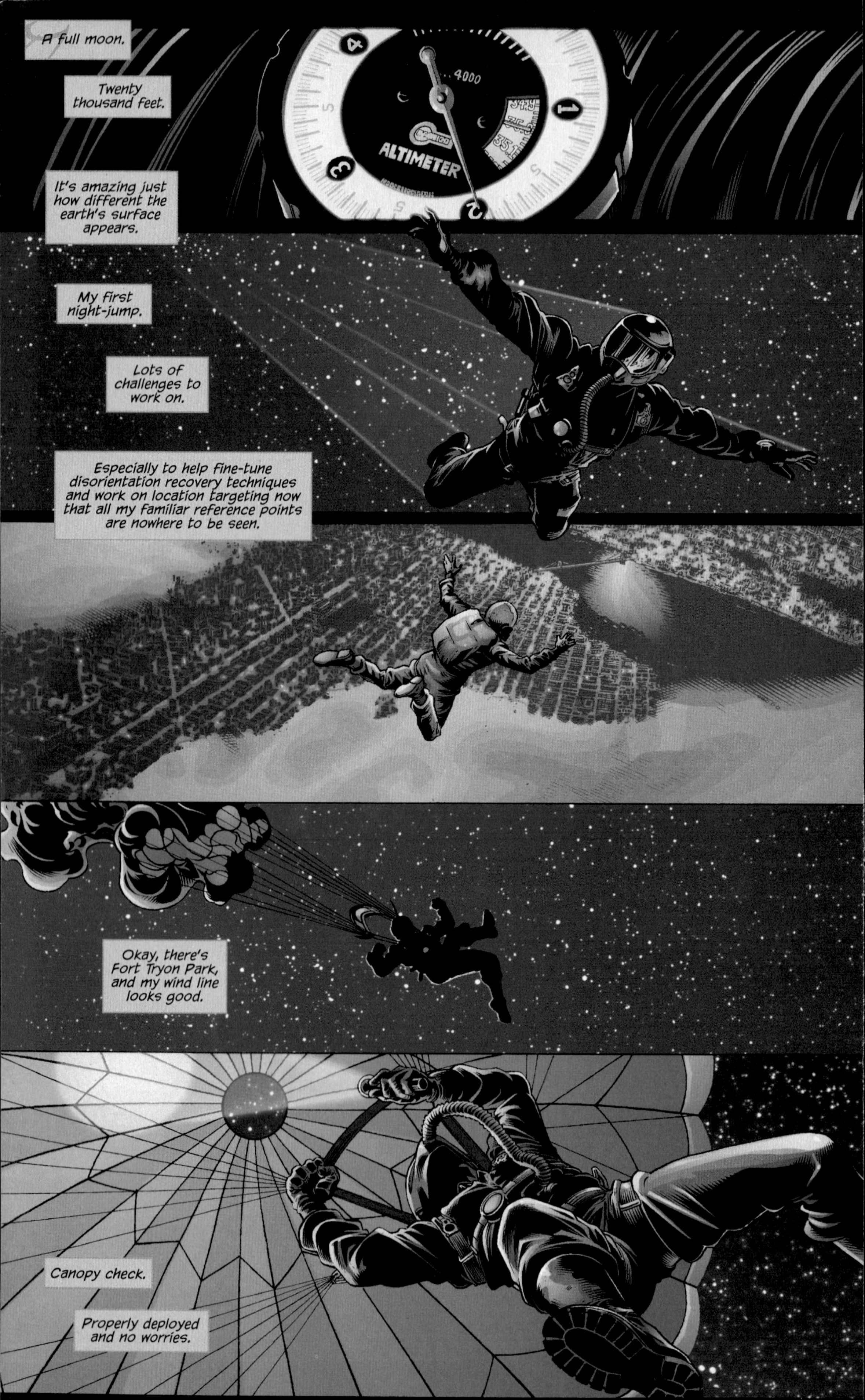
A full moon.
Twenty thousand feet.
4000
ALTIMETER
It's amazing just how different the earth's surface appears.
My first night-jump.
Lots of challenges to work on.
Especially to help fine-tune disorientation recovery techniques and work on location targeting now that all my familiar reference points are nowhere to be seen.
Okay, there's Fort Tryon Park, and my wind line looks good.
Canopy check.
Properly deployed and no worries.

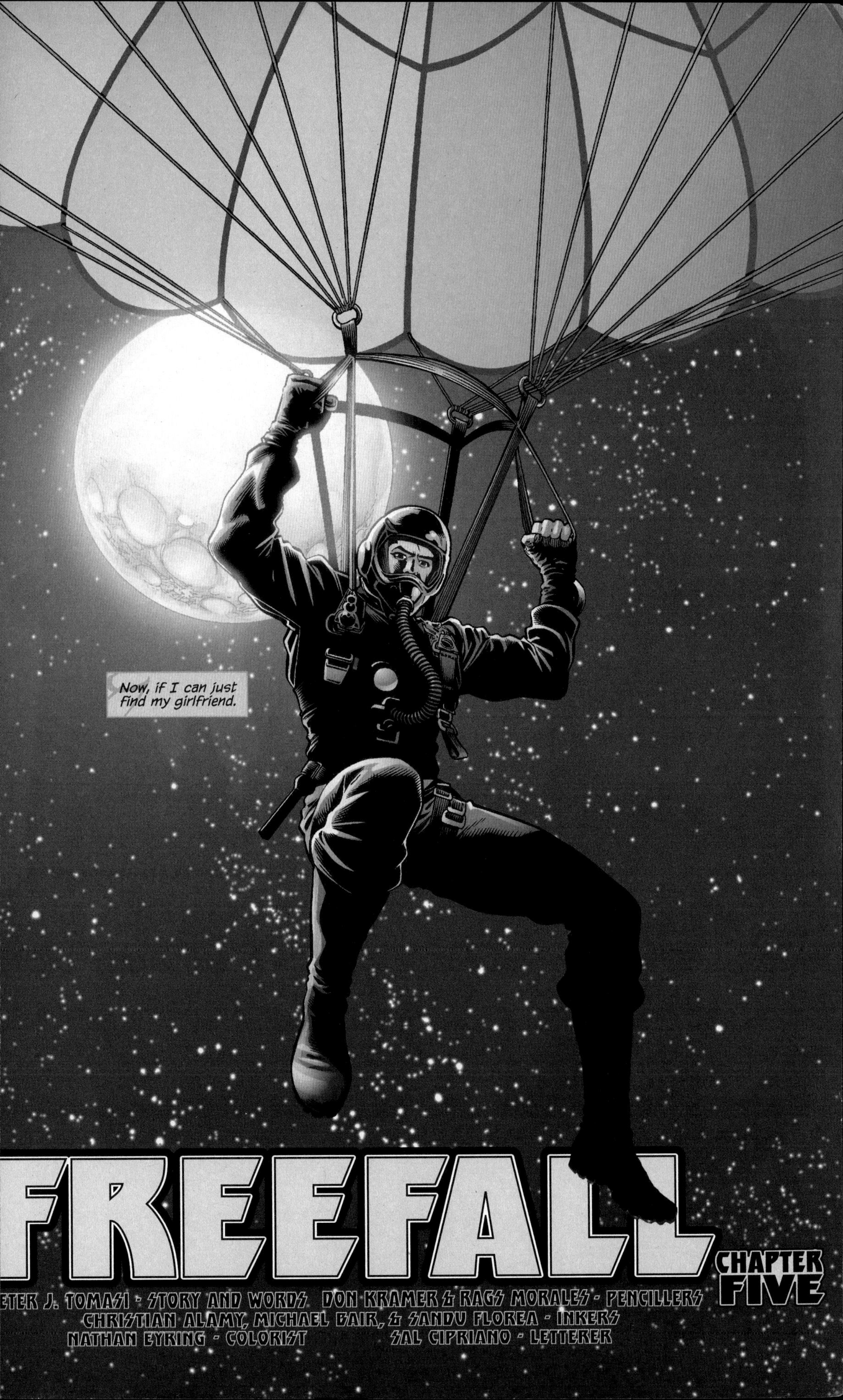
Now, if I can just find my girlfriend.
FREEFALL
CHAPTER FIVE
ETER J. TOMASI - STORY AND WORDS DON KRAMER & RAGS MORALES - PENCILLERS
CHRISTIAN ALAMY, MICHAEL BAIR, & SANDU FLOREA - INKERS
NATHAN EYRING - COLORIST SAL CIPRIANO - LETTERER

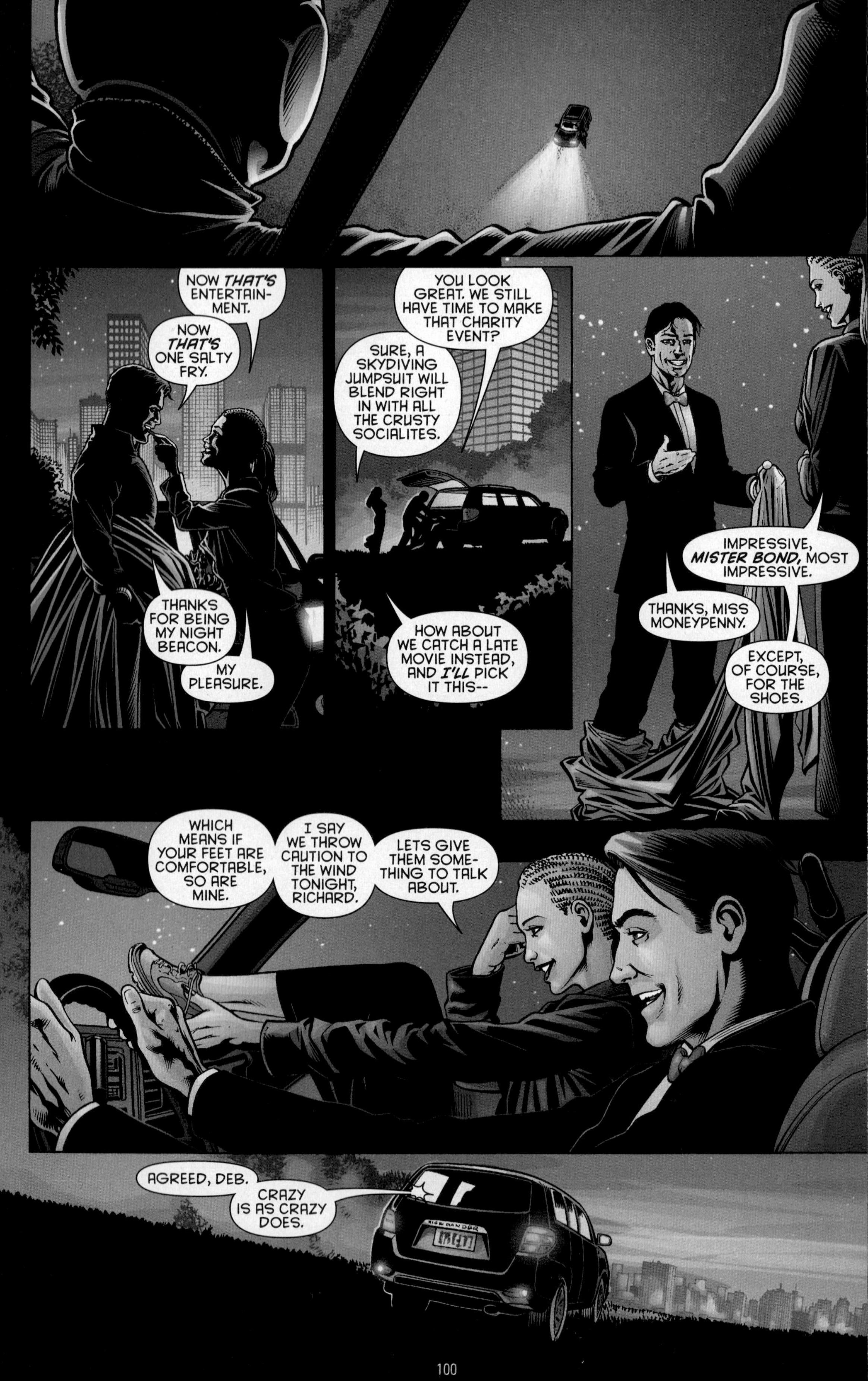
NOW THAT'S ENTERTAIN-MENT.
NOW THAT'S ONE SALTY FRY.
THANKS FOR BEING MY NIGHT BEACON.
MY PLEASURE.
YOU LOOK GREAT. WE STILL HAVE TIME TO MAKE THAT CHARITY EVENT?
SURE, A SKYDIVING JUMPSUIT WILL BLEND RIGHT IN WITH ALL THE CRUSTY SOCIALITES.
HOW ABOUT WE CATCH A LATE MOVIE INSTEAD, AND I'LL PICK IT THIS--
IMPRESSIVE, MISTER BOND, MOST IMPRESSIVE.
THANKS, MISS MONEYPENNY.
EXCEPT, OF COURSE, FOR THE SHOES.
WHICH MEANS IF YOUR FEET ARE COMFORTABLE, SO ARE MINE.
I SAY WE THROW CAUTION TO THE WIND TONIGHT, RICHARD.
LETS GIVE THEM SOME-THING TO TALK ABOUT.
AGREED, DEB.
CRAZY IS AS CRAZY DOES.

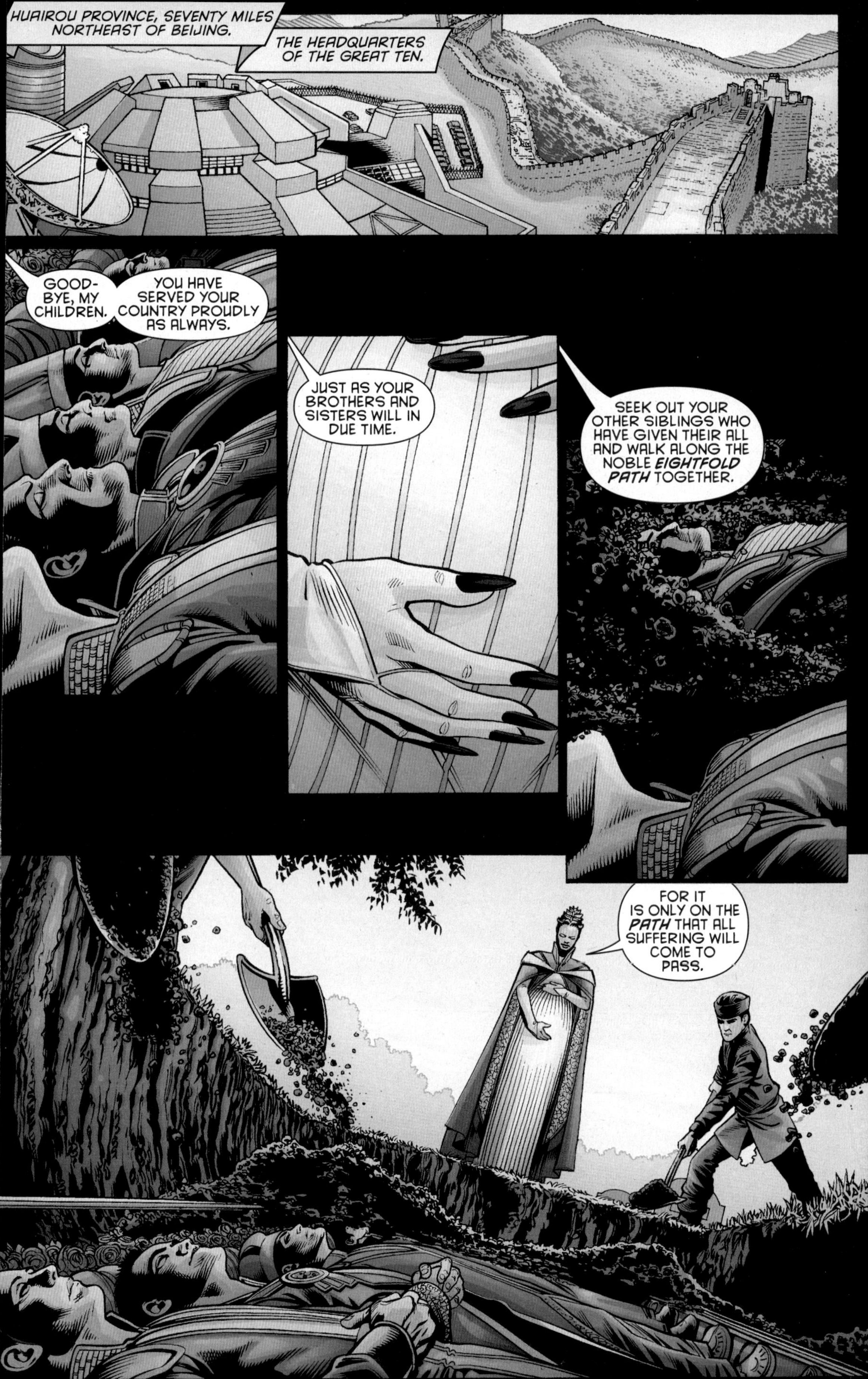
HUAIROU PROVINCE, SEVENTY MILES NORTHEAST OF BEIJING.
THE HEADQUARTERS OF THE GREAT TEN.
GOOD-BYE, MY CHILDREN.
YOU HAVE SERVED YOUR COUNTRY PROUDLY AS ALWAYS.
JUST AS YOUR BROTHERS AND SISTERS WILL IN DUE TIME.
SEEK OUT YOUR OTHER SIBLINGS WHO HAVE GIVEN THEIR ALL AND WALK ALONG THE NOBLE EIGHTFOLD PATH TOGETHER.
FOR IT IS ONLY ON THE PATH THAT ALL SUFFERING WILL COME TO PASS.

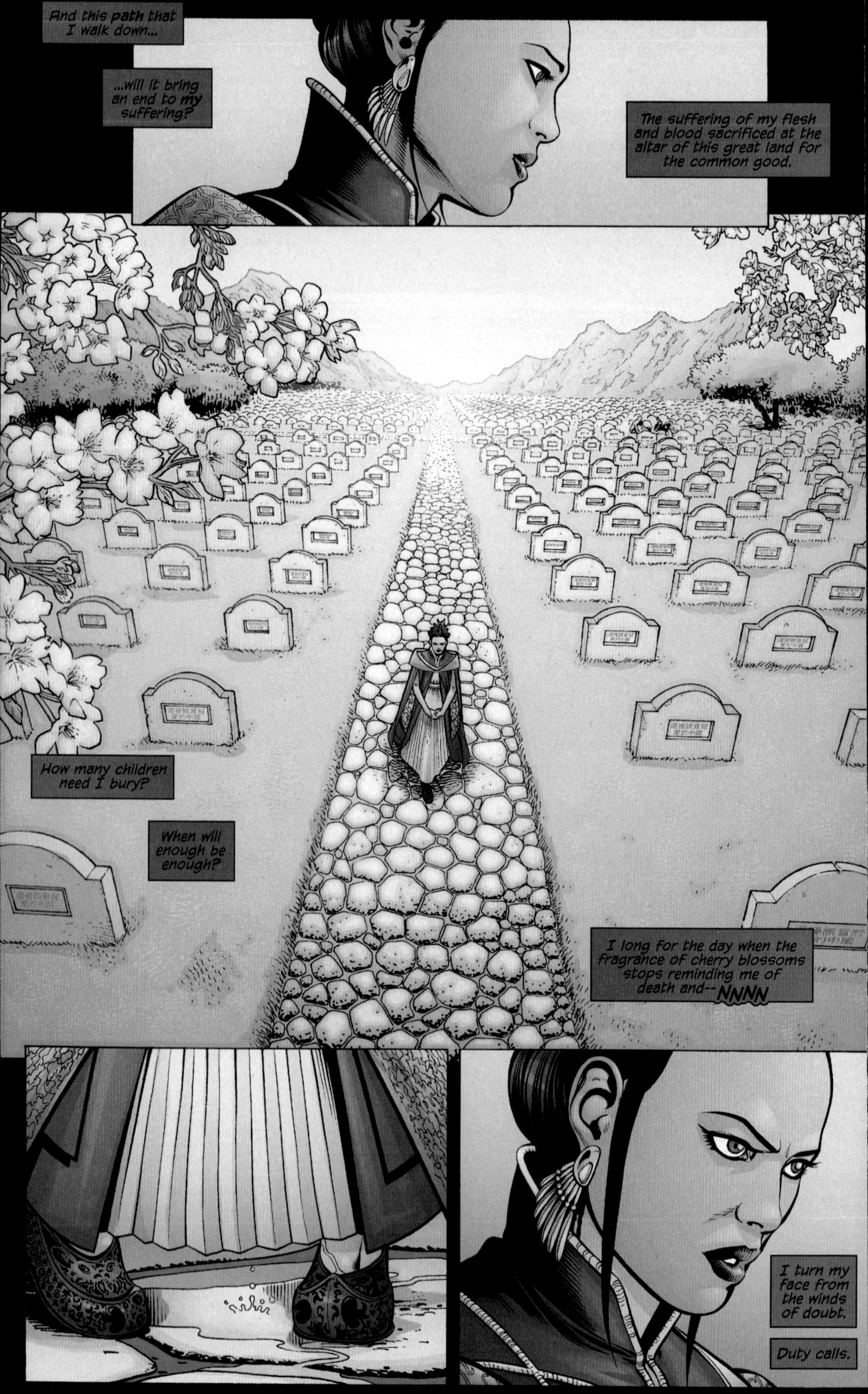
And this path that I walk down...
...will it bring an end to my suffering?
The suffering of my flesh and blood sacrificed at the altar of this great land for the common good.
How many children need I bury?
When will enough be enough?
I long for the day when the fragrance of cherry blossoms stops reminding me of death and--NNNN
I turn my face from the winds of doubt.
Duty calls.

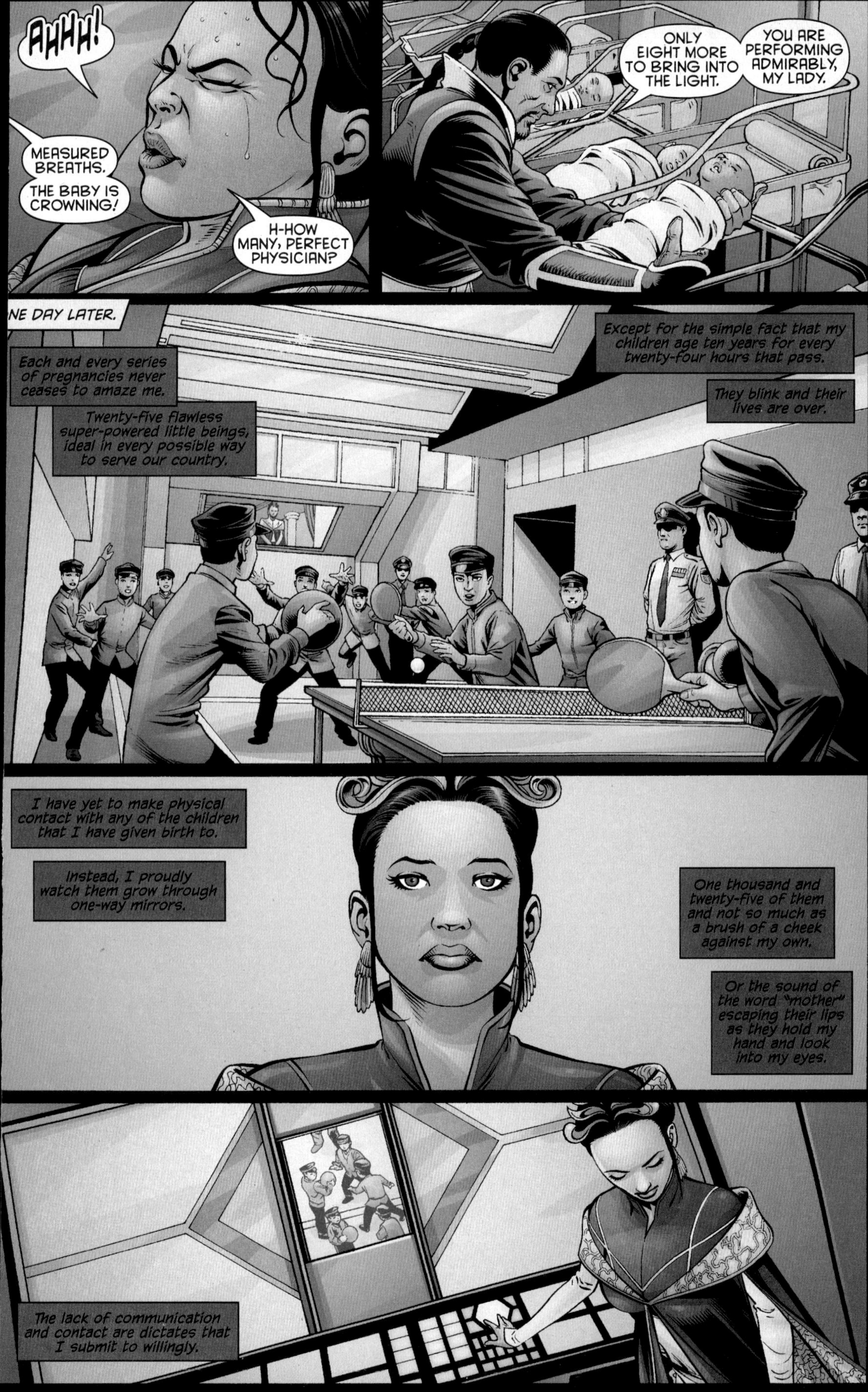
AHHH!
MEASURED BREATHS.
THE BABY IS CROWNING!
H-HOW MANY, PERFECT PHYSICIAN?
ONLY EIGHT MORE TO BRING INTO THE LIGHT.
YOU ARE PERFORMING ADMIRABLY, MY LADY.
NE DAY LATER.
Each and every series of pregnancies never ceases to amaze me.
Twenty-five flawless super-powered little beings, ideal in every possible way to serve our country.
Except for the simple fact that my children age ten years for every twenty-four hours that pass.
They blink and their lives are over.
I have yet to make physical contact with any of the children that I have given birth to.
Instead, I proudly watch them grow through one-way mirrors.
One thousand and twenty-five of them and not so much as a brush of a cheek against my own.
Or the sound of the word "mother" escaping their lips as they hold my hand and look into my eyes.
The lack of communication and contact are dictates that I submit to willingly.

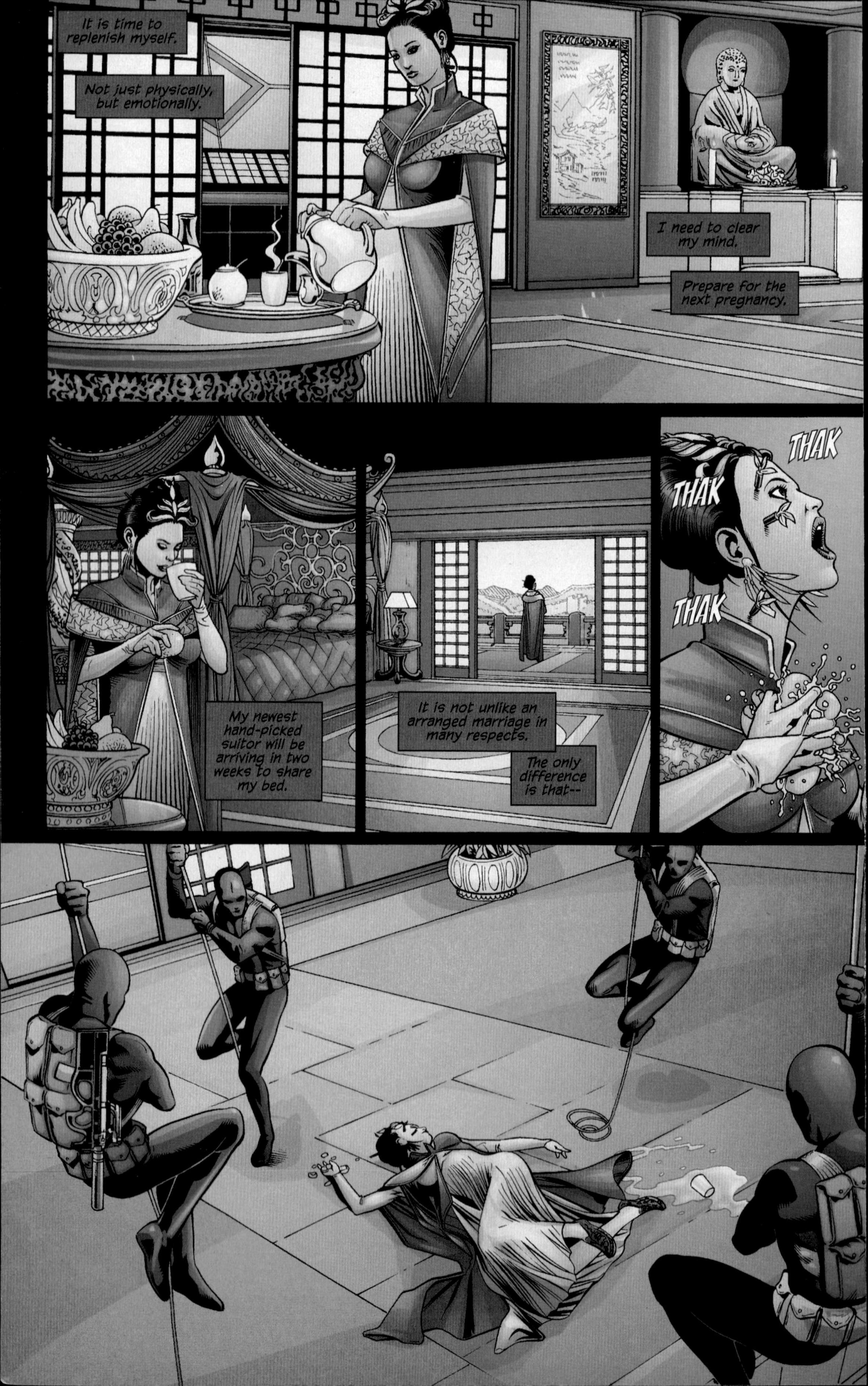
It is time to replenish myself.
Not just physically, but emotionally.
I need to clear my mind.
Prepare for the next pregnancy.
My newest hand-picked suitor will be arriving in two weeks to share my bed.
It is not unlike an arranged marriage in many respects.
The only difference is that--
THAK
THAK
THAK

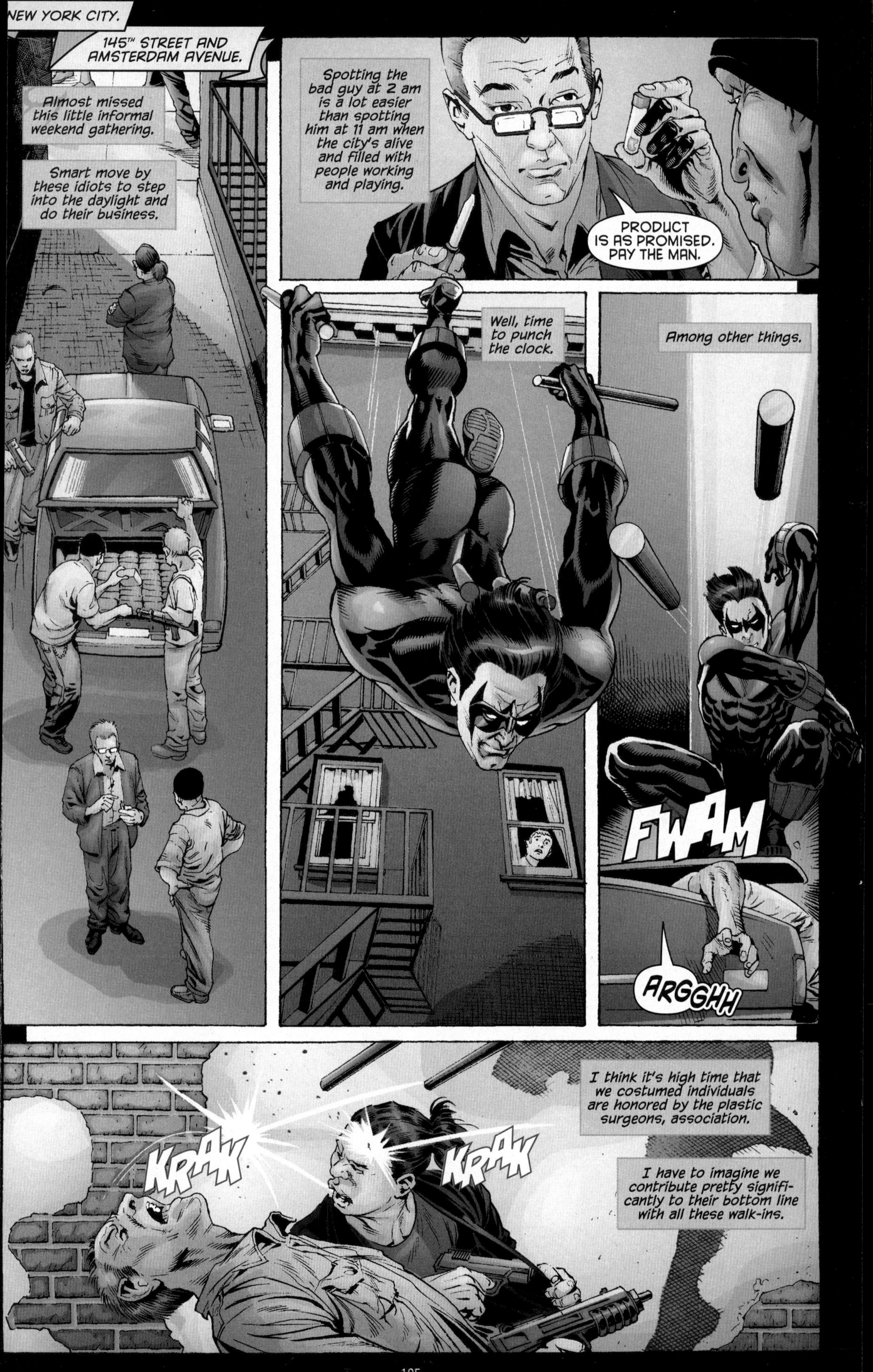
NEW YORK CITY.
145TH STREET AND AMSTERDAM AVENUE.
Almost missed this little informal weekend gathering.
Smart move by these idiots to step into the daylight and do their business.
Spotting the bad guy at 2 am is a lot easier than spotting him at 11 am when the city's alive and filled with people working and playing.
PRODUCT IS AS PROMISED. PAY THE MAN.
Well, time to punch the clock.
Among other things.
FWAM
ARGGHH
I think it's high time that we costumed individuals are honored by the plastic surgeons, association.
I have to imagine we contribute pretty significantly to their bottom line with all these walk-ins.
KRAK
KRAK

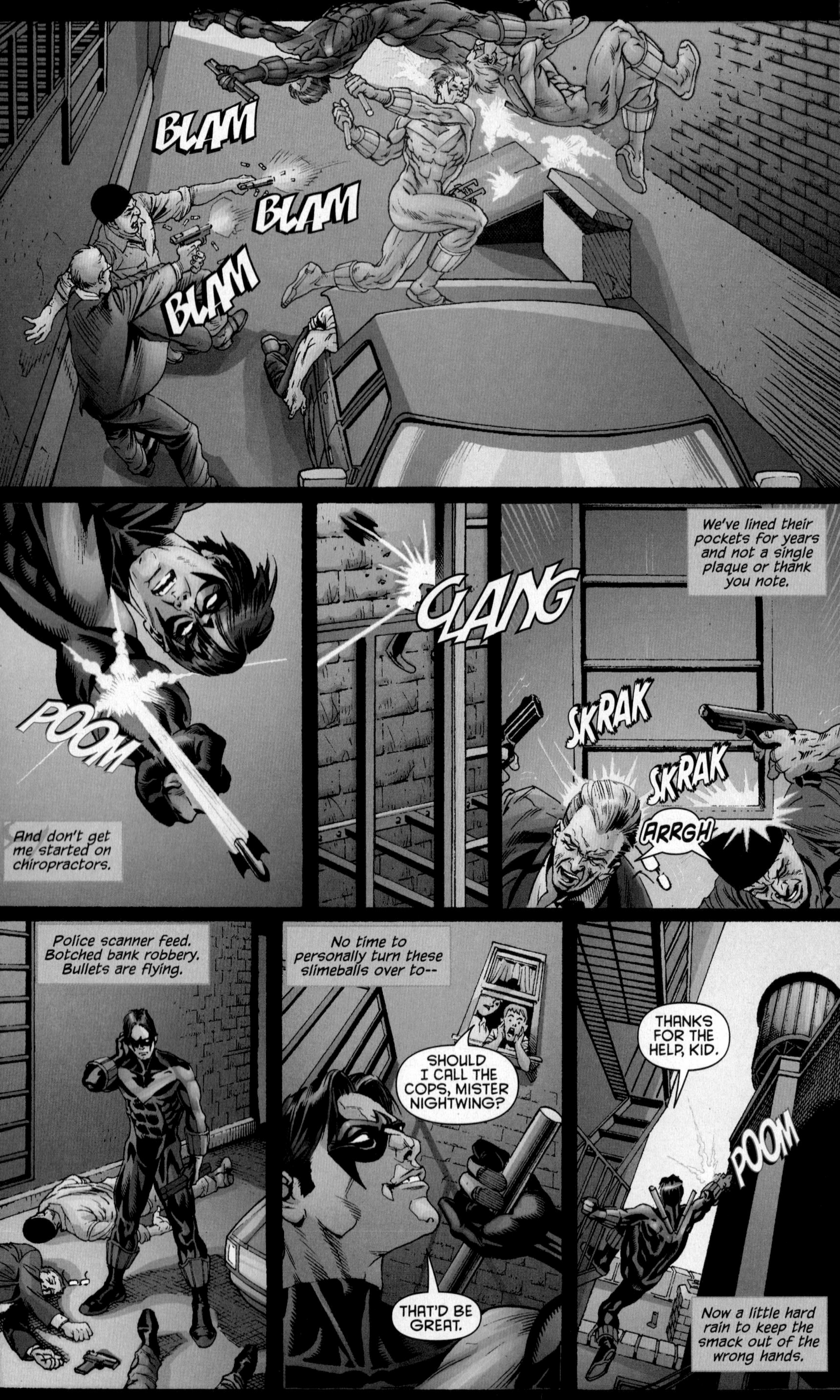
BLAM
BLAM
BLAM
We've lined their pockets for years and not a single plaque or thank you note.
POOM
And don't get me started on chiropractors.
CLANG
SKRAK
SKRAK
ARRGH
Police scanner feed. Botched bank robbery. Bullets are flying.
No time to personally turn these slimeballs over to--
SHOULD I CALL THE COPS, MISTER NIGHTWING?
THAT'D BE GREAT.
THANKS FOR THE HELP, KID.
POOM
Now a little hard rain to keep the smack out of the wrong hands.

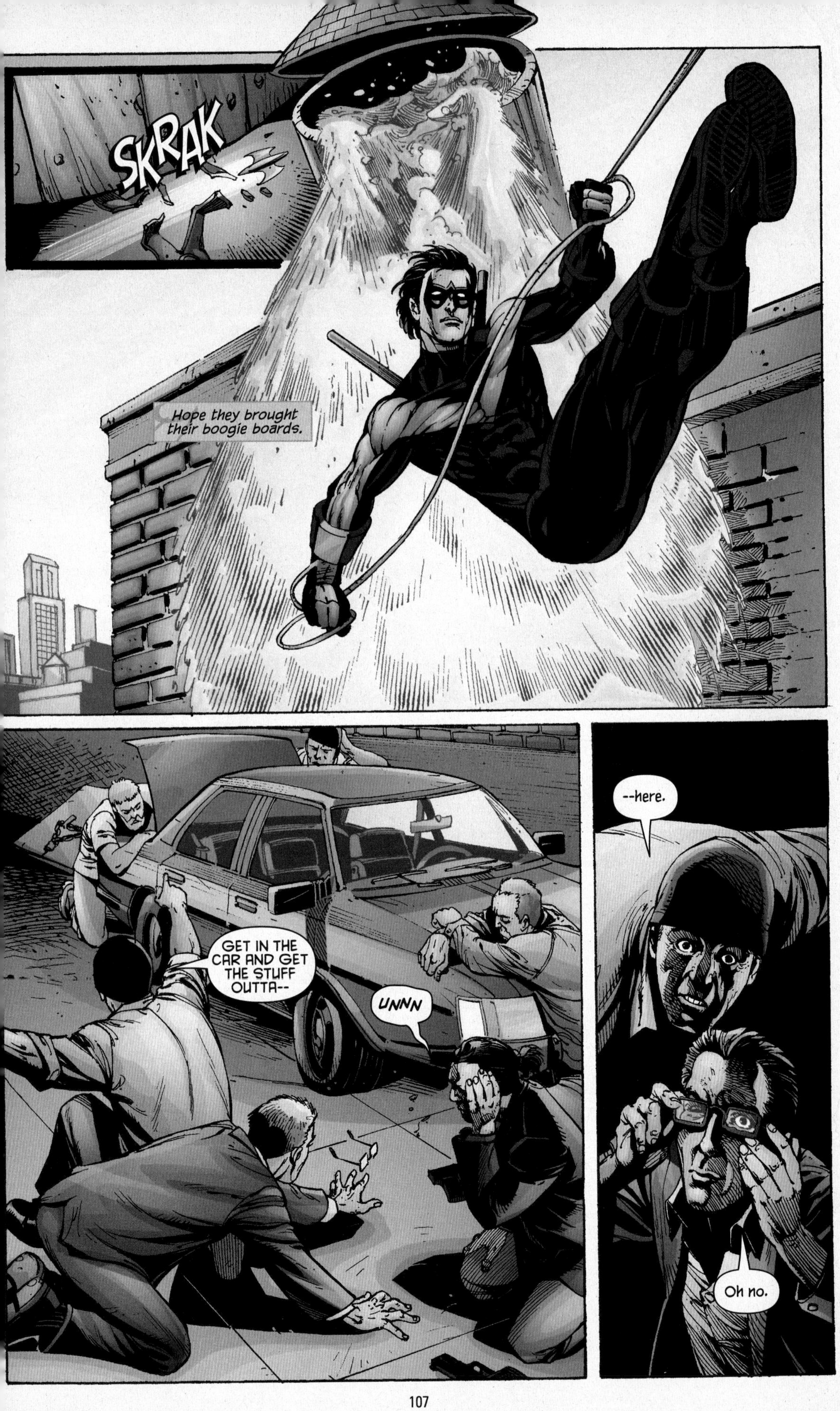
SKRAK
Hope they brought their boogie boards.
GET IN THE CAR AND GET THE STUFF OUTTA--
UNNN
--here.
Oh no.

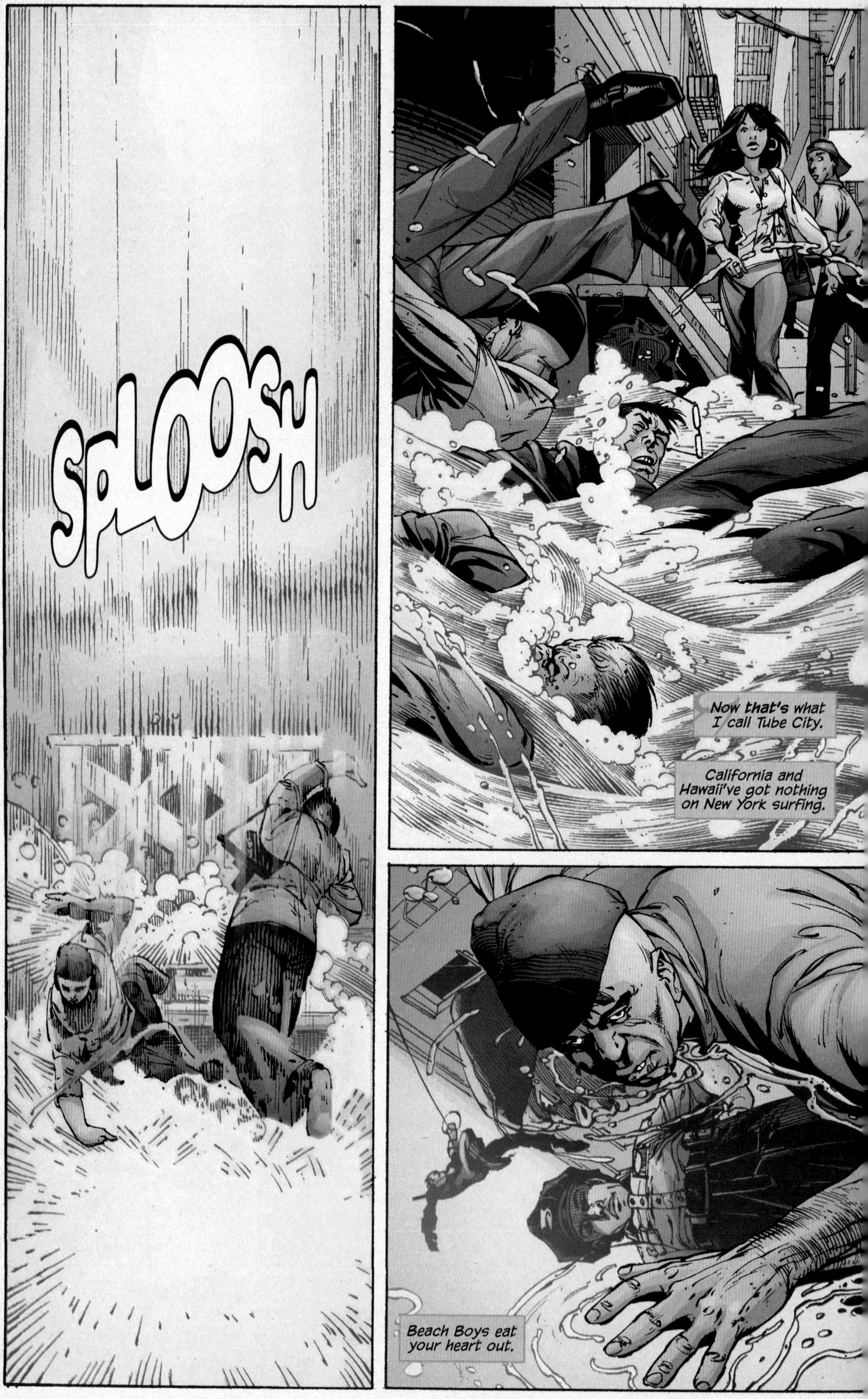
SPLOOSH
Now that's what I call Tube City.
California and Hawaii've got nothing on New York surfing.
Beach Boys eat your heart out.

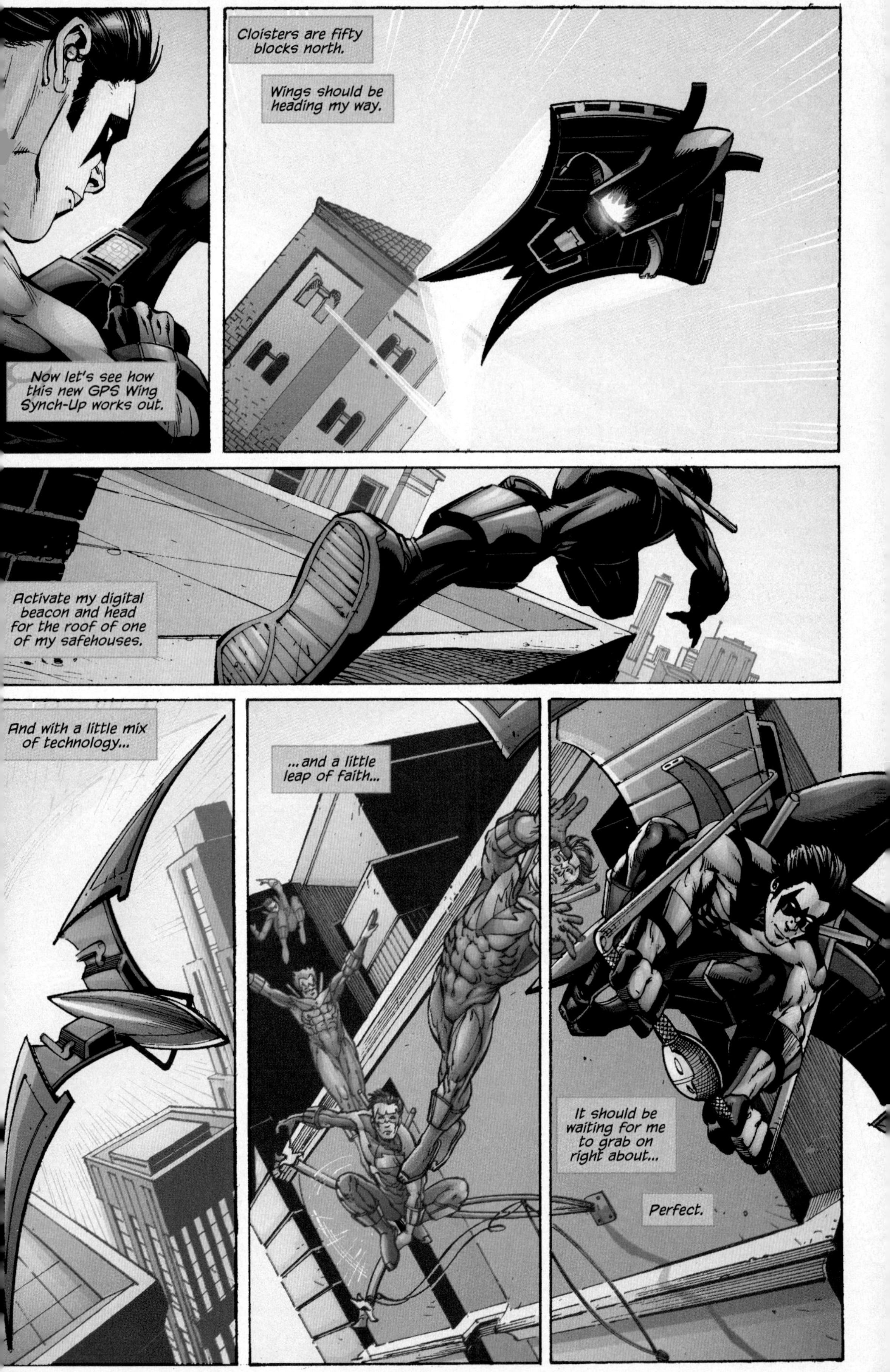

Now let's see how this new GPS Wing Synch-Up works out.
Cloisters are fifty blocks north.
Wings should be heading my way.
Activate my digital beacon and head for the roof of one of my safehouses.
And with a little mix of technology...
...and a little leap of faith...
It should be waiting for me to grab on right about...
Perfect.

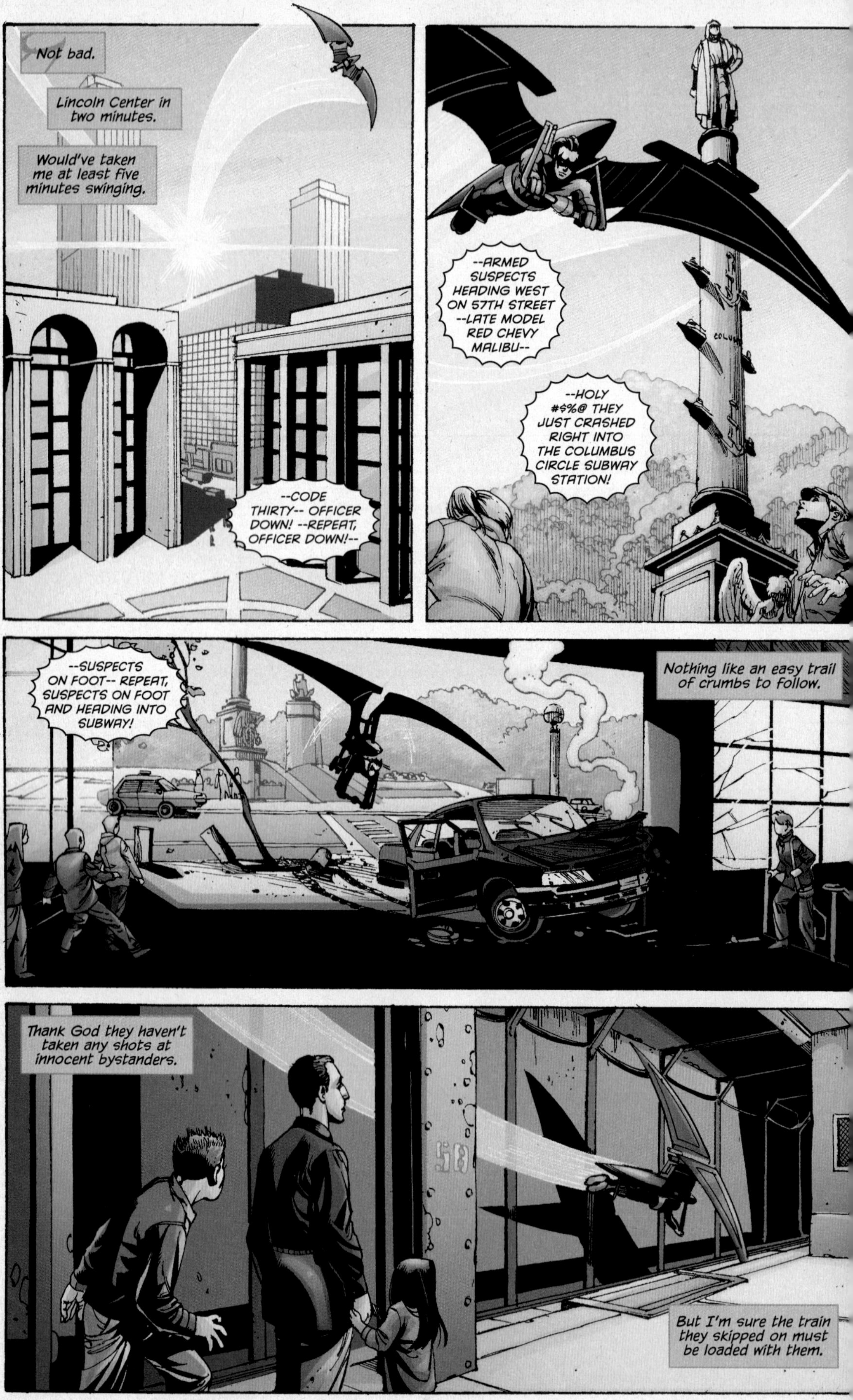
Not bad.
Lincoln Center in two minutes.
Would've taken me at least five minutes swinging.
--CODE THIRTY-- OFFICER DOWN! --REPEAT, OFFICER DOWN!--
--ARMED SUSPECTS HEADING WEST ON 57TH STREET --LATE MODEL RED CHEVY MALIBU--
--HOLY #$%@ THEY JUST CRASHED RIGHT INTO THE COLUMBUS CIRCLE SUBWAY STATION!
--SUSPECTS ON FOOT-- REPEAT, SUSPECTS ON FOOT AND HEADING INTO SUBWAY!
Nothing like an easy trail of crumbs to follow.
Thank God they haven't taken any shots at innocent bystanders.
But I'm sure the train they skipped on must be loaded with them.

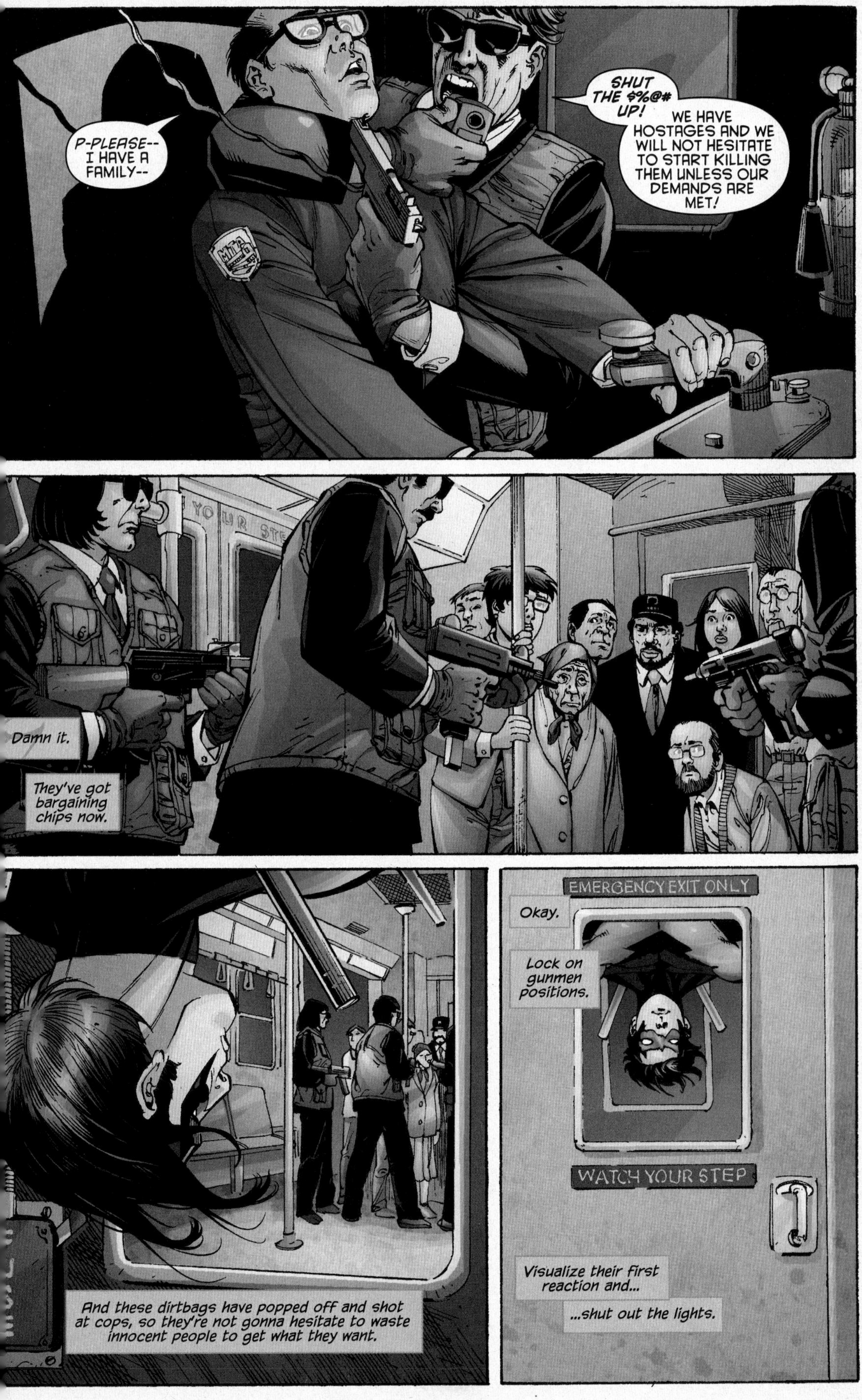
P-PLEASE-- I HAVE A FAMILY--
SHUT THE $%@# UP!
WE HAVE HOSTAGES AND WE WILL NOT HESITATE TO START KILLING THEM UNLESS OUR DEMANDS ARE MET!
Damn it.
They've got bargaining chips now.
And these dirtbags have popped off and shot at cops, so they're not gonna hesitate to waste innocent people to get what they want.
EMERGENCY EXIT ONLY
Okay.
Lock on gunmen positions.
WATCH YOUR STEP
Visualize their first reaction and...
...shut out the lights.

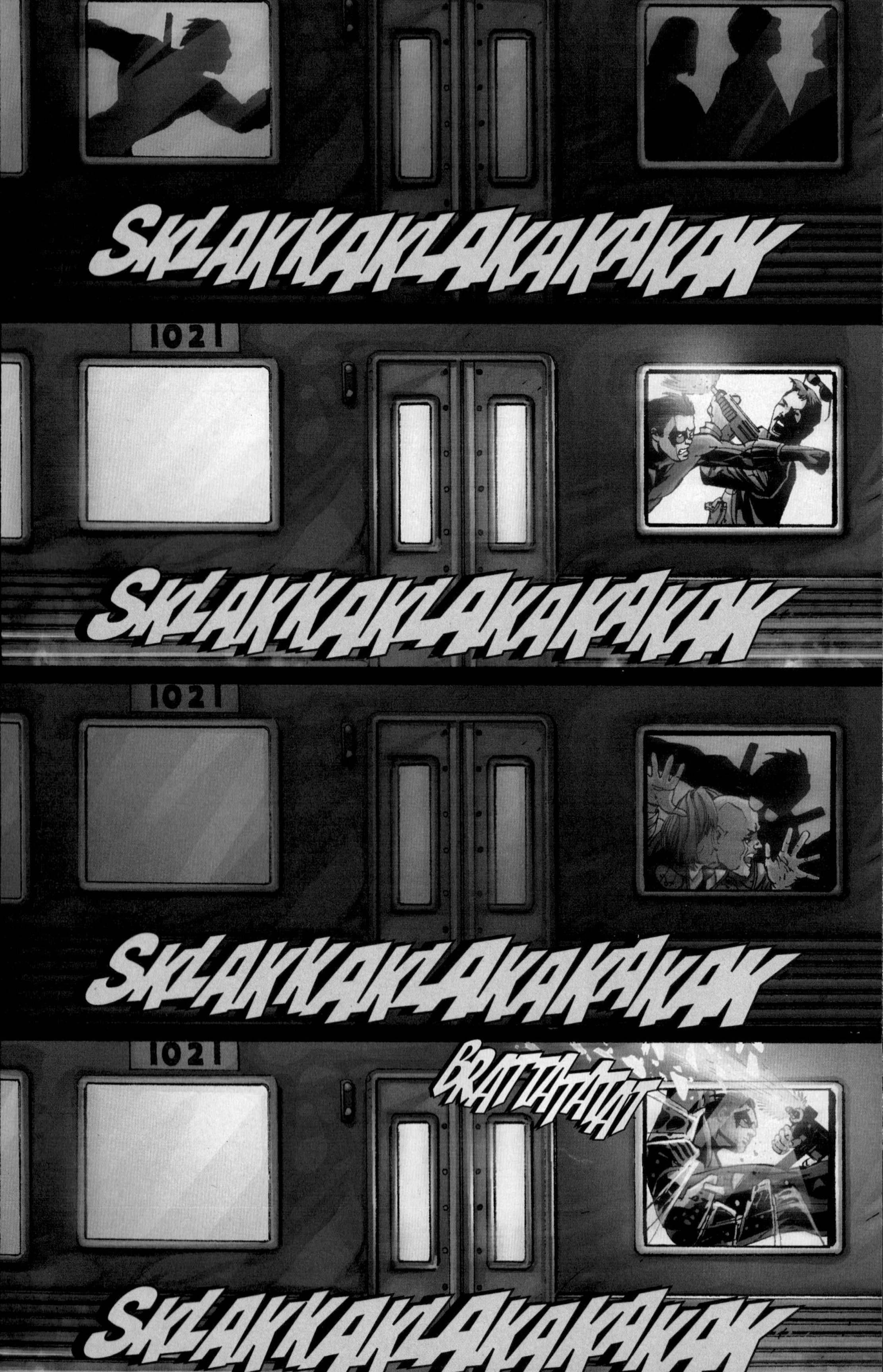
SKLAKKAKLAKAKAKAK
1021
SKLAKKAKLAKAKAKAK
1021
SKLAKKAKLAKAKAKAK
1021
BRATTATATAT
SKLAKKAKLAKAKAKAK

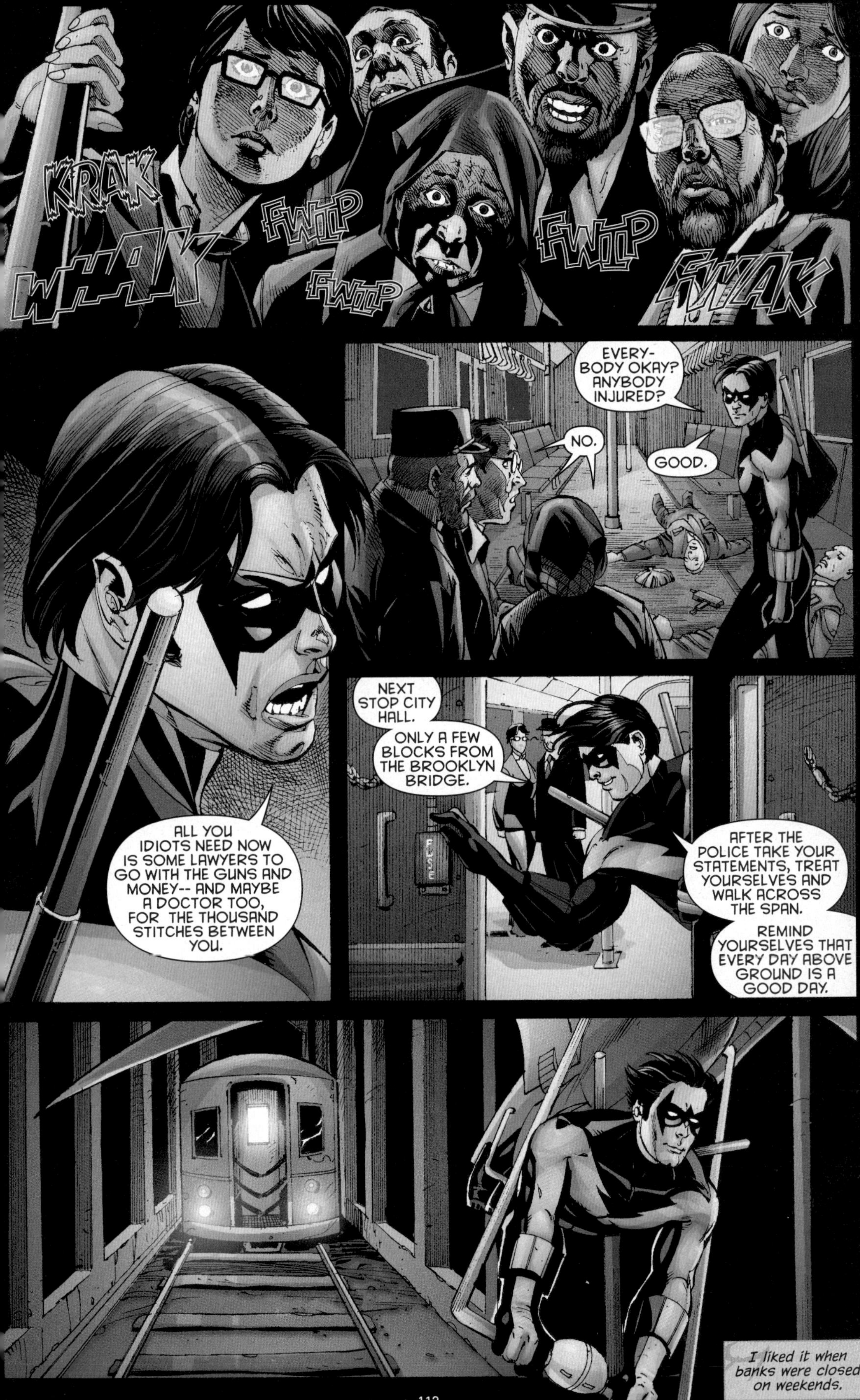
KRAK
WHAK
FWIP
FWIP
FWIP
FWAK
EVERY-BODY OKAY? ANYBODY INJURED?
NO.
GOOD.
ALL YOU IDIOTS NEED NOW IS SOME LAWYERS TO GO WITH THE GUNS AND MONEY-- AND MAYBE A DOCTOR TOO, FOR THE THOUSAND STITCHES BETWEEN YOU.
NEXT STOP CITY HALL.
ONLY A FEW BLOCKS FROM THE BROOKLYN BRIDGE.
AFTER THE POLICE TAKE YOUR STATEMENTS, TREAT YOURSELVES AND WALK ACROSS THE SPAN.
REMIND YOURSELVES THAT EVERY DAY ABOVE GROUND IS A GOOD DAY.
I liked it when banks were closed on weekends.

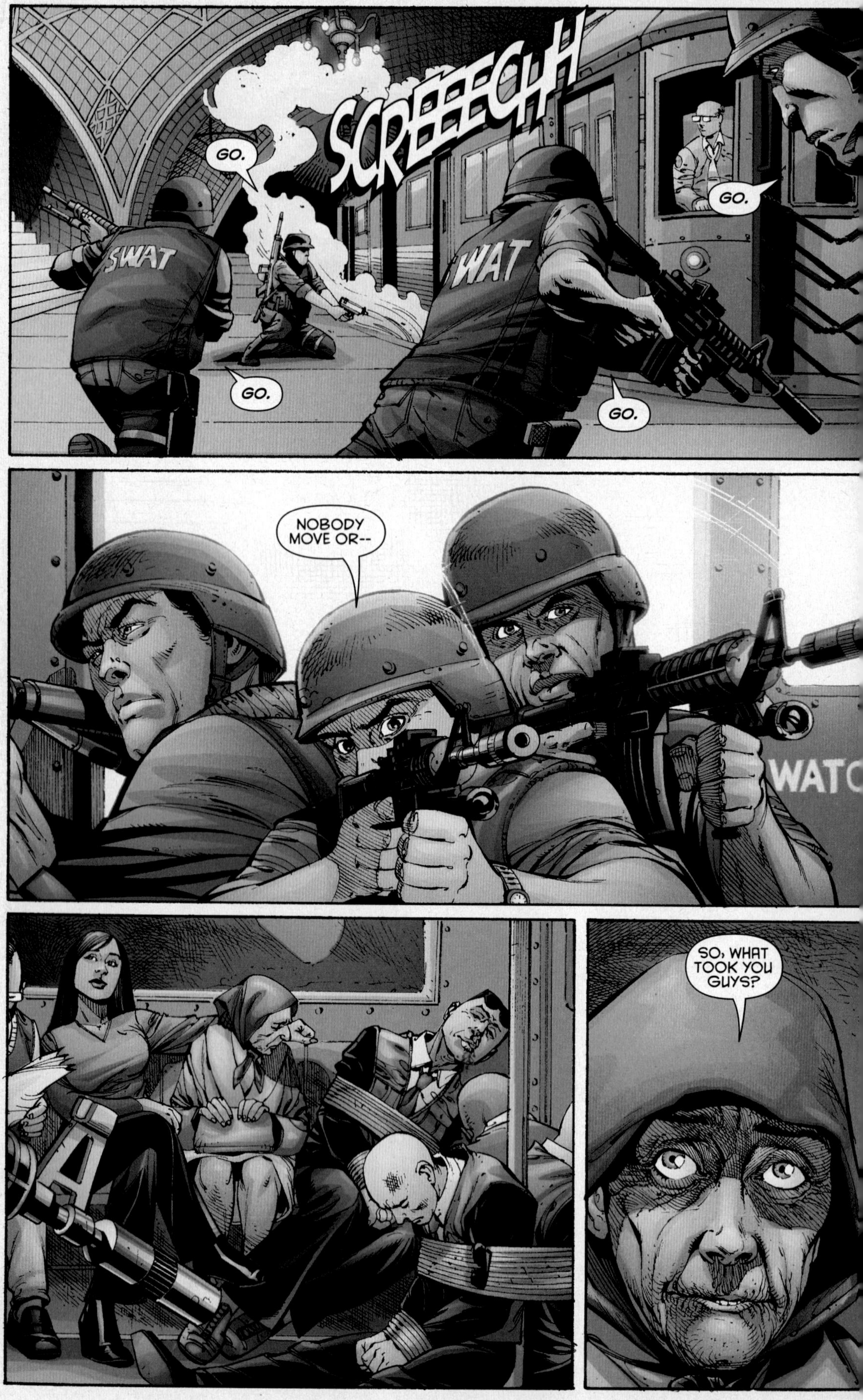
SCREEEECHH
GO.
GO.
GO.
GO.
NOBODY MOVE OR--
SWAT
SO, WHAT TOOK YOU GUYS?

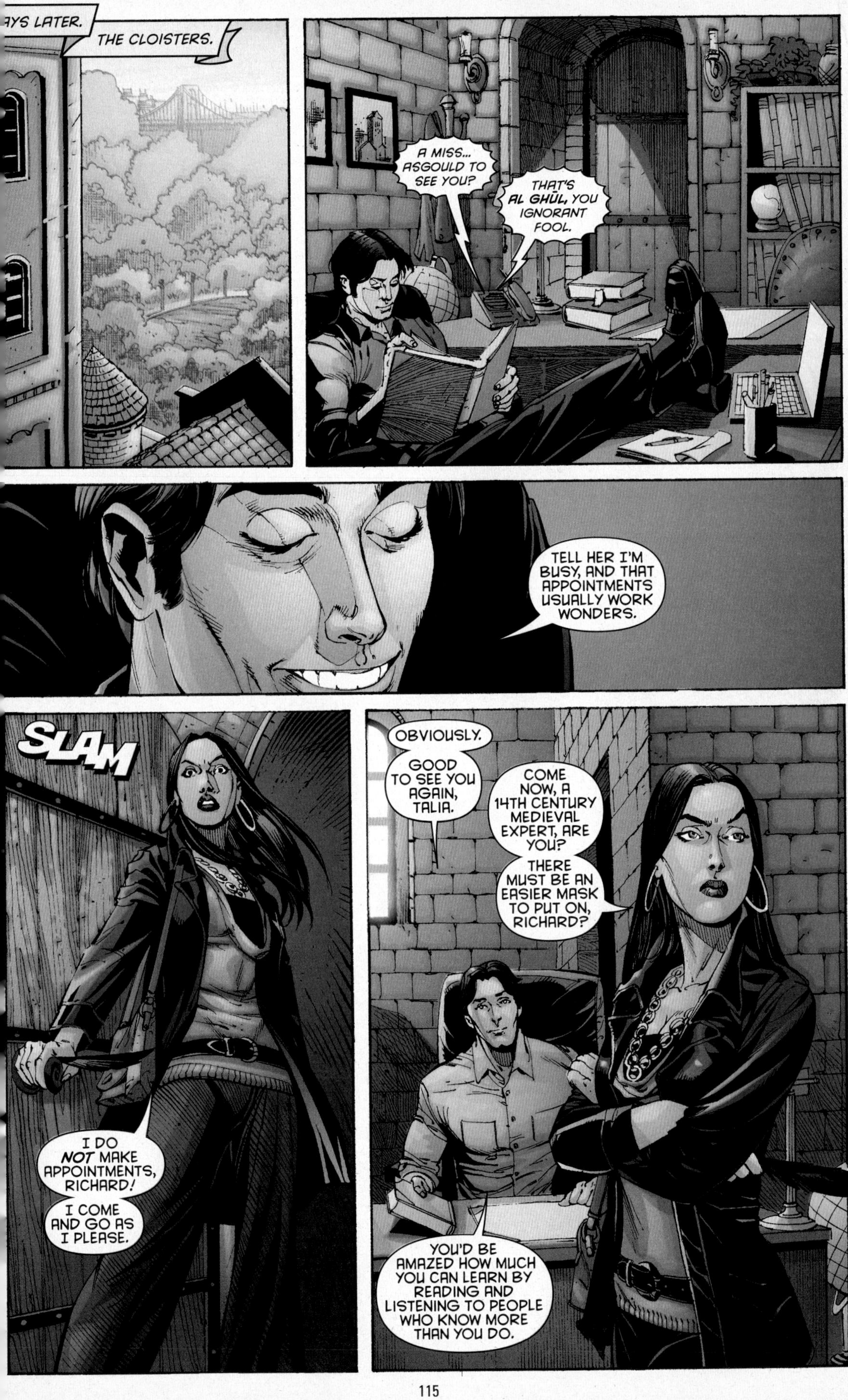
AYS LATER.
THE CLOISTERS.
A MISS... ASGOULD TO SEE YOU?
THAT'S **AL GHŪL,** YOU IGNORANT FOOL.
TELL HER I'M BUSY, AND THAT APPOINTMENTS USUALLY WORK WONDERS.
SLAM
I DO ***NOT*** MAKE APPOINTMENTS, RICHARD!
I COME AND GO AS I PLEASE.
OBVIOUSLY.
GOOD TO SEE YOU AGAIN, TALIA.
COME NOW, A 14TH CENTURY MEDIEVAL EXPERT, ARE YOU?
THERE MUST BE AN EASIER MASK TO PUT ON, RICHARD?
YOU'D BE AMAZED HOW MUCH YOU CAN LEARN BY READING AND LISTENING TO PEOPLE WHO KNOW MORE THAN YOU DO.

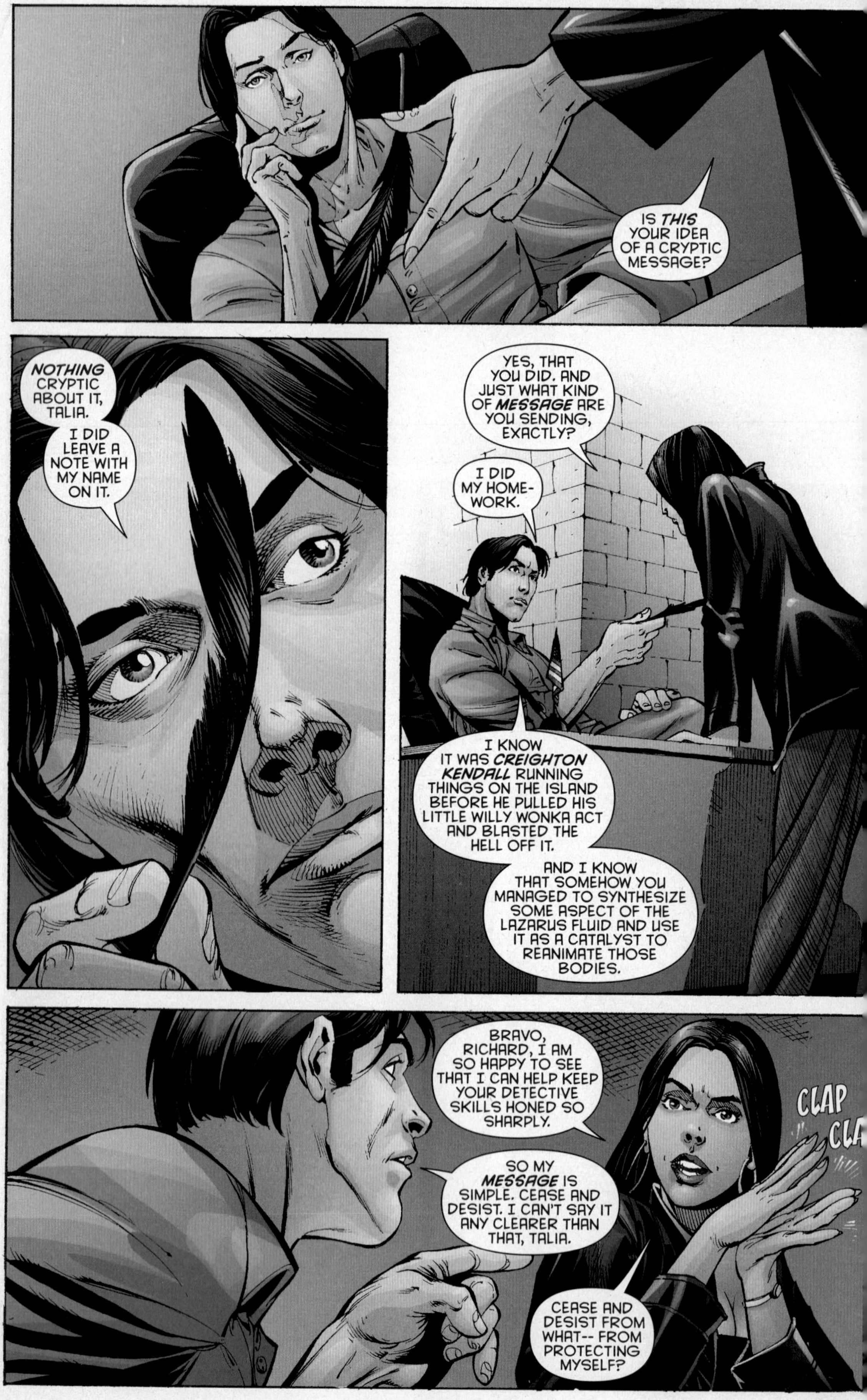

IS *THIS* YOUR IDEA OF A CRYPTIC MESSAGE?
NOTHING CRYPTIC ABOUT IT, TALIA.
I DID LEAVE A NOTE WITH MY NAME ON IT.
YES, THAT YOU DID. AND JUST WHAT KIND OF *MESSAGE* ARE YOU SENDING, EXACTLY?
I DID MY HOME-WORK.
I KNOW IT WAS *CREIGHTON KENDALL* RUNNING THINGS ON THE ISLAND BEFORE HE PULLED HIS LITTLE WILLY WONKA ACT AND BLASTED THE HELL OFF IT.
AND I KNOW THAT SOMEHOW YOU MANAGED TO SYNTHESIZE SOME ASPECT OF THE LAZARUS FLUID AND USE IT AS A CATALYST TO REANIMATE THOSE BODIES.
BRAVO, RICHARD, I AM SO HAPPY TO SEE THAT I CAN HELP KEEP YOUR DETECTIVE SKILLS HONED SO SHARPLY.
CLAP
SO MY *MESSAGE* IS SIMPLE. CEASE AND DESIST. I CAN'T SAY IT ANY CLEARER THAN THAT, TALIA.
CEASE AND DESIST FROM WHAT-- FROM PROTECTING MYSELF?

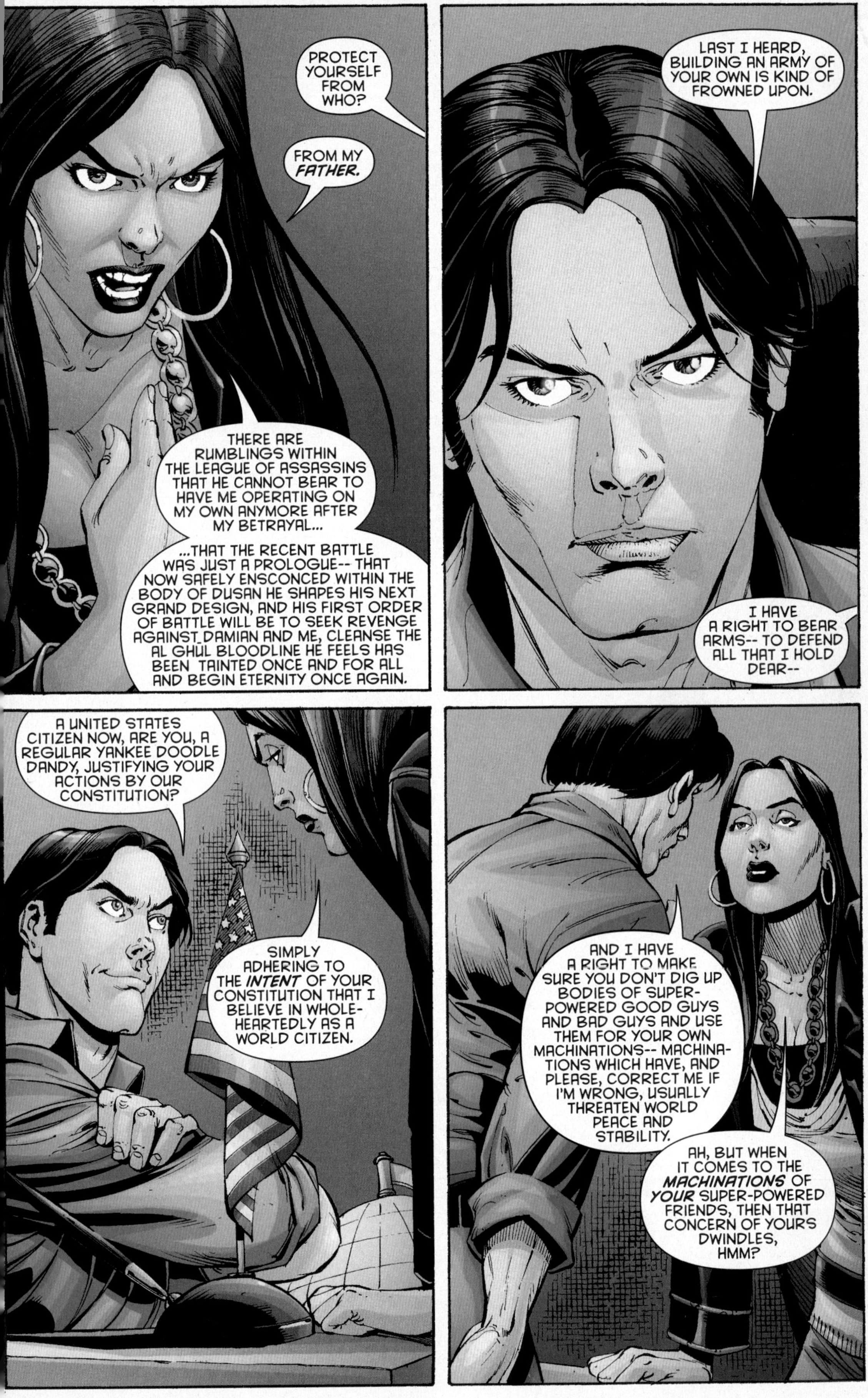
PROTECT YOURSELF FROM WHO?
FROM MY *FATHER.*
THERE ARE RUMBLINGS WITHIN THE LEAGUE OF ASSASSINS THAT HE CANNOT BEAR TO HAVE ME OPERATING ON MY OWN ANYMORE AFTER MY BETRAYAL...
...THAT THE RECENT BATTLE WAS JUST A PROLOGUE-- THAT NOW SAFELY ENSCONCED WITHIN THE BODY OF DUSAN HE SHAPES HIS NEXT GRAND DESIGN, AND HIS FIRST ORDER OF BATTLE WILL BE TO SEEK REVENGE AGAINST DAMIAN AND ME, CLEANSE THE AL GHŪL BLOODLINE HE FEELS HAS BEEN TAINTED ONCE AND FOR ALL AND BEGIN ETERNITY ONCE AGAIN.
LAST I HEARD, BUILDING AN ARMY OF YOUR OWN IS KIND OF FROWNED UPON.
I HAVE A RIGHT TO BEAR ARMS-- TO DEFEND ALL THAT I HOLD DEAR--
A UNITED STATES CITIZEN NOW, ARE YOU, A REGULAR YANKEE DOODLE DANDY, JUSTIFYING YOUR ACTIONS BY OUR CONSTITUTION?
SIMPLY ADHERING TO THE *INTENT* OF YOUR CONSTITUTION THAT I BELIEVE IN WHOLE-HEARTEDLY AS A WORLD CITIZEN.
AND I HAVE A RIGHT TO MAKE SURE YOU DON'T DIG UP BODIES OF SUPER-POWERED GOOD GUYS AND BAD GUYS AND USE THEM FOR YOUR OWN MACHINATIONS-- MACHINATIONS WHICH HAVE, AND PLEASE, CORRECT ME IF I'M WRONG, USUALLY THREATEN WORLD PEACE AND STABILITY.
AH, BUT WHEN IT COMES TO THE *MACHINATIONS* OF *YOUR* SUPER-POWERED FRIENDS, THEN THAT CONCERN OF YOURS DWINDLES, HMM?

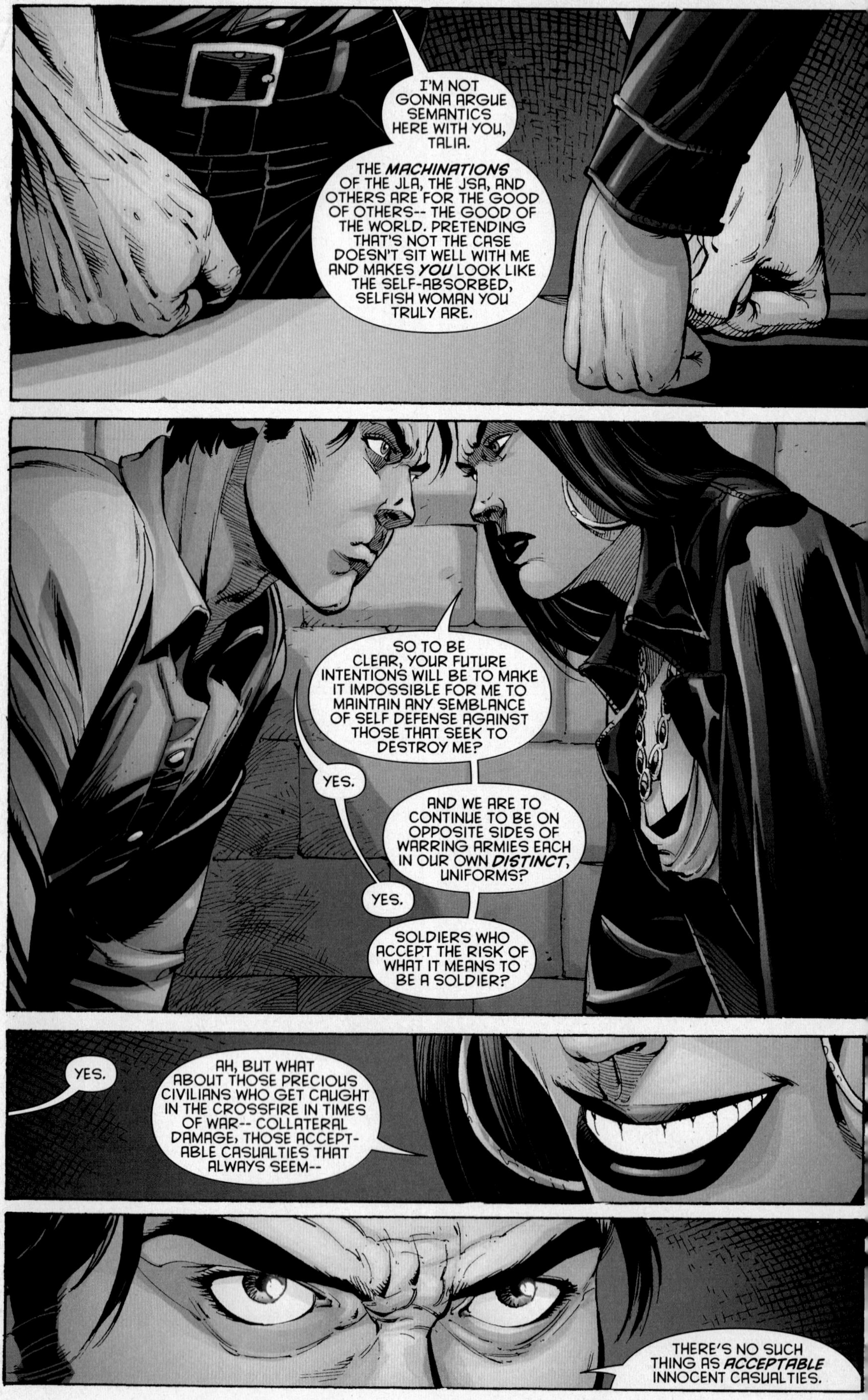
I'M NOT GONNA ARGUE SEMANTICS HERE WITH YOU, TALIA.
THE *MACHINATIONS* OF THE JLA, THE JSA, AND OTHERS ARE FOR THE GOOD OF OTHERS-- THE GOOD OF THE WORLD. PRETENDING THAT'S NOT THE CASE DOESN'T SIT WELL WITH ME AND MAKES *YOU* LOOK LIKE THE SELF-ABSORBED, SELFISH WOMAN YOU TRULY ARE.
SO TO BE CLEAR, YOUR FUTURE INTENTIONS WILL BE TO MAKE IT IMPOSSIBLE FOR ME TO MAINTAIN ANY SEMBLANCE OF SELF DEFENSE AGAINST THOSE THAT SEEK TO DESTROY ME?
YES.
AND WE ARE TO CONTINUE TO BE ON OPPOSITE SIDES OF WARRING ARMIES EACH IN OUR OWN *DISTINCT*, UNIFORMS?
YES.
SOLDIERS WHO ACCEPT THE RISK OF WHAT IT MEANS TO BE A SOLDIER?
YES.
AH, BUT WHAT ABOUT THOSE PRECIOUS CIVILIANS WHO GET CAUGHT IN THE CROSSFIRE IN TIMES OF WAR-- COLLATERAL DAMAGE, THOSE ACCEPT-ABLE CASUALTIES THAT ALWAYS SEEM--
THERE'S NO SUCH THING AS *ACCEPTABLE* INNOCENT CASUALTIES.

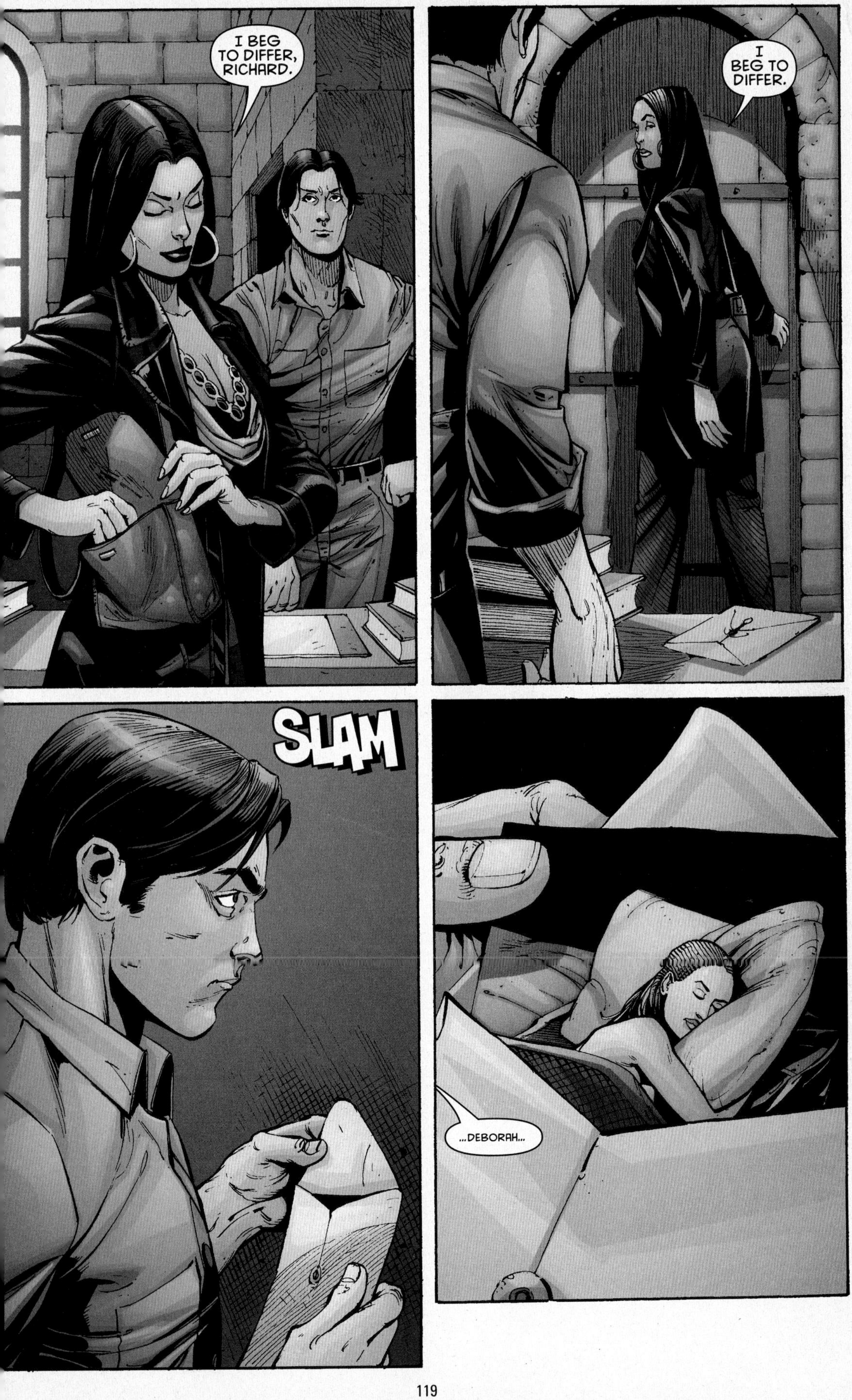
I BEG TO DIFFER, RICHARD.
I BEG TO DIFFER.
SLAM
...DEBORAH...

NIGHTWING #
Cover art by Andy Ku

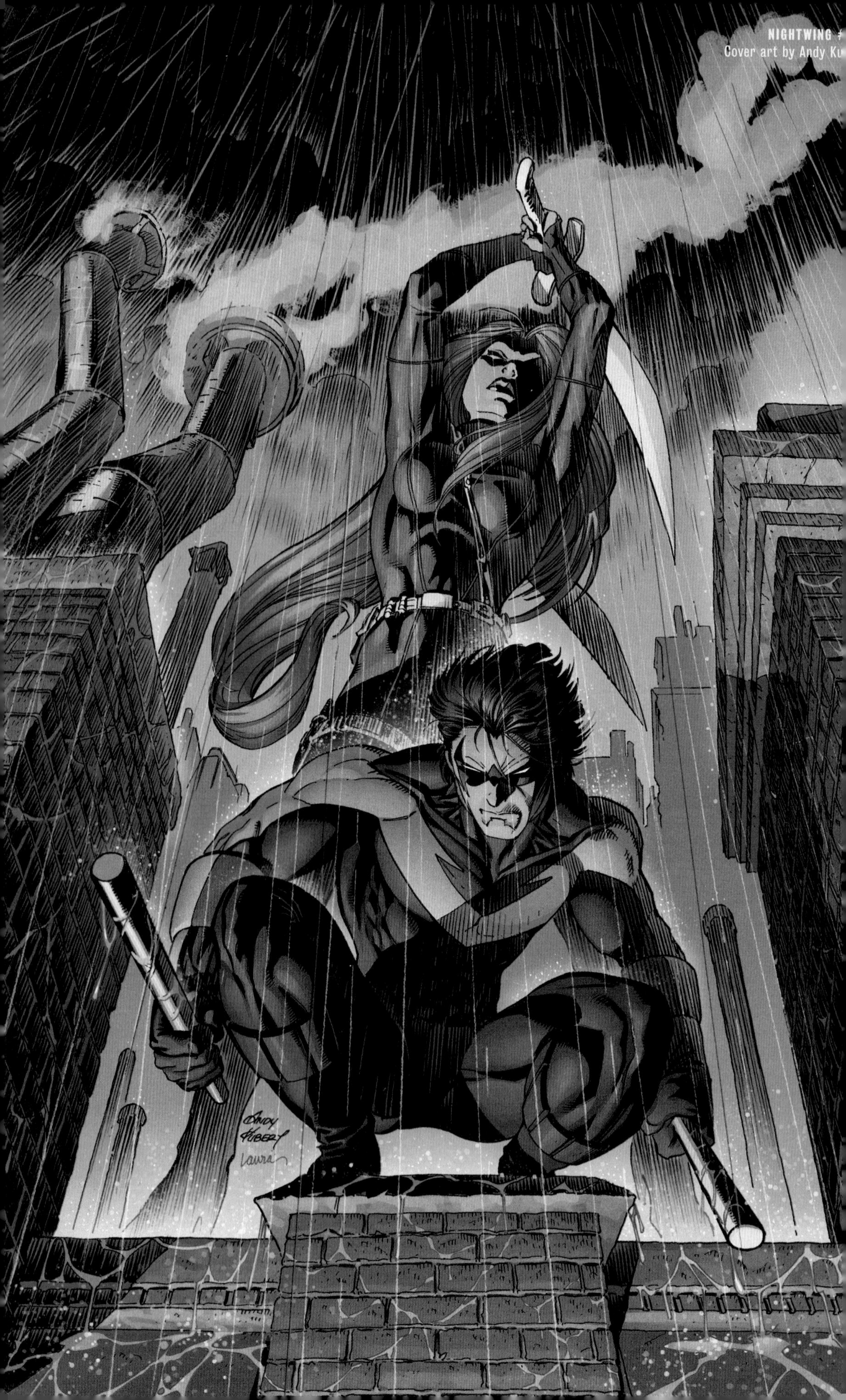
ANDY
KUBERT
Laura

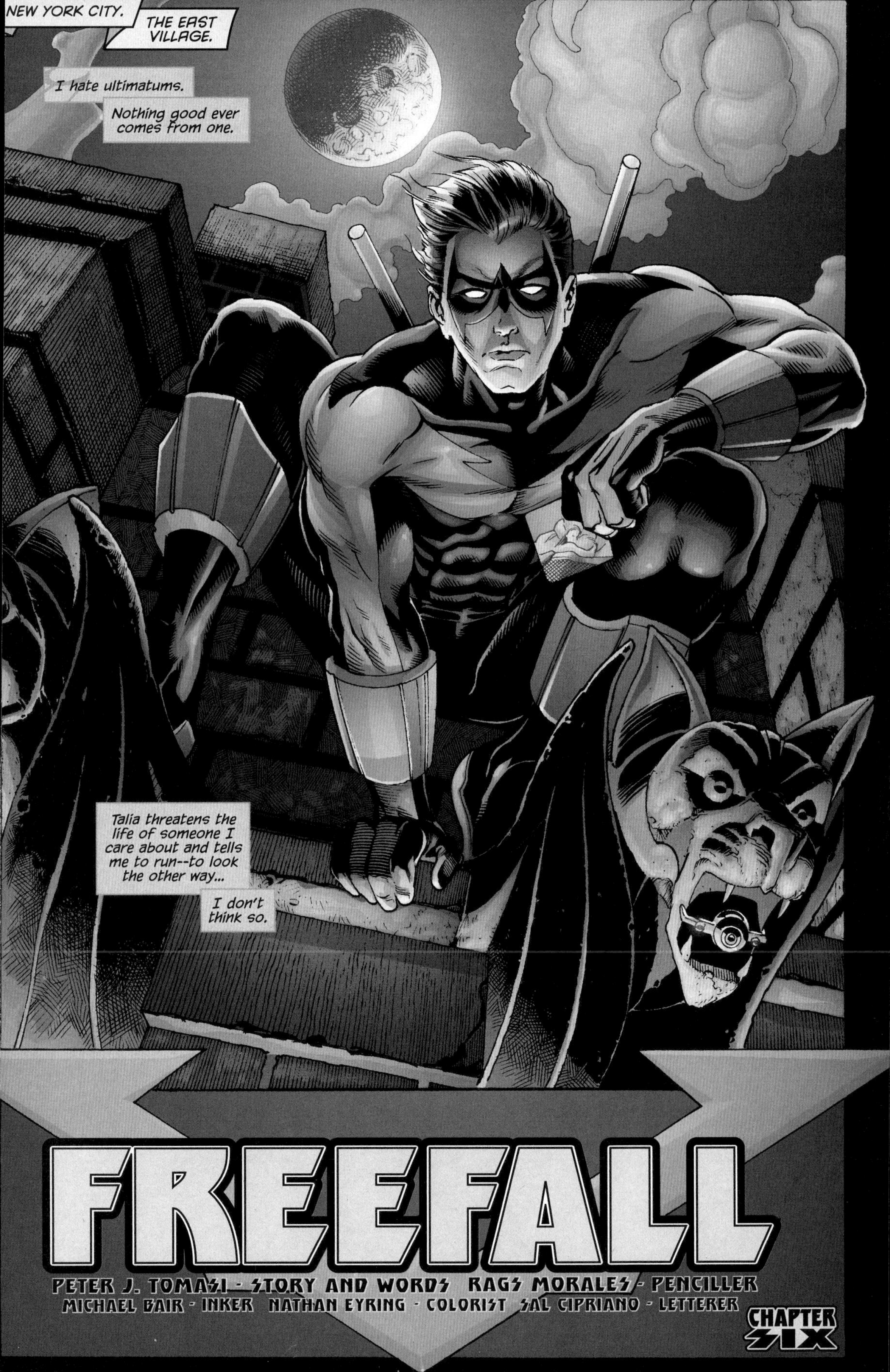

NEW YORK CITY.
THE EAST VILLAGE.
I hate ultimatums.
Nothing good ever comes from one.
Talia threatens the life of someone I care about and tells me to run--to look the other way...
I don't think so.
FREEFALL
PETER J. TOMASI - STORY AND WORDS RAGS MORALES - PENCILLER
MICHAEL BAIR - INKER NATHAN EYRING - COLORIST SAL CIPRIANO - LETTERER
CHAPTER SIX

THE HUDSON HIGHLANDS. POLLEPEL ISLAND. SIXTY MILES NORTH OF NEW YORK CITY.

THERE IT IS, THE HAMMER ARMORY.

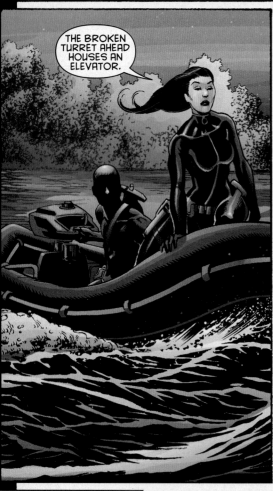

THE BROKEN TURRET AHEAD HOUSES AN ELEVATOR.

REMAIN HERE UNTIL I RETURN.

AS YOU WISH, MISS TALIA.

UNDER THE HUDSON RIVER.

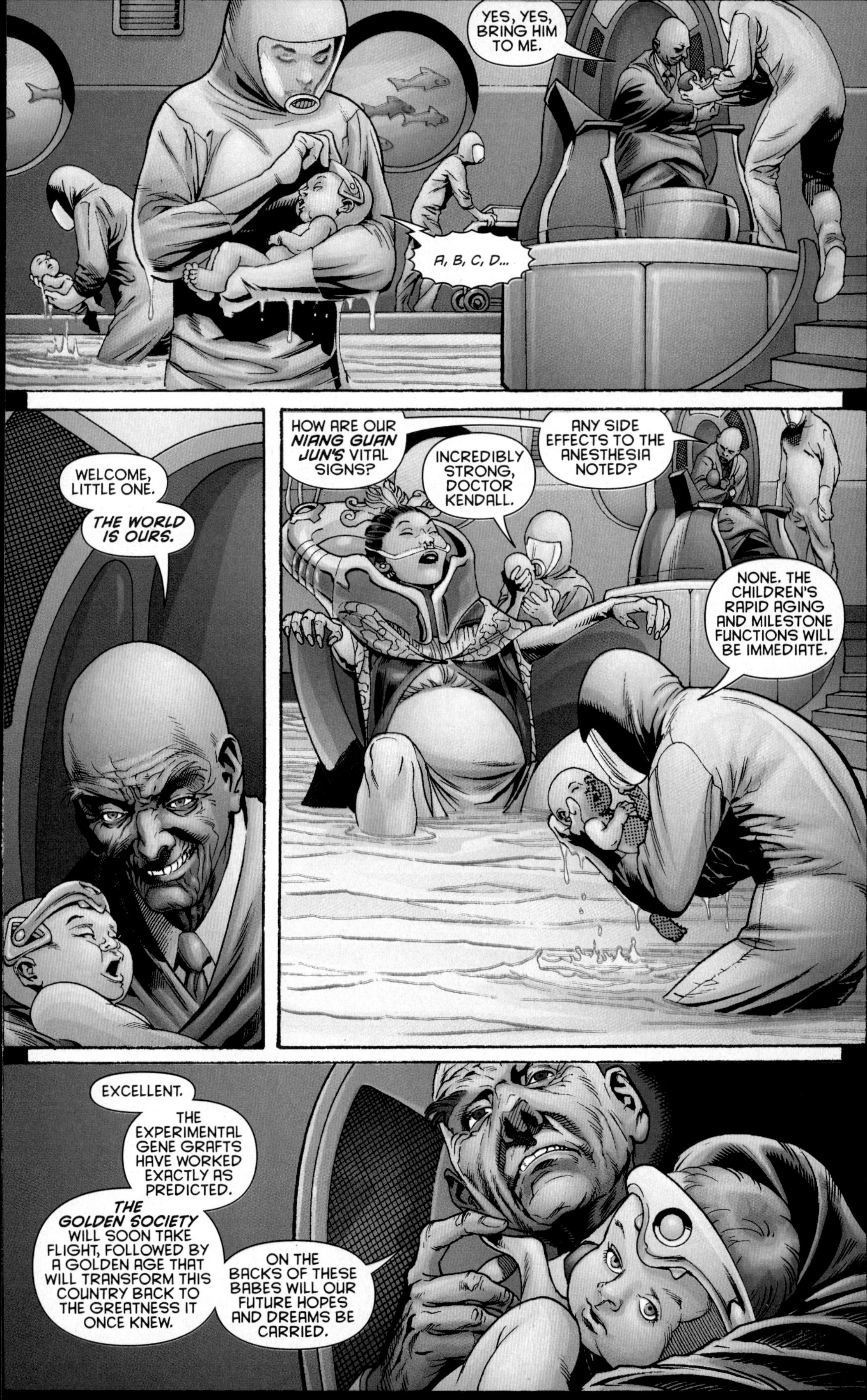
YES, YES, BRING HIM TO ME.
A, B, C, D...
WELCOME, LITTLE ONE.
THE WORLD IS OURS.
HOW ARE OUR NIANG GUAN JUN'S VITAL SIGNS?
INCREDIBLY STRONG, DOCTOR KENDALL.
ANY SIDE EFFECTS TO THE ANESTHESIA NOTED?
NONE. THE CHILDREN'S RAPID AGING AND MILESTONE FUNCTIONS WILL BE IMMEDIATE.
EXCELLENT.
THE EXPERIMENTAL GENE GRAFTS HAVE WORKED EXACTLY AS PREDICTED.
THE GOLDEN SOCIETY WILL SOON TAKE FLIGHT, FOLLOWED BY A GOLDEN AGE THAT WILL TRANSFORM THIS COUNTRY BACK TO THE GREATNESS IT ONCE KNEW.
ON THE BACKS OF THESE BABES WILL OUR FUTURE HOPES AND DREAMS BE CARRIED.

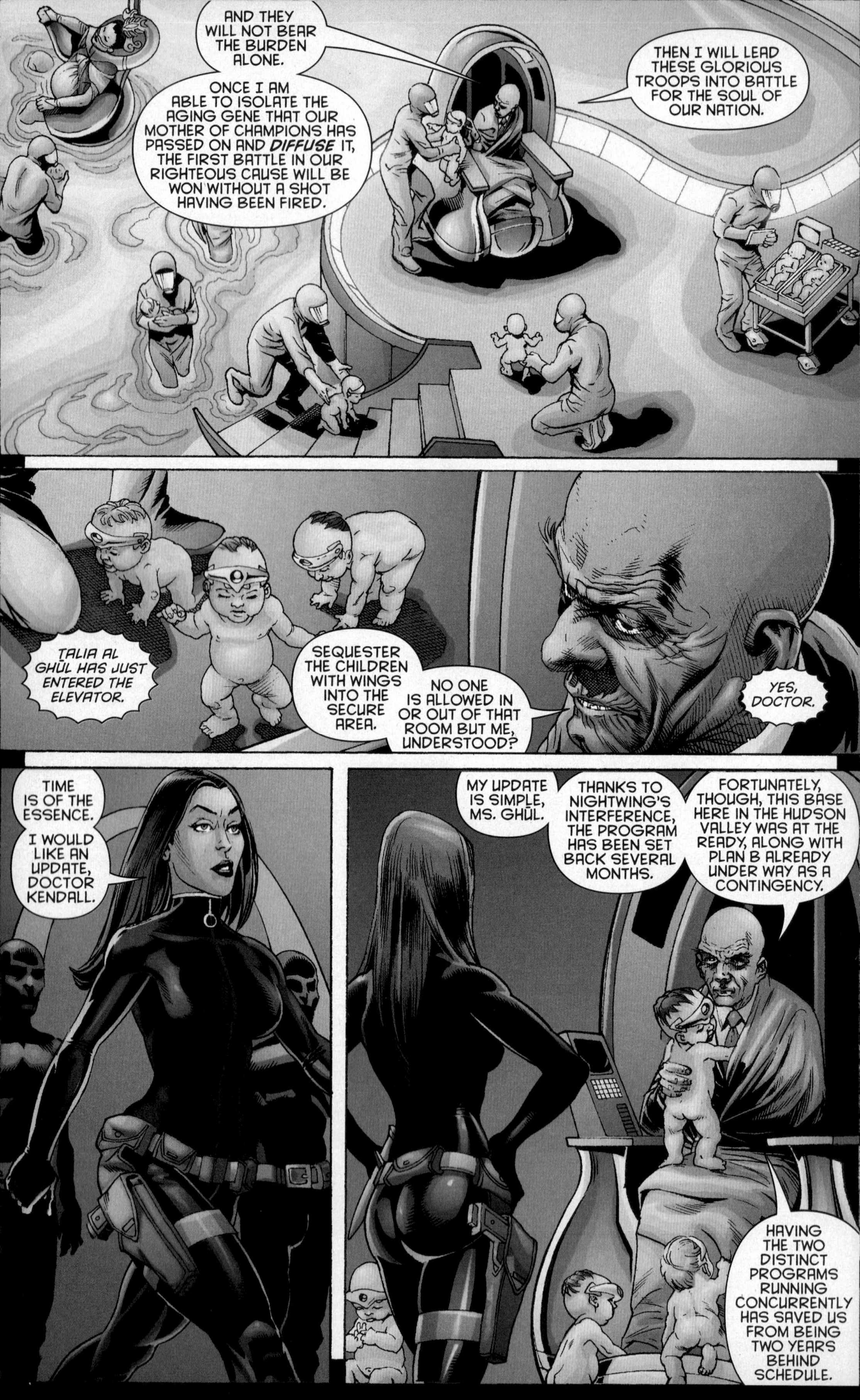
AND THEY WILL NOT BEAR THE BURDEN ALONE.
ONCE I AM ABLE TO ISOLATE THE AGING GENE THAT OUR MOTHER OF CHAMPIONS HAS PASSED ON AND *DIFFUSE* IT, THE FIRST BATTLE IN OUR RIGHTEOUS CAUSE WILL BE WON WITHOUT A SHOT HAVING BEEN FIRED.
THEN I WILL LEAD THESE GLORIOUS TROOPS INTO BATTLE FOR THE SOUL OF OUR NATION.
TALIA AL GHŪL HAS JUST ENTERED THE ELEVATOR.
SEQUESTER THE CHILDREN WITH WINGS INTO THE SECURE AREA.
NO ONE IS ALLOWED IN OR OUT OF THAT ROOM BUT ME, UNDERSTOOD?
YES, DOCTOR.
TIME IS OF THE ESSENCE.
I WOULD LIKE AN UPDATE, DOCTOR KENDALL.
MY UPDATE IS SIMPLE, MS. GHŪL.
THANKS TO NIGHTWING'S INTERFERENCE, THE PROGRAM HAS BEEN SET BACK SEVERAL MONTHS.
FORTUNATELY, THOUGH, THIS BASE HERE IN THE HUDSON VALLEY WAS AT THE READY, ALONG WITH PLAN B ALREADY UNDER WAY AS A CONTINGENCY.
HAVING THE TWO DISTINCT PROGRAMS RUNNING CONCURRENTLY HAS SAVED US FROM BEING TWO YEARS BEHIND SCHEDULE.

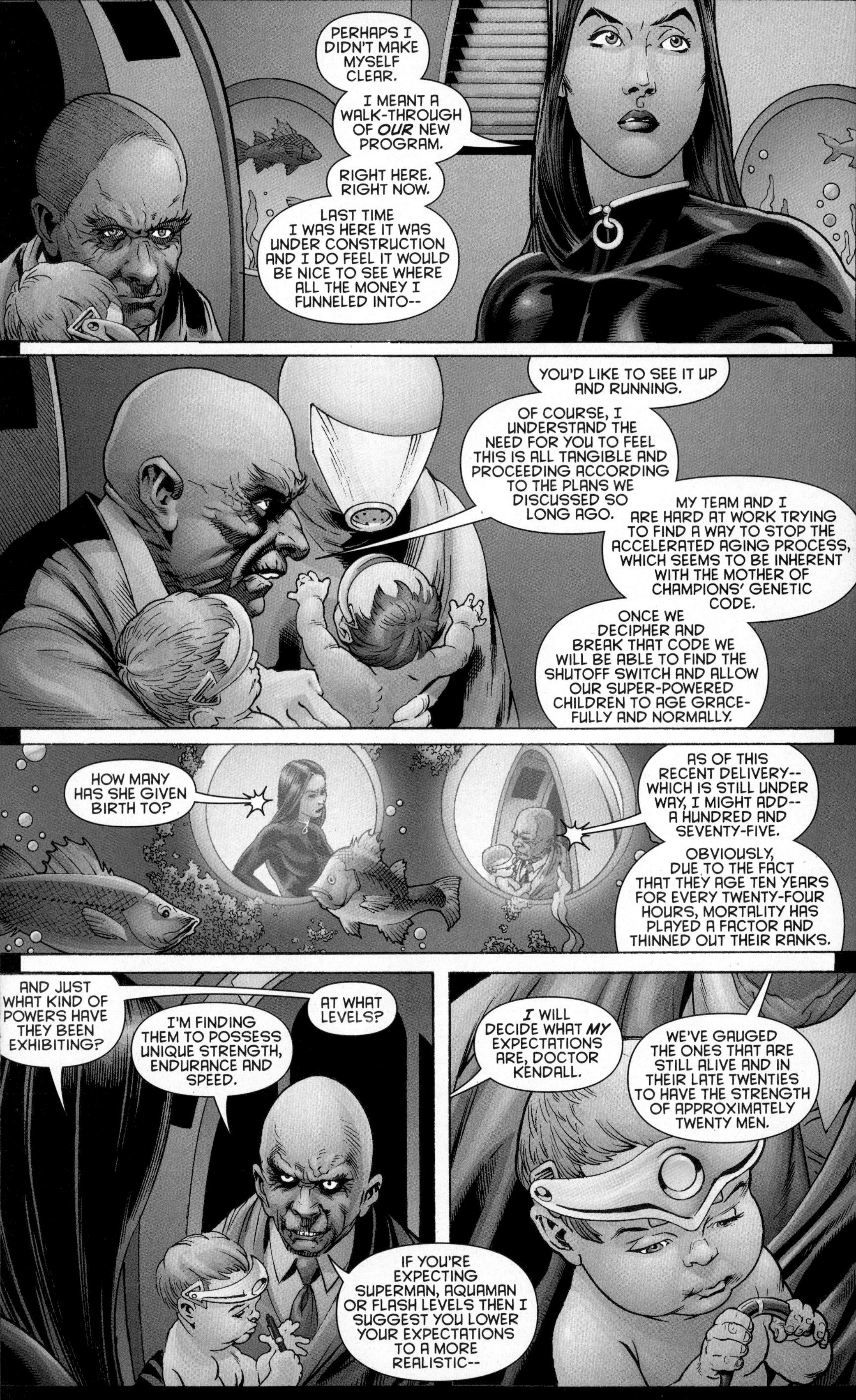
PERHAPS I DIDN'T MAKE MYSELF CLEAR.
I MEANT A WALK-THROUGH OF OUR NEW PROGRAM.
RIGHT HERE. RIGHT NOW.
LAST TIME I WAS HERE IT WAS UNDER CONSTRUCTION AND I DO FEEL IT WOULD BE NICE TO SEE WHERE ALL THE MONEY I FUNNELED INTO--
YOU'D LIKE TO SEE IT UP AND RUNNING.
OF COURSE, I UNDERSTAND THE NEED FOR YOU TO FEEL THIS IS ALL TANGIBLE AND PROCEEDING ACCORDING TO THE PLANS WE DISCUSSED SO LONG AGO.
MY TEAM AND I ARE HARD AT WORK TRYING TO FIND A WAY TO STOP THE ACCELERATED AGING PROCESS, WHICH SEEMS TO BE INHERENT WITH THE MOTHER OF CHAMPIONS' GENETIC CODE.
ONCE WE DECIPHER AND BREAK THAT CODE WE WILL BE ABLE TO FIND THE SHUTOFF SWITCH AND ALLOW OUR SUPER-POWERED CHILDREN TO AGE GRACEFULLY AND NORMALLY.
HOW MANY HAS SHE GIVEN BIRTH TO?
AS OF THIS RECENT DELIVERY-- WHICH IS STILL UNDER WAY, I MIGHT ADD-- A HUNDRED AND SEVENTY-FIVE.
OBVIOUSLY, DUE TO THE FACT THAT THEY AGE TEN YEARS FOR EVERY TWENTY-FOUR HOURS, MORTALITY HAS PLAYED A FACTOR AND THINNED OUT THEIR RANKS.
AND JUST WHAT KIND OF POWERS HAVE THEY BEEN EXHIBITING?
I'M FINDING THEM TO POSSESS UNIQUE STRENGTH, ENDURANCE AND SPEED.
AT WHAT LEVELS?
IF YOU'RE EXPECTING SUPERMAN, AQUAMAN OR FLASH LEVELS THEN I SUGGEST YOU LOWER YOUR EXPECTATIONS TO A MORE REALISTIC--
I WILL DECIDE WHAT MY EXPECTATIONS ARE, DOCTOR KENDALL.
WE'VE GAUGED THE ONES THAT ARE STILL ALIVE AND IN THEIR LATE TWENTIES TO HAVE THE STRENGTH OF APPROXIMATELY TWENTY MEN.

BUT I DO BELIEVE YOU'RE LOOKING MORE ALONG THE LINES FOR STRENGTH IN NUMBERS, YES?

CORRECT.

HOW IS IT THAT SHE CAN CONTINUE GIVING BIRTH VAGINALLY WHILE UNCONSCIOUS? WILL THERE BE AFTER-EFFECTS THAT MAY JEOPARDIZE--

HER COMFORT HAS BEEN TAKEN INTO ACCOUNT AT EVERY LEVEL.

AS YOU CAN SEE, THAT SHOULD NOT BE A PROBLEM.

OUR... "GUEST" SITTING IN THE POOL AT THE MOMENT IS FERTILE ENOUGH TO BIRTH LEGIONS UPON LEGIONS FOR YOU, JUST AS LONG AS HER PHYSICAL WELL-BEING IS TENDED TO.

ALONG WITH THE ARTIFICIAL INSEMINATION, I'VE CREATED A SPECIAL CHEMICAL THAT NOT ONLY INDUCES LABOR BUT ALSO MIMICS CONTRACTIONS TO AID IN PUSHING THE NEWBORNS THROUGH THE BIRTH CANAL AT A QUICKER RATE SO WE CAN BEGIN THE PROCESS ANEW AND LOWER THE RISK OF INJURY TO HER AND YOUR POTENTIAL ARMY.

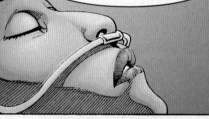

TO PREVENT ANY MORE UNFORESEEN DELAYS OR UNWELCOME INTERRUPTIONS, NIGHTWING WILL BE PAYING FOR HIS--

I HAVE SEEN TO IT THAT HE IS... PREOCCUPIED FOR THE TIME BEING--REALIGNED HIS PRIORITIES, SO TO SPEAK-- GIVING US THE SPACE WE NEED TO COMPLETE THIS PROJECT.

UNLESS NIGHTWING INTERFERES AGAIN, HE IS TO BE LEFT ALONE.

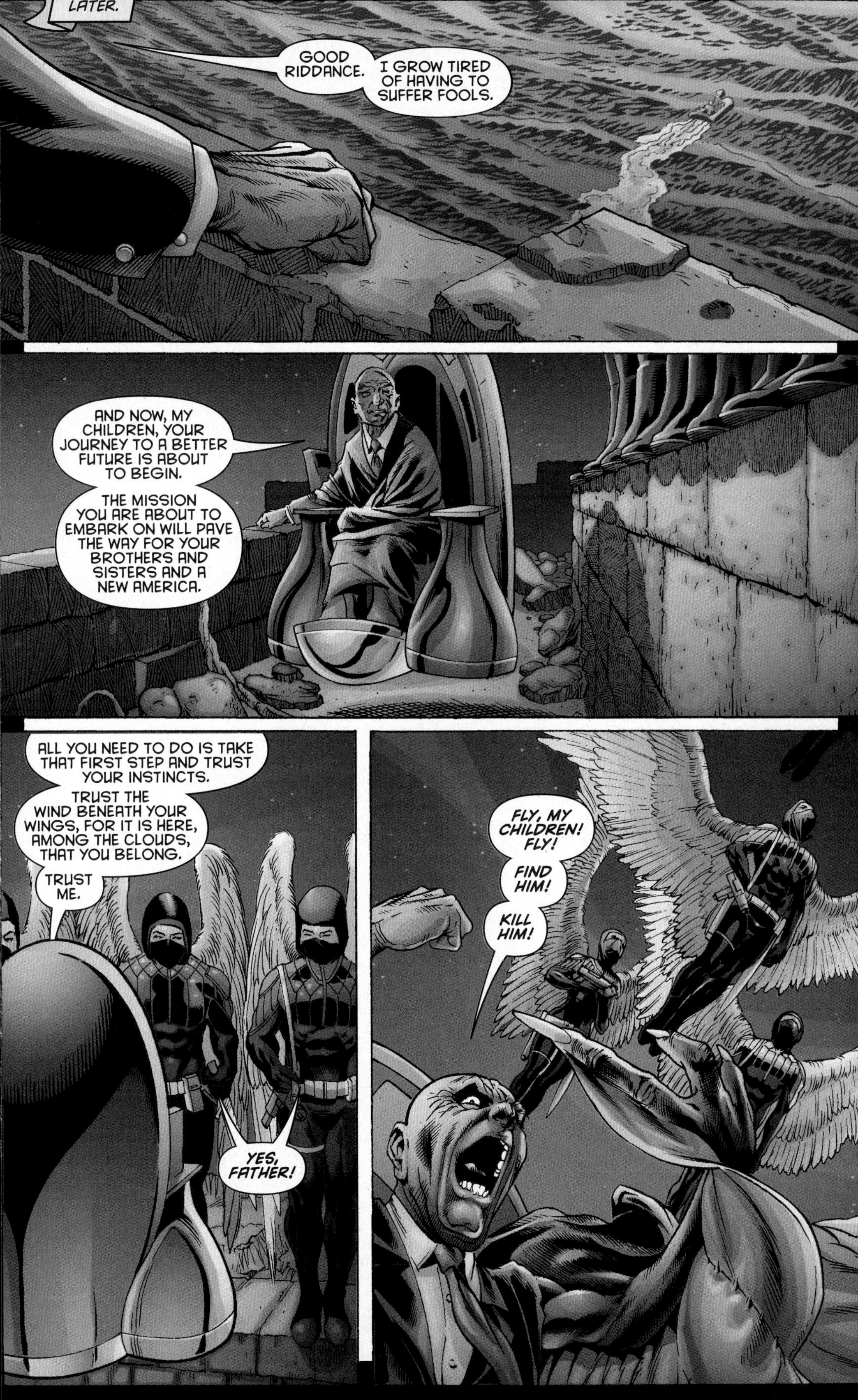
LATER.
GOOD RIDDANCE.
I GROW TIRED OF HAVING TO SUFFER FOOLS.
AND NOW, MY CHILDREN, YOUR JOURNEY TO A BETTER FUTURE IS ABOUT TO BEGIN.
THE MISSION YOU ARE ABOUT TO EMBARK ON WILL PAVE THE WAY FOR YOUR BROTHERS AND SISTERS AND A NEW AMERICA.
ALL YOU NEED TO DO IS TAKE THAT FIRST STEP AND TRUST YOUR INSTINCTS.
TRUST THE WIND BENEATH YOUR WINGS, FOR IT IS HERE, AMONG THE CLOUDS, THAT YOU BELONG.
TRUST ME.
YES, FATHER!
FLY, MY CHILDREN! FLY!
FIND HIM!
KILL HIM!

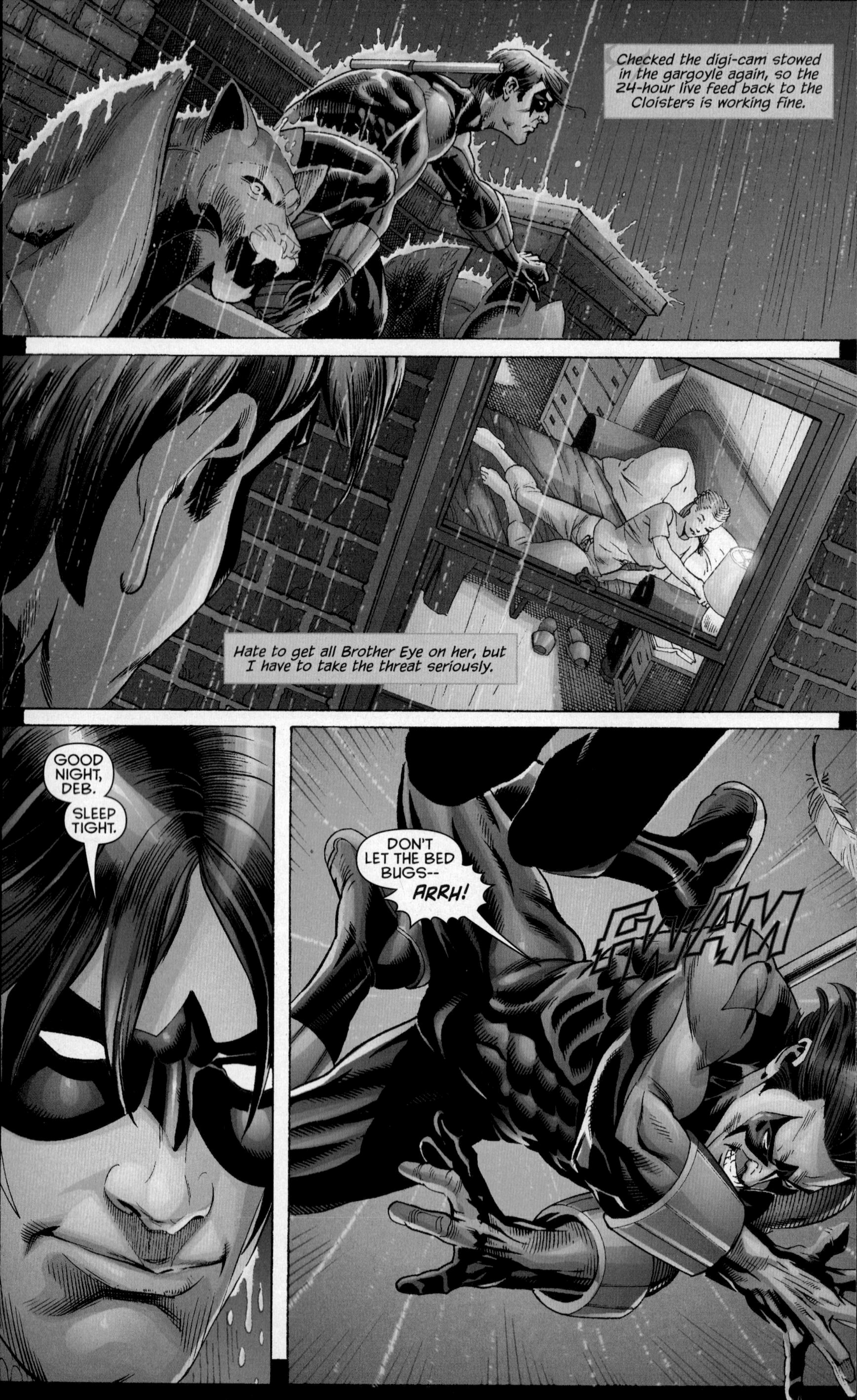
Checked the digi-cam stowed in the gargoyle again, so the 24-hour live feed back to the Cloisters is working fine.
Hate to get all Brother Eye on her, but I have to take the threat seriously.
GOOD NIGHT, DEB.
SLEEP TIGHT.
DON'T LET THE BED BUGS-- ARRH!
FWAM

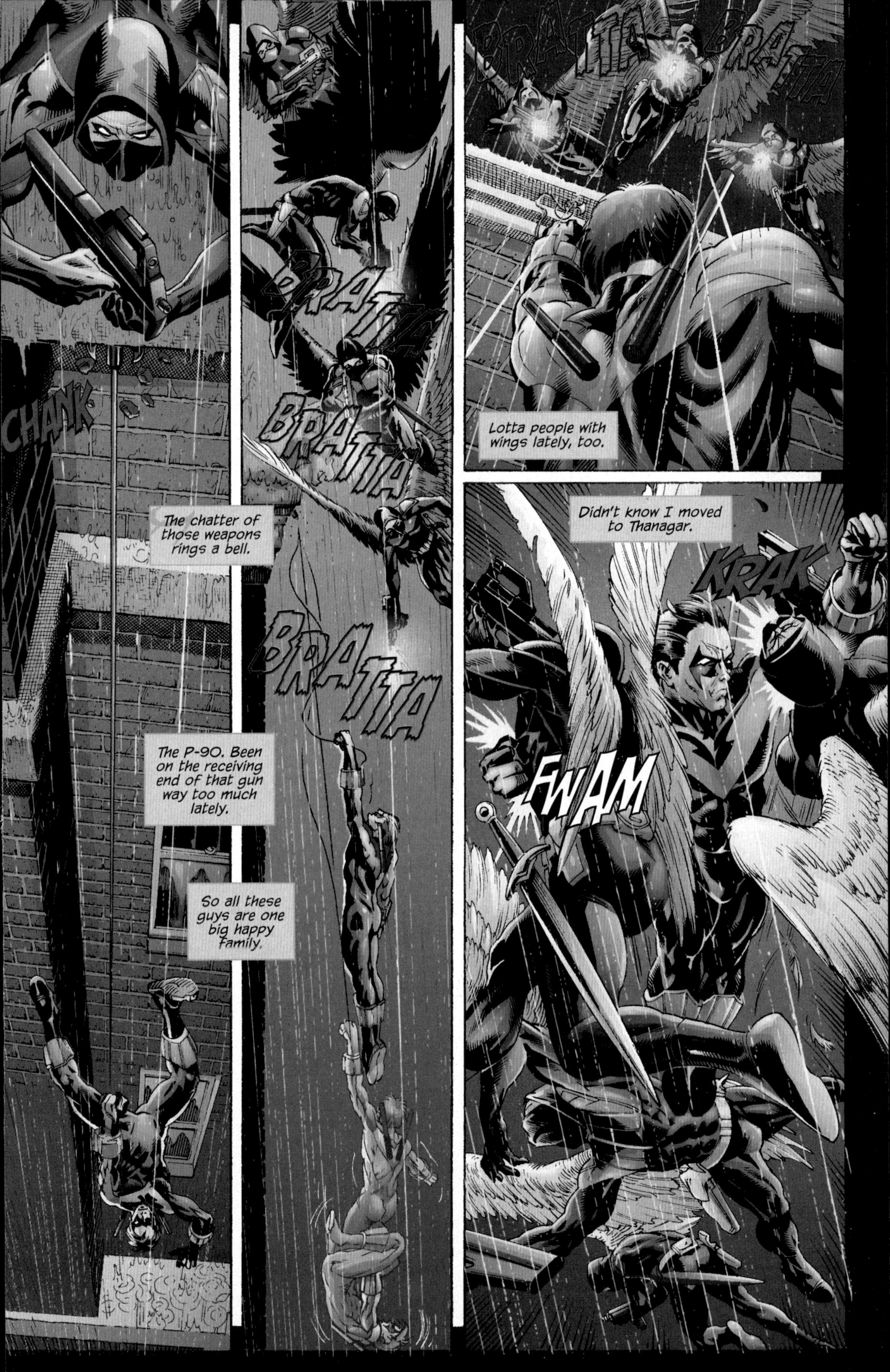
CHANK
BRATTA
BRATTA
The chatter of those weapons rings a bell.
BRATTA
The P-90. Been on the receiving end of that gun way too much lately.
So all these guys are one big happy family.
BRATTA BRATTA
Lotta people with wings lately, too.
Didn't know I moved to Thanagar.
KRAK
FWAM

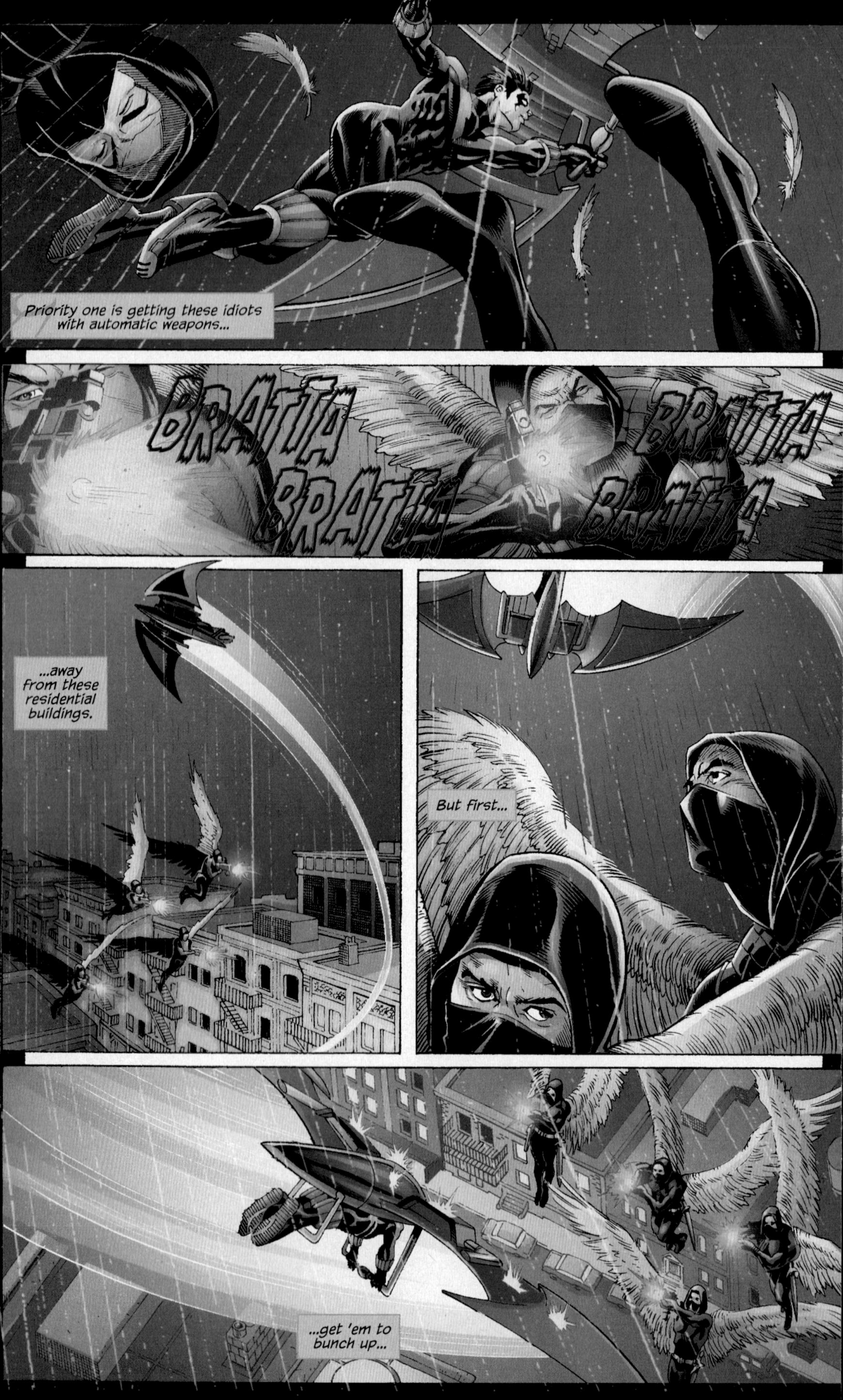
Priority one is getting these idiots with automatic weapons...
BRATTA BRATTA
BRATTA BRATTA
...away from these residential buildings.
But first...
...get 'em to bunch up...

...and clip some wings!

ARGHH!

ARGHH!

SHRRIPP

Now it's time...

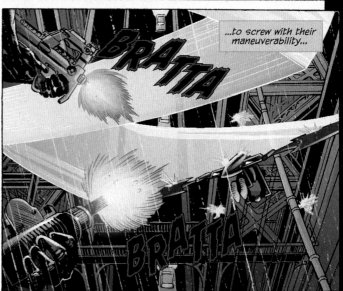

...to screw with their maneuverability...

BRATTA

BRATTA

...and give 'em a reason to paint the Manhattan Bridge soon.

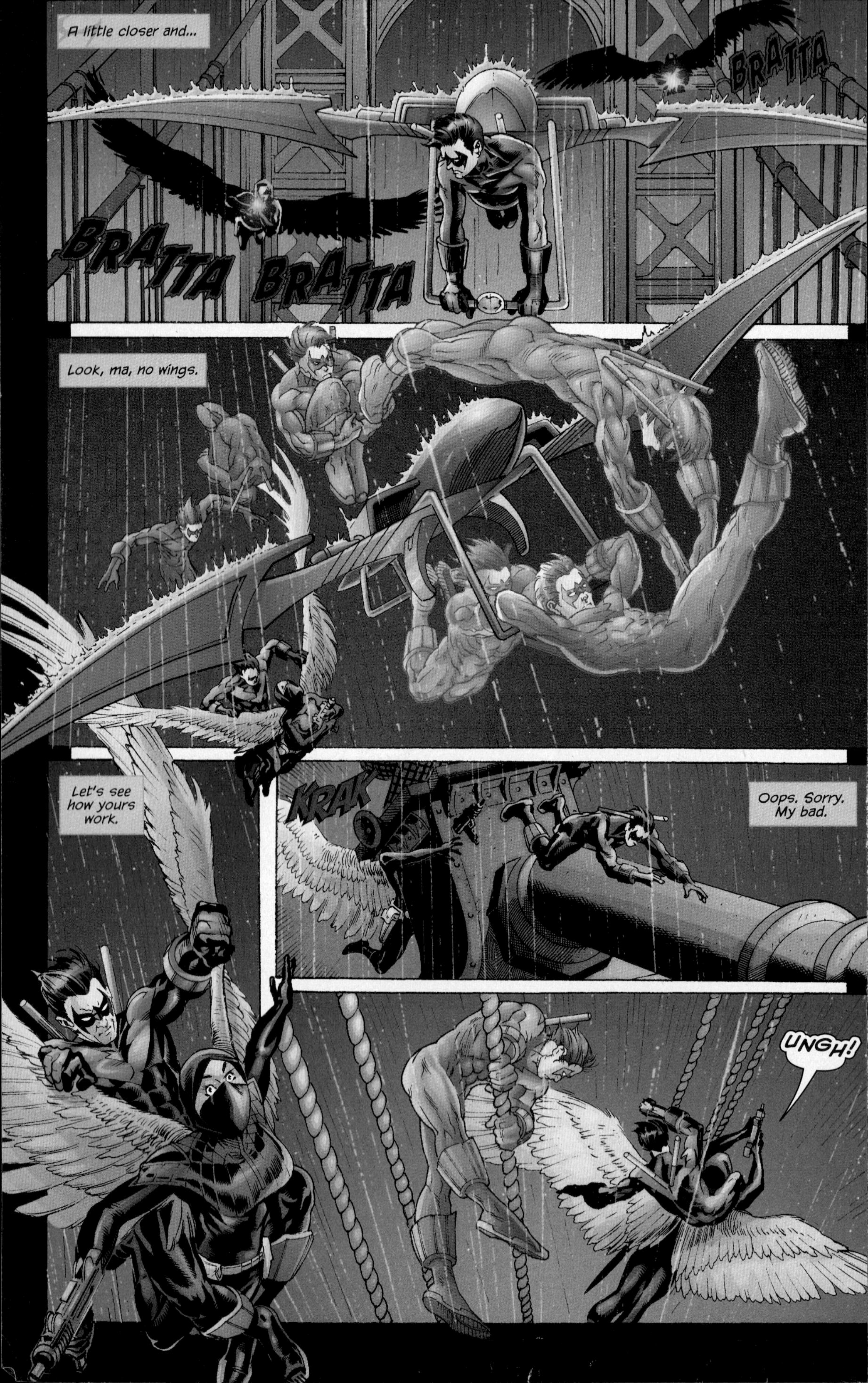
A little closer and...
BRATTA
BRATTA BRATTA
Look, ma, no wings.
Let's see how yours work.
KRAK
Oops. Sorry. My bad.
UNGH!

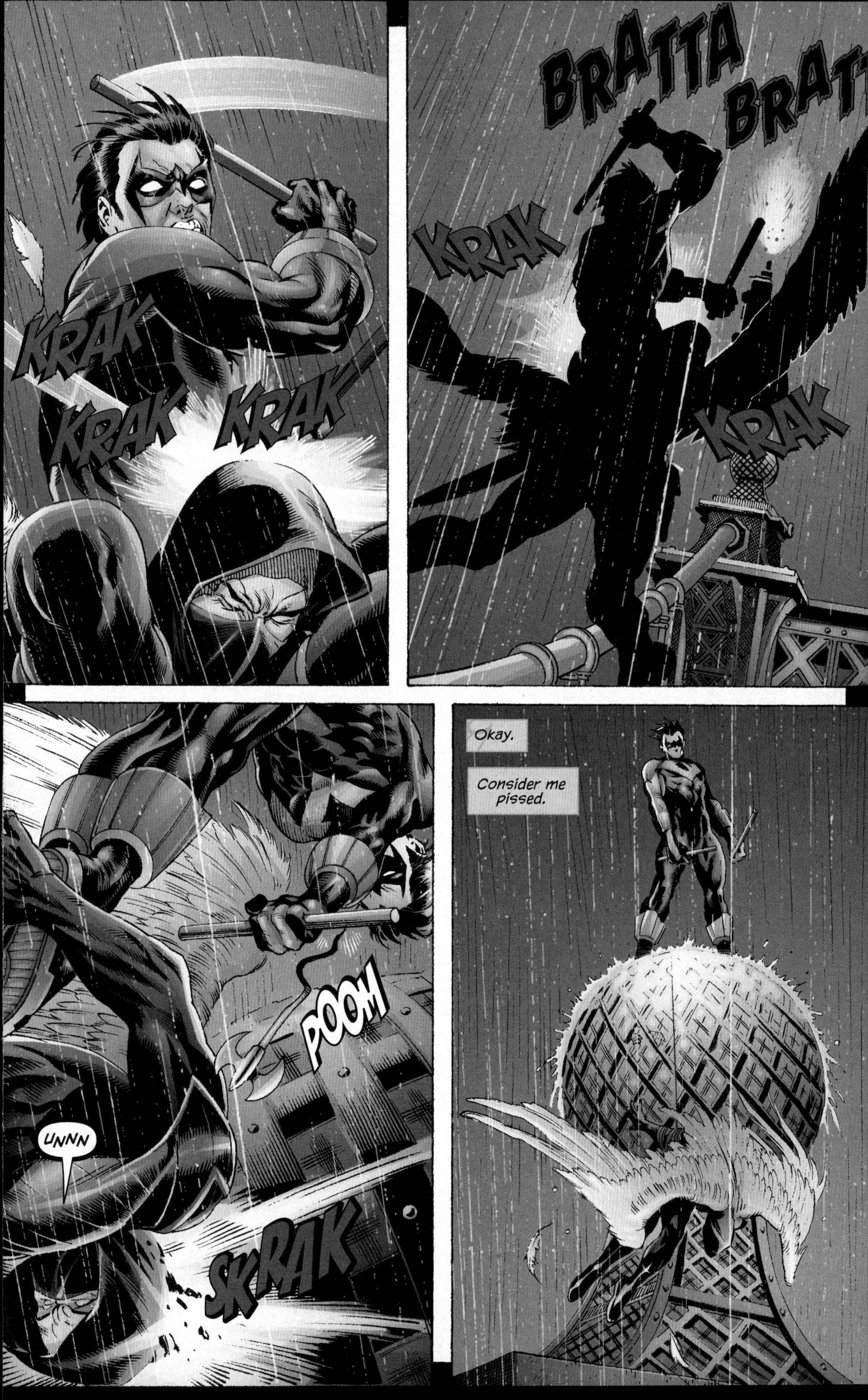
KRAK
KRAK
KRAK
BRATTA
BRATT
KRAK
KRAK
POOM
UNNN
SKRAK
Okay.
Consider me pissed.

GOTHAM CITY.

ARKHAM ASYLUM.

HOME FOR THE CRIMINALLY INSANE.

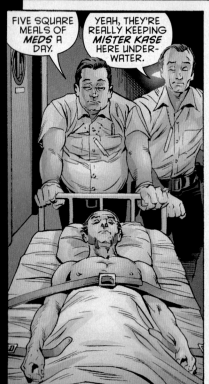

FIVE SQUARE MEALS OF *MEDS* A DAY.

YEAH, THEY'RE REALLY KEEPING *MISTER KASE* HERE UNDER-WATER.

THEY SURE ARE.

HE'S SO DEEP HE MIGHT AS WELL BE DEAD.

~yawn~

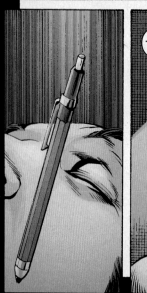

LET'S GO TURN ON THE GAME.

SLAM

HOURS LATER.

WHA--

WHEEEEEE

I'VE GOT A 10-56A IN CELL 708!

REPEAT! I'VE GOT A 10-56A IN CELL 708!

TALK ABOUT DETERMINED--THIS PATIENT TORE THROUGH HIS BRACHIAL, ULNAR AND RADIAL ARTERIES WITH A DAMN PEN.

HOW MANY BAGS HAVE WE HUNG, NURSE?

THIS IS THE SEVENTH BAG, DOCTOR. HE'S AT 5.6 LITERS.

WELL, MISTER KASE HERE HAS RECEIVED A FULL BODY BLOOD TRANSFUSION COURTESY OF ARKHAM.

I'M SURE HE'LL BE QUITE UPSET TO LEARN THAT HIS SINGULAR EFFORT TO REACH THE PEARLY GATES HAS BEEN DENIED AT THIS TIME.

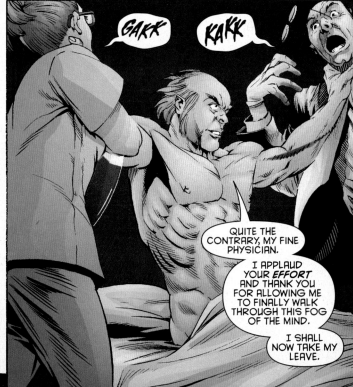

GAKK

KAKK

QUITE THE CONTRARY, MY FINE PHYSICIAN.

I APPLAUD YOUR *EFFORT* AND THANK YOU FOR ALLOWING ME TO FINALLY WALK THROUGH THIS FOG OF THE MIND.

I SHALL NOW TAKE MY LEAVE.

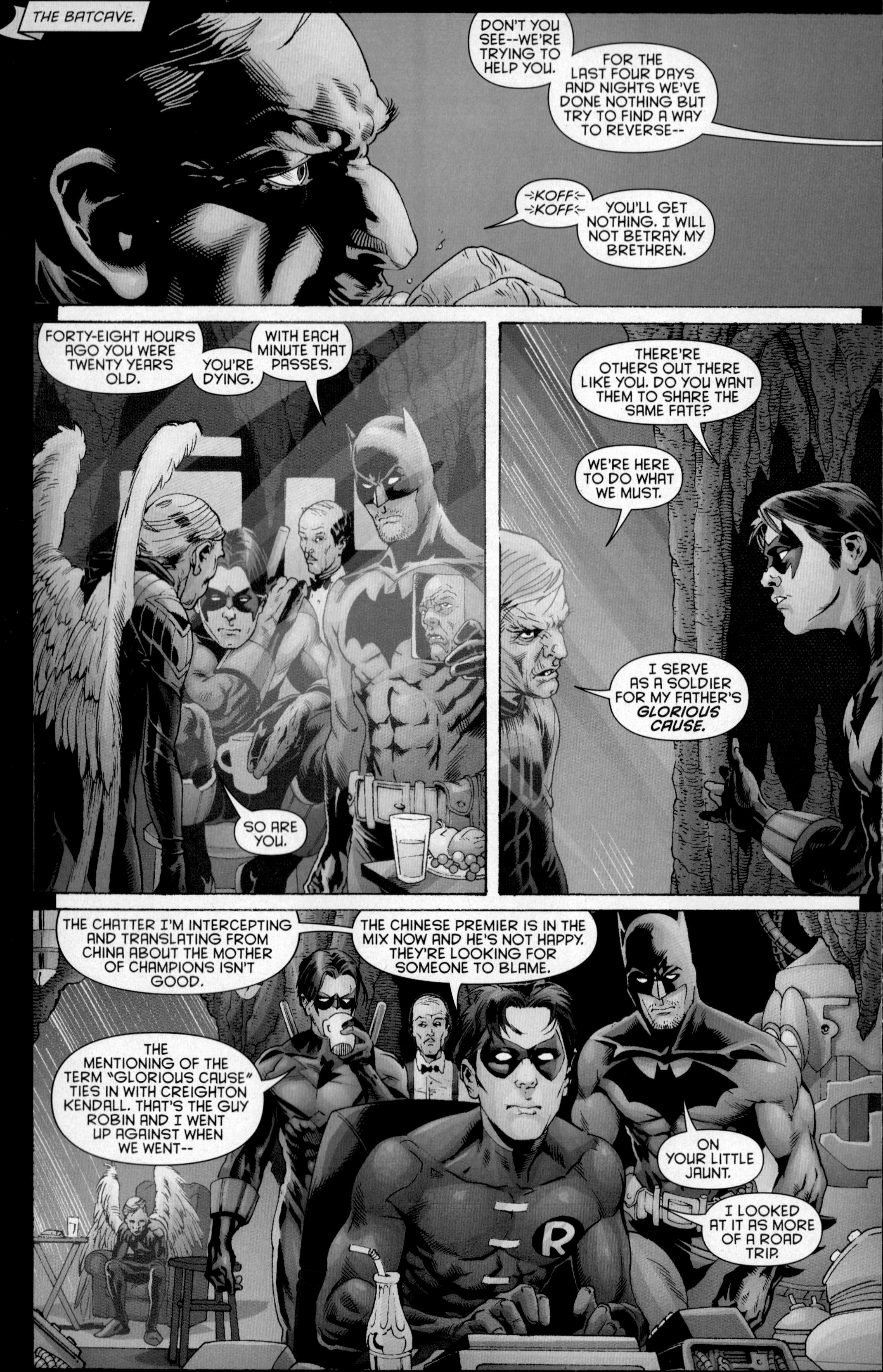
THE BATCAVE.
DON'T YOU SEE--WE'RE TRYING TO HELP YOU.
FOR THE LAST FOUR DAYS AND NIGHTS WE'VE DONE NOTHING BUT TRY TO FIND A WAY TO REVERSE--
KOFF KOFF
YOU'LL GET NOTHING. I WILL NOT BETRAY MY BRETHREN.
FORTY-EIGHT HOURS AGO YOU WERE TWENTY YEARS OLD.
YOU'RE DYING.
WITH EACH MINUTE THAT PASSES.
SO ARE YOU.
THERE'RE OTHERS OUT THERE LIKE YOU. DO YOU WANT THEM TO SHARE THE SAME FATE?
WE'RE HERE TO DO WHAT WE MUST.
I SERVE AS A SOLDIER FOR MY FATHER'S GLORIOUS CAUSE.
THE CHATTER I'M INTERCEPTING AND TRANSLATING FROM CHINA ABOUT THE MOTHER OF CHAMPIONS ISN'T GOOD.
THE CHINESE PREMIER IS IN THE MIX NOW AND HE'S NOT HAPPY. THEY'RE LOOKING FOR SOMEONE TO BLAME.
THE MENTIONING OF THE TERM "GLORIOUS CAUSE" TIES IN WITH CREIGHTON KENDALL. THAT'S THE GUY ROBIN AND I WENT UP AGAINST WHEN WE WENT--
ON YOUR LITTLE JAUNT.
I LOOKED AT IT AS MORE OF A ROAD TRIP.

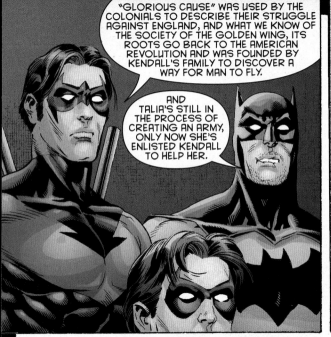

"GLORIOUS CAUSE" WAS USED BY THE COLONIALS TO DESCRIBE THEIR STRUGGLE AGAINST ENGLAND, AND WHAT WE KNOW OF THE SOCIETY OF THE GOLDEN WING, ITS ROOTS GO BACK TO THE AMERICAN REVOLUTION AND WAS FOUNDED BY KENDALL'S FAMILY TO DISCOVER A WAY FOR MAN TO FLY.

AND TALIA'S STILL IN THE PROCESS OF CREATING AN ARMY, ONLY NOW SHE'S ENLISTED KENDALL TO HELP HER.

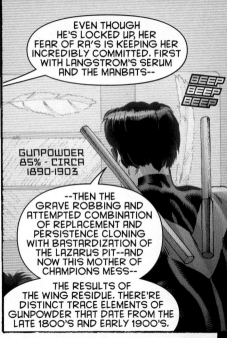

EVEN THOUGH HE'S LOCKED UP, HER FEAR OF RA'S IS KEEPING HER INCREDIBLY COMMITTED. FIRST WITH LANGSTROM'S SERUM AND THE MANBATS--

BEEP BEEP BEEP

GUNPOWDER 85% - CIRCA 1890-1903

--THEN THE GRAVE ROBBING AND ATTEMPTED COMBINATION OF REPLACEMENT AND PERSISTENCE CLONING WITH BASTARDIZATION OF THE LAZARUS PIT--AND NOW THIS MOTHER OF CHAMPIONS MESS--

THE RESULTS OF THE WING RESIDUE. THERE'RE DISTINCT TRACE ELEMENTS OF GUNPOWDER THAT DATE FROM THE LATE 1800'S AND EARLY 1900'S.

I'LL RUN A CROSS-CHECK ON POSSIBLE LOCATIONS.

COMMISSIONER GORDON ON THE EMERGENCY LINE. THERE'S A PROBLEM AT ARKHAM.

OUR MR. KASE--OTHERWISE KNOWN AS RA'S AL GHUL--HAS ESCAPED. THERE ARE FATALITIES.

DAMN IT. HE'S PROBABLY LOST TO THE SHADOWS ALREADY.

TIM AND I WILL FOLLOW UP AT ARKHAM, DICK.

AND I'VE GOT SOMETHING THAT NEEDS TO BE DONE WHILE THE GUNPOWDER LEAD IS PROCESSED.

ALFRED, ATTEND TO OUR GUEST'S NEEDS AND CONTACT ME WHEN THE CROSS-CHECK IS DONE.

FWOOOSH

VROOOM

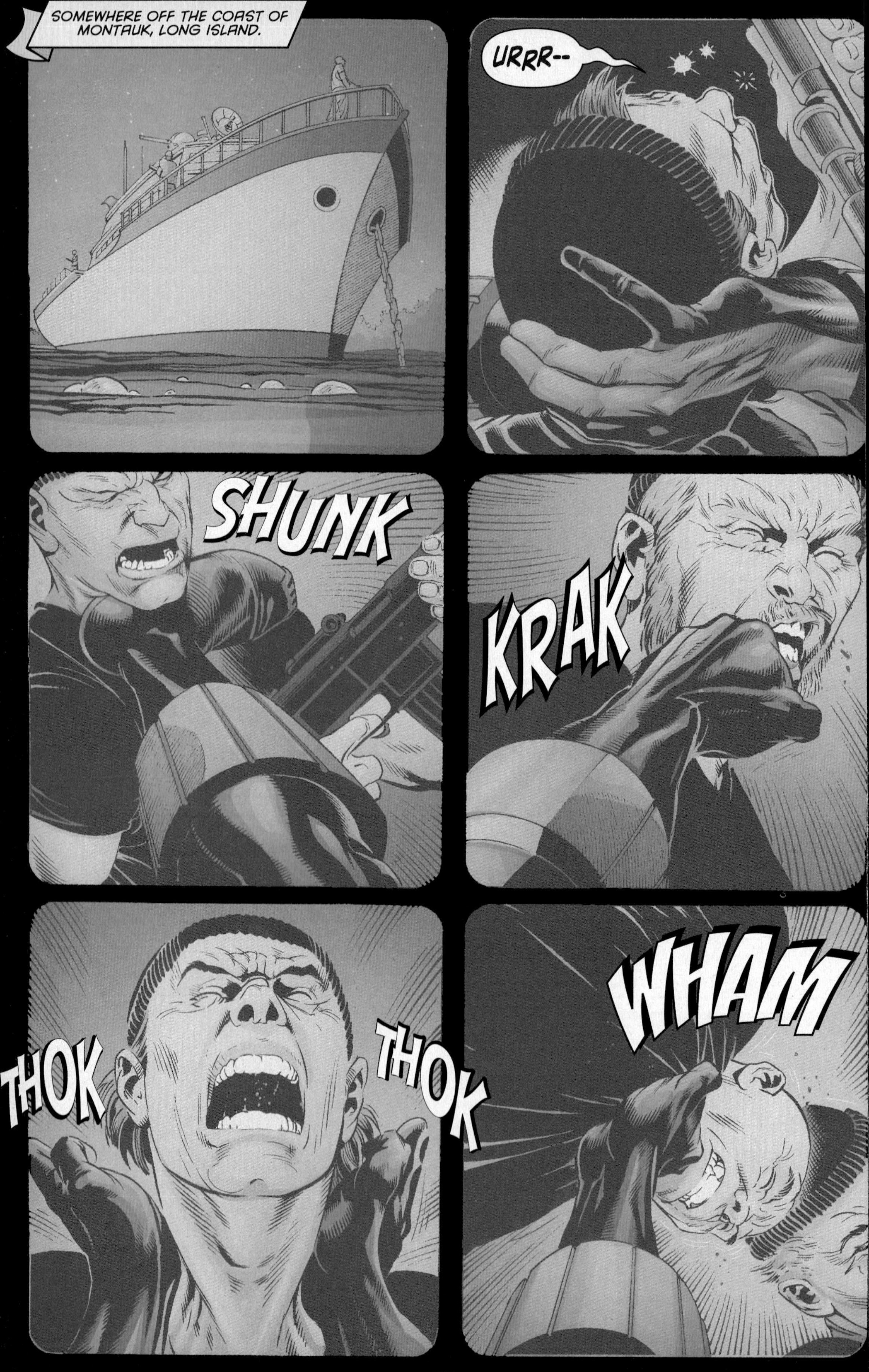
SOMEWHERE OFF THE COAST OF MONTAUK, LONG ISLAND.
URRR--
SHUNK
KRAK
THOK
THOK
WHAM

I HAD A TRAINING MISSION IN PROGRESS-- A SIMPLE SEARCH AND RETRIEVE DIRECTIVE TO ACQUIRE SOME CHEMICALS THAT I REQUIRED--AND I NOW HAVE STANDING IN FRONT OF ME SEVERAL OF OUR BADLY DAMAGED SOLDIERS ALONG WITH ONE MISSING IN ACTION!

I WILL NOT PUT UP WITH THIS MUCH LONGER--IF YOU WISH FOR ME TO CONTINUE, NIGHTWING MUST--

ENOUGH!

I WILL TAKE CARE OF IT.

I SURELY HOPE--

--SO BECAUSE HIS INSINUATION INTO OUR PLANS IS

I NEED YOU TO--

SEVERAL OF YOU ARE SPORTING FRESH BRUISES AND FACIAL CONTU-SIONS.

WHY IS THAT?

I APOLOGIZE, MISS TALIA, THERE WAS A DISAGREE-MENT BELOW DECK LAST NIGHT--AND SOME OF US RESORTED TO--

SEE TO IT THAT IT NEVER HAPPENS AGAIN OR YOU WILL FIND YOURSELF FLOATING ON THE OPEN WATER AS SHARK BAIT, UNDERSTOOD?

I WILL NOT STAND FOR HOSTILITY AMID THE RANKS.

YES, MA'AM.

HERE IS THE INFORMATION.

GET HER AND BRING HER HERE.

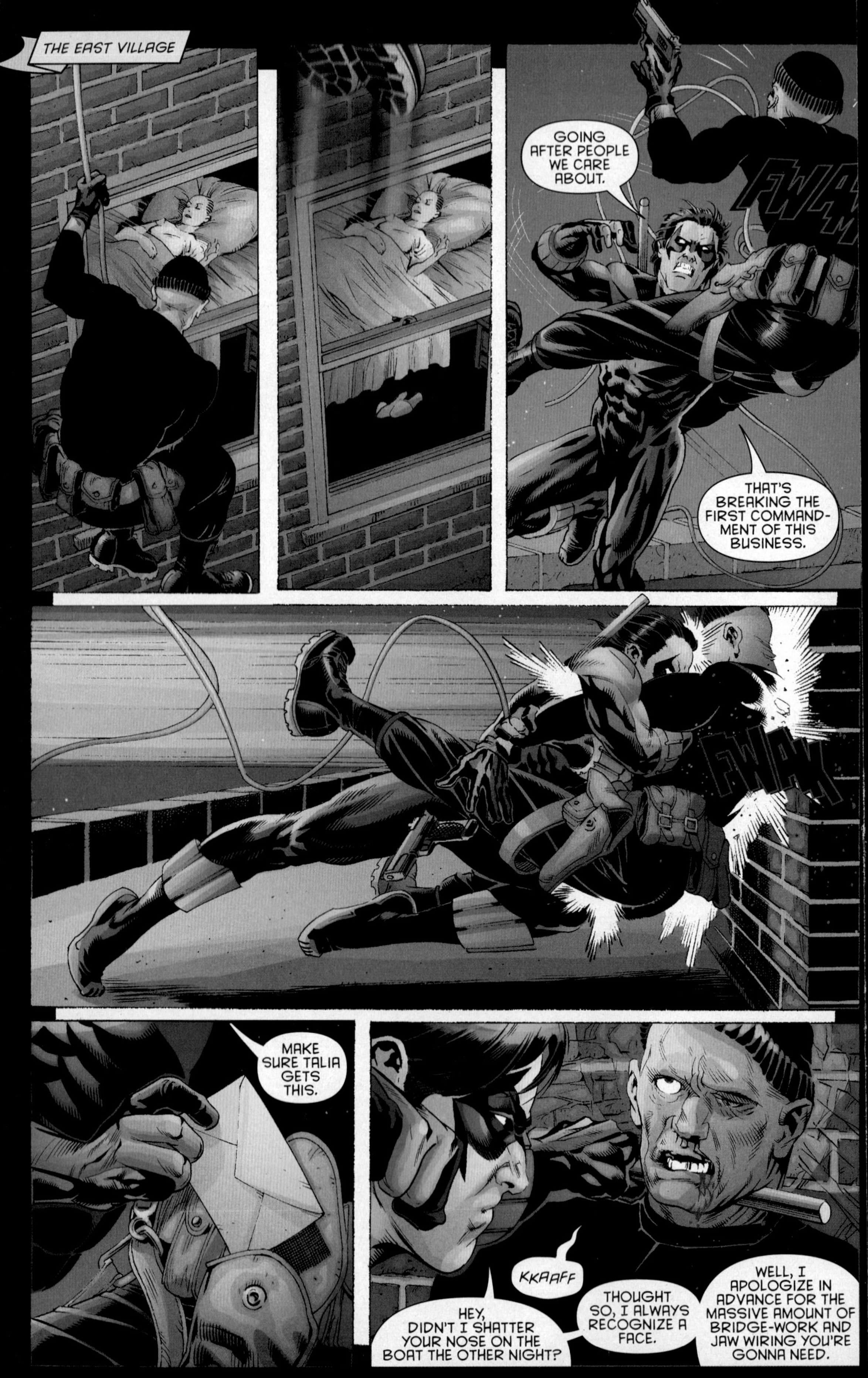
THE EAST VILLAGE
GOING AFTER PEOPLE WE CARE ABOUT.
FWAK
THAT'S BREAKING THE FIRST COMMAND-MENT OF THIS BUSINESS.
FWAK
MAKE SURE TALIA GETS THIS.
KKAAFF
HEY, DIDN'T I SHATTER YOUR NOSE ON THE BOAT THE OTHER NIGHT?
THOUGHT SO, I ALWAYS RECOGNIZE A FACE.
WELL, I APOLOGIZE IN ADVANCE FOR THE MASSIVE AMOUNT OF BRIDGE-WORK AND JAW WIRING YOU'RE GONNA NEED.

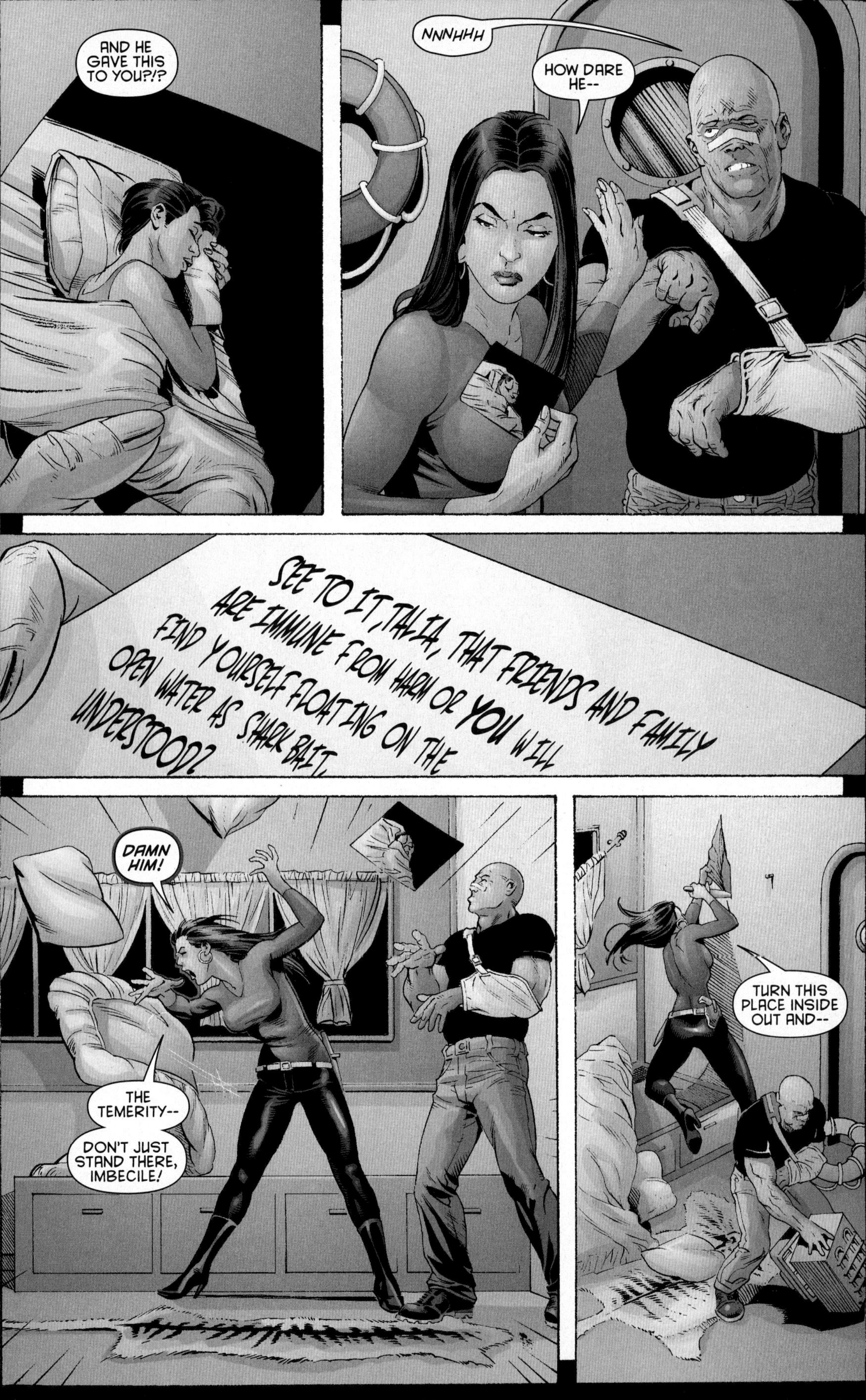
AND HE GAVE THIS TO YOU?!?
NNNHHH
HOW DARE HE--
SEE TO IT, TALIA, THAT FRIENDS AND FAMILY ARE IMMUNE FROM HARM OR YOU WILL FIND YOURSELF FLOATING ON THE OPEN WATER AS SHARK BAIT. UNDERSTOOD?
DAMN HIM!
THE TEMERITY--
DON'T JUST STAND THERE, IMBECILE!
TURN THIS PLACE INSIDE OUT AND--

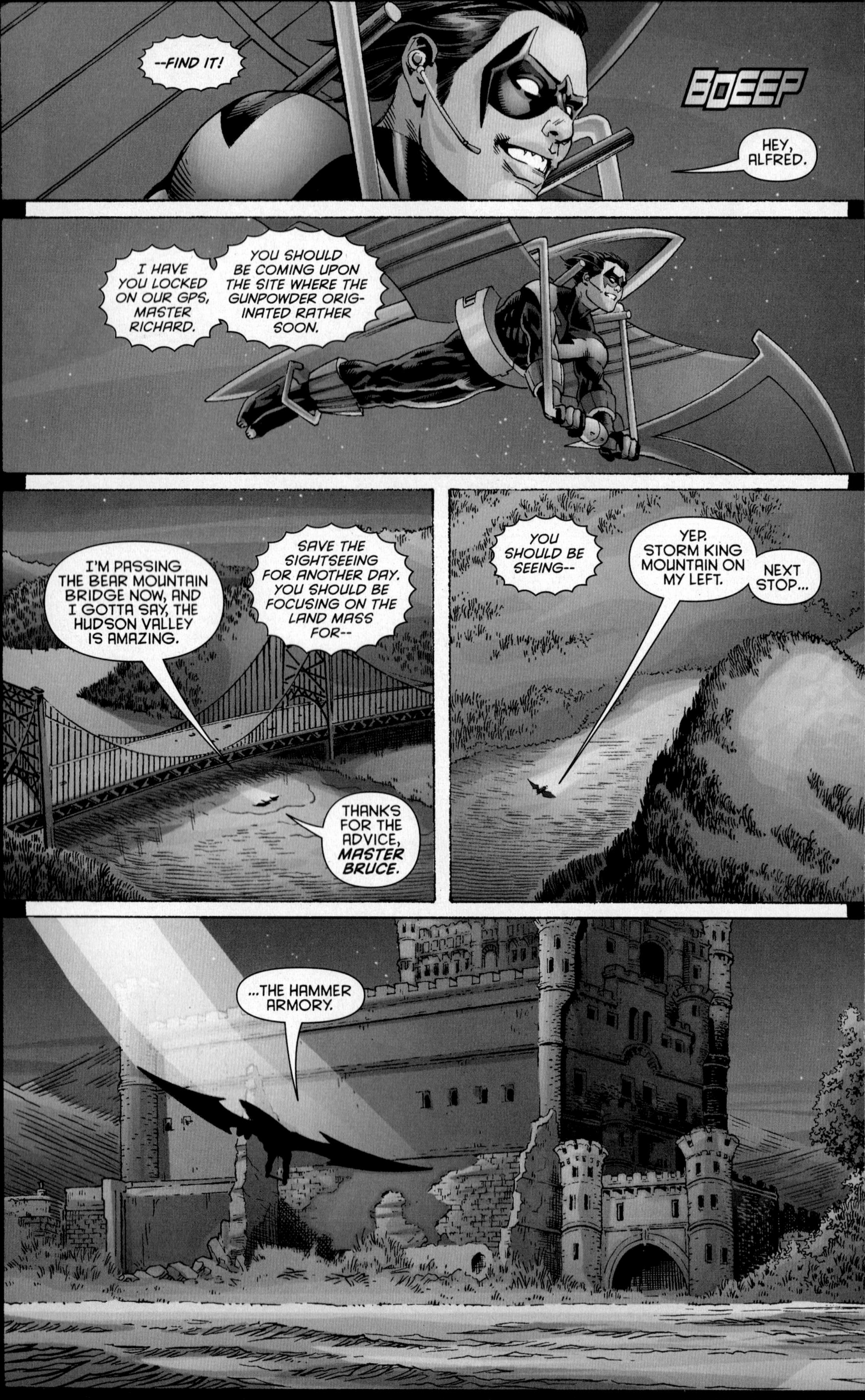
--FIND IT!
BDEEP
HEY, ALFRED.
I HAVE YOU LOCKED ON OUR GPS, MASTER RICHARD.
YOU SHOULD BE COMING UPON THE SITE WHERE THE GUNPOWDER ORIGINATED RATHER SOON.
I'M PASSING THE BEAR MOUNTAIN BRIDGE NOW, AND I GOTTA SAY, THE HUDSON VALLEY IS AMAZING.
SAVE THE SIGHTSEEING FOR ANOTHER DAY. YOU SHOULD BE FOCUSING ON THE LAND MASS FOR--
THANKS FOR THE ADVICE, MASTER BRUCE.
YOU SHOULD BE SEEING--
YEP. STORM KING MOUNTAIN ON MY LEFT.
NEXT STOP...
...THE HAMMER ARMORY.

NIGHTWING #146
Cover art by Andy Kubert

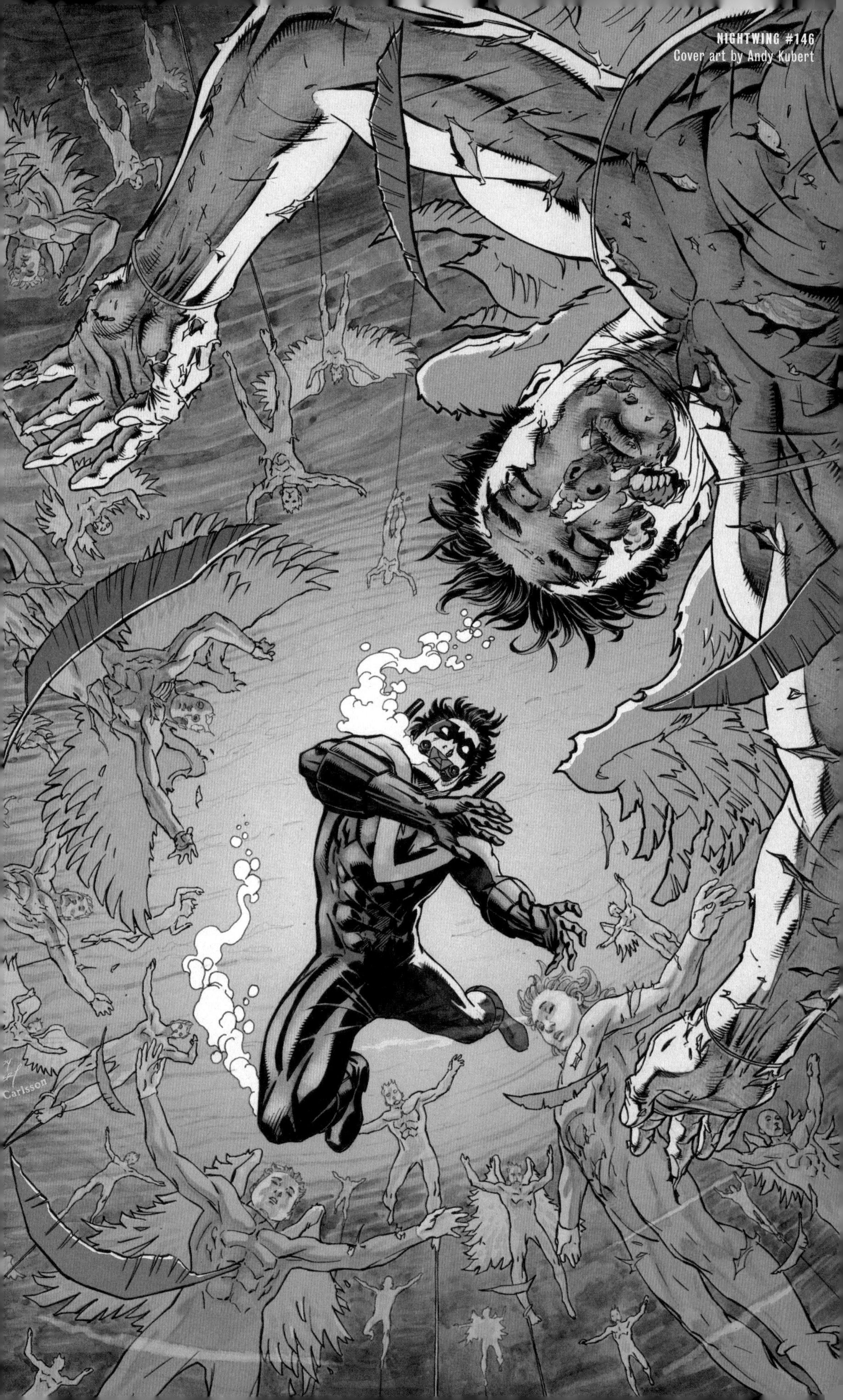
Carlsson

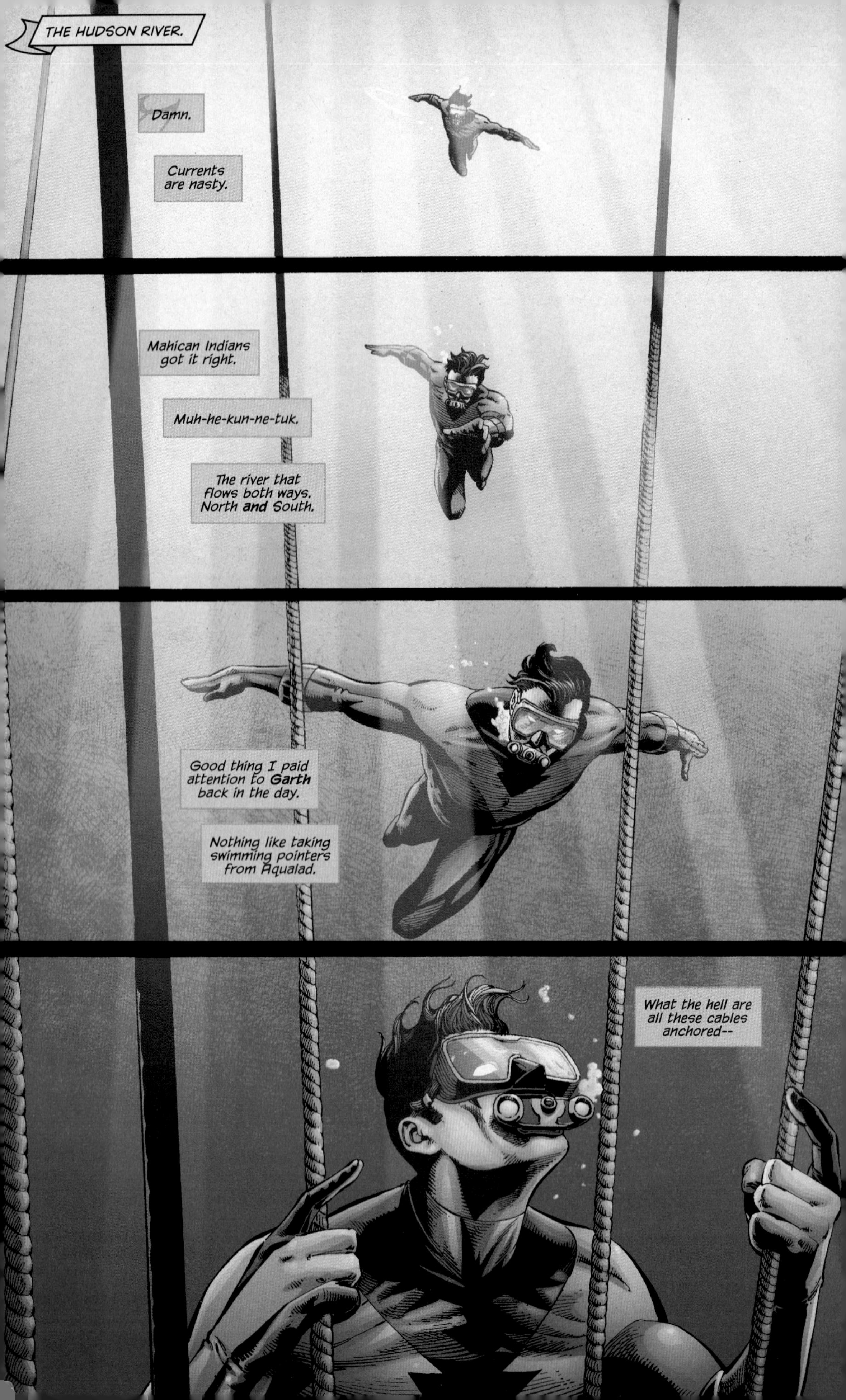
THE HUDSON RIVER.
Damn.
Currents are nasty.
Mahican Indians got it right.
Muh-he-kun-ne-tuk.
The river that flows both ways. North and South.
Good thing I paid attention to Garth back in the day.
Nothing like taking swimming pointers from Aqualad.
What the hell are all these cables anchored--

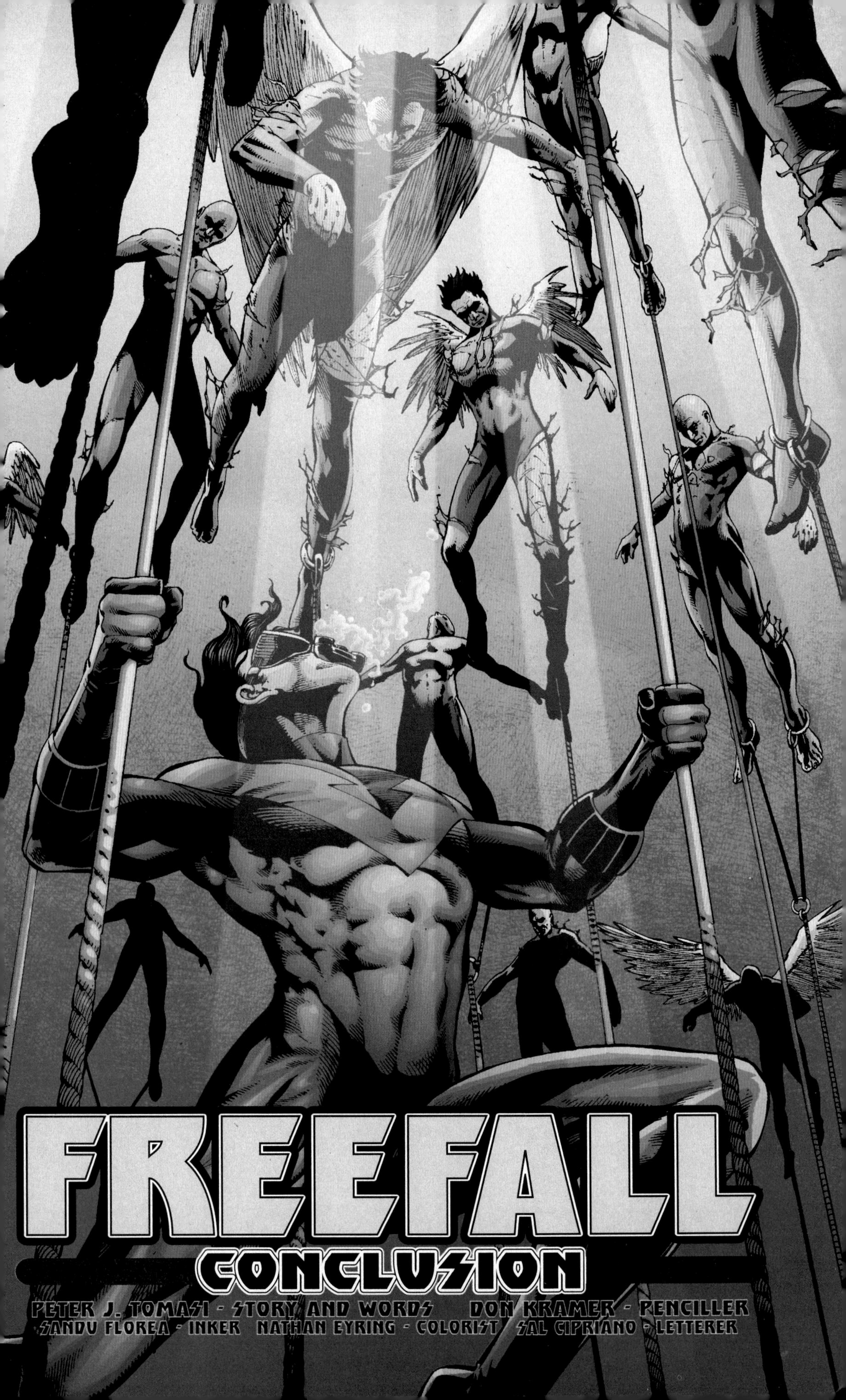
FREEFALL
CONCLUSION
PETER J. TOMASI - STORY AND WORDS
DON KRAMER - PENCILLER
SANDU FLOREA - INKER
NATHAN EYRING - COLORIST
SAL CIPRIANO - LETTERER

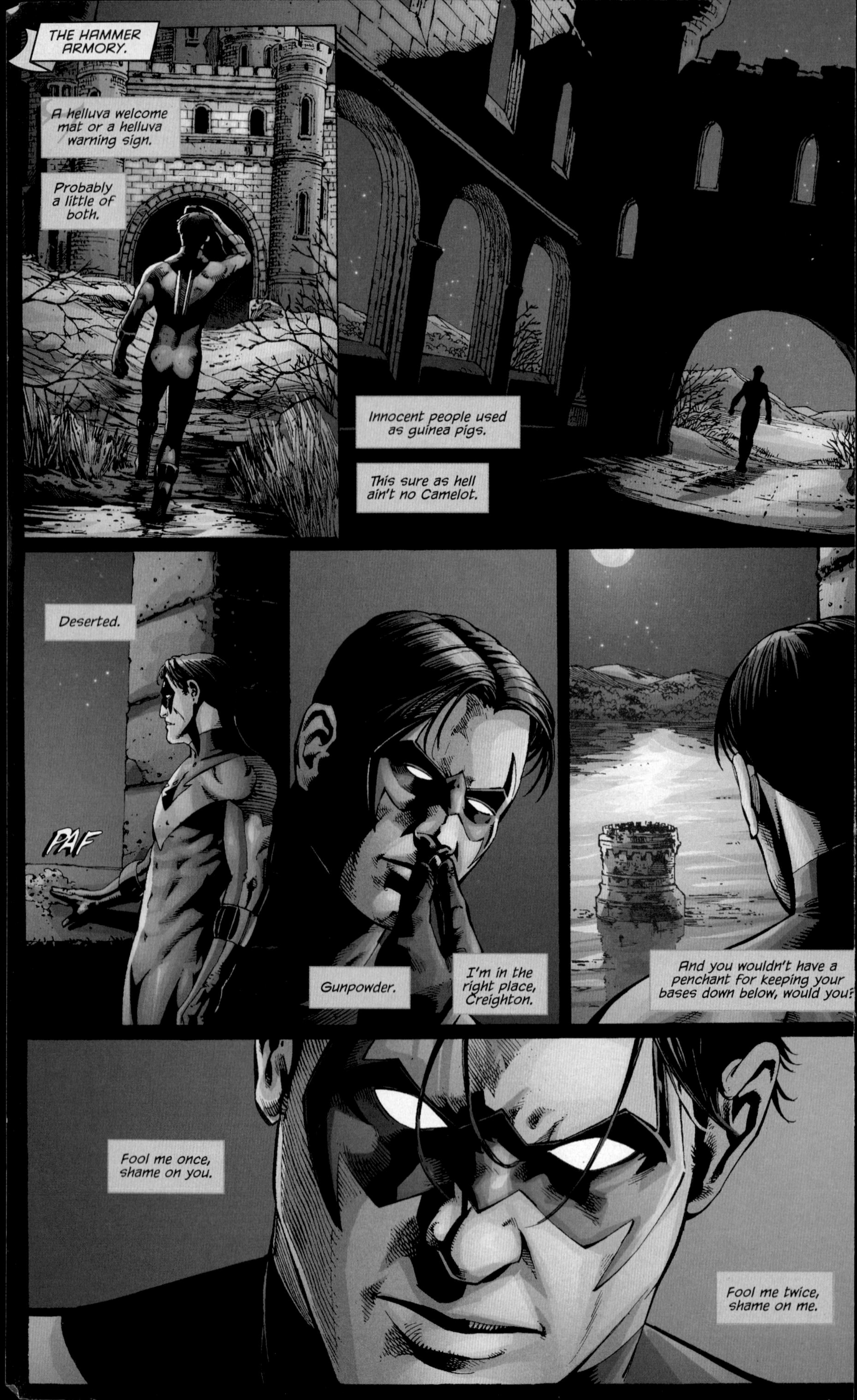
THE HAMMER ARMORY.
A helluva welcome mat or a helluva warning sign.
Probably a little of both.
Innocent people used as guinea pigs.
This sure as hell ain't no Camelot.
Deserted.
PAF
Gunpowder.
I'm in the right place, Creighton.
And you wouldn't have a penchant for keeping your bases down below, would you?
Fool me once, shame on you.
Fool me twice, shame on me.

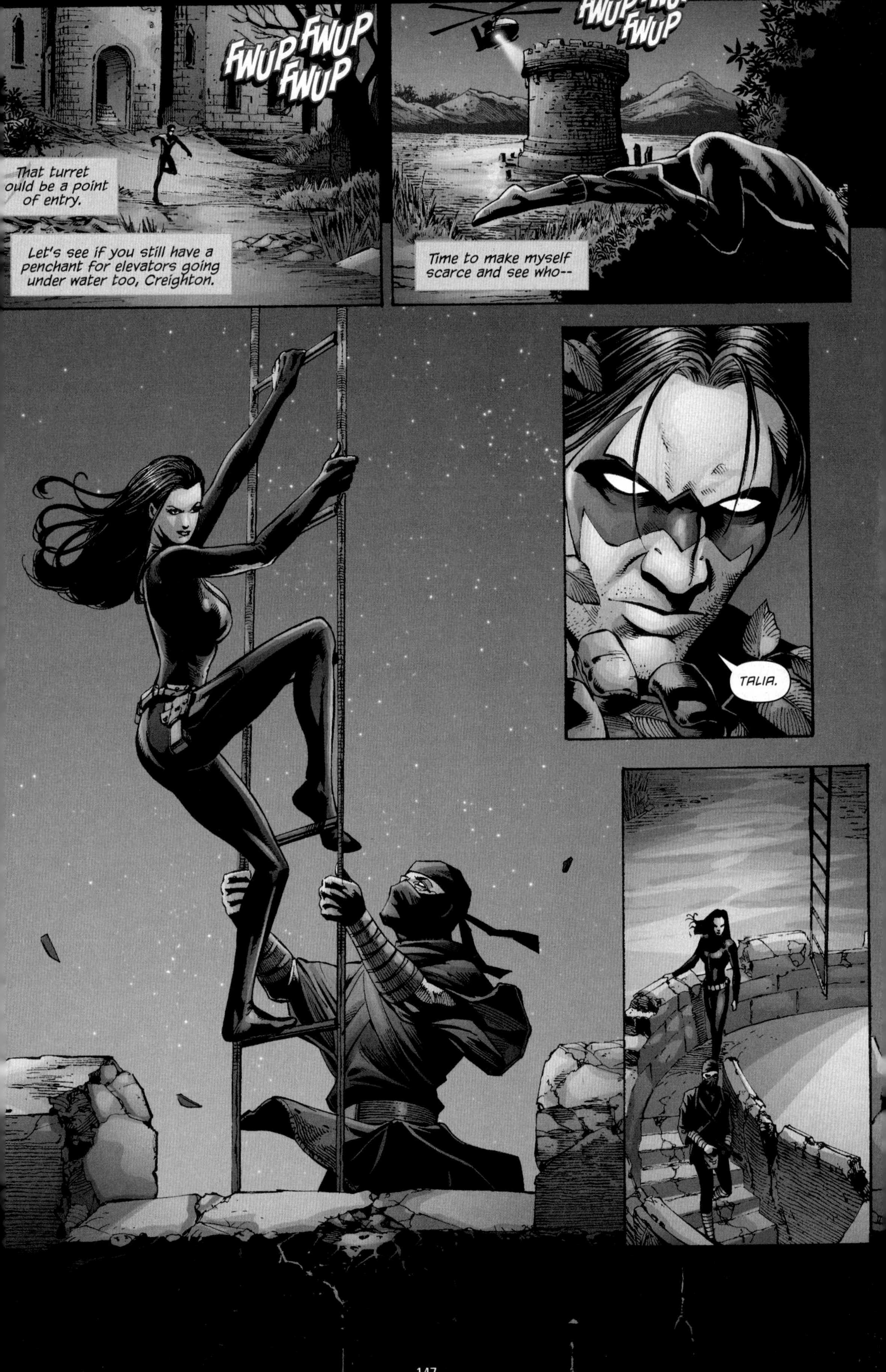
FWUP FWUP
FWUP
That turret ould be a point of entry.
Let's see if you still have a penchant for elevators going under water too, Creighton.
FWUP FWUP
FWUP
Time to make myself scarce and see who--
TALIA.

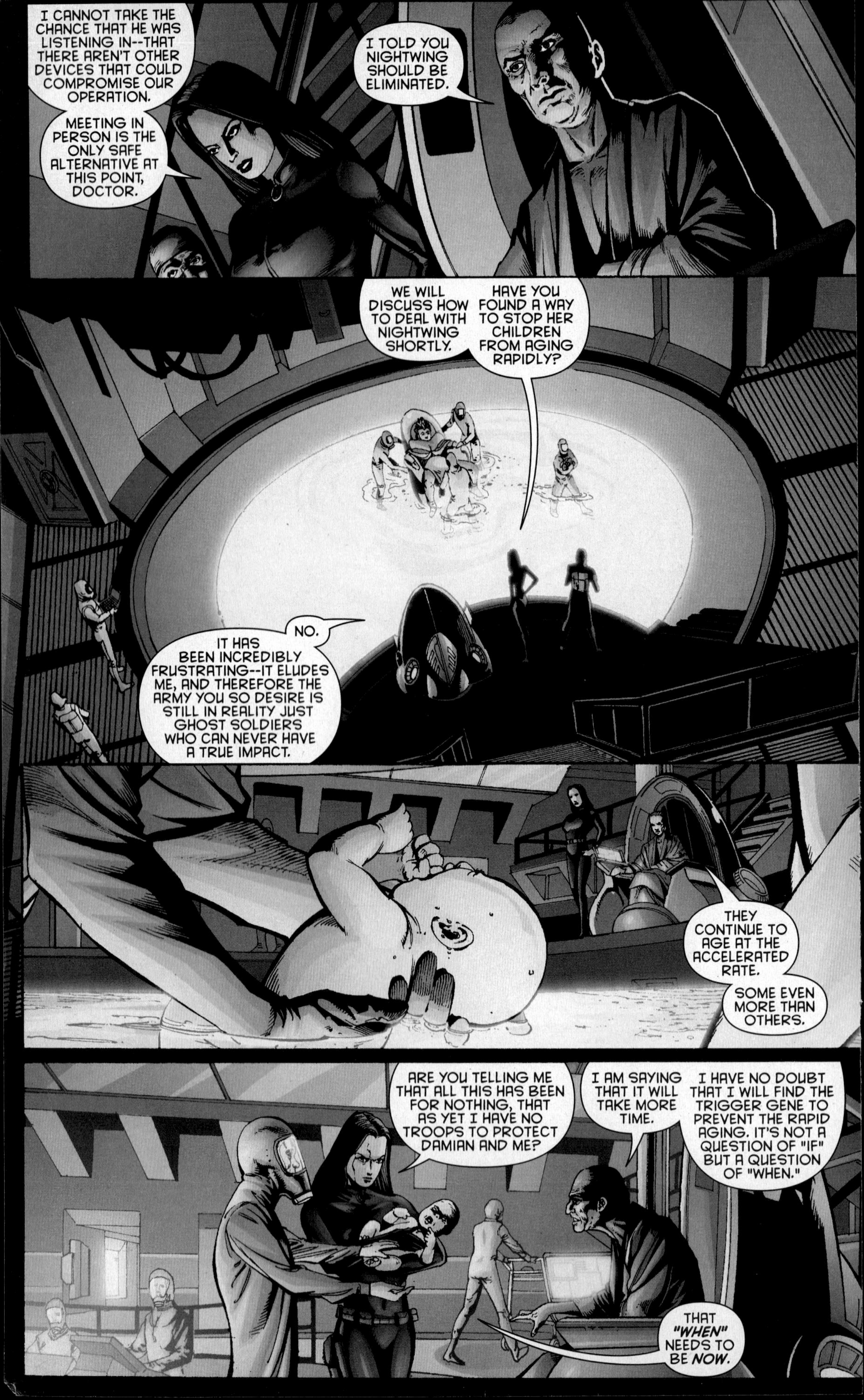
I CANNOT TAKE THE CHANCE THAT HE WAS LISTENING IN--THAT THERE AREN'T OTHER DEVICES THAT COULD COMPROMISE OUR OPERATION.
MEETING IN PERSON IS THE ONLY SAFE ALTERNATIVE AT THIS POINT, DOCTOR.
I TOLD YOU NIGHTWING SHOULD BE ELIMINATED.
WE WILL DISCUSS HOW TO DEAL WITH NIGHTWING SHORTLY.
HAVE YOU FOUND A WAY TO STOP HER CHILDREN FROM AGING RAPIDLY?
NO.
IT HAS BEEN INCREDIBLY FRUSTRATING--IT ELUDES ME, AND THEREFORE THE ARMY YOU SO DESIRE IS STILL IN REALITY JUST GHOST SOLDIERS WHO CAN NEVER HAVE A TRUE IMPACT.
THEY CONTINUE TO AGE AT THE ACCELERATED RATE.
SOME EVEN MORE THAN OTHERS.
ARE YOU TELLING ME THAT ALL THIS HAS BEEN FOR NOTHING, THAT AS YET I HAVE NO TROOPS TO PROTECT DAMIAN AND ME?
I AM SAYING THAT IT WILL TAKE MORE TIME.
I HAVE NO DOUBT THAT I WILL FIND THE TRIGGER GENE TO PREVENT THE RAPID AGING. IT'S NOT A QUESTION OF "IF" BUT A QUESTION OF "WHEN."
THAT *"WHEN"* NEEDS TO BE ***NOW***.

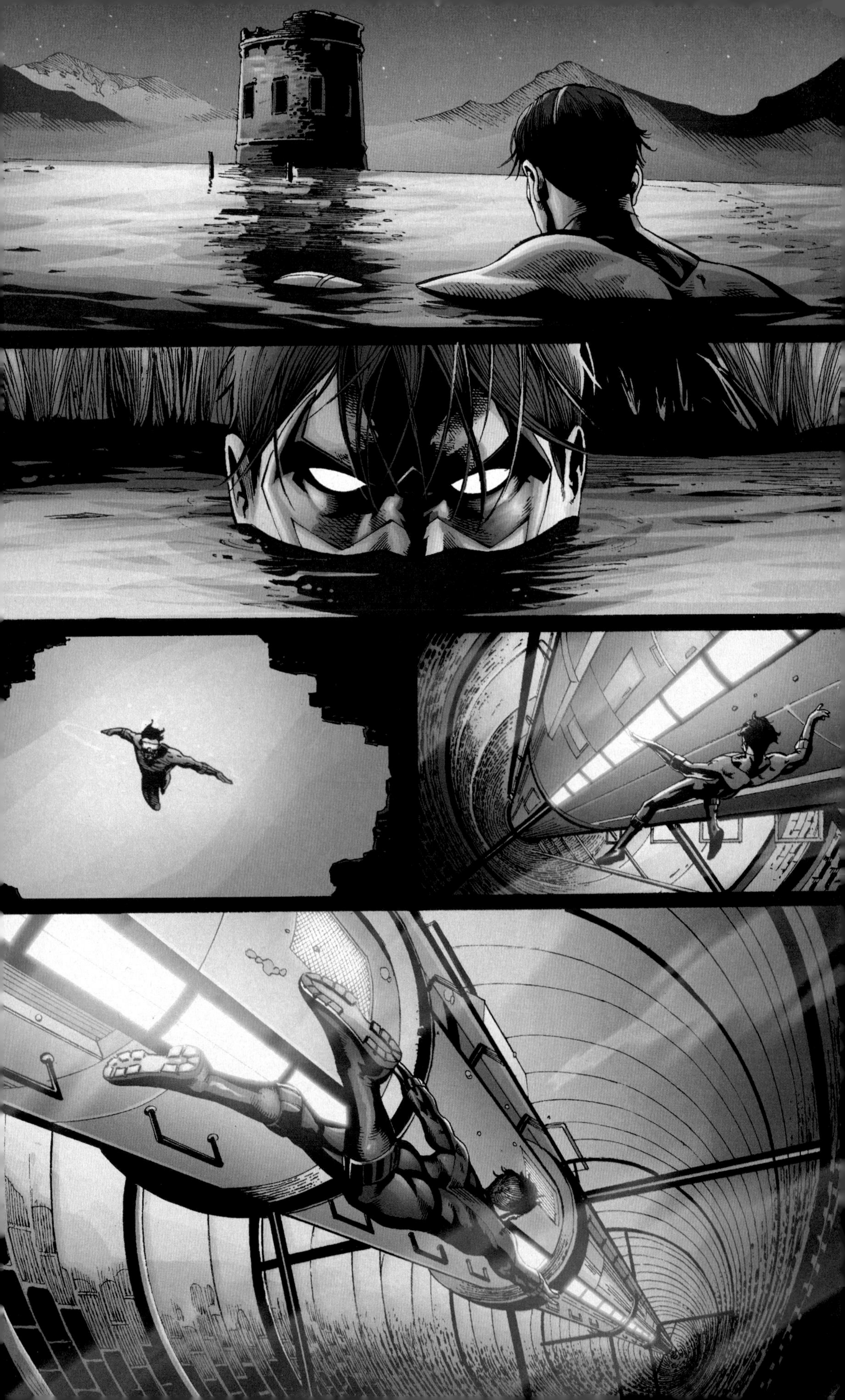

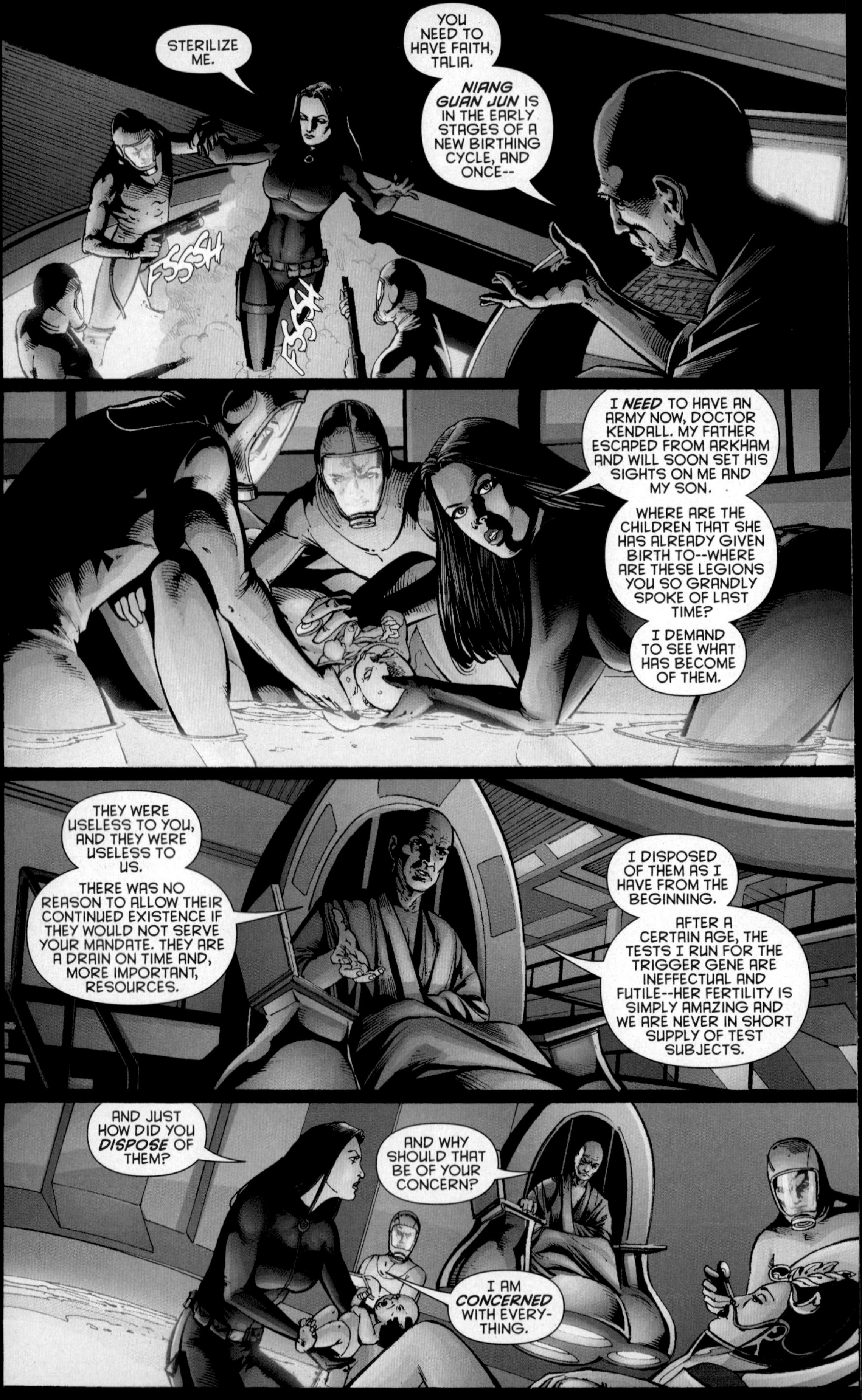
STERILIZE ME.
YOU NEED TO HAVE FAITH, TALIA.
NIANG GUAN JUN IS IN THE EARLY STAGES OF A NEW BIRTHING CYCLE, AND ONCE--
FSSSH
FSSSH
I NEED TO HAVE AN ARMY NOW, DOCTOR KENDALL. MY FATHER ESCAPED FROM ARKHAM AND WILL SOON SET HIS SIGHTS ON ME AND MY SON.
WHERE ARE THE CHILDREN THAT SHE HAS ALREADY GIVEN BIRTH TO--WHERE ARE THESE LEGIONS YOU SO GRANDLY SPOKE OF LAST TIME?
I DEMAND TO SEE WHAT HAS BECOME OF THEM.
THEY WERE USELESS TO YOU, AND THEY WERE USELESS TO US.
THERE WAS NO REASON TO ALLOW THEIR CONTINUED EXISTENCE IF THEY WOULD NOT SERVE YOUR MANDATE. THEY ARE A DRAIN ON TIME AND, MORE IMPORTANT, RESOURCES.
I DISPOSED OF THEM AS I HAVE FROM THE BEGINNING.
AFTER A CERTAIN AGE, THE TESTS I RUN FOR THE TRIGGER GENE ARE INEFFECTUAL AND FUTILE--HER FERTILITY IS SIMPLY AMAZING AND WE ARE NEVER IN SHORT SUPPLY OF TEST SUBJECTS.
AND JUST HOW DID YOU DISPOSE OF THEM?
AND WHY SHOULD THAT BE OF YOUR CONCERN?
I AM CONCERNED WITH EVERY-THING.

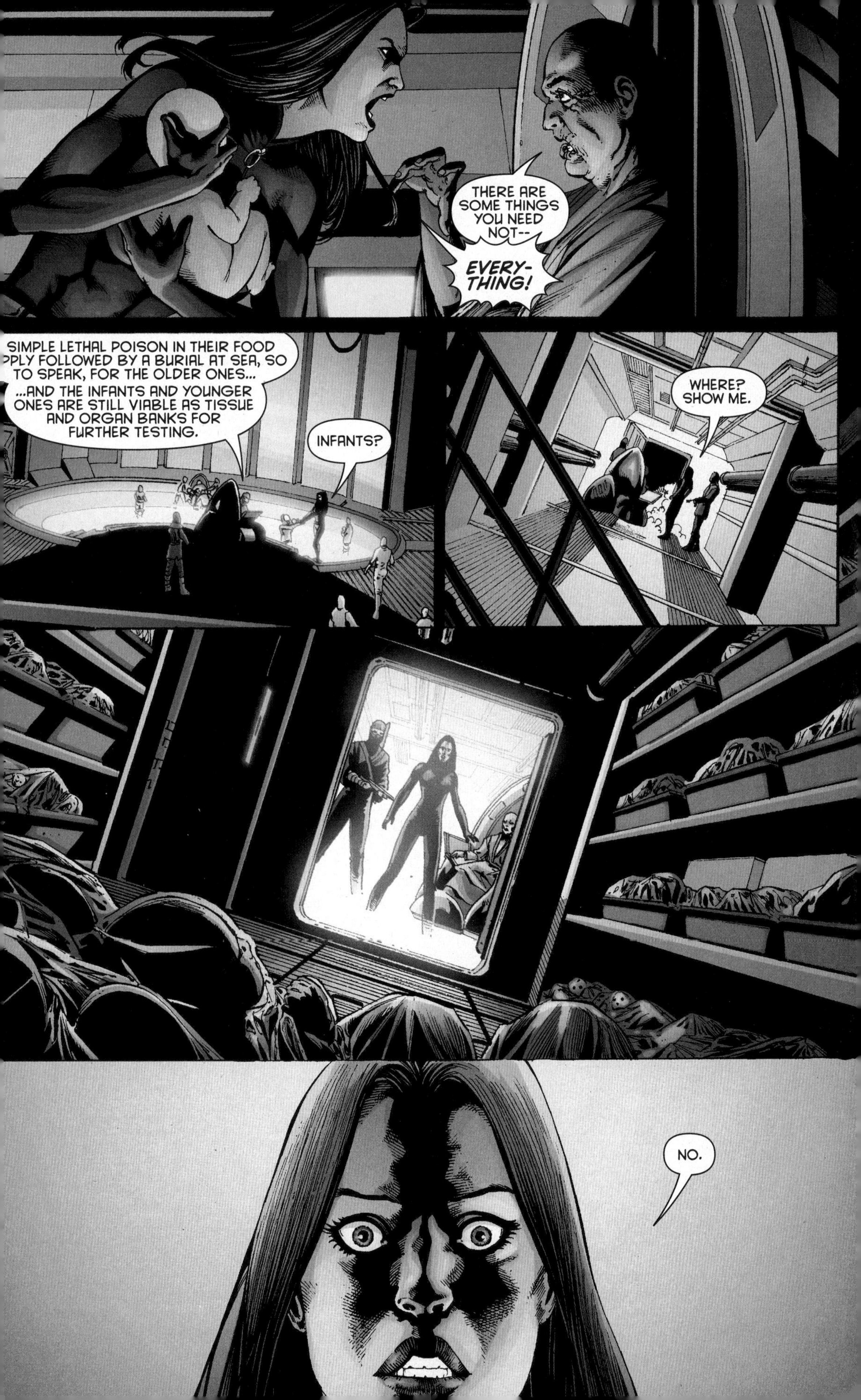
THERE ARE SOME THINGS YOU NEED NOT--
EVERY-THING!
SIMPLE LETHAL POISON IN THEIR FOOD PPLY FOLLOWED BY A BURIAL AT SEA, SO TO SPEAK, FOR THE OLDER ONES...
...AND THE INFANTS AND YOUNGER ONES ARE STILL VIABLE AS TISSUE AND ORGAN BANKS FOR FURTHER TESTING.
INFANTS?
WHERE? SHOW ME.
NO.

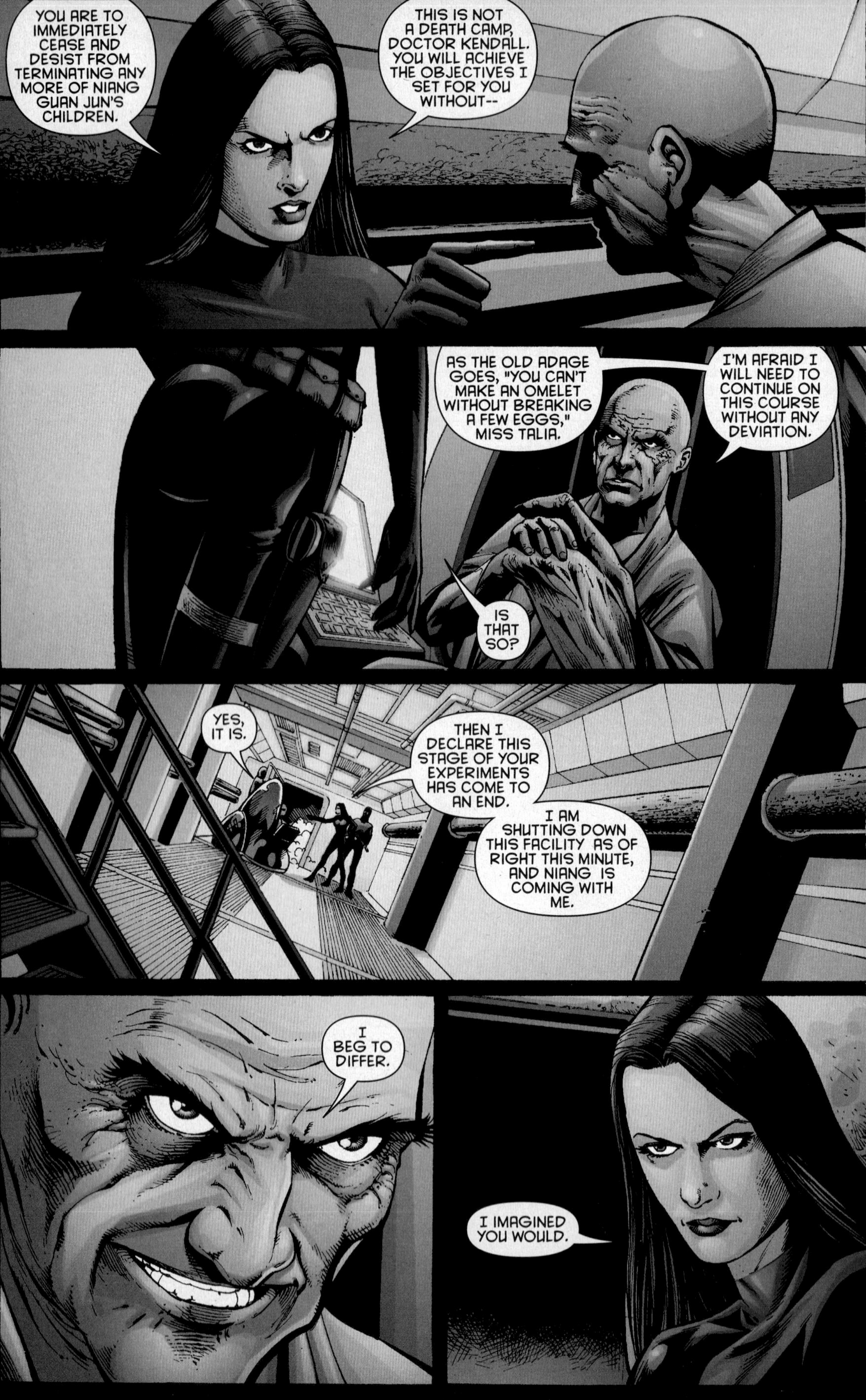
YOU ARE TO IMMEDIATELY CEASE AND DESIST FROM TERMINATING ANY MORE OF NIANG GUAN JUN'S CHILDREN.
THIS IS NOT A DEATH CAMP, DOCTOR KENDALL. YOU WILL ACHIEVE THE OBJECTIVES I SET FOR YOU WITHOUT--
AS THE OLD ADAGE GOES, "YOU CAN'T MAKE AN OMELET WITHOUT BREAKING A FEW EGGS," MISS TALIA.
I'M AFRAID I WILL NEED TO CONTINUE ON THIS COURSE WITHOUT ANY DEVIATION.
IS THAT SO?
YES, IT IS.
THEN I DECLARE THIS STAGE OF YOUR EXPERIMENTS HAS COME TO AN END.
I AM SHUTTING DOWN THIS FACILITY AS OF RIGHT THIS MINUTE, AND NIANG IS COMING WITH ME.
I BEG TO DIFFER.
I IMAGINED YOU WOULD.

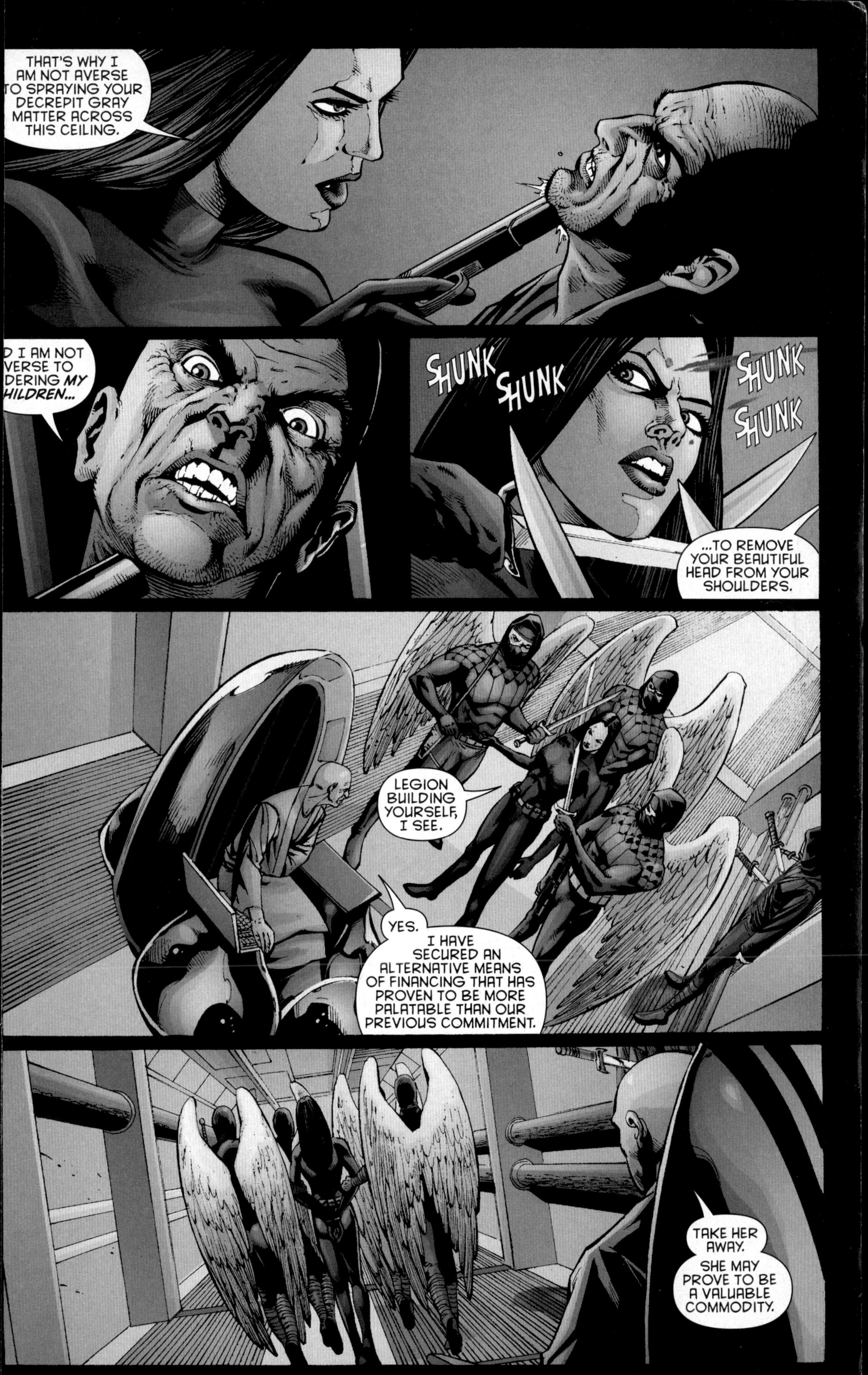
THAT'S WHY I AM NOT AVERSE TO SPRAYING YOUR DECREPIT GRAY MATTER ACROSS THIS CEILING.
D I AM NOT VERSE TO DERING *MY HILDREN...*
SHUNK SHUNK
SHUNK SHUNK
...TO REMOVE YOUR BEAUTIFUL HEAD FROM YOUR SHOULDERS.
LEGION BUILDING YOURSELF, I SEE.
YES.
I HAVE SECURED AN ALTERNATIVE MEANS OF FINANCING THAT HAS PROVEN TO BE MORE PALATABLE THAN OUR PREVIOUS COMMITMENT.
TAKE HER AWAY.
SHE MAY PROVE TO BE A VALUABLE COMMODITY.

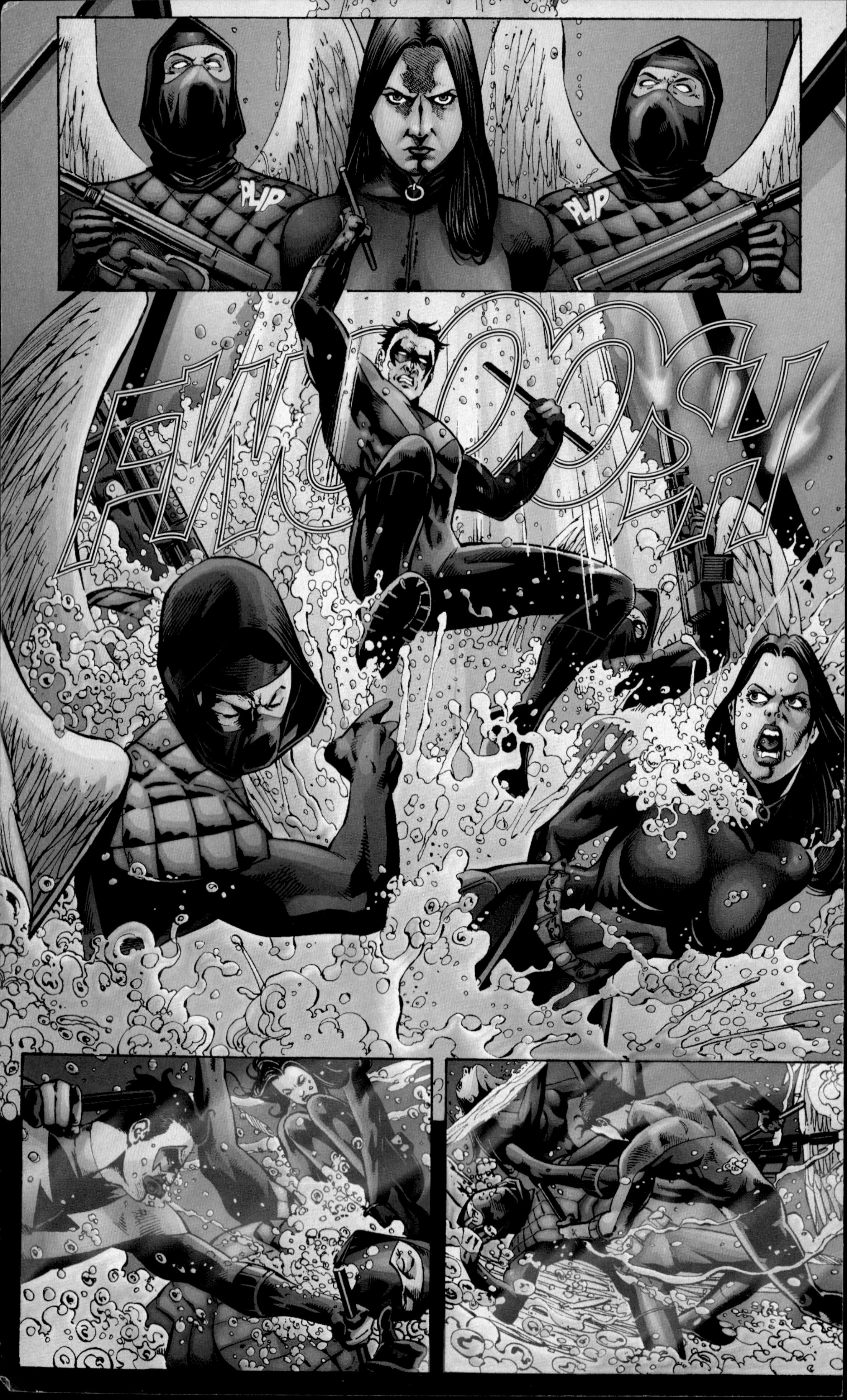
PLIP
PLIP
FWOOSH

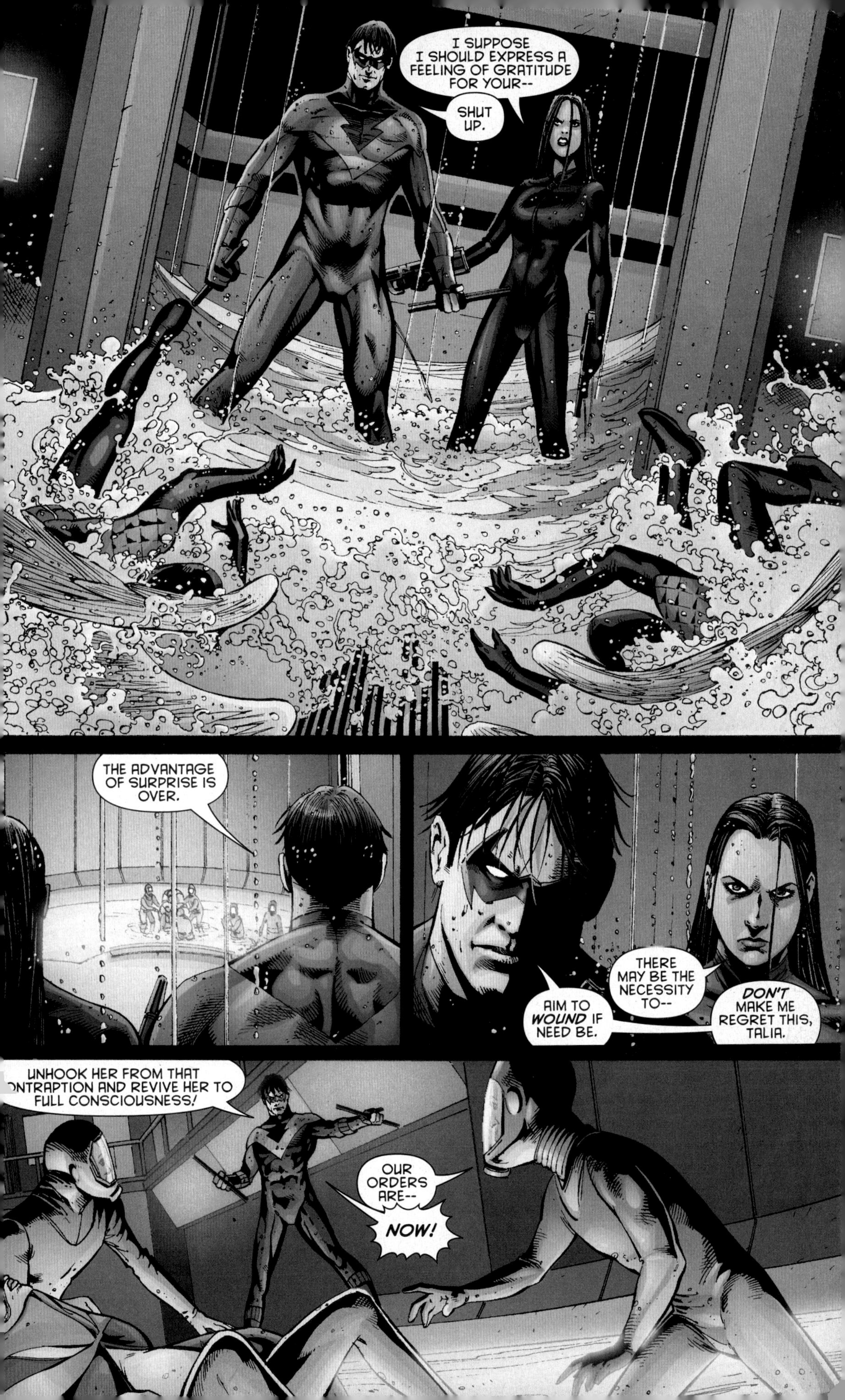

I SUPPOSE I SHOULD EXPRESS A FEELING OF GRATITUDE FOR YOUR--
SHUT UP.
THE ADVANTAGE OF SURPRISE IS OVER.
THERE MAY BE THE NECESSITY TO--
AIM TO *WOUND* IF NEED BE.
DON'T MAKE ME REGRET THIS, TALIA.
UNHOOK HER FROM THAT ONTRAPTION AND REVIVE HER TO FULL CONSCIOUSNESS!
OUR ORDERS ARE--
NOW!

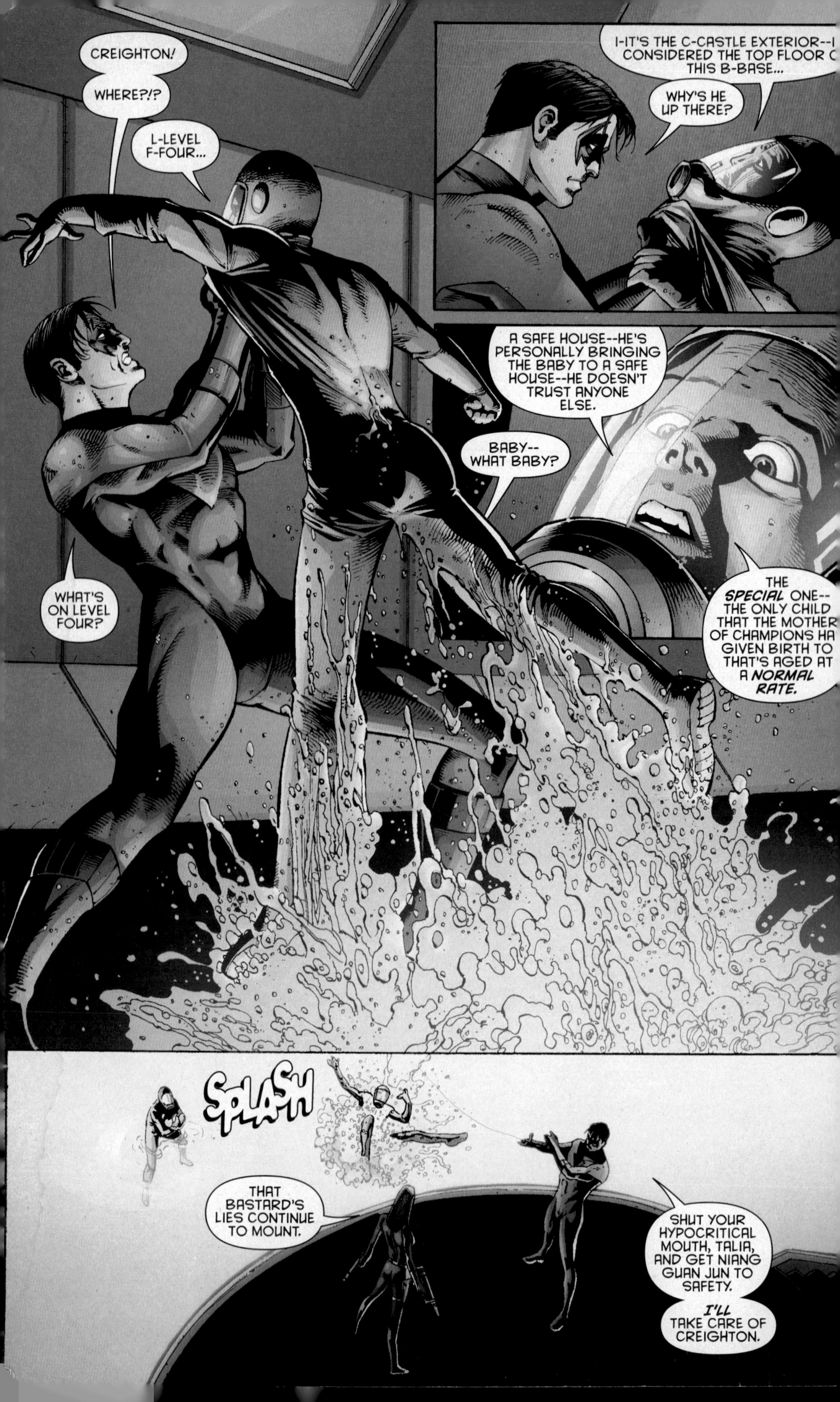
CREIGHTON!
WHERE?!?
L-LEVEL F-FOUR...
I-IT'S THE C-CASTLE EXTERIOR--I CONSIDERED THE TOP FLOOR O THIS B-BASE...
WHY'S HE UP THERE?
A SAFE HOUSE--HE'S PERSONALLY BRINGING THE BABY TO A SAFE HOUSE--HE DOESN'T TRUST ANYONE ELSE.
BABY-- WHAT BABY?
WHAT'S ON LEVEL FOUR?
THE SPECIAL ONE-- THE ONLY CHILD THAT THE MOTHER OF CHAMPIONS HA GIVEN BIRTH TO THAT'S AGED AT A NORMAL RATE.
SPLASH
THAT BASTARD'S LIES CONTINUE TO MOUNT.
SHUT YOUR HYPOCRITICAL MOUTH, TALIA, AND GET NIANG GUAN JUN TO SAFETY.
I'LL TAKE CARE OF CREIGHTON.

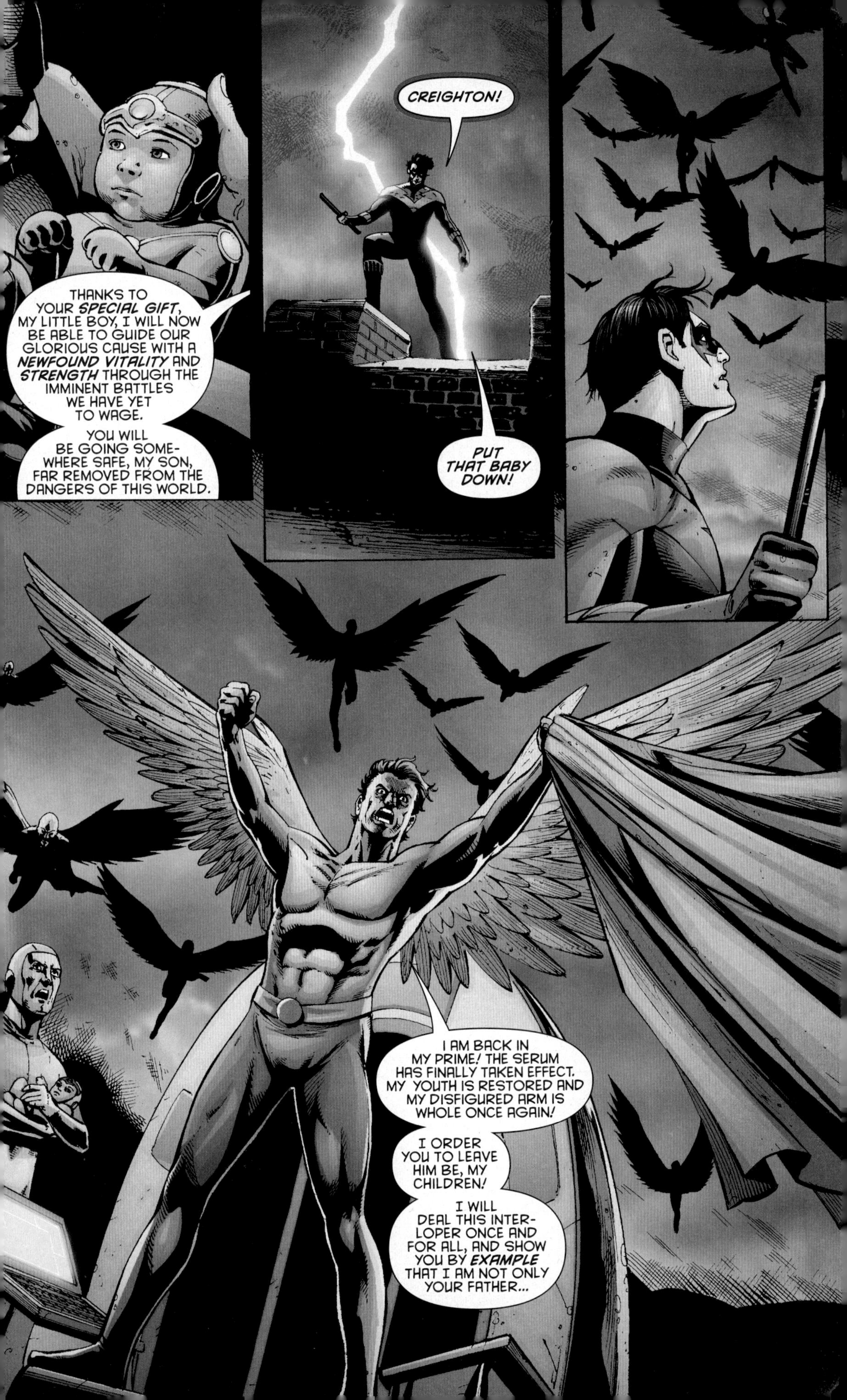
THANKS TO YOUR SPECIAL GIFT, MY LITTLE BOY, I WILL NOW BE ABLE TO GUIDE OUR GLORIOUS CAUSE WITH A NEWFOUND VITALITY AND STRENGTH THROUGH THE IMMINENT BATTLES WE HAVE YET TO WAGE.
YOU WILL BE GOING SOME-WHERE SAFE, MY SON, FAR REMOVED FROM THE DANGERS OF THIS WORLD.
CREIGHTON!
PUT THAT BABY DOWN!
I AM BACK IN MY PRIME! THE SERUM HAS FINALLY TAKEN EFFECT. MY YOUTH IS RESTORED AND MY DISFIGURED ARM IS WHOLE ONCE AGAIN!
I ORDER YOU TO LEAVE HIM BE, MY CHILDREN!
I WILL DEAL THIS INTER-LOPER ONCE AND FOR ALL, AND SHOW YOU BY EXAMPLE THAT I AM NOT ONLY YOUR FATHER...

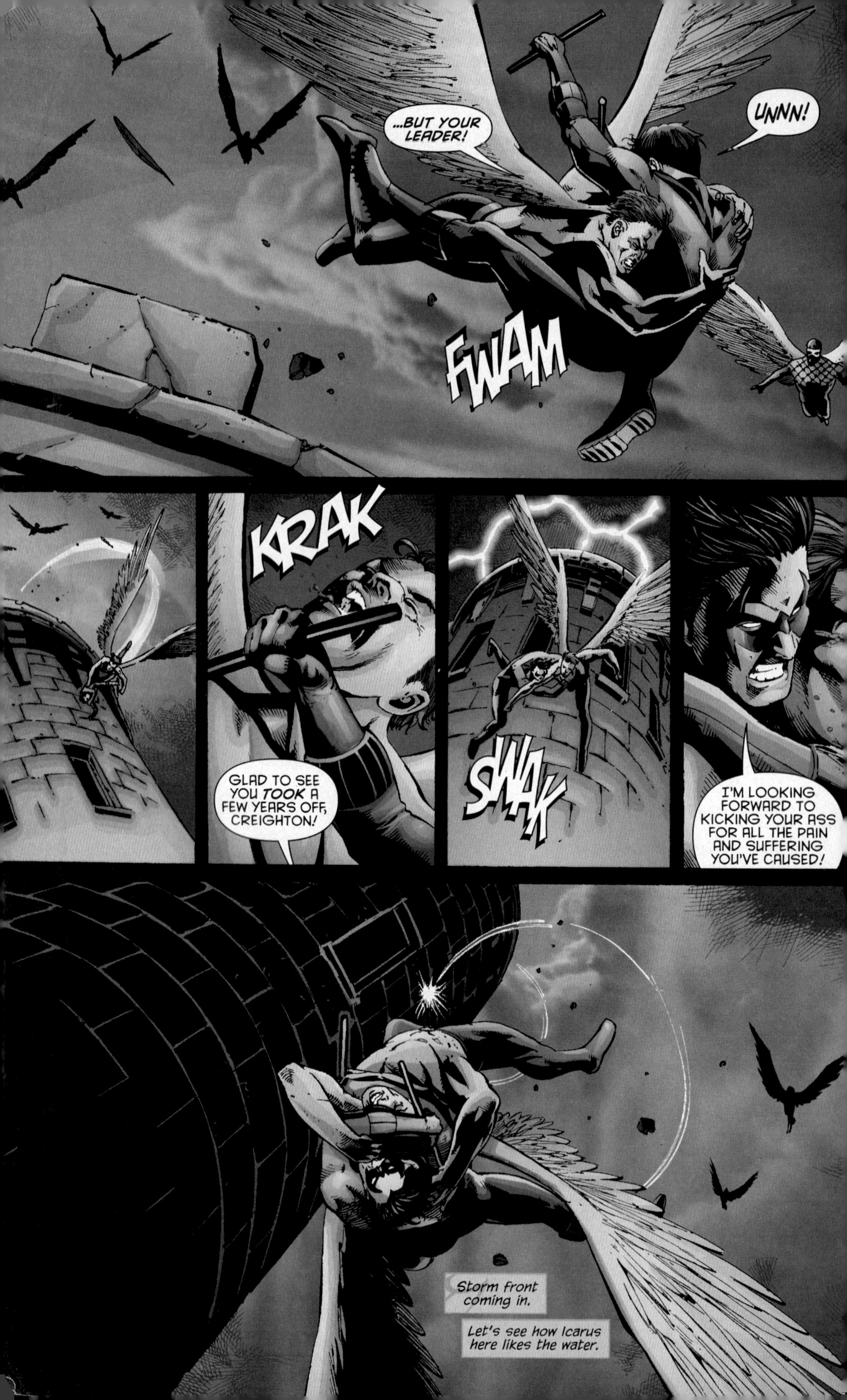
...BUT YOUR LEADER!
UNNN!
FWAM
KRAK
GLAD TO SEE YOU *TOOK* A FEW YEARS OFF, CREIGHTON!
SWAK
I'M LOOKING FORWARD TO KICKING YOUR ASS FOR ALL THE PAIN AND SUFFERING YOU'VE CAUSED!
Storm front coming in.
Let's see how Icarus here likes the water.

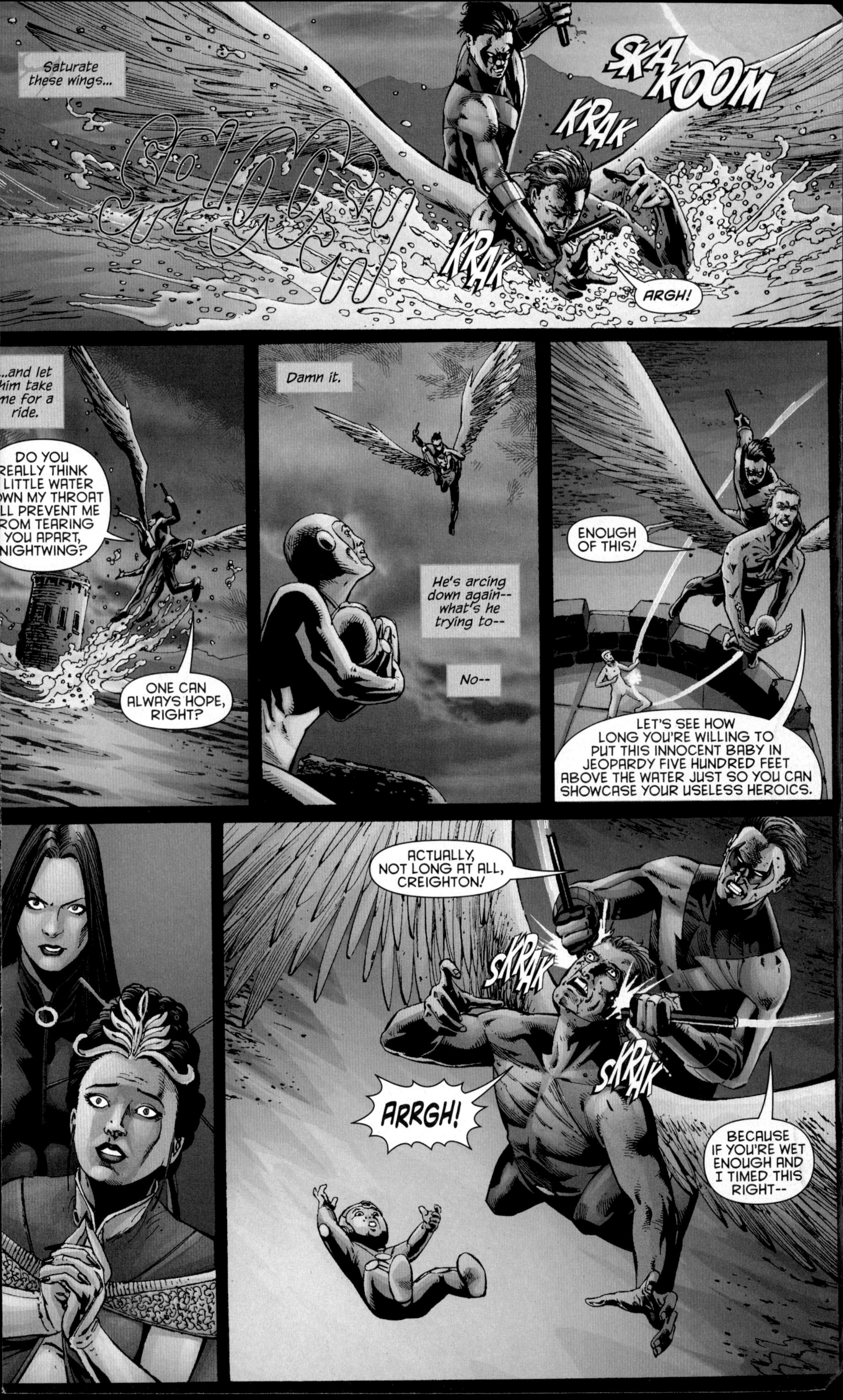
Saturate these wings...
SKA KOOM
KRAK
SPLOOSH
KRAK
ARGH!
...and let him take me for a ride.
DO YOU REALLY THINK A LITTLE WATER DOWN MY THROAT WILL PREVENT ME FROM TEARING YOU APART, NIGHTWING?
ONE CAN ALWAYS HOPE, RIGHT?
Damn it.
He's arcing down again-- what's he trying to--
No--
ENOUGH OF THIS!
LET'S SEE HOW LONG YOU'RE WILLING TO PUT THIS INNOCENT BABY IN JEOPARDY FIVE HUNDRED FEET ABOVE THE WATER JUST SO YOU CAN SHOWCASE YOUR USELESS HEROICS.
ACTUALLY, NOT LONG AT ALL, CREIGHTON!
SKRAK
ARRGH!
SKRAK
BECAUSE IF YOU'RE WET ENOUGH AND I TIMED THIS RIGHT--

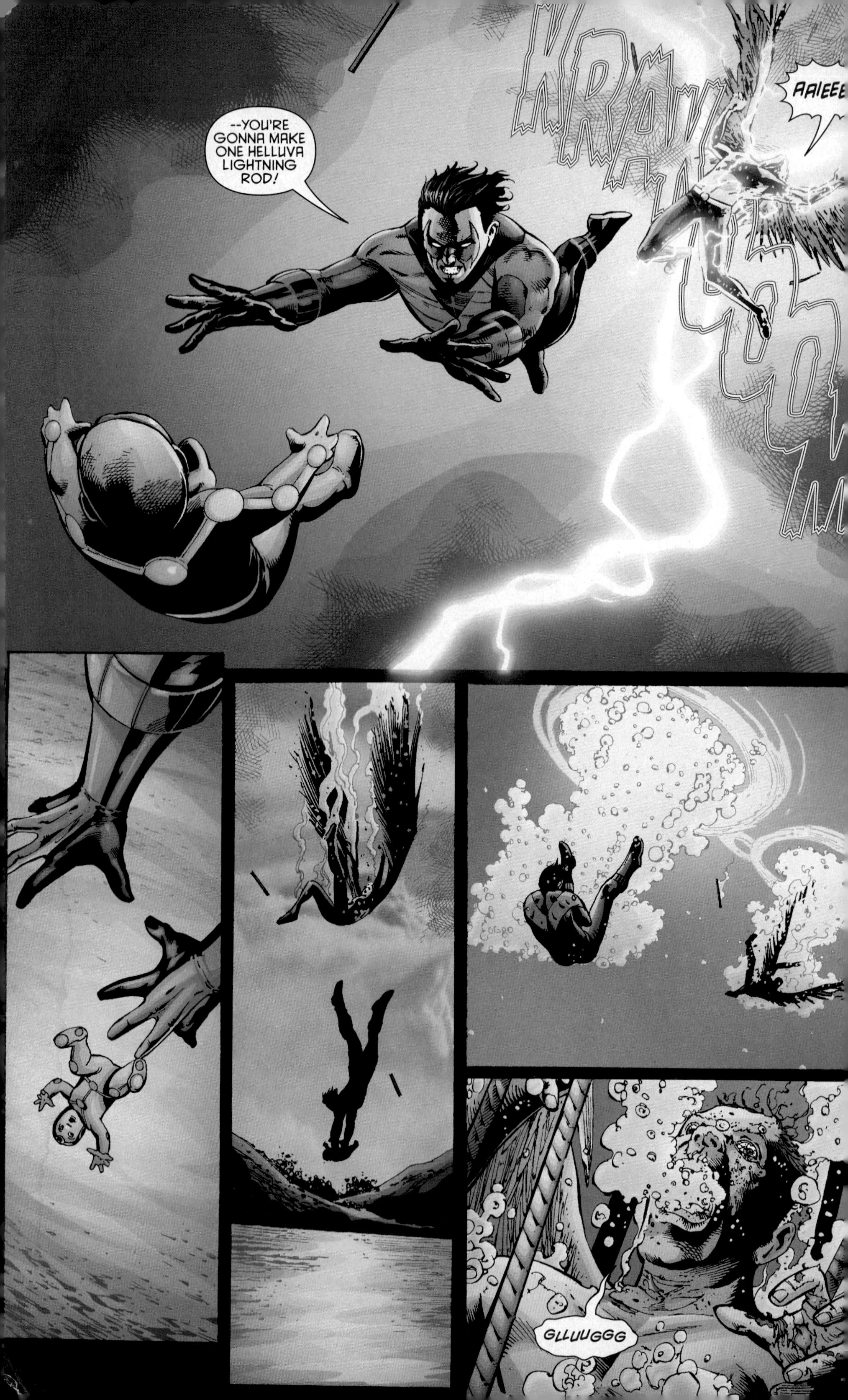
--YOU'RE GONNA MAKE ONE HELLUVA LIGHTNING ROD!
AAIEEE
GLLUUGGG

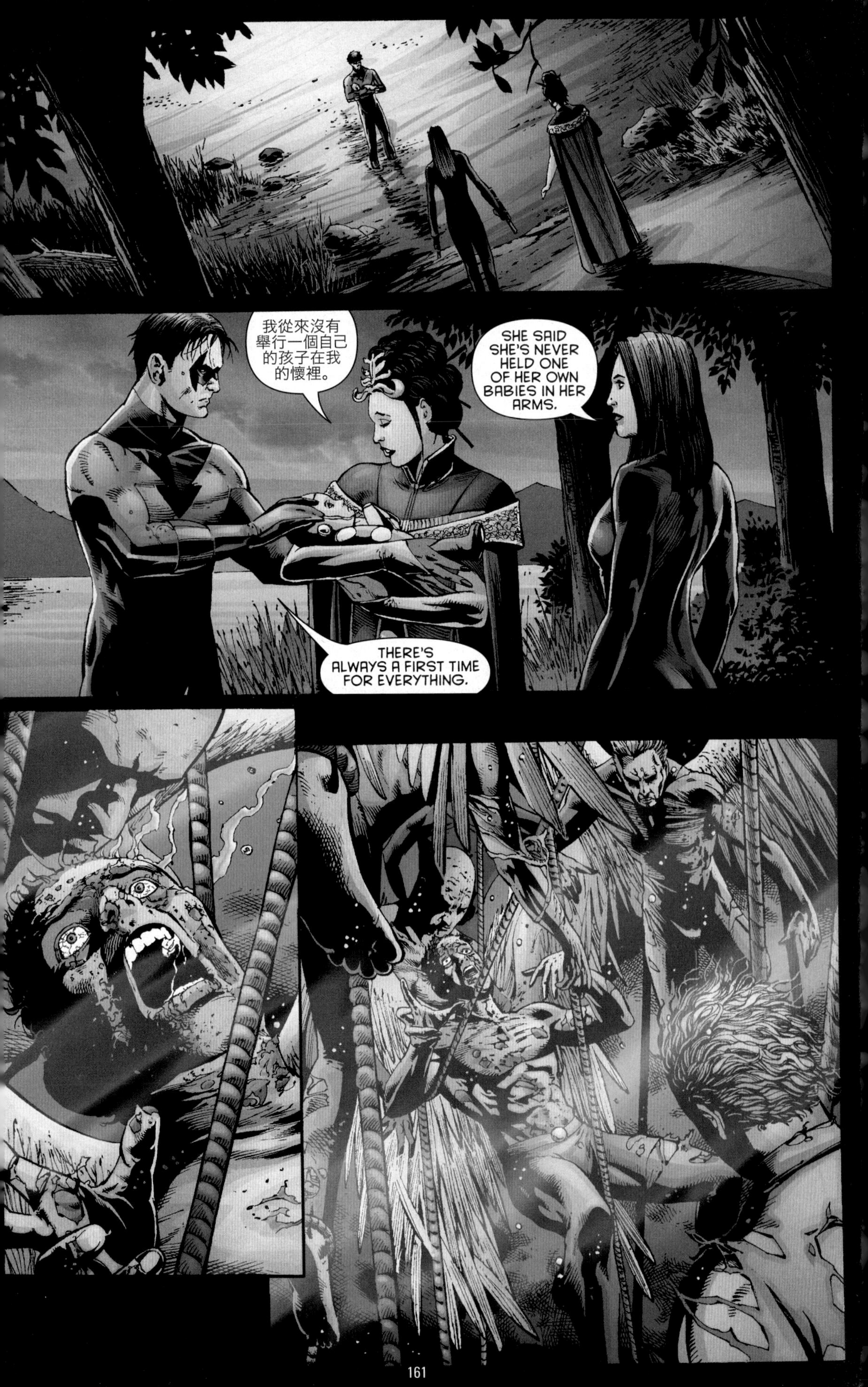
我從來沒有
舉行一個自己
的孩子在我
的懷裡。
SHE SAID
SHE'S NEVER
HELD ONE
OF HER OWN
BABIES IN HER
ARMS.
THERE'S
ALWAYS A FIRST TIME
FOR EVERYTHING.

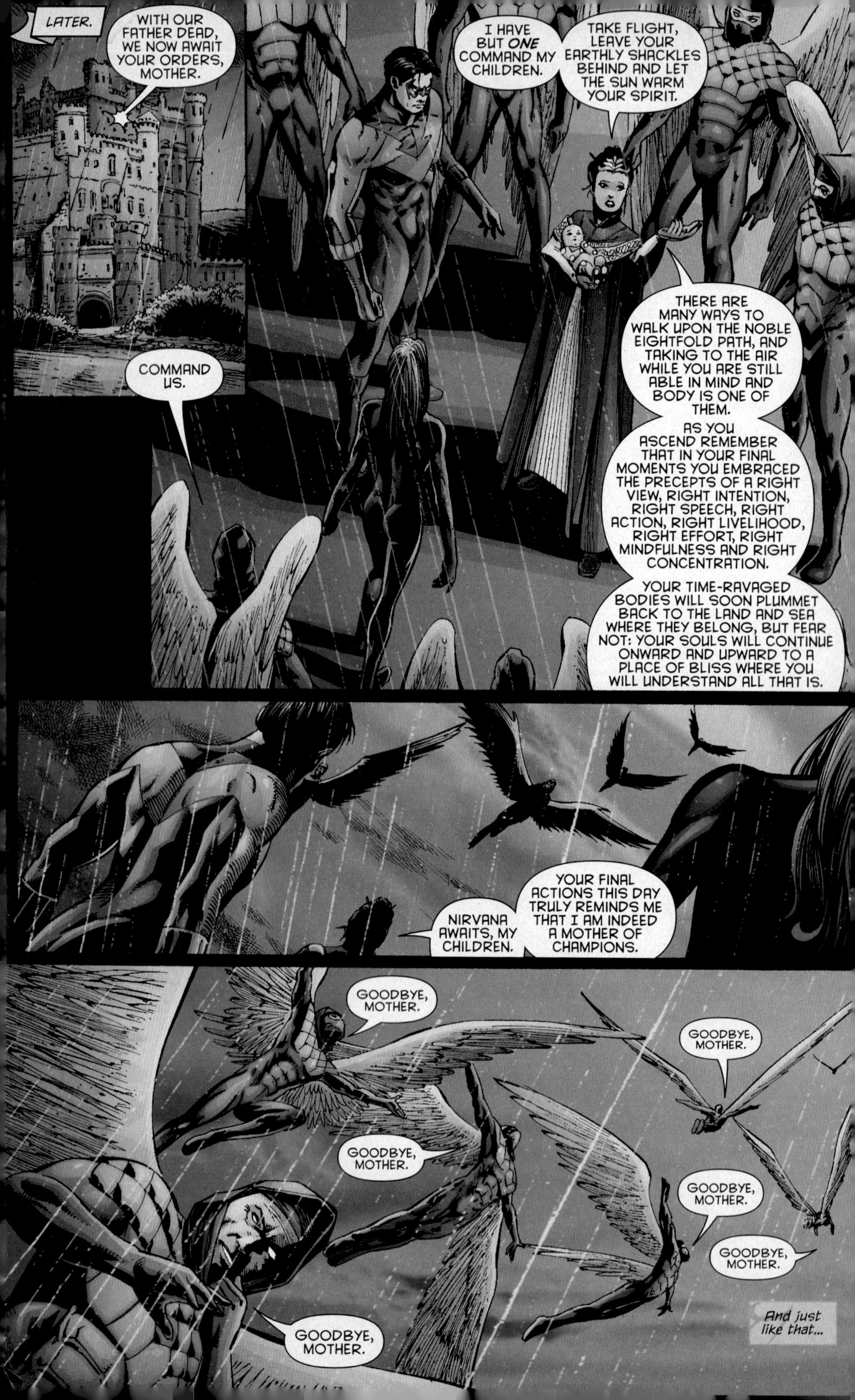
LATER.
WITH OUR FATHER DEAD, WE NOW AWAIT YOUR ORDERS, MOTHER.
COMMAND US.
I HAVE BUT ONE COMMAND MY CHILDREN.
TAKE FLIGHT, LEAVE YOUR EARTHLY SHACKLES BEHIND AND LET THE SUN WARM YOUR SPIRIT.
THERE ARE MANY WAYS TO WALK UPON THE NOBLE EIGHTFOLD PATH, AND TAKING TO THE AIR WHILE YOU ARE STILL ABLE IN MIND AND BODY IS ONE OF THEM.
AS YOU ASCEND REMEMBER THAT IN YOUR FINAL MOMENTS YOU EMBRACED THE PRECEPTS OF A RIGHT VIEW, RIGHT INTENTION, RIGHT SPEECH, RIGHT ACTION, RIGHT LIVELIHOOD, RIGHT EFFORT, RIGHT MINDFULNESS AND RIGHT CONCENTRATION.
YOUR TIME-RAVAGED BODIES WILL SOON PLUMMET BACK TO THE LAND AND SEA WHERE THEY BELONG, BUT FEAR NOT: YOUR SOULS WILL CONTINUE ONWARD AND UPWARD TO A PLACE OF BLISS WHERE YOU WILL UNDERSTAND ALL THAT IS.
YOUR FINAL ACTIONS THIS DAY TRULY REMINDS ME THAT I AM INDEED A MOTHER OF CHAMPIONS.
NIRVANA AWAITS, MY CHILDREN.
GOODBYE, MOTHER.
GOODBYE, MOTHER.
GOODBYE, MOTHER.
GOODBYE, MOTHER.
GOODBYE, MOTHER.
GOODBYE, MOTHER.
And just like that...

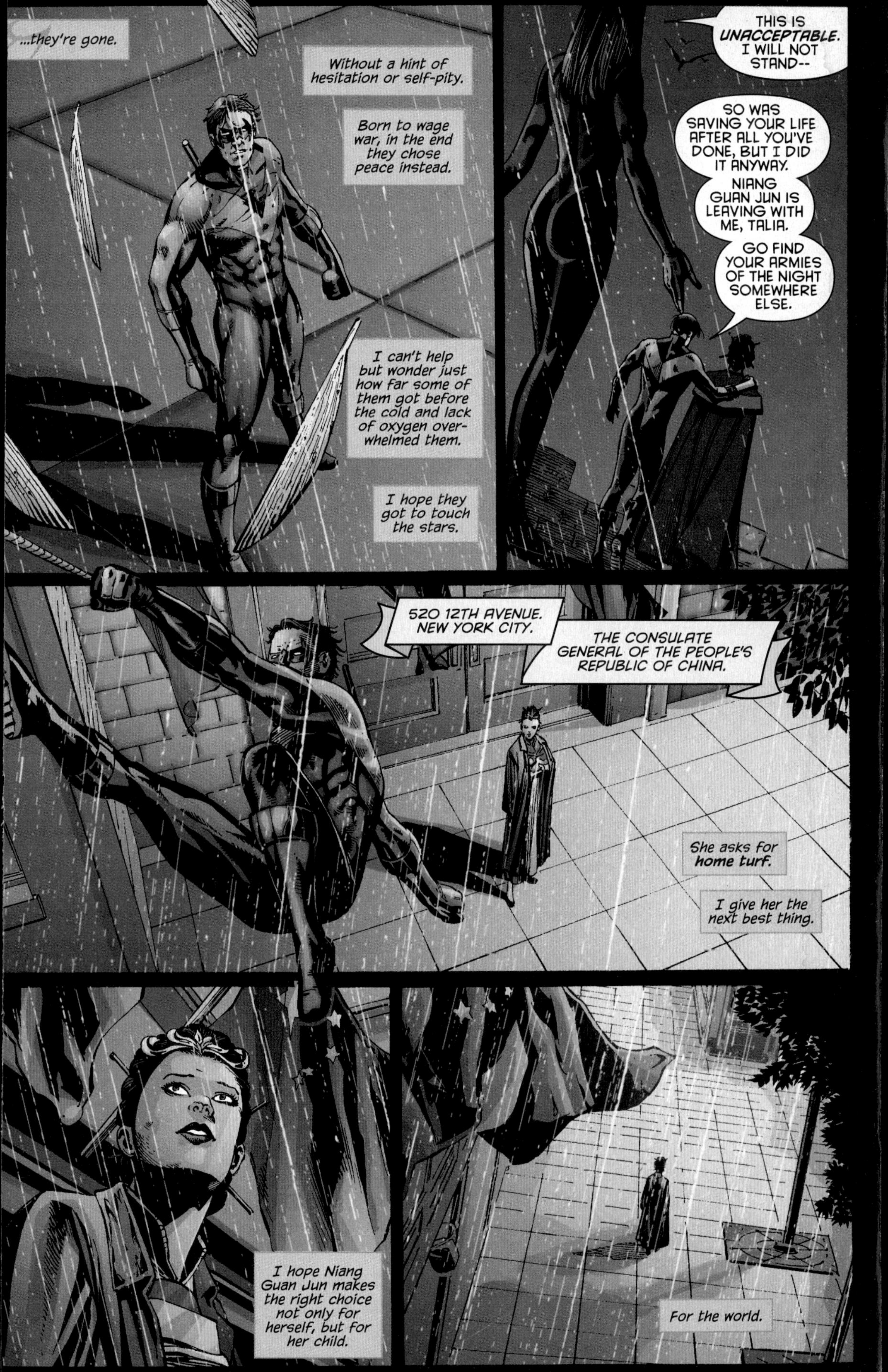
...they're gone.
Without a hint of hesitation or self-pity.
Born to wage war, in the end they chose peace instead.
I can't help but wonder just how far some of them got before the cold and lack of oxygen over-whelmed them.
I hope they got to touch the stars.
THIS IS UNACCEPTABLE. I WILL NOT STAND--
SO WAS SAVING YOUR LIFE AFTER ALL YOU'VE DONE, BUT I DID IT ANYWAY.
NIANG GUAN JUN IS LEAVING WITH ME, TALIA.
GO FIND YOUR ARMIES OF THE NIGHT SOMEWHERE ELSE.
520 12TH AVENUE. NEW YORK CITY.
THE CONSULATE GENERAL OF THE PEOPLE'S REPUBLIC OF CHINA.
She asks for home turf.
I give her the next best thing.
I hope Niang Guan Jun makes the right choice not only for herself, but for her child.
For the world.

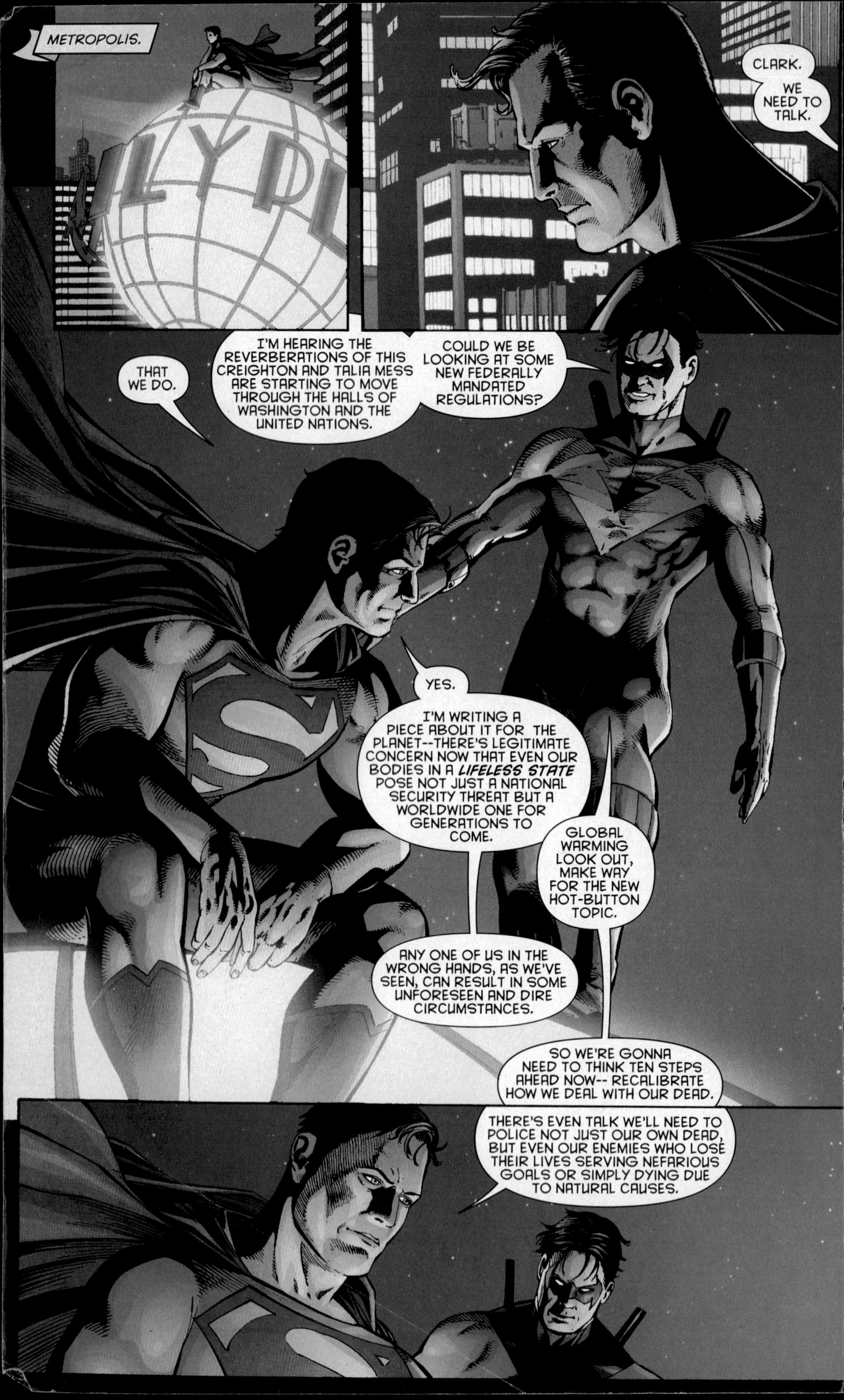
METROPOLIS.
CLARK.
WE NEED TO TALK.
THAT WE DO.
I'M HEARING THE REVERBERATIONS OF THIS CREIGHTON AND TALIA MESS ARE STARTING TO MOVE THROUGH THE HALLS OF WASHINGTON AND THE UNITED NATIONS.
COULD WE BE LOOKING AT SOME NEW FEDERALLY MANDATED REGULATIONS?
YES.
I'M WRITING A PIECE ABOUT IT FOR THE PLANET--THERE'S LEGITIMATE CONCERN NOW THAT EVEN OUR BODIES IN A *LIFELESS STATE* POSE NOT JUST A NATIONAL SECURITY THREAT BUT A WORLDWIDE ONE FOR GENERATIONS TO COME.
GLOBAL WARMING LOOK OUT, MAKE WAY FOR THE NEW HOT-BUTTON TOPIC.
ANY ONE OF US IN THE WRONG HANDS, AS WE'VE SEEN, CAN RESULT IN SOME UNFORESEEN AND DIRE CIRCUMSTANCES.
SO WE'RE GONNA NEED TO THINK TEN STEPS AHEAD NOW-- RECALIBRATE HOW WE DEAL WITH OUR DEAD.
THERE'S EVEN TALK WE'LL NEED TO POLICE NOT JUST OUR OWN DEAD, BUT EVEN OUR ENEMIES WHO LOSE THEIR LIVES SERVING NEFARIOUS GOALS OR SIMPLY DYING DUE TO NATURAL CAUSES.

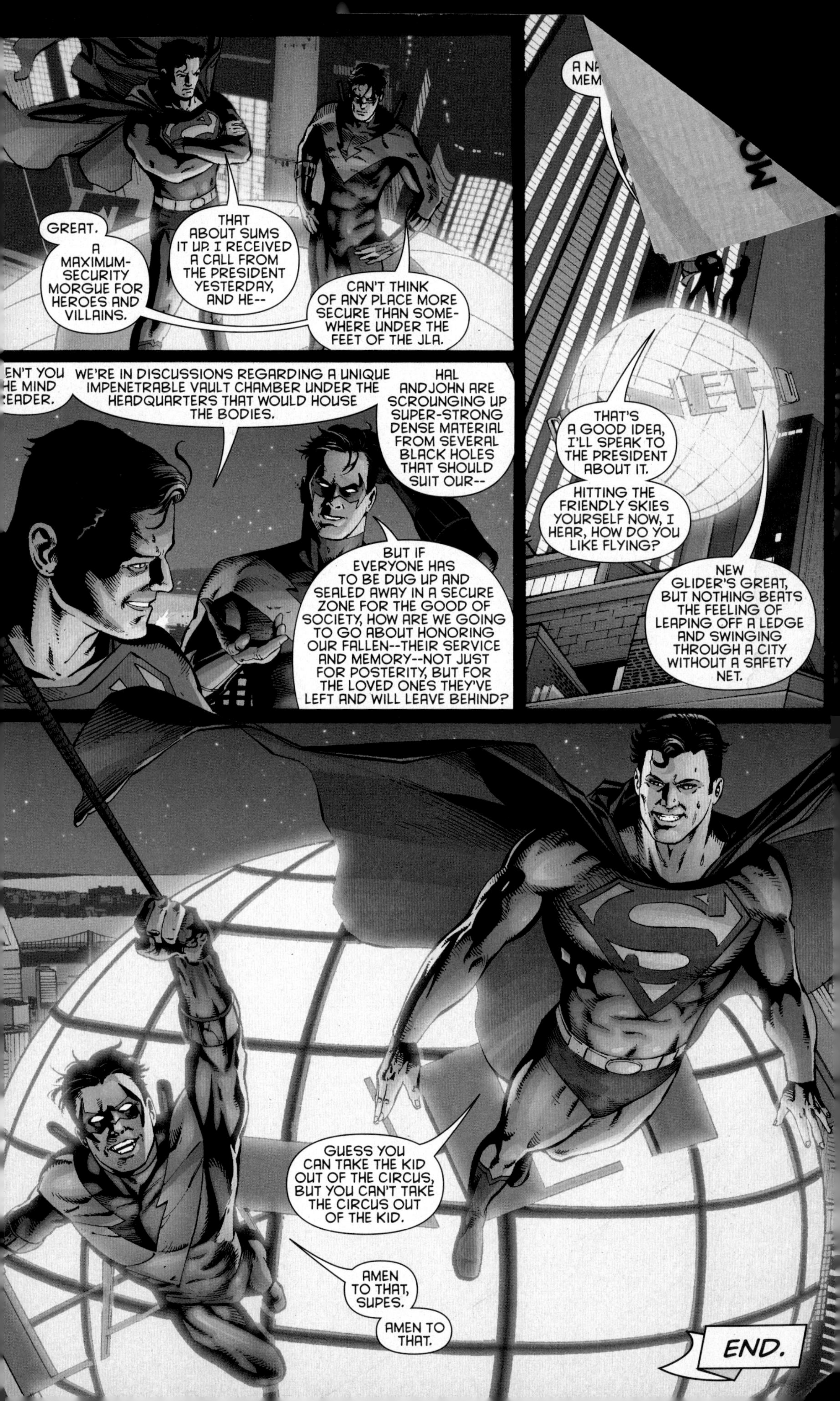
GREAT. A MAXIMUM-SECURITY MORGUE FOR HEROES AND VILLAINS.
THAT ABOUT SUMS IT UP. I RECEIVED A CALL FROM THE PRESIDENT YESTERDAY, AND HE--
CAN'T THINK OF ANY PLACE MORE SECURE THAN SOMEWHERE UNDER THE FEET OF THE JLA.
WE'RE IN DISCUSSIONS REGARDING A UNIQUE IMPENETRABLE VAULT CHAMBER UNDER THE HEADQUARTERS THAT WOULD HOUSE THE BODIES.
HAL AND JOHN ARE SCROUNGING UP SUPER-STRONG DENSE MATERIAL FROM SEVERAL BLACK HOLES THAT SHOULD SUIT OUR--
BUT IF EVERYONE HAS TO BE DUG UP AND SEALED AWAY IN A SECURE ZONE FOR THE GOOD OF SOCIETY, HOW ARE WE GOING TO GO ABOUT HONORING OUR FALLEN--THEIR SERVICE AND MEMORY--NOT JUST FOR POSTERITY, BUT FOR THE LOVED ONES THEY'VE LEFT AND WILL LEAVE BEHIND?
THAT'S A GOOD IDEA, I'LL SPEAK TO THE PRESIDENT ABOUT IT.
HITTING THE FRIENDLY SKIES YOURSELF NOW, I HEAR, HOW DO YOU LIKE FLYING?
NEW GLIDER'S GREAT, BUT NOTHING BEATS THE FEELING OF LEAPING OFF A LEDGE AND SWINGING THROUGH A CITY WITHOUT A SAFETY NET.
GUESS YOU CAN TAKE THE KID OUT OF THE CIRCUS, BUT YOU CAN'T TAKE THE CIRCUS OUT OF THE KID.
AMEN TO THAT, SUPES.
AMEN TO THAT.
END.

MORE CLASSIC TALES OF THE DARK KNIGHT

**BATMAN: HUSH
VOLUME ONE**

JEPH LOEB
JIM LEE

**BATMAN: HUSH
VOLUME TWO**

JEPH LOEB
JIM LEE

**BATMAN:
THE LONG HALLOWEEN**

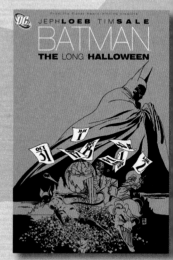

JEPH LOEB
TIM SALE

**BATMAN:
DARK VICTORY**

JEPH LOEB
TIM SALE

**BATMAN:
HAUNTED KNIGHT**

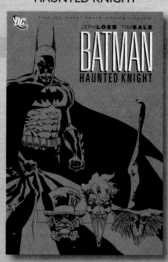

JEPH LOEB
TIM SALE

**BATMAN:
YEAR 100**

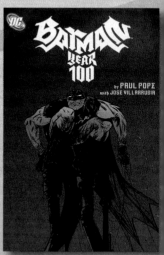

PAUL POPE

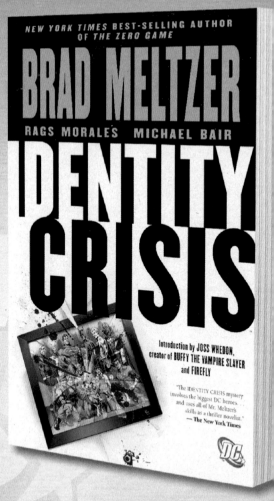